Citroen 19, 20, 21 1966-74 Aut

By Kenneth Ball
Associate Member, Guild of Motoring Writers
and the Autopress Team of Technical Writers.

Citroen ID19, D19, D Spéciale 1966-74
Citroen ID20, D20, D Super, D Super 5 1968-74
Citroen DS19 1966-68
Citroen DS20 1968-73
Citroen DS21 1966-72

Autobooks

Autopress Ltd. Golden Lane Brighton BN1 2QJ England

The AUTOBOOK series of Workshop Manuals is the largest in the world and covers the majority of British and Continental motor cars, as well as all major Japanese and Australian models. For a full list see the back of this manual.

CONTENTS

ISBN 0 85147 532 9

First Edition 1972
Second Edition, fully revised 1973
Reprinted 1973
Third Edition, fully revised 1974
Reprinted 1975

742

Printed and bound in Brighton England for Autopress Ltd by G Beard & Son Ltd B

ACKNOWLEDGEMENT

My thanks are due to Citroen Cars Ltd. for their unstinted co-operation and also for supplying data and illustrations.

I am also grateful to a considerable number of owners who have discussed their cars at length and many of whose suggestions have been included in this manual.

Kenneth Ball
Associate Member, Guild of Motoring Writers
Ditchling Sussex England.

INTRODUCTION

This do-it-yourself Workshop Manual has been specially written for the owner who wishes to maintain his car in first class condition and to carry out his own servicing and repairs. Considerable savings on garage charges can be made, and one can drive in safety and confidence knowing the work has been done properly.

Comprehensive step-by-step instructions and illustrations are given on all dismantling, overhauling and assembling operations. Certain assemblies require the use of expensive special tools, the purchase of which would be unjustified. In these cases information is included but the reader is recommended to hand the unit to the agent for attention.

Throughout the Manual hints and tips are included which will be found invaluable, and there is an easy to follow fault diagnosis at the end of each chapter.

Whilst every care has been taken to ensure correctness of information it is obviously not possible to guarantee complete freedom from errors or to accept liability arising from such errors or omissions.

Instructions may refer to the righthand or lefthand sides of the vehicle or the components. These are the same as the righthand or lefthand of an observer standing behind the car and looking forward.

CHAPTER 1

THE ENGINE

1 :1 Types, features, models, capacities

Citroen DS cars with a central hydraulic power system used in conjunction with the specialized hydro-pneumatic suspension associated with these cars, as well as for brakes, steering and a semi-automatic gearchange, were introduced in 1955 and followed by the simplified ID version. Front wheel drive four-cylinder in-line water-cooled engine units of 1911 cc capacity (78 x 100 mm bore and stroke) and with three-bearing crankshafts were similar in each type.

Completely new and larger engines of two sizes were introduced in 1966, again of the four-cylinder in-line type but oversquare units with a short stroke counter-balanced crankshaft carried on five main bearings to give smoother performance. Other features incorporated with the new engines included a higher mounting of the chain-driven camshaft, giving shorter pushrods to assist the valve gear operating at higher engine speeds, all-synchromesh lower gearing at forward speeds, improved brakes and self-levelling headlights. The smaller engine size was fitted in the DS19 series and the larger version in an additional model called the DS21, as follows:

Type	*Capacity cc*	*Bore mm*	*Stroke mm*	*Compression Ratio*	*Bhp*
DS19A	1985	86	85.5	8.75:1	90
DS21	2175	90	85.5	8.75:1	109

These engines are of the overhead valve type, the valves being mounted in an aluminium cylinder head as before and inclined at an angle of 60 deg. to each other (see **FIG 1 :1**). The valves are operated by long and short rockers, with the inlet valve rockers on a common shaft and the exhaust rockers on separate short shafts. Sparking plugs are fitted centrally in the head at the lower ends of tubes projecting through the rocker cover. The pistons operate in removable cylinder barrels or wet liners in the cast-iron cylinder block, the piston crowns being shaped as part of the hemispherical combustion chambers to suit the increased compression ratio.

The front wheel transmission system, including gearbox, differential and drive shafts, forms a complete power unit with the engine. A flywheel and a single dry plate clutch at the front end of the five-bearing crankshaft transmit the drive to a fourspeed gearbox with synchromesh engagement of all forward gears. The gearbox mainshaft from the clutch passes over the final drive pinion and differential assembly mounted on the end of the lower or second motion shaft. Disc brakes are

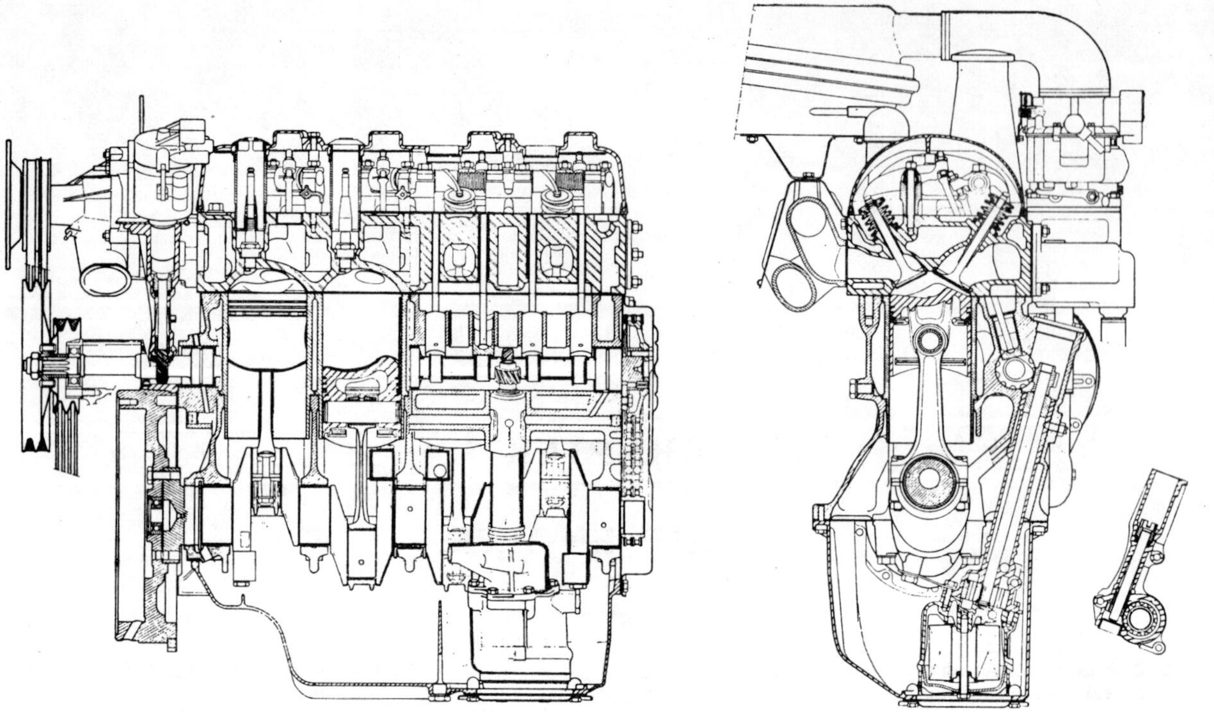

FIG 1 :1 Longitudinal and sectional views of the DX engine. DY engines are similar except that the distributor is on the oil pump gear at the rear end of the camshaft. In all D engines since October, 1968, the distributor is positioned at the front of the engine

mounted on the inboard end of each front wheel drive shaft and constant velocity type outer universal joints transmit power from the drive shafts to the wheels. Wheel attachment is by five studs instead of the former central nut.

The distributor and oil pump are driven through spur gears from the camshaft. The lubricating system is of the forced feed type, oil being circulated by a gear type oil pump in the sump with a filter on the intake. Cooling is by a conventional radiator, water pump and fan system, the cooling water coming into direct contact with the outer surfaces of the detachable liners in the cylinder block. Belts from a drive pulley at the front end of the camshaft drive are connected to pulleys on the water pump, the generator or alternator, the hydraulic pressure pump providing power for the suspension system and other equipment and the centrifugal regulator where fitted.

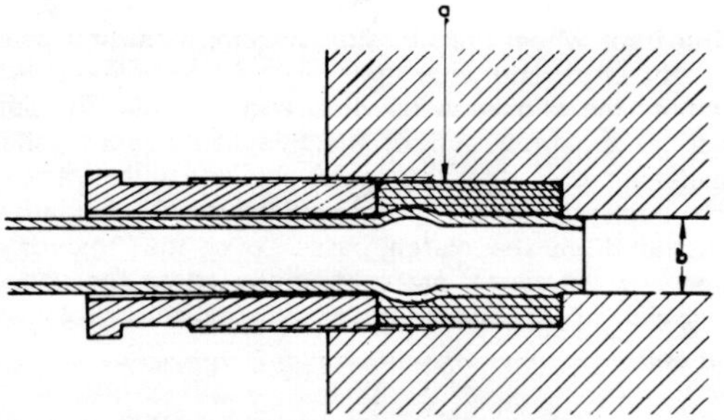

FIG 1 :2 Sealing sleeve (a). Pipe must enter small bore (b)

In the ID series, the former long stroke (78 x 100 mm) 1911 cc three-bearing engine continued to be used in the ID19A until September, 1966. A dual Solex carburetter was employed and power raised from 73 to 83 bhp, with a compression ratio of 8.1:1 by changes in the cylinder head and valve mechanism. Otherwise between 1966 and 1970 the two new engine types formed the basis for a varied range of models, each with particular features and purposes and optional provisions for manual or semi-automatic gearchange, power-assisted steering and other conveniences.

The DS19 was introduced in February, 1966, with the new 1985cc engine, all synchromesh gearbox and power-assisted steering. The following September an ID19B model with the 1985cc engine replaced the ID19A. The new model employed a single Solex carburetter with the former compression ratio of 8.1:1 to give a power rating of 84 bhp. Confort models were variants which included power steering and reclining seats. The ratios of the second and third gears of the DS19 were changed in 1967 and the Pallas version received the new lighting system in which the headlights turn with the steering.

Late in 1968 the DS19 was redesignated as the DS20 and a further model brought out called the ID20,

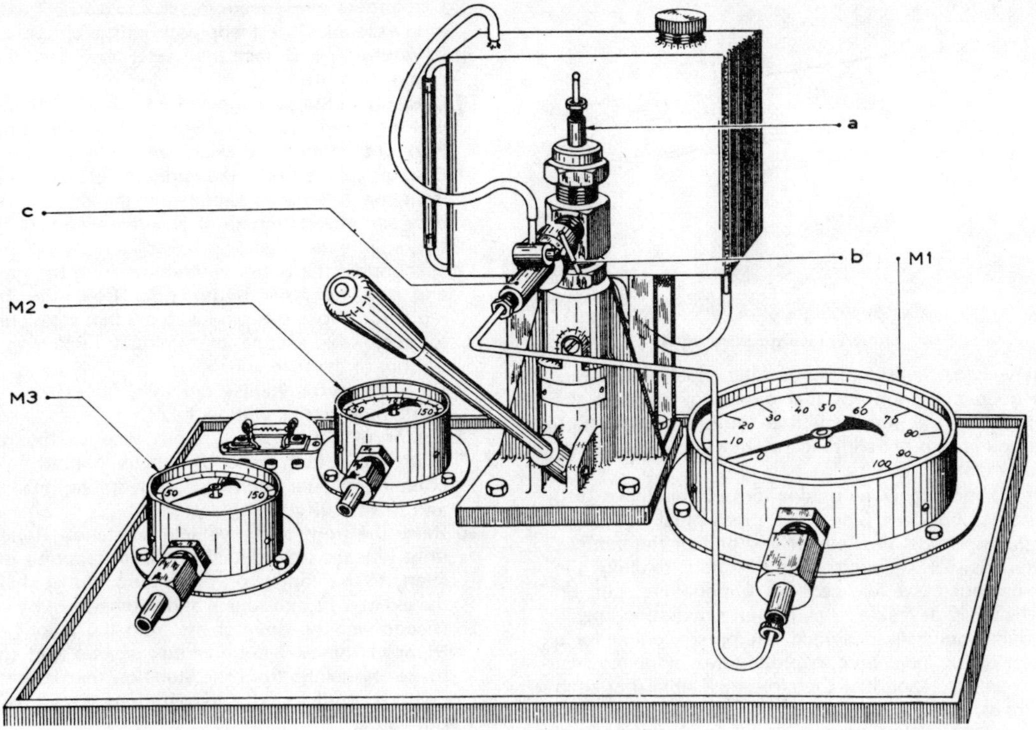

FIG 1 : 3 Test bench and apparatus

Key to Fig 1 : 3 **a** Pump orifice **b** Bleed screw **c** Pressure outlet **M1, M2, M3** Pressure gauges

equipped to Confort standards. These models incorporated a more powerful version of the 1985 cc engine, developing 103 bhp or 13 bhp more than the DS19, mainly by increasing the compression ratio and fitting new jets on the downdraught twin-choke Weber carburetter. Then came the D20 Super and the D19 Special in 1969, using the 1985 cc engine of 91 bhp with manual and semi-automatic transmission respectively and replacing the ID20 and the ID19B. These models had a revised facia and similar specifications of the Confort type.

Over the same period the DS21 series, using the 2175 cc engine, continued with an increased output of 115 bhp in late 1968 and a still greater output of 139 bhp in late 1969 when electronic fuel injection was made optionally available. A DS21 drop-head coupé was manufactured shortly after the new engines came into production, but very few were imported into Britain.

Included in the variants of both engine sizes were the DS19 Pallas and the DS21 Pallas as super-luxury types, especially in relation to upholstery and seating and with standard equipment optional on other cars.

The current range includes the Safari 20, D Special and D Super 5 using both capacities of engines.

1 : 2 Procedure when working on the car

To ensure the correct functioning of the hydraulic systems extreme precautions must be taken to ensure that the hydraulic fluid and all component parts are kept perfectly clean and protected from dust and possible knocks. Seals and rubber pipes must not be exposed to dust, strong light or heat. Before starting work carefully clean the area in which the operations are being undertaken. A union and its connecting parts should be washed with alcohol before disconnection.

Special caps, plugs and a blank flange, which are obtainable from service agents, are provided for sealing all openings in the units as dismantling proceeds. These items must also be thoroughly cleaned before using. Sealing sleeves (see **FIG 1 : 2**) should be renewed after each dismantling operation and should be set back 2 mm from the end of the pipe. Centralize the pipe in the bore and make sure that the end of the pipe enters the small bore at 'b'. Screw on the union nut by hand. On certain units the axis of the bore is oblique relative to the face of the boss for the unit. Lightly tighten the nut to a torque of 4.3 to 5.7 lb ft (.6 to .8 kg m). This light tightening is sufficient to ensure a good seal. Excessive tightening will cause leakage.

Before commencing an overhaul, if there is any irregularity of operation it must be ensured that the hydraulic circuit is under pressure before doing anything else. With the engine running at idling speed, unscrew the pressure regulator bleed screw 1 to $1\frac{1}{2}$ turns, when the pressure release should be perceptible. Tighten the bleed screw, and the valve must cut out in less than 20 seconds. The moment of cut-out is indicated by a reduction in the noise of operation. If the result is negative, check (a) that there is sufficient hydraulic fluid in

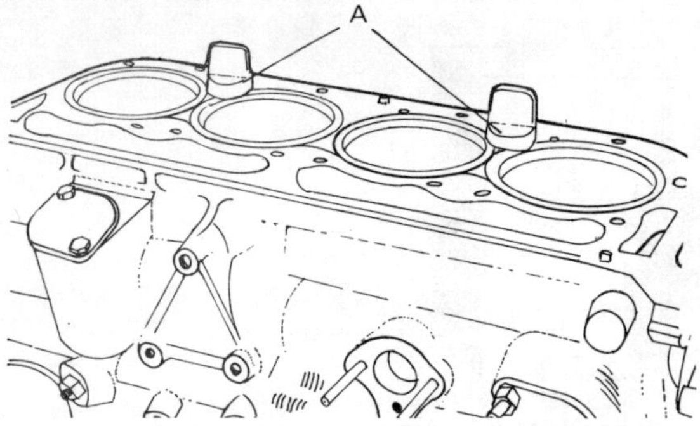

FIG 1 : 4 Liner retaining screws **A**

the reservoir, (b) that the reservoir filter is perfectly clean, and in good condition, (c) that air is not entering the suction pipe of the pump, (d) that the belts of the high pressure pump are not slipping, (e) that the bleed screw is securely closed.

After all work, check all unions for possible leaks, also the clearance between pipes. The pipes must not touch each other nor must they touch any part of the vehicle.

Operations for draining, flushing and refilling the whole hydraulic system can be undertaken, but on completion it is desirable to carry out a hydraulic check. This requires specially designed equipment, either for a rapid test or for more precise procedures involving test bench operations, and it is therefore advisable that such work should be undertaken by a suitably equipped service agent. A view of the test bench employed is given in **FIG 1 : 3.**

1 : 3 Removing engine

Removal of the engine and gearbox as an assembly in cars with semi-automatic gearchange is undertaken as follows:

1 Remove the front wings together with the air filter and its support. Then drain the radiator and cylinder block, keeping the water with its antifreeze content. The radiator is drained by opening the tap under the bottom tank on the righthand side and the cylinder block by removing the hexagon screw plug behind the starter.

2 Release the pressure in all the hydraulic circuits (see **Section 1 : 2**), and drain the hydraulic fluid reservoir.

3 Remove the radiator inlect duct assembly with the crossmember supporting the spare wheel and remove the battery and its tray.

4 Disconnect the hydraulic reservoir and leave it lying on the lefthand sidemember.

5 Remove the steering rack (see **Chapter 9**), also the two front suspension spheres.

6 Disconnect the exhaust downpipe from the flexible exhaust pipe only. Remove the screws securing the fixing clamp of the flexible exhaust pipe and its retaining screw on the exhaust silencer. Withdraw the pipe towards the silencer.

7 Disconnect the generator/alternator and the distributor leads together with the lead to the thermometer transmitter.

8 Disconnect the choke cable from the carburetter. Remove the two return springs and the rear support bracket for the vertical accelerator control rod.

9 Disconnect the speedometer cable, the gearchange pipe assembly, the feedpipe from the clutch-lock and its return pipe. Detach the heater hose from the water pump inlet tube.

10 Disconnect the supply pipe for the front lefthand brake unit and remove its retaining clip. Disconnect the lead for the brake pad wear warning light.

11 Disconnect the outlet pipe from the pressure regulator, from the three-way union and the connecting pipe between the clutch re-engagement control and the hydraulic gear selector.

12 Disconnect the petrol inlet elbow from the fuel pump and the reservoir return pipe from the pressure regulator. Close this pipe with a 9 mm screw or a plug to avoid the escape of the fluid remaining at the bottom of the reservoir.

13 Disconnect the heater tap inlet hose from the hot water pipe on the cylinder head.

14 Disconnect the rubber return pipe to the reservoir from the clutch re-engagement control, also the connecting pipe between the hydraulic gear selector and the centrifugal regulator.

15 Raise the front of the vehicle on stands. Remove the front wheels, then detach the nuts securing the drive shafts to the flanges on the gearbox outlet shafts with the aid of a 17 mm socket and extension.

16 Disconnect the drive shafts from the pivot bearings. Remove the two countersunk screws and then the tri-axe housings from the studs on the flanges of the gearbox outlet shafts to withdraw the drive shafts outwards.

17 Disconnect the handbrake cable from the mechanical brake caliper levers, after having completely unscrewed the locknut and the adjusting nut of the threaded sleeve.

18 Remove the screws securing the front engine crossmember to the body sidemembers and the securing screws holding the rear engine mountings. Note the adjustment packing pieces between the crossmember and sidemembers.

19 Make a final check to ensure that no cables, pipes or other connections between the unit and the car have been overlooked, then pass a sling or a sheathed chain under the water pump cover, raise the engine and disengage it from the car. If mechanical lifting facilities are not available, the weight of the unit should be reduced by removing the cylinder head, manifolds, generator, starter, etc., when it should be able to be lifted out manually with the aid of an assistant. Mount the assembly on a stand. Pay particular attention to the pipes remaining on the car and do not damage or distort them.

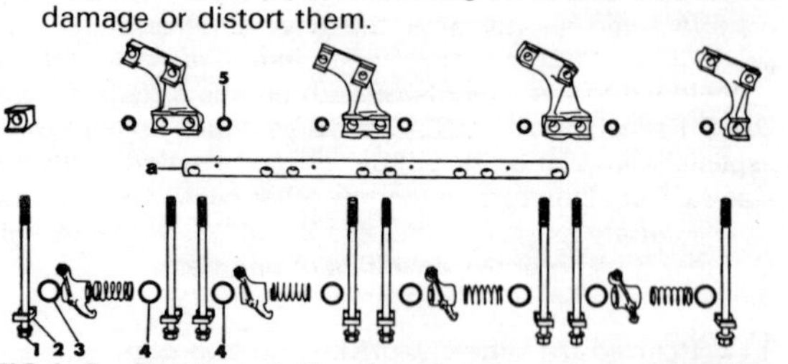

FIG 1 : 5 Details of the inlet rocker shaft assembly

Key to Fig 1 : 5 1 Long screw 2 Fixing cap 3 Thick washer 4 Thin washer 5 Ring seal **a** Lubrication hole

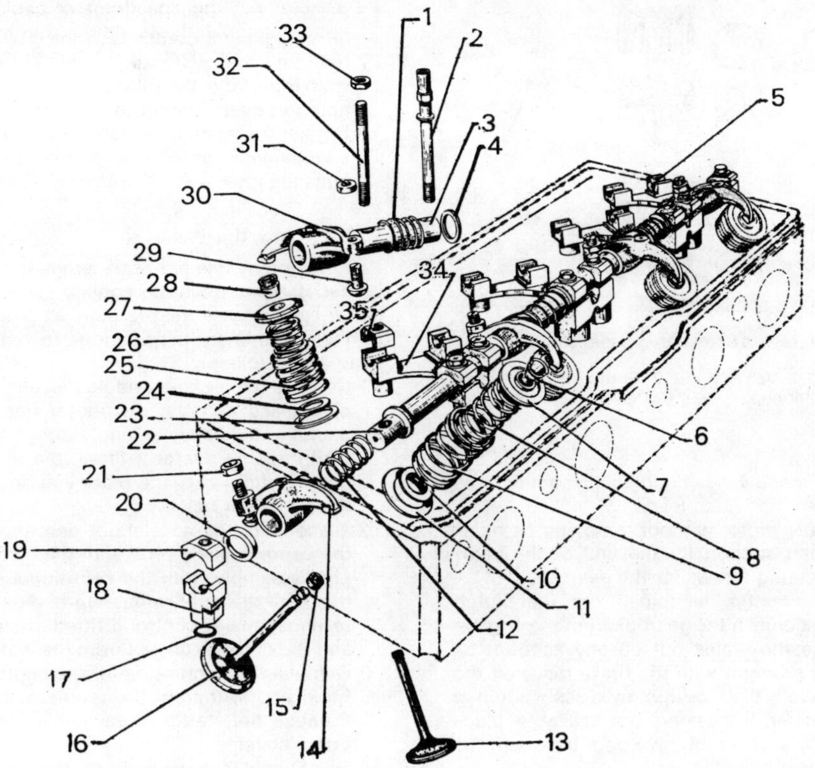

FIG 1:6 An exploded view of the rocker and valve assemblies

Key to Fig 1:6 1 Spring 2 Long screw 3 Exhaust rocker shaft 4 Spacing washer 5 Rocker shaft bracket 6 Seal, inlet valves only 7 Cap 8 Inner spring 9 Outer spring 10 Thrust washer 11 Thrust washer 12 Spring 13 Inlet valve 14 Inlet rocker 15 Split cotters 16 Exhaust valve 17 Washer 18 Rocker bracket 19 Cap 20 Spacer 21 Nut 22 Inlet rocker shaft 23 Thrust washer 24 Thrust washer 25 Outer spring 26 Inner spring 27 Cap 28 Split cotters 29 Tappet adjusting screw 30 Exhaust rocker 31 Nut 32 Stud for rocker bracket 33 Nut 34 Exhaust rocker shaft bracket 35 Cap

Where a manual gearchange is employed, operations are similar except for the following differences:

1 In Operation 9, disconnect (a) the assembly of gearchange control lever, cable bracket and cable, (b) the gearchange control rod from the cross tube and (c) the cross tube from the shaft on the gearbox cover. Free the tube from its support bearing on the chassis and remove the rubber strap holding the speedometer cable and the gearchange selection cable on the crossmember.

2 There are no hydraulic components as mentioned in Operations 12 and 14. Instead, disconnect the clutch cable by removing the return spring from the clutch fork and loosening the clutch clearance adjusting screw (see **Chapter 6**). Remove the pushrod and free the end of the cable from the lever on the bellhousing and the sheath from the clutch housing.

Removal of ancillary equipment as described in the following instructions will be required as necessary to undertake the overhaul operations described in later Sections. Details are for semi-automatic gearchange models, but manual gearchange requirements are similar except for references to the particular hydraulic components concerned with clutch and gearbox.

1 Remove the exhaust downpipe and place the engine-gearbox assembly on a stand.

2 Disconnect the radiator tie-rod, the upper and lower radiator hoses and remove the radiator.

3 Disconnect the connecting pipe between the hydraulic brake units and the lead for the brake pad wear warning light.

4 Remove the pads from the hydraulic brake units (see **Chapter 10**), the pipe connecting the righthand hydraulic brake unit to the centrifugal regulator and the screws securing the brake units on the gearbox outlet housings.

5 Disconnect and remove the righthand brake unit from the engine crossmember. Remove the crossmember together with the lefthand unit.

6 Continue to remove the engine fan, the pipe between high pressure pump and pressure regulator, the belts (see **Chapters 2** and **5**), the generator and the pipe between the centrifugal regulator and the clutch lock.

7 Remove the high pressure pump, and the lefthand mechanical brake caliper.

8 Remove the drive pulley and the washers for adjusting the pulley alignment. Use a file to remove the metal of the nut turned down into the shaft for locking

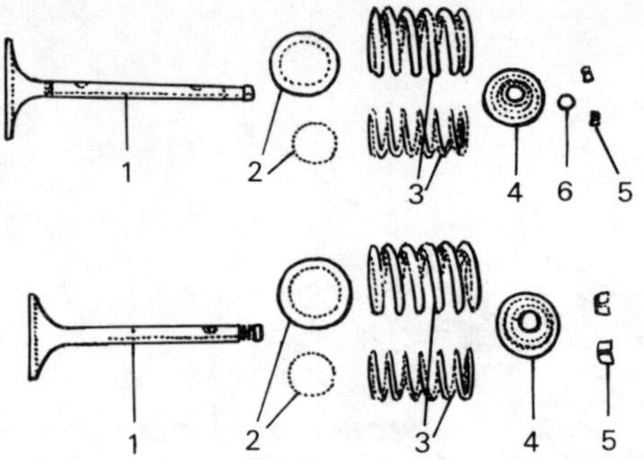

FIG 1:7 Details of the valve assemblies

Key to Fig 1:7 1 Valves 2 Spring thrust washers 3 Springs 4 Upper cups 5 Cotters 6 Seal, inlet valves only

purposes. With manual gearchange, disconnect the return spring from the clutch lever.

9 Remove the starter motor without removing its heat-shield, the bearing support for the end of the cam-shaft and the securing screws for the gearbox.

10 Disconnect the pressure feedpipe from the clutch cylinder, then disconnect the gearbox from the engine. Note that the gearbox must not on any account be moved about by rolling it with the brake discs on the ground. Fit old worn discs or dummy discs machined to 350 mm diameter. If these are not available, place a rubber mat or a sheet of plywood between the ground and the gearbox.

11 Remove the heat-shield from the exhaust manifold, the exhaust manifolds and the heater pipe with the metal bracket for the manifold shield.

12 Disconnect the hydraulic piping on the centrifugal regulator. Remove the centrifugal regulator, the water pump and gasket with the tie-rod, and the bracket under the engine holding the exhaust downpipe.

13 Remove the fuel pump, the insulation distance piece, the pushrod guide, the paper joint and the pushrod.

14 Remove the rubber sleeves connecting the carburetter, air filter and breather, then remove the carburetter and its packing piece.

15 Remove the pressure regulator assembly with its support bracket and disconnect the piping on the clutch re-engagement control.

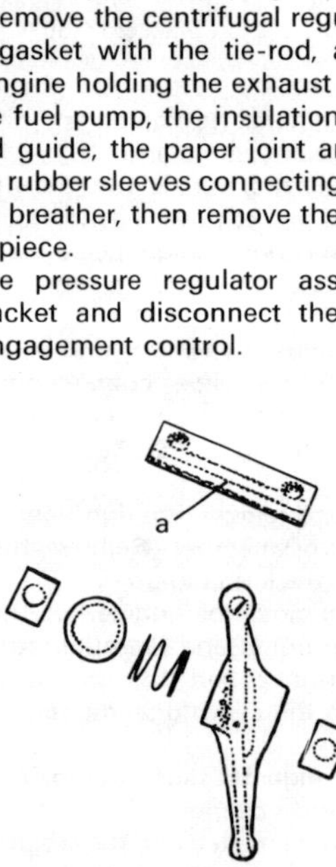

FIG 1:8 Exhaust rocker assembly showing lubrication hole at a

16 Remove the inlet manifold together with the clutch re-engagement control and the gaskets.

17 Remove the distributor and its drive tower, the sparking plugs, the oil dipstick and the positive cable going to the starter motor.

18 Detach the hydraulic pipe assembly of the clutch re-engagement control and remove the engine mounting arms together with the rubber mountings.

1:4 Lifting the head

If the engine has not been removed from the car it will be necessary to drain the cooling system, disconnect the battery and release the pressure, as previously described. Further preliminary preparations to remove the cylinder head are as follows:

1 Remove the air filter and its flexible pipe, the sparking plug leads and the distributor head, the pipe connecting the accelerating idling device with the centrifugal regulator if fitted, the radiator tie-rod, the engine lifting clip, the battery earth wire, the fan and the generator belts.

2 Disconnect the accelerator control, the choke cable, the petrol delivery pipe from the carburetter, the feed-pipe assembly from the centrifugal regulator if fitted, the pipe assembly and return pipe from the clutch re-engagement control if fitted, the upper water hose and the dynamo tie-rod from the water pump.

3 Remove the fulcrum pin of the centrifugal regulator if fitted and withdraw the regulator towards the right. Remove the starter motor cable clip from the water pump cover.

4 Disconnect the wire from the thermometer transmitter on the water pump cover, the lower water suction hose from the pump, the rocker lubrication pipe shown in **FIG 1:27** from the cylinder head and the high pressure pump tie-rod if fitted from the water pump. Remove the front righthand suspension sphere and exhaust shield.

5 Disconnect the exhaust downpipes from the manifolds, the screw fixing the downpipe clamp from its bracket, the exhaust manifolds from the cylinder head and the heater hose from the pipe on the cylinder head.

6 Remove the cylinder head cover and its gasket, the sparking plugs and the sealing cups from the sparking plug wells with their rubber joints.

7 Unscrew completely the cylinder head screws, slackening each a little at a time in the reverse order to that shown for tightening in **FIG 1:9.** Proceed to remove the exhaust rocker units and the inlet rocker assembly (see **FIG 1:6**).

8 Unscrew the inlet rocker assembly screws without removing them from their brackets. Remove the assembly with the screws in place, in order to keep the parts in their correct positions. Then remove the exhaust rocker assemblies and brackets, noting the order of removal for refitting. To remove the rear screw from the inlet rocker line, remove the rubber plug from the engine recess in the scuttle, cut the felt and remove the screw through this hole.

9 The rocker pushrods can now be removed, giving each a slight twist to free it. Store them in their correct order for refitting, pushing them the right way up through numbered holes in a card. To remove the

exhaust rocker pushrod from No. 4 cylinder raise the cylinder head slightly.

10 Lift off the head and gasket, observing the centring dowels. If the head does not come away freely, tap it along each side with a mallet or with light hammer blows on a piece of wood. Note that if the engine is turned after the head has been lifted (e.g. for decarbonizing) the liners may come out of the cylinder bores. The liners should therefore be held in position by the two screws 3074T shown in **FIG 1 : 4.**

1 : 5 Servicing the head, attention to valves

Referring to **FIG 1 : 5,** dismantle the inlet rocker shaft by removing the fixing screws, the caps, the washers, the springs and the rocker arms. Carefully clean the inside of the shaft with a metal pin and make sure that the lubrication holes in the shaft are clear. Keep each rocker and its parts in a numbered container or otherwise ensure that they go back in the same locations. Valves and their parts should be kept in sequence in the same way.

Check the rocker shaft for wear, particularly on the underside, also the rocker bores for scores and wear. Inspect the ends of the adjusting screws. If wear is uneven, renew, together with the corresponding pushrod. Similarly inspect the pushrod contact faces and check that no bending has occurred. Withdraw the valve tappets, for which a special extractor tool is available. Keep them in their correct order for refitting, if still serviceable, in their original bores, and examine for scores, wear or cracks.

If decarbonizing is necessary, scrape most of the carbon from the cylinder head before removing the valves, to prevent damage to the valve seats. Temporarily replace the cylinder head screws to avoid carbon scrapings entering the holes. If carborundum is used, extreme care must be taken to remove all traces from the valve chambers or gas passages, as even small quantities entering the engine will cause rapid wear. Remove all traces of old gasket material and finally clean the cylinder head with paraffin and petrol.

Remove the valves by first compressing the valve springs, using either a suitable spring-type compressor or the special compressor 3084T used by service agents with a support MR 4156.40. Referring to **FIG 1 : 7,** free the split cotters 5. Remove the cotters, the upper spring retaining cup 4, the springs 3 and the sealing ring 6 on inlet valves. A sealing ring is not fitted on exhaust valves as the action of the valve will rotate and destroy the ring. Clean the valves and the valve ports by removing carbon deposits, for which a file card will be useful. Inspect the valve seats and the seatings in the head for wear and deep pitting. Exhaust valves are liable to be burnt, when they will appear brown and discoloured. Examine the valve springs for loss of temper or fracture. Try each valve in its guide for undue side movement, indicating wear of either bore or valve stem or both. Valve seats may be refaced to the specified angles of 120 deg. for inlet valves and 90 deg. for exhaust valves by a service agent with the necessary facilities. As the cylinder head is aluminium it is impossible to renew the valve seats without special tooling. If necessary the valve guides may be renewed by a service agent equipped with the special tools required. New valve guides are finally reamered to

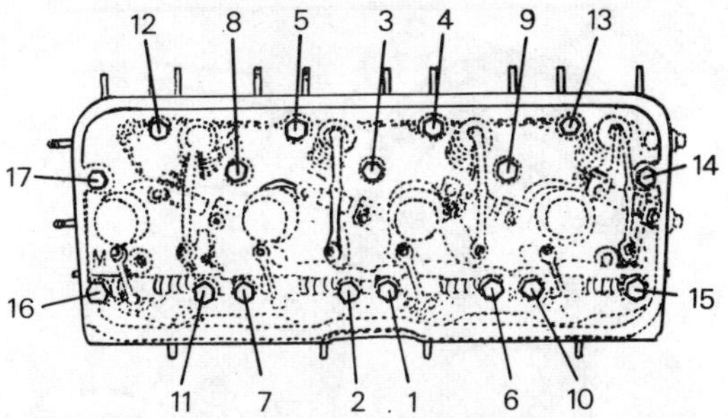

FIG 1 : 9 Cylinder head screws sequence of tightening

a diameter of 9+.015—.010 mm for exhaust valves or 8+.015—.010 mm for inlet valves. Each valve should then be ground into its appropriate seat, using a light application of medium or fine grinding paste. Thoroughly flush out the cylinder head water passages and refit the valve assemblies by reversing the sequence of removal operations. Lubricate the faces and stems of the valves, fit new valve springs if required, also a new sealing ring on the stems of inlet valves only, before fitting the split cotters.

Reassembly of the tappets, pushrods, cylinder head and rocker assemblies is in general the reverse of the removal operations, fitting the pushrods and tappets according to the marks made when dismantling. Take care that a tappet does not fall into an empty bore upside down, when its recovery would involve dismantling the engine. To refit the cylinder head, the contacting faces of head and block must be clean and dry. Remove the screws holding the cylinder barrels and fit a new gasket. Ensure that the cylinder head dowels are in position, centre the gasket and locate the cylinder head on the dowels. Offer up the cylinder head with the exhaust rocker pushrod of No. 4 cylinder in position, as once the cylinder head is in position this pushrod cannot be fitted. Note that when fitting the pushrods the exhaust pushrods are the longer.

When reassembling the inlet rocker shaft, note that the end of the shaft with the lubrication hole 'a' nearest the end (see **FIG 1 : 5**) is the front end. Commence the assembly from this end. Oil the inlet rocker shaft and with the lubrication holes facing downwards and towards the valves, commence fitting in the order of one long screw 1 with its fixing cap 2, the thick washer 3, one rocker, one spring, one thin washer 4 and one long screw. Continue the assembly in the same order, the thick washer 3 being replaced by a thin washer 4 for the other cylinders.

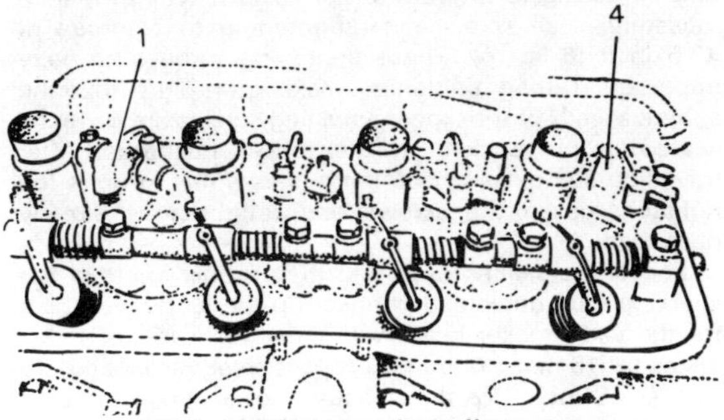

FIG 1 : 10 Valve rocker adjustment

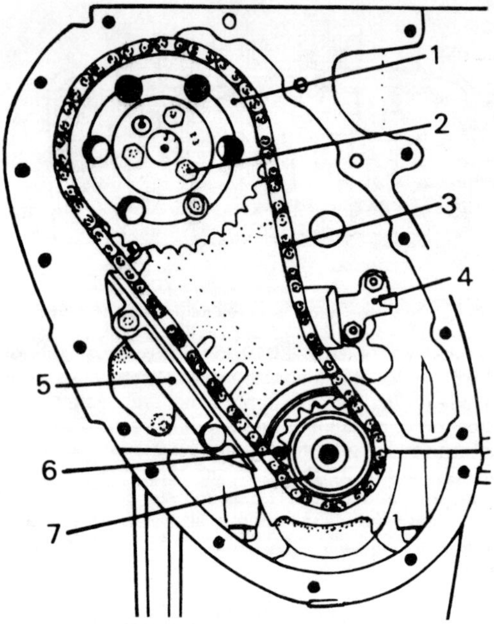

FIG 1:11 The timing gear

Key to Fig 1:11 1 Timing pinion 2 Pinion retaining screws 3 Chain 4 Chain tensioner 5 Chain guide 6 Crankshaft pinion 7 Crankshaft

Fit the bearers on the long screws, positioned as shown in the illustration. The front bearer has a chamfer which must face the rocker pushrod to allow its entry. Place a ring seal 5 on the long screws between the brackets and the cylinder head except on the front screw. Make quite sure that the cylinder head is correctly seated on its dowels and locate the assembly in position. Pass the head of the rear screw through the hole previously made in the engine recess felt.

Assemble the exhaust rockers (see **FIG 1:8**), the lubrication holes 'a' facing downwards and towards the valves. Fit the fixing caps. Tighten the nuts on the studs securing the exhaust rockers to a torque of 18 ± 2 lb ft ($2.5 \pm .3$ kg m). The nuts holding the rocker shaft assembly on No. 1 and No. 3 cylinders also hold the cylinder head.

Fit the cylinder head screws without tightening. Then tighten all the screws in the order shown in **FIG 1:9**, first tightening to a torque of 21.75 lb ft (3 kg m) then loosening each screw and retightening to a torque of 43.5 lb ft (6 kg m). These tightening torques are very important. During tightening make quite sure that the spherical ends of the tappet adjusting screws are correctly seated in the socket on the rocker pushrods. After travelling 300 miles or 500 km it is essential to drain the radiator, loosen the screws and retighten as already described.

Locate the sealing cups and their rubber joints in the sparking plug tubes and connect up the lubrication pipe for the valve rocker gear. Adjust the valve rocker clearances to .15 mm (.006 inch) for the inlet valves and .20 mm (.008 inch) for the exhaust valves when cold, or .20 mm (.008 inch) and .25 mm (.010 inch) respectively, with the engine hot. Adjust the valves of one cylinder with the piston at top dead centre, end of compression. The valves of the corresponding cylinders are then in balance, that is to say, the inlet valve is at the start of admission and the exhaust valve at the end of exhaust. Turn the engine by means of the starting handle, after operating the auxiliary clutch control where fitted, and adjust the valves of individual cylinders as follows:

1 1st cylinder with the valves of the 4th cylinder at the point of balance (see **FIG 1:10**).
2 3rd cylinder with the valves of the 2nd cylinder at the point of balance.
3 4th cylinder with the valves of the 1st cylinder at the point of balance.
4 2nd cylinder with the valves of the 3rd cylinder at the point of balance.

Refit the cylinder head cover, using a new gasket, and tighten the screws to a torque of 5.5 lb ft (.75 kg m).

Proceed to refit and reconnect the items removed for access identified in **Section 1:4,** then connect up the battery and start the engine. Unscrew the pressure control valve bleed screw, leave the engine running for a few minutes and retighten the bleed screw. Where appropriate, bleed the centrifugal regulator and the brakes (see **Chapters 6** and **10**). Check the unions for leakage.

1:6 Removing timing gear and camshaft

With the engine removed from the car as in **Section 1:3** remove the timing cover (see **FIG 1:12**) after unscrewing the three retaining nuts with distance pieces and the remaining screws with plain washers. Referring to **FIG 1:11,** now remove the chain guide 5 and the chain tensioner 4, taking care not to let the components fly apart. Take out the screws 2 holding the timing pinion 1 on the camshaft and remove the pinion and the chain. Note that the crankshaft pinion 6 in **FIG 1:11** is a force fit on the shaft 7 and its renewal can only be carried out in a workshop with specialized equipment.

To remove the camshaft it is necessary first to remove the sump and oil pump (see **Section 1:8**), the distributor (see **Chapter 4**), the cylinder head (see **Section 1:4**), the tappets (see **Section 1:5**) and the timing chain and pinion assembly as already described. Then remove the clamp or securing fork 4 shown in **FIG 1:13,** when the camshaft (see **FIG 1:14**) may be withdrawn from the rear of the engine.

1:7 Refitting timing gear and camshaft

Before reassembling, all parts should be examined for wear and new components fitted if necessary. If the skew gear is badly worn or damaged the oil pump driving gear may also have to be renewed. Check the camshaft thrust plate and timing chain for wear. Also check the shape of the teeth on the timing wheel with those on a new timing wheel, as worn teeth will cause rapid wear of a new chain. To refit the camshaft and timing gear, use new gaskets and proceed as follows:

1 Lubricate the bearing surfaces and insert the camshaft in the cylinder block, carefully guiding it to avoid damage to the bearing surfaces.

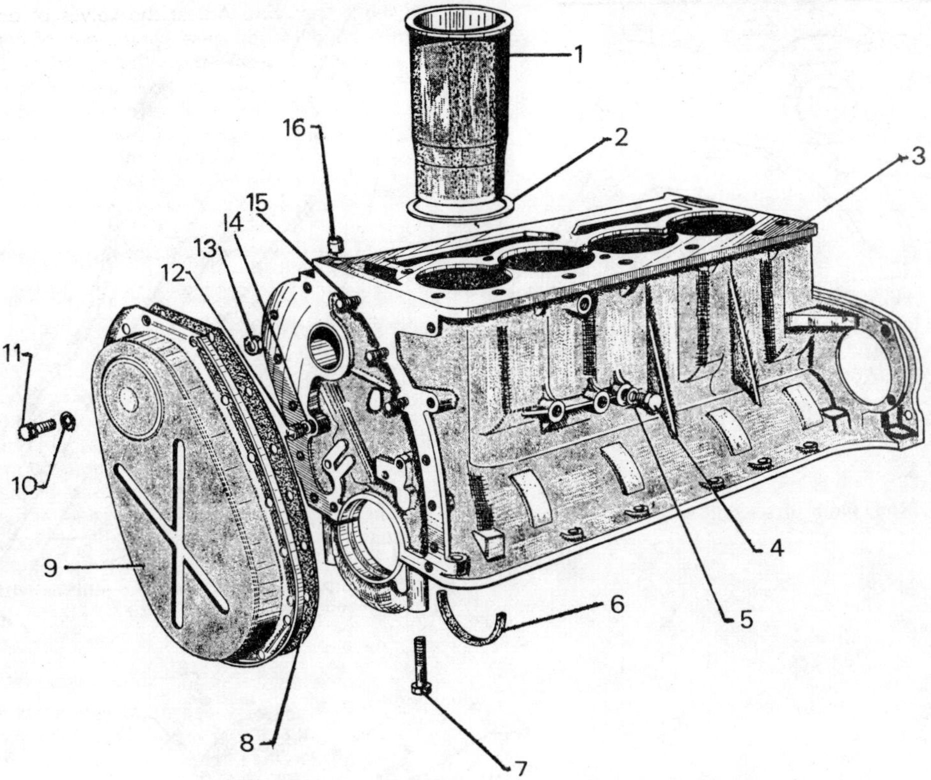

FIG 1:12 An exploded view of the cylinder block

Key to Fig 1:12 1 Cylinder barrel 2 Joint 3 Cylinder block 4 Drain plug 5 Washer 6 Joint 7 Bearing cap screw 8 Joint 9 Timing cover 10 Washer 11 Bolt 12 Timing chain lubricator 13 Nut 14 Securing nut 15 Stud 16 Centring pin

2 Fit the clamp fork in the camshaft groove. The end float of the shaft should be .05 to .07 mm, which is adjustable according to the thickness of the securing clamp. A selection of clamps is available to give an end float within the specified dimensions.

3 Ensure that the positioning dowel for the camshaft pinion is in position then tighten the clamp securing screws with shakeproof washers under the heads to a torque of between 10.0 and 13.5 lb ft (1.4 to 1.9 kg m).

4 Bring the pistons of cylinders Nos. 1 and 4 to about TDC. Place the timing chain on the crankshaft pinion, then the camshaft pinion in the chain.

5 Position the pinions so that the taut side of the chain is on the side farther from the tensioner, and so that a straightedge passing through the centres of the two pinions (see **FIG 1:15**) passes also through the mark (centre punch on one tooth) on the camshaft pinion and through the mark (etched electrically between two teeth) on the crankshaft pinions. The marks should face each other.

6 Turn the camshaft until the centring dowel and the tapped holes are in line with the holes drilled in the pinion. Tighten the securing screws.

7 Referring to **FIG 1:16,** insert the cylinder 3 of the chain tensioner in the body 2, the spring 4 in the cylinder, then the assembly of the slider pad 6 and plunger carrying the pad 5 in the body. The spring will be partly compressed.

8 Through the tapped hole for the plug, insert a 3 mm Allen key and turn it clockwise to engage the plunger pin 5 in the spiral in the cylinder assembly 3. The slide pad carrier 6 must butt against the body 2.

9 Without moving any parts insert the filter 1 in the housing and fit the tensioner on the crankcase. Tighten the screw to 12 lb ft (1.7 kg m), then tighten the screwed plug, inserting and turning over a lock tab.

10 Locate the chain guide 5 (see **FIG 1:11**) in place. Insert the screws 8 without tightening them, with plain washers under the heads. Position the guide to leave a clearance of .1 to .5 mm, then tighten the screws.

11 Insert a new cork gasket and fit the timing cover. Tighten the nuts with spacers under and the screws with plain washers under to a torque of 12 lb ft (1.7 kg m). Reassemble the remaining components in the reverse order of their removal.

1:8 Removing sump and oil pump

The engine and gearbox assembly having been removed from the car as described in **Section 1:3,** the assembly should preferably be suspended from a pulley

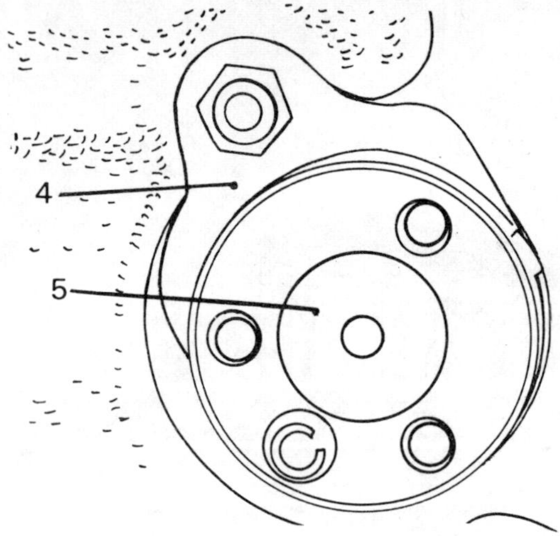

FIG 1:13 The clamp fork 4 on the camshaft 5

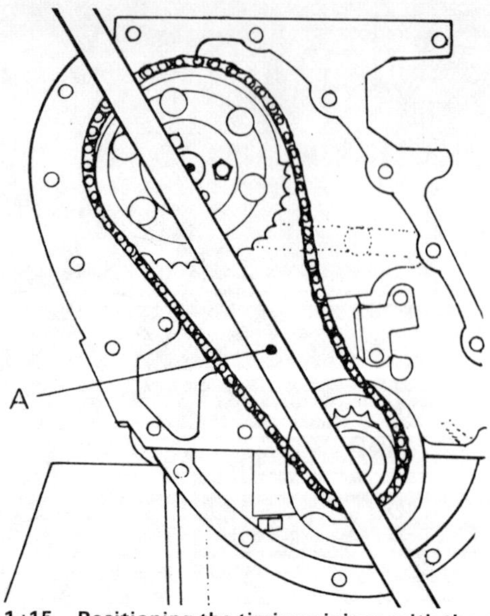

FIG 1:15 Positioning the timing pinions with the aid of a straightedge A

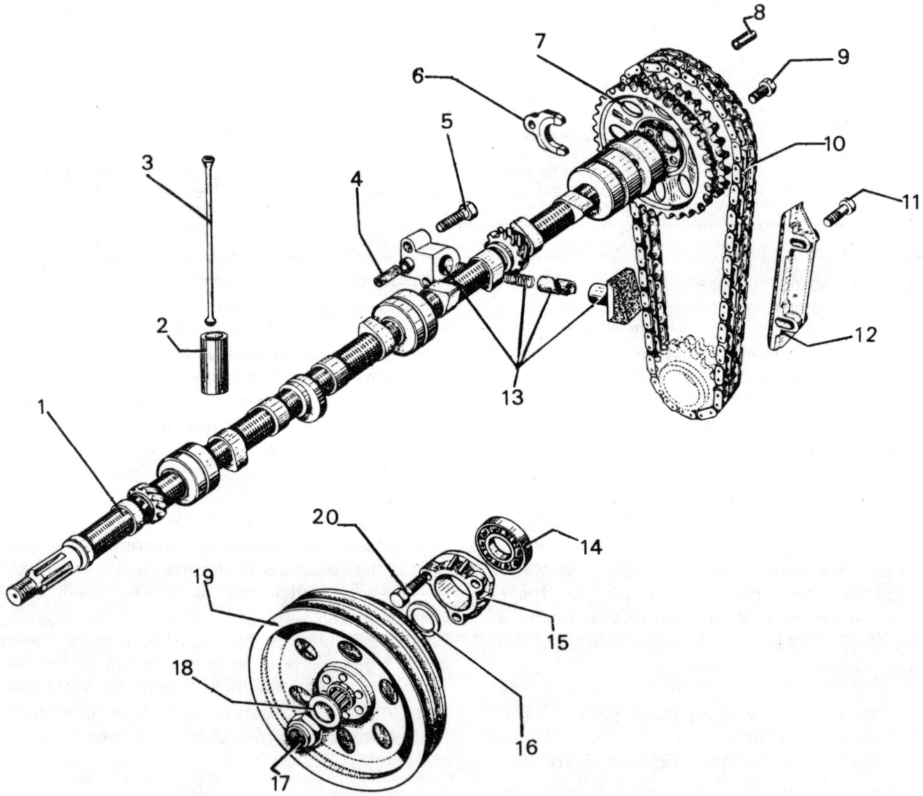

FIG 1:14 An exploded view of the camshaft and timing chain components

Key to Fig 1:14 1 Camshaft 2 Tappet 3 Pushrod 4 Filter 5 Bolt 6 Clamp fork 7 Camshaft pinion 8 Dowel 9 Bolt 10 Timing chain 11 Bolt 12 Chain guide 13 Chain tensioner assembly 14 Ballbearing 15 Hub 16 Washer 17 Attaching nut 18 Washer 19 Pulley 20 Bolt

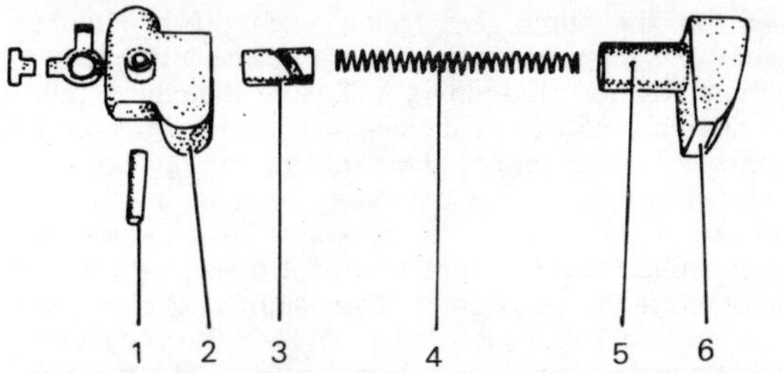

FIG 1:16 An exploded view of the chain tensioner

Key to Fig 1:16 1 Filter 2 Body 3 Cylinder 4 Spring 5 Plunger pin 6 Slider pad

block. After draining the engine oil, remove the bracket securing the exhaust downpipe, then remove the retaining screws and disengage the sump. Detach the cork gasket from the groove of the bearing cap at the flywheel end and carefully clean the groove.

Loosen the locknut 4 (see **FIG 1:17**) and remove the pointed screw 5 holding the oil pump. Then loosen the screw holding the securing clip for the oil pump on No. 3 bearing, free the pump and withdraw it.

When refitting the pump in its housing, ensure that the conical hole in the body of the pump is in line with the tapped hole in the cylinder block. Coat the pointed screw with non-setting sealing compound and tighten it to a torque of 3.25 to 4.75 lb ft (.5 to .7 kg m). Tighten the locknut with non-setting sealing compound applied to its bearing face. Tighten the screw securing the pump lug on No. 3 bearing to a torque of 21.5 to 28.5 lb ft (3 to 4 kg m).

Remove the oil filter access plate under the sump and clean the sump and plate before refitting, for which the use of a detergent followed by hosing out will be effective. Examine the contact faces for distortion or damage and remove all traces of jointing compound or sealer. Fit a new cork gasket in the groove of the bearing cap at the flywheel end. Smear hermetic compound between the gasket and the bearing cap, also the two faces of the sump which meet the cylinder block.

Offer up the sump and insert a long screw to the left-hand side of the bearing at the timing gear end and two long screws on the righthand side of the engine, i.e., the second and third screws counting from the timing end bearing. Tighten all the screws to a torque of 10.5 to 14 lb ft (1.4 to 1.9 kg m).

When refitting the inspection cover, grease the face of the paper joint which contacts the sump and smear hermetic compound on the other face. Tighten the screws retaining the inspection cover to a torque of 6.25 to 8.5 lb ft (.9 to 1.2 kg m). Fit the drain plug with a new gasket and tighten it to a torque of 17.5 to 24.5 lb ft (2.5 to 3.5 kg m).

For routine maintenance, removal of the inspection cover after draining the sump allows access for the renewal of the engine oil filter every 6000 miles or 10,000 km. To renew the filter, remove the centre screw, the strainer assembly and the filter element. Clean the strainer assembly with petrol and dry it under a compressed air jet but never refit a used filter element. Refit the assembly into the filter housing so that the red triangles shown in **FIG 1:18**, one on the strainer and the

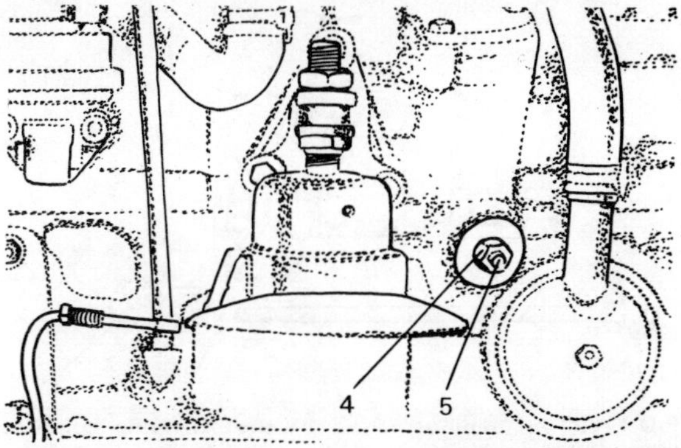

FIG 1:17 Oil pump retaining screw 5 and locknut 4

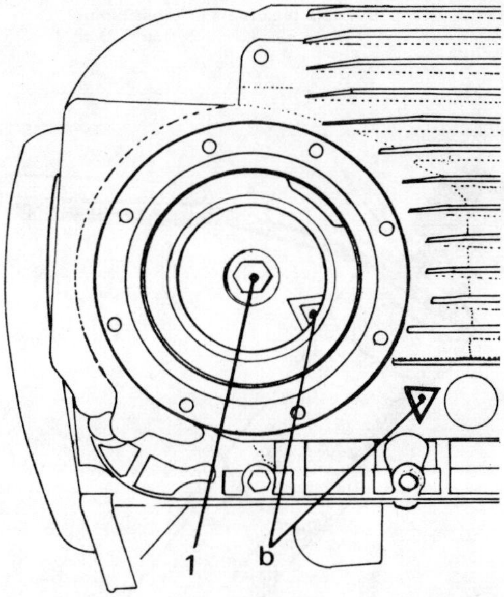

FIG 1:18 Oil pump strainer assembly showing the centre screw 1 and the red locating symbols at b

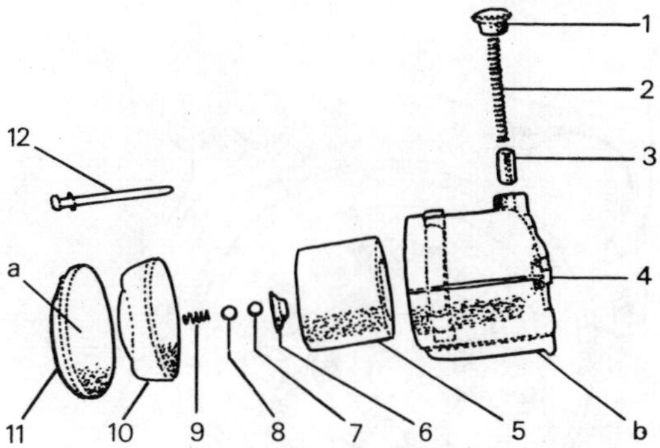

FIG 1:19 An exploded view of the oil pump filter

Key to Fig 1:19 1 Plug 2 Spring 3 Piston 4 Filter body 5 Filter element 6 Cup 7 Ring seal 8 Flat washer 9 Spring 10 Bowl 11 Pre-filter 12 Screw **a** Guides **b** Suction boss

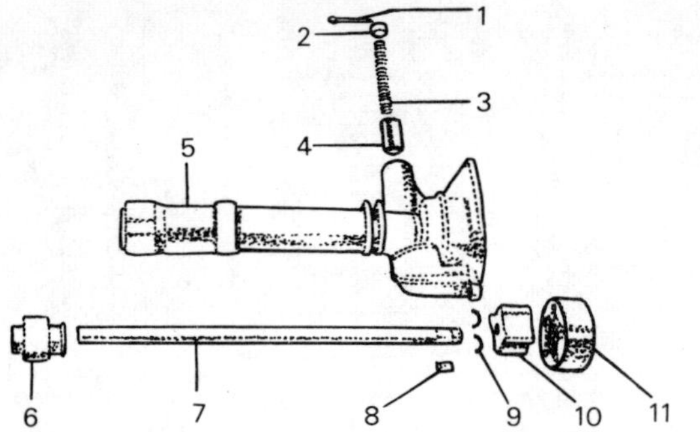

FIG 1:20 An exploded view of the oil pump spindle assembly

Key to Fig 1:20 1 Pin 2 Thrust cup 3 Spring 4 Piston 5 Housing 6 Drive pinion 7 Spindle 8 Key 9 Half cotters 10 Pump pinion 11 Loose pinion

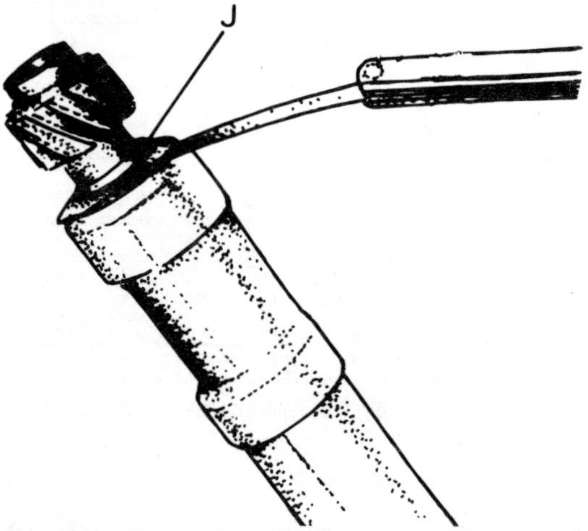

FIG 1:21 Measuring oil pump pinion clearance at J

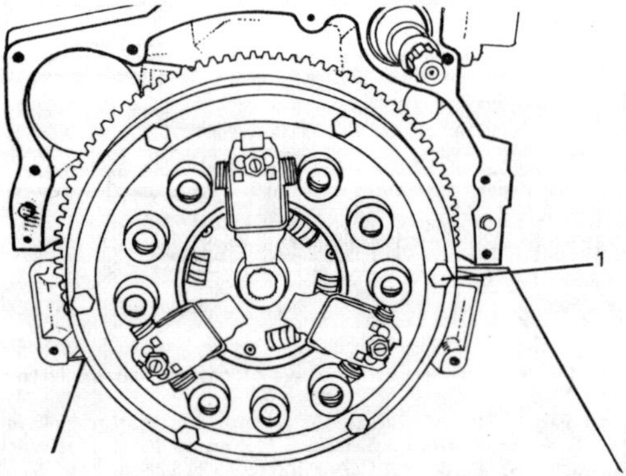

FIG 1:22 The clutch, showing the retaining screws I

other on the sump, are facing each other. Hold the assembly against the filter body and insert the screw 1 by hand without tightening it. Ensure that the screw is not slanting, as if it is it means that it is not correctly engaged in the tapped hole of the pump body but between the boss and the filter element. In this case lubrication of the engine is not ensured. Also ensure that the pre-filter cover cannot turn. If it does, the pre-filter is not correctly positioned. Then tighten the screw to between 6 to 7 lb ft (.8 to 1 kg m). Refit the access plate on the sump as previously described and refill the sump.

1:9 Dismantling and reassembling oil pump

Referring to **FIG 1:19,** remove (a) the screw 12 with its flat washer, (b) the cup 6 holding the filter, (c) the ring seal 7, (d) the flat washer 8, (e) the spring 9, (f) the bowl 10, (g) the pre-filter 11, (h) the filter element 5, (j) the plug 1, (k) the spring 2 (l) the piston 3, (m) the filter body 4. Withdraw the loose pinion from the pump.

Remove the drive pinion using a suitable extractor or the service tool 1964T and a spacer 10 mm diameter x 40 mm long. Referring to **FIG 1:20,** remove (a) the spindle 7, (b) the half-cotters 9, (c) the key 8, (d) the pump pinion 10. Remove the oil pressure control valve by taking out (a) the pin 1, (b) the thrust cup 2, (c) the spring 3, (d) the piston 4.

The bush of the support tube cannot be dismantled. If it is worn it is essential to change the pump body. Check that the filter sealing face on the pump body is not scored. If it is it should be resurfaced.

To reassemble the pump, connect the pinion 10 to the spindle, using the key 8 and the split stop cotters 9. Place this assembly in the pump body. Fit the drive pinion 6 on the spindle using a press, and maintaining a clearance of .4 to .5 mm between the pump body and the pinion as shown in **FIG 1:21.**

Refit the pressure control valve and the remaining components in the reverse order of their dismantling. When locating the filter body 4 (see **FIG 1:19**) on the bottom of the pump, insert the securing screws and position the fixing lug on the side opposite to the hole for the pointed screw on the pump body. Also, fit the filter assembly so that the guides 'a' are on each side of the suction boss 'b'.

1:10 Removing clutch and flywheel

With the engine and gearbox assembly removed from the car, the gearbox must first be disconnected from the engine as follows:

1 Remove the radiator, the belts and the drive pulley, setting aside the adjusting washers. Remove the starter motor.

2 Disconnect the pipe at the pressure regulator which connects the regulator to the high pressure pump, also the pump stay. Then remove the assembling screws to detach the gearbox from the engine. Do not roll the gearbox with the brake discs on the ground, as emphasized in **Section 1:3.**

Proceed to mark the position of the clutch housing on the engine flywheel. Remove the screws 1 (see **FIG 1:22**) holding the clutch mechanism to remove the latter and the clutch disc.

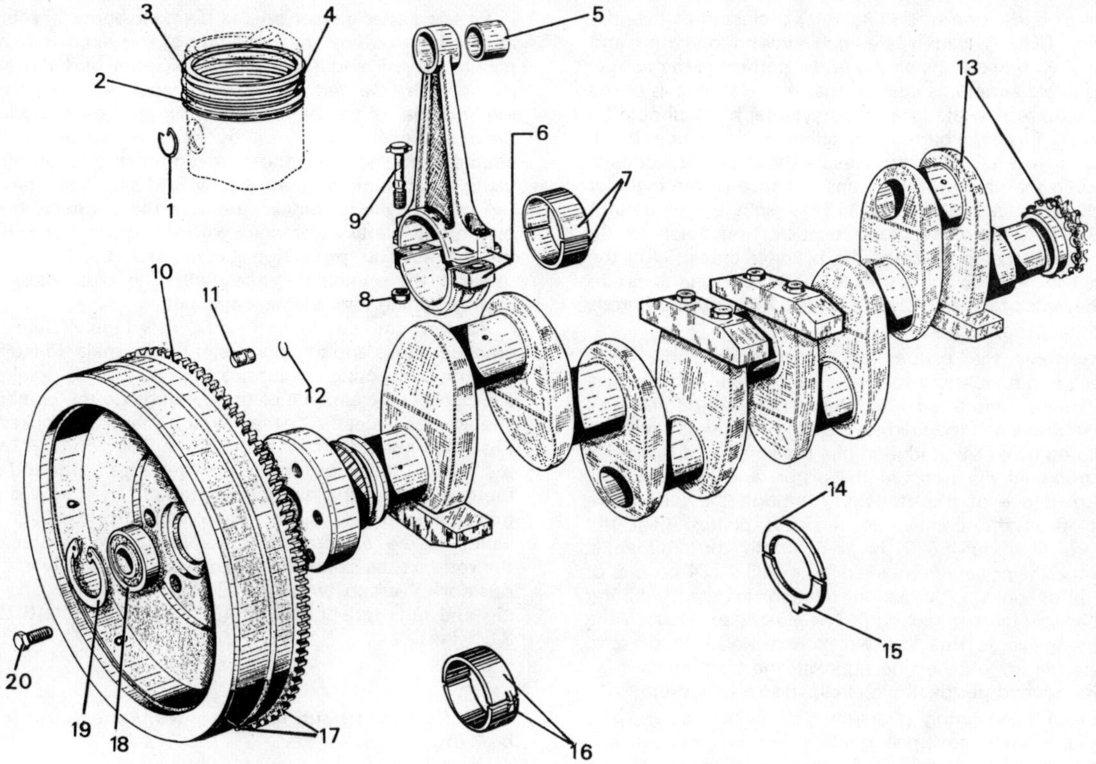

FIG 1:23 An exploded view of the crankshaft, connecting rod and piston assemblies

Key to Fig 1:23 1 Circlip 2 Scraper ring 3 Compression ring 4 Compression ring 5 Small-end bush 6 Connecting rod and cap 7 Big-end bearing liners 8 Nut 9 Big-end bolt 10 Starter gear ring 11 Dowel 12 Circlip 13 Crankshaft pinion 14 Upper thrust half-ring 15 Lower thrust half-ring 16 Front bearing 17 Flywheel 18 Bearing 19 Circlip 20 Attaching screw

Detach the retaining bolts securing the flywheel (see **FIG 1:23**) and whilst supporting it tap it off the crankshaft flange evenly, using a copper or lead hammer. Examine the friction face of the flywheel for scores or cracks. Scores can be removed by machining within specified limits. Examine the ballbearing in the flywheel bore for roughness or wear and renew if necessary. The condition of the ring gear should also be examined. If replacement is necessary it is advisable to use the special facilities and experience at the disposal of a service workshop.

1:11 Splitting big-ends, removing rods, pistons and cylinder liners

Access to the connecting rod big-end assemblies and removal of connecting rods, pistons and cylinder barrels (see **FIGS 1:12** and **1:23**) requires the removal of the cylinder head, sump and oil pump as described in previous Sections.

The connecting rod and connecting rod cap are numbered with the same number on both parts. When the connecting rods are fitted to the engine this number is to be facing towards the camshaft side. Before dismantling mark the connecting rods with figures (do not use a file or a punch) showing the order of assembly in the engine. Commence the marking with No. 1 connecting rod at the clutch end. If the bearings or pistons and barrels are to be used again it is absolutely essential to fit them in the same place they occupied before dismantling. The barrels must be fitted so that they are in the same relative positions to the pistons as they were before dismantling.

Remove the connecting rod caps and the screws holding the barrels in place, when the assemblies of connecting rods, pistons, barrels and gaskets may be withdrawn. There are two types of barrels of different heights, marked yellow or blue on the stock. If the barrels are difficult to lift out of their housings in the cylinder block, gentle leverage may be initially applied by two screwdrivers diametrically opposed. Check the bores for distortion.

1:12 Pistons, rings and gudgeon pins

Before separating a piston from its connecting rod the piston rings should be removed, using a piston ring expander. The gudgeon pins are free in the connecting rods and may be removed by extracting one of the retaining circlips in each case, thus separating the pistons.

New assemblies of barrels and pistons are provided matched, as are the pistons and gudgeon pins. Note that the position of the barrel in relation to the piston is not important with brand-new components. There are two types of barrel corresponding to two classes of cylinder blocks. Class 1 barrels are marked with one ring and Class 2 with two rings on the upper portion of the flange.

To avoid errors it is advised that the relationship of the barrel top face to the face of the cylinder block should be checked. Place the barrels in position in the cylinder block without their gaskets and measure the difference in level between the barrel top face and the face of the cylinder block using a dial gauge 1754T, with a comparator 2437T. The barrel top face must be from flush to .04 mm below the top face of the cylinder block. With the gasket in position the barrel top face must stand proud of the block face by .12 to .16 mm. Remove the barrels from the cylinder block.

Assemble the pistons and connecting rods. Note that it is not possible to replace the small-end bushes. The bushes are fitted after being nitrogen-cooled and special tooling is required for reaming the bore. Lubricate with engine oil the gudgeon pin, the small-end bush and the gudgeon pin bores in the piston and locate a new circlip in one of the grooves. Although the pins are a push-fit in the connecting rod and piston, heat the pistons to about 60°C, in an oil bath for preference. Arrange the projection marked 'a' in **FIG 1 : 24** on one of the gudgeon-pin bosses in relation to the matching number on the connecting rod as illustrated. Then fit the gudgeon pin so that the two etched marks on the end of the pin are on the side opposite the boss marked 'a'. Fit the second gudgeon pin circlip, also a new one.

Using piston ring pliers, fit the piston rings. It is advisable to fit new piston rings, but first remove any carbon or other deposits from the ring grooves. Also, if the liners have had some service the internal oil glaze must be removed. Referring to **FIG 1 : 25**, fit the rings in the following order:

1 The oil ring 1. Place in position (a) the expander 2 by hand, (b) the oil ring with the aid of piston ring pliers. The gaps in these two parts must be at 180 deg. to each other.

2 The scraper ring 3. This is tapered and carries an oil scraper groove which must always face towards the piston skirt when the ring is fitted.

3 The compression ring 4. This is chromed and has two small outer chamfers. Fit the ring so that the mark 'TOP' and the inner chamfer are towards the top.

Arrange the gaps in the piston rings so that the compression ring has the gap towards the number on the big-end of the connecting rod and the scraper and oil rings have their gaps at 120 deg. from the gap in the first ring.

Prepare the cylinder barrels for insertion by wire-brushing the exteriors to remove any scale deposits. Avoid damaging the bearing surfaces, however, which must be perfectly clean. Oil the pistons and the barrels. If the assemblies of connecting rods—pistons—barrels and connecting rod bearings are to be used again, they must be assembled in accordance with the markings made when dismantling. To fit the assemblies a special bush 3072T is fitted over the rings from the skirt of the piston, with an interior chamfer in the bush towards the top of the piston. Note that the entry of the oil ring in the bush requires a considerable force which must be reduced when the ring begins to slide into the bush, so as to avoid breaking the scraper ring by striking it with the edge of the bush.

Fit the paper gasket on the cylinder barrel, the black lines which outline the positions of the extra thickness parallel to the end faces of the big-end and the extra thicknesses (the part with brown paper) in contact with the shoulder of the barrel. Work the joint onto the liner. Service agents work it on by hand as far as the first shoulder on the liner and then complete the fitting by using a flat punched plate No. MR.4134. Then from the top of the cylinder block introduce the connecting rod, piston and barrel assemblies with the pistons at TDC in the barrel. The projection 'a' in **FIG 1 : 24** must be towards the engine flywheel, with the connecting rod number facing towards the camshaft.

To refit the connecting rods, thoroughly clean the crankpin bores and the oilways in the journals. Make sure that the connecting rod lubricating holes in the crankpins are clear. The clearance of the bearings on the crankpins should not exceed .06 mm, which may be checked as described for the main bearings in **Section 1 : 13.** Oil the bearing faces and fit the half bearings in the rod and the cap. Ensure that the lugs engage in the grooves and that the reference marks made when dismantling coincide if the existing bearings are being refitted. Fit the rods on the crankshaft taking care not to reverse the position of a cap on a rod. Tighten the connecting rod big-end nuts to a torque of 48.25 to 53.5 lb ft (6.75 to 7.5 kg m).

1 : 13 Removing and refitting crankshaft and main bearings

With the piston and connecting rod assemblies removed as already described, removal of the crankshaft (see **FIG 1 : 23**) is undertaken as follows:

1 Remove the main bearing caps (see **FIG 1 : 26**). The crankshaft bearing caps are marked with a figure, except for the bearing at the flywheel end which is not marked. A No. 4 bearing is fitted at the timing gear end. Note that the caps are fitted with the figures facing towards the camshaft.

2 Remove the bearings, and the half thrust rings on the central bearing No. 2. If the crankshaft shell-bearings are to be used again, mark them so that they can be returned to the same position they occupied before dismantling. Withdraw the crankshaft.

3 Examine the condition of the journals and main bearings. Clean the shaft and in particular the oil passages. The shaft may be checked for alignment by supporting it between centres and taking indicator readings on the main journals.

4 Check the crankshaft to bearing clearance but do not use steel feeler strip, otherwise the bearing surface will be damaged. Clearances can be checked by using a piece of Plastigage strip across the centre of the journal, assembling the cap and half bearing and tightening to the specified torque. The bearing and journal must be free from oil, in which Plastigage is soluble. The flattened Plastigage when removed and measured at its widest point will give the clearance in thousands of an inch in relation to the scale provided with the material. Clearances on crankshaft bearings should not exceed .06 mm. The crankshaft main journal diameters may be machined to 64.04 mm dia. or 63.54 mm dia. Note that it is possible to

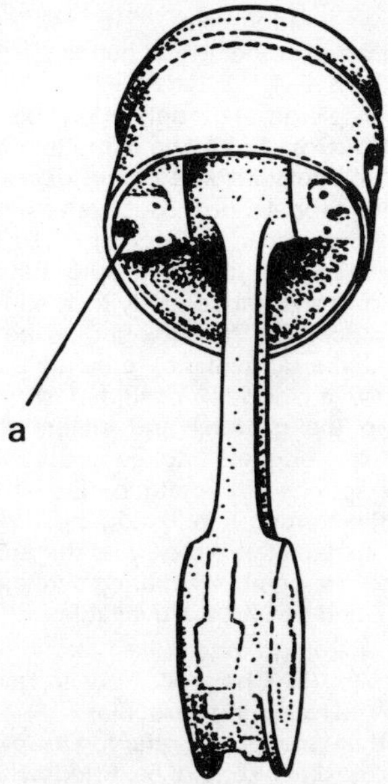

FIG 1 : 24 Piston and connecting rod assembly showing the projection a

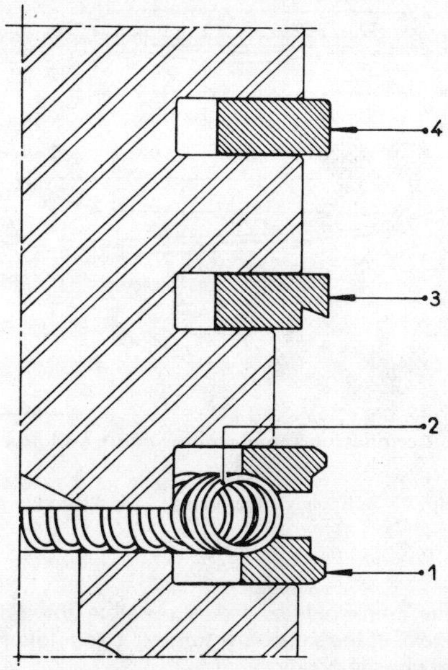

FIG 1 : 25 Diagram showing piston ring location

Key to Fig 1 : 25 1 Oil ring 2 Expander 3 Scraper ring 4 Compression ring

renew the connecting rod and crankshaft bearings separately. It is advised that when required standard exchange assemblies should be used, which are available ready for fitting. The crankshaft pinion cannot be renewed.

5 The main bearing housing bores should be checked by assembling the caps to the crankcase without the bearings to ensure that the bearing caps have not been filed. If so, it is not possible to fit the standard crankshaft/connecting rod assemblies. It is then necessary to renew the cylinder block or to rebore the cylinder block bearings, for which the assistance of a service agent with the necessary equipment should be obtained.

When refitting the crankshaft, if the main bearings are to be used again they must be fitted according to the marks made when dismantling. It will be necessary to obtain the specified end float of .045 to .160 mm by means of the half rings (see **FIG 1 : 23**) situated on each side of the central main bearing, with a locating lug on the half rings in the bearing caps. There are two classes of rings marked I and II on the steel face, Class I of thicknesses 3.10 to 3.14 mm and Class II of thicknesses 3.14 to 3.18 mm. The two half rings placed on the same side of the bearing must both be of the same thickness, although the half rings placed on one side of the bearing may be of a different thickness from those placed on the other side. Proceed as follows:

1 Place the half rings so that the faces covered with anti-friction metal are in contact with the crankshaft.
2 Oil the bearings. Place a half ring Class I on each side of the bearing.
3 Put the crankshaft in position and fit the two intermediate bearing caps and tighten the screws to a torque of 36 lb ft (5 kg m).

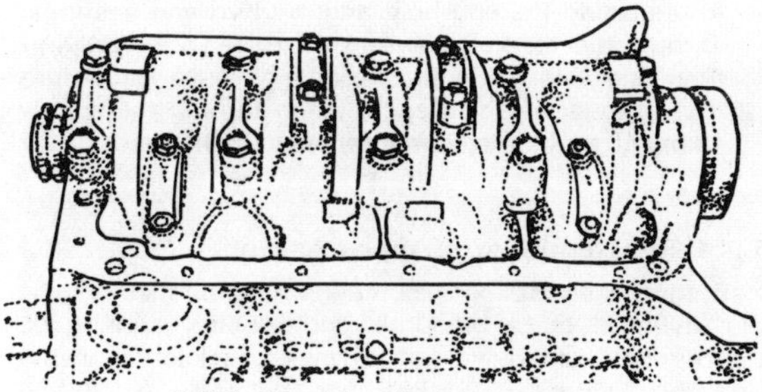

FIG 1 : 26 Main bearing caps

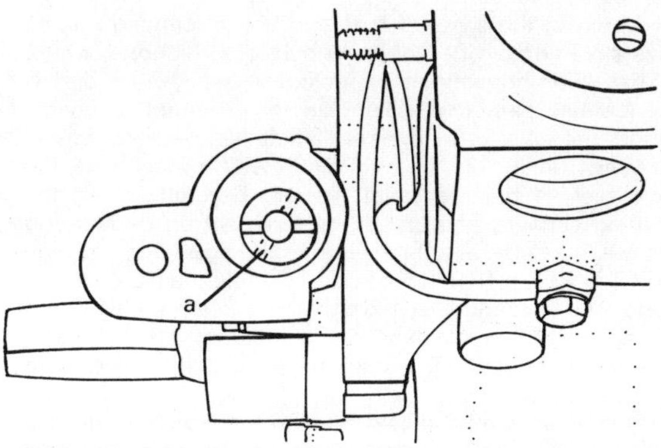

FIG 1 : 27 Distributor drive (DX) showing driving slot at a

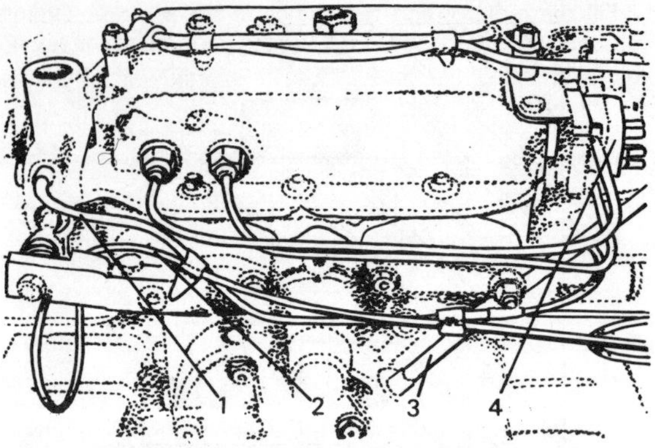

FIG 1 : 28 Connecting speedometer cable and pipework

Key to Fig 1 : 28 1 Feed pipe for the clutch lock 2 Return pipe 3 Speedometer cable 4 Gearchange pipe assembly

4 Push the crankshaft as far as possible towards the timing gear, at the same time turning it and holding the two half rings in position.

5 Using a feeler gauge, measure the clearance, which should lie between .045 mm and .160 mm. If it is greater replace one or both of the rings by rings of Class II. Push them round the crankshaft journal without removing the shaft.

6 Fit the cap of the central bearing, with its half rings for adjusting the end float and the two end bearings. Tighten the fixing screws to 36 lb ft (5 kg m) and then finally to 72 lb ft (10 kg m). Make quite sure that there are no hard spots when turning the crankshaft and that the end float remains unchanged.

1 :14 Reassembling stripped engine

Before reassembling a completely dismantled engine the cylinder block and all components should be thoroughly cleaned and all oilways checked to ensure that they are clear. Gaskets and oil seals should be renewed as required, carefully cleaning the joint faces free from old gasket material and jointing compound. All bearing surfaces and moving parts should be lightly oiled before assembly.

Much of the work of reassembling a stripped engine has already been described in previous Sections, where it has been convenient to include it with other details concerning particular assemblies. In sequence of operations, the refitting of the crankshaft has been described in **Section 1 :13,** which is followed by refitting the flywheel on the crankshaft flange. Carefully clean the mating surfaces and locate the flywheel on its centring dowel. Insert the attaching screws and tighten to a torque of 42 to 47 lb ft (5.9 to 6.5 kg m). Couple the clutch to the flywheel, ensuring that the bearing faces are clean, and using a gearbox mainshaft or a mandrel MR.3676.350 to centre the disc. The mandrel should slide evenly to ensure concentricity with the flywheel bearing. Note that there are twelve drilled holes in the clutch casing but only six are used for assembly. Fit the clutch mechanism so that three of its screws are in line with the toggles. Tighten the screws to a torque of 25 lb ft (3.5 kg m) with shakeproof washers under the heads. Remove the mandrel.

Refitting of the piston and connecting rod assemblies is described in **Section 1 :12,** the sump and oil pump in **Section 1 :8,** the camshaft and timing gear in **Section 1 :7** and the valve tappets, pushrods, valves, rocker shaft assembly and cylinder head in **Section 1 :5.** To connect the gearbox to the engine, first make sure that the dowels for centring the gearbox are correctly located in the holes in the cylinder block. The gearbox should be resting on a trolley or similar arrangement, for which the service practice is to use a specially designed support fixture 1799.T. Offer up the gearbox and ensure that it is in alignment with the engine. Engage the splines of the mainshaft in the splines of the clutch disc by turning the mainshaft with the starting handle dog, pushing the gearbox meanwhile to facilitate entry into the splines. Then insert and tighten the gearbox securing screws, for which spanners 2431.T and 1677.T are available.

Refit the remaining assemblies and components removed as detailed in **Chapter 3** but in reverse order, giving regard to the following particulars:

1 For refitting the water pump, refer to **Chapter 5.**

2 The exhaust gaskets should be fitted with the joint turnover towards the manifolds.

3 Fit the two exhaust manifolds together, leaving the securing nuts fingertight. Final tightening is carried out when the engine is installed.

4 When the pressure regulator and its bracket are refitted locate the assembly as high as possible within the limits allowed by the clearance of the holes and the securing screws.

5 To fit the distributor and its drive tower, bring the No. 1 piston (next to the flywheel) to TDC, then place a gasket smeared with grease on the distributor drive. Grease the lips of the seal and offer up the distributor drive. Before engaging the pinion the offset driving slot 'a' (see **FIG 1 :27**) must be facing forwards at 45 deg. to the camshaft, with the offset towards the engine. After engaging the pinion, secure the drive on the crankcase with two long screws in the upper part and one short screw in the lower part and plain washers under the heads. The drive slot should then be parallel to the centre line of the camshaft and the small side of the sleeve must still always be towards the engine.

6 The fan securing screws are to be tightened to a torque of 7 to 10 lb ft (1 to 1.4 kg m).

7 For refitting the driving belts refer to **Chapter 2** and for the brake units to **Chapter 10.**

1 :15 Refitting engine in car

Operations in general for installing the engine and gearbox assembly are as follows. For more detailed instructions on refitting individual items reference should be made to later Chapters covering the assemblies concerned.

1 Lift the assembly and place it in position. Allow the engine to rest on its mountings. Place the packing pieces, found when dismantling between the front engine crossmember and the body sidemembers. Tighten the screws using plain and shakeproof washers.

2 There must be a difference of 80 ± 2 mm between the distance from the lefthand disc to the body and that from the righthand disc to the body. Alter the packing shims if necessary.
3 Fix the rear engine mountings on the rear supports, using shakeproof washers and thrust plates under the screw heads.
4 Connect the reservoir return pipe to the pressure regulator and the pressure regulator outlet pipe to the three-way union.
5 Fit the flexible bearing onto the carburetter control relay and place it on its bracket on the scuttle front. Align the bearing and tighten the securing nuts using flat and shakeproof washers.
6 Pass the vertical accelerator control rod through the trunnion in the lever and hook on the springs. Adjust the control (see **Chapter 3**).
7 Renew the handbrake cable and adjust it (see **Chapter 10**).
8 Place the drive shafts in position. Fit the tri-axe housings on the studs in the flanges of the gearbox outlet shafts. Assemble the nuts and tighten them to a torque of from 60 to 80 lb ft (8.5 to 11.0 kg m), using a 17 mm socket and extension. Fit the drive shaft flanges on the wheel hubs with two countersunk head screws on each side.
9 Referring to **FIG 1:28**, connect the speedometer cable 3, the gearchange pipe assembly 4 and the feedpipe 1 for the clutch lock and its reservoir return pipe 2.
10 Connect the exhaust downpipe to the flexible exhaust pipe. Fit the downpipe in its support under the engine. Tighten the nut using plain and shakeproof washers. Tighten the fixing clamp of the downpipe connection to the flexible exhaust pipe. Connect the heater hose to the hot water supply pipe on the cylinder head.
11 Fit the steering rack (see **Chapter 9**).
12 Connect the supply pipe to the front lefthand brake unit, also the holding clip for this pipe, and the lead for the brake pad wear warning light.
13 Fit the hydraulic reservoir and assemble the battery tray, the battery, and the battery top frame. Connect the cables to the battery terminals.
14 Fit the fuel pump hose, and the heater hose to the heater unit.
15 Connect the generator or alternator leads, the distributor leads (LT and HT) and the lead for the thermometer transmitter. Fit the front wheels and lower the car to the ground.
16 Fit the air filter and the rubber union between the filter and the rocker cover. Connect the rubber elbow between the carburetter and the air filter.
17 Couple up the connecting pipe between the clutch re-engagement control and the hydraulic gear selector where fitted.
18 Couple up the connecting pipe between the hydraulic gear selector and the centrifugal regulator where fitted.
19 Adjust, if necessary, the initial ignition advance setting (see **Chapter 4**).
20 Connect the carburetter choke control and adjust it (see **Chapter 3**).
21 Fill the reservoir with the recommended fluid (see **Chapter 2**) and fit the two front suspension spheres.
22 Fill the radiator and the engine cylinder block. Open the heater tap, start up the engine and check the level after a few minutes running, then top up if necessary.
23 Have pressure applied by an assistant to the hydraulic brake pedal to centralize the brake. Tighten the screws securing the brake units on the gearbox outlet housings to between 94 and 100 lb ft (13 to 14 kg m). Bleed the brakes as described in **Chapter 10.**
24 Raise the engine and secure the exhaust downpipe to the manifolds. Adjust the idling as described in **Chapter 3.**
25 Refit the wings and connect the wiring harnesses. Refit the radiator air intake duct with the spare wheel crossmember and reassemble the wheel.

After a final inspection to ensure that all components have been properly connected, undo the screw on the pressure control valve. Start the engine, let it run for a few minutes and check for any oil or water leaks. Retighten the bleed screw so as to put the hydraulic system under pressure and check all unions for leakage.

1:16 Fault diagnosis

(a) Engine will not start

1 Defective coil
2 Faulty distributor capacitor
3 Dirty, pitted or incorrectly set contact breaker points
4 Ignition wires loose or insulation faulty
5 Water on sparking plug leads
6 Corrosion of battery terminals or discharged condition
7 Faulty or jammed starter
8 Sparking plug leads wrongly connected
9 Vapour lock in fuel pipes
10 Defective fuel pump
11 Overchoking
12 Underchoking
13 Blocked petrol filter or carburetter jets
14 Leaking valves
15 Sticking valves
16 Valve timing incorrect
17 Ignition timing incorrect

(b) Engine stalls

Check 1, 2, 3, 4, 10, 11, 12, 13, 14 and 15 in (a)
1 Sparking plugs defective or gap incorrect
2 Retarded ignition
3 Mixture too weak
4 Water in fuel system
5 Petrol tank breather choked
6 Incorrect valve clearance

(c) Engine idles badly

Check 1 and 6 in (b)
1 Air leak in manifold joints
2 Slow-running jet blocked or out of adjustment
3 Air leak in carburetter
4 Over-rich mixture
5 Worn piston rings
6 Worn valve stems or guides
7 Weak exhaust valve springs

(d) Engine misfires

Check 1, 2, 3, 4, 5, 8, 10, 13, 14, 15, 16 and 17 in (a) and 1, 2, 3 and 6 in (b)
1 Weak or broken valve springs

(e) Engine overheats

See **Chapter 5**

(f) Compression low

Check 14 and 15 in (a); 5 and 6 in (c) and 1 in (d)
1 Worn piston ring grooves
2 Scored or worn cylinder bores

(g) Engine lacks power

Check 3, 10, 11, 13, 14, 15 and 16 in (a); 1, 2, 3 and 6 in (b); 5 and 6 in (c) and 1 in (d). Also check (e) and (f)
1 Leaking joint washers
2 Fouled spark plugs

(h) Burnt valves or seats

Check 14 and 15 in (a); 6 in (b) and 1 in (d). Also check (e)
1 Excessive carbon around valve seat and head

(j) Sticking valves

Check 1 in (d)
1 Bent valve stem
2 Scored valve stem, or guide
3 Incorrect valve clearance

(k) Excessive cylinder wear

Check 11 in (a) and check (c)
1 Lack of oil
2 Dirty oil
3 Piston rings gummed up or broken
4 Badly fitting piston rings
5 Connecting rods bent

(l) Excessive oil consumption

Check 5 and 6 in (c) and check (k)
1 Ring gaps too wide
2 Scored cylinders
3 Oil level too high
4 External oil leaks
5 Ineffective valve stem oil seals

(m) Crankshaft and connecting rod failure

Check 1 in (k)
1 Restricted oilways
2 Worn journals or crankpins
3 Loose bearing caps
4 Extremely low oil pressure
5 Bent connecting rod

(n) Internal water leakage (see **Chapter 5**)

(o) Poor circulation (see **Chapter 5**)

(p) Corrosion (see **Chapter 5**)

(q) High fuel consumption (see **Chapter 3**)

(r) Engine vibration

1 Loose generator bolts
2 Rear engine supports out of adjustment
3 Exhaust pipe mountings too tight

CHAPTER 2

THE HYDRAULIC PRESSURE SYSTEM

2:1 General description

Hydraulic power for operating the brakes and often the clutch in ordinary cars is usually initiated by individual action by the driver as required, with separate fluid pressure arrangements being incorporated in particular features such as power steering equipment and automatic transmission.

In the Citroen cars under description, however, a single central pressure system is employed to give a continuous source of hydraulic power when the engine is running, thus eliminating much of the physical effort involved in conventional arrangements. The engine drives a seven-cylinder pump supplying hydraulic fluid under pressure to an accumulator, from which it is bled off as required to serve particular purposes. Full use of this power source in DS cars is made by applying it to controlling a hydro-pneumatic suspension system as well as the brakes and steering, the operation of the clutch and the selection of the gears.

A diagrammatic view of the hydraulic system is shown in **FIG 2:1.** Fluid is drawn from a reservoir by a high pressure pump which supplies the main accumulator. Pressure in the accumulator is controlled by a valve, which returns fluid to the reservoir at an upper limit of 2130 to 2420 lb/sq inch (150 to 170 kg/sq cm) and cuts in again at 1850 to 1990 lb/sq inch (130 to 140 kg/sq cm). With hydraulic gearchange, the main accumulator supplies high pressure fluid to the gearchange and clutch control block, the centrifugal clutch control unit, the steering pressure distributor or servo control and the distributor block. The latter feeds the front suspension circuit supplying the front brake accumulator, also the brakes and rear suspension directly. The operating pedal for the brakes takes the form of a plunger with a small circular head and very limited movement. When depressed it opens valves in the brake pressure distribution unit to allow fluid under pressure to be transmitted to each circuit with almost negligible effort.

Hydraulic gear operation takes place in conjunction with the clutch release also actuated by the change-speed lever forward of the steering wheel, fluid being delivered under pressure which varies with engine speed, gearlever movement and accelerator position. No clutch pedal is provided and clutch action begins automatically by movement of the gearlever into the required position with a light touch. The fast idling speed on the carburetter is set to give a slow creep when first gear is engaged but to idle slower when the footbrake is applied.

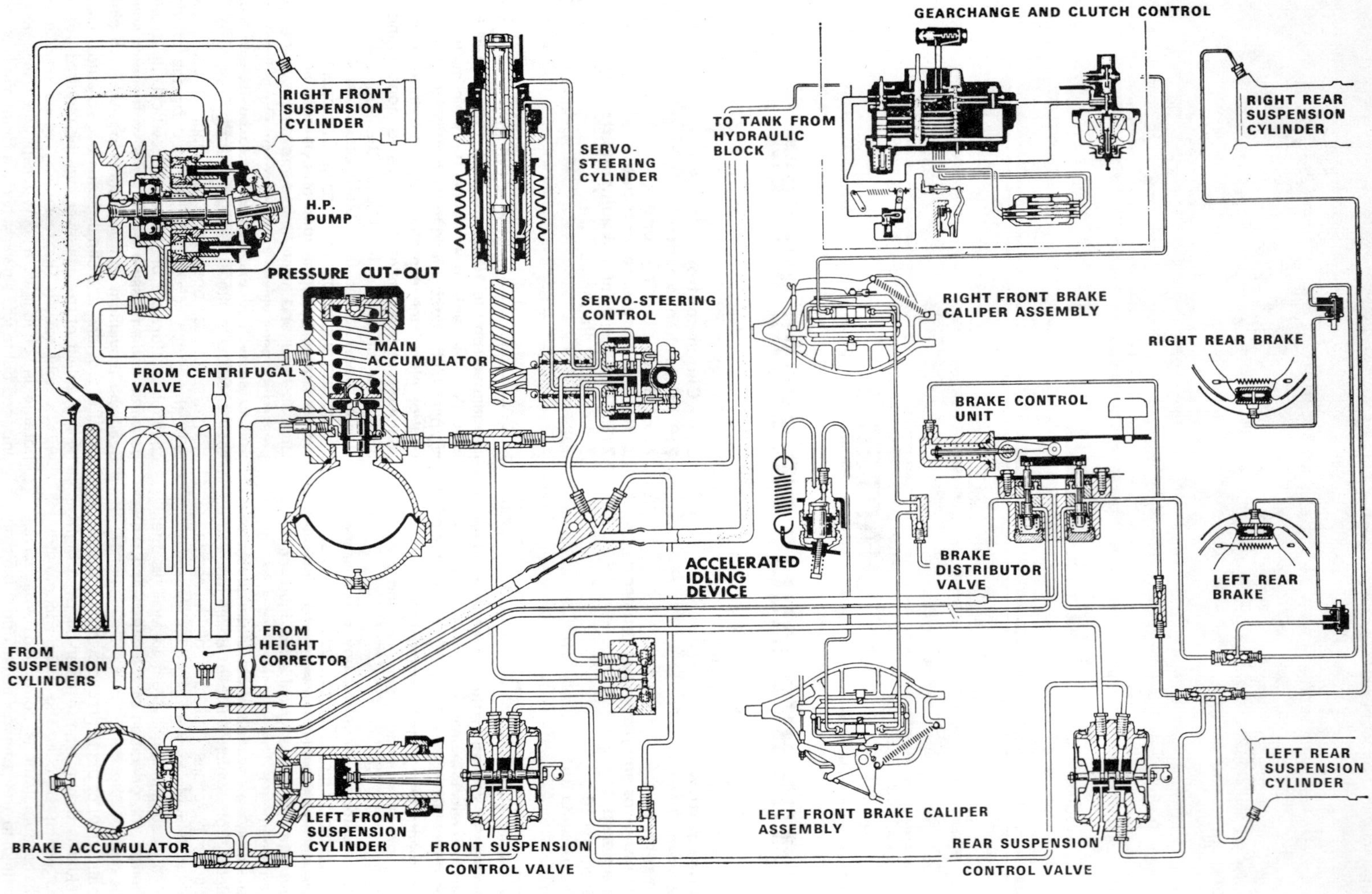

FIG 2:1 A diagrammatic view of the hydraulic system including gearchange and clutch control

The centrifugal clutch unit controls the clutch system pressure during starting and braking but not for gear-changing. Its purpose is to withdraw the clutch at engine speeds below approximately 1200 rev/min. At higher speeds automatic withdrawal of the clutch coincides with gearlever action in the selection of gears and taking up the drive. An auxiliary clutch control on the facia panel overrides the automatic control and allows clutch engagement when the engine is stopped and the gear-lever in neutral. In cars with manual gearchange a conventional clutch pedal is used with a changespeed lever located below the steering wheel. Operation of the front inboard disc brakes and the usual drum brakes mounted on the rear wheels is by a conventional Lockheed hydraulic system and a full-sized brake pedal.

2:2 The reservoir

The supply of fluid for the hydraulic system is contained in the reservoir situated in front of the battery as shown in **FIG 2:2** and also at 45 in **FIG 2:3.** The level of the fluid should be between the high and low marks on the transparent gauge A in the former illustration with the car at its maximum height. Raise the car to this position by starting the engine and accelerate slightly to save time, then set the lever A shown in **FIG 2:12** to position 5 and wait until the car has settled at its maximum height. Finally check the level remains steady between the gauge marks and return the height lever to the normal position 2.

For topping up the fluid in the reservoir it is essential that only the fluid specified by the manufacturers should be used. Prior to September, 1966, a synthetic fluid was employed but since that date all cars of the D type with the exception of certain export models have their hydraulic circuits filled with the green mineral based LHM hydraulic fluid. Vehicles intended for USA and Canada did not receive this modification until March, 1969. On all cars using the LHM fluid the main hydraulic reservoir and the hydraulic units are painted green or have green identification marks. Petrol is used for cleaning the hydraulic components concerned and only the LHM mineral fluid should be used for their lubrication before fitting. It is also essential to use only those seals, tubes and diaphragms specially made for use with the LHM fluid and parts of the same dimensions intended for use with the LHM fluid and parts of the same dimensions intended for use with other fluids should never be fitted. The same requirements for using compatible components, of course, applies to earlier cars using the former synthetic fluid, when alcohol was specified for cleaning the parts concerned.

For the later cars, however, no other fluid than LHM may be used, especially those of a synthetic origin or brake fluids which can cause the seals and joints of the LHM hydraulic system rapidly to deteriorate and become ineffective. In an emergency it is permissible to use either an engine oil of type SAE.10 or SAE.20 or the hydraulic transducer fluid A, type A. The reservoir must then be drained at the earliest opportunity and the specified fluid substituted. To drain the reservoir, lower the car to its minimum height at position 6 (see **FIG 2:12**) and open the bleed screw on the pressure regulator. Unclip the tube B at C (see **FIG 2:2**) from the lower clips and bend the tube downwards. Remove the plug D and drain the

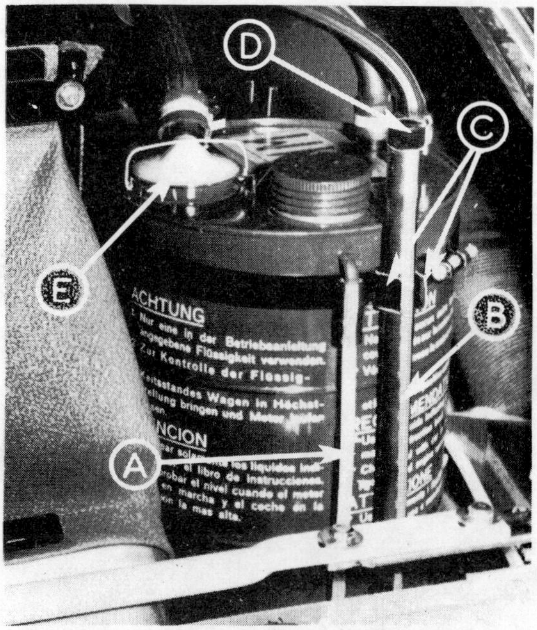

FIG 2:2 **Hydraulic fluid reservoir**

Key to Fig 2:2 **A** Level gauge **B** Drain tube **C** Clips **D** Blanking plug **E** Filter

reservoir. When refilled return the height lever to the normal position 2. A filter is located at E in the reservoir and should be removed and cleaned every 6000 miles or 10,000 km. Disengage the spring retaining the outlet pipe, withdraw the pipe by pulling it upwards and remove the filter. Clean it by immersing it in petrol and blowing it dry with compressed air from the outside. Refit it in the reverse manner of removal.

All operations on the hydraulic system and its components must be undertaken with strict regard to the precautions to be observed described in **Chapter 1.** To remove the reservoir release the pressure, drain the reservoir, then remove the spare wheel, the spare wheel support member and the mechanical headlamp control. Disconnect the rubber pipes from the steel pipes on the reservoir and the pump suction pipe from the plunger pipe. Remove the clips securing the reservoir and disconnect the rubber pipes underneath the reservoir. These are identified in **FIG 2:4** as follows:

1 The overflow return pipe from the suspension cylinders.
2 The return pipe from the pressure regulator and the three-way union (steering, height corrector and hydraulic gear selector).
3 The return pipe of the clutch re-engagement control.
4 The return pipe of the brake control.
5 The overflow return pipes from the height correctors and clutch lock.

Reverse the removal procedure to refit the reservoir. On completion, fill up the reservoir with the approved fluid and fill the high pressure pump with fluid through the reservoir outlet filter housing. Loosen the bleed screw, start up the engine, put the circuits under pressure,

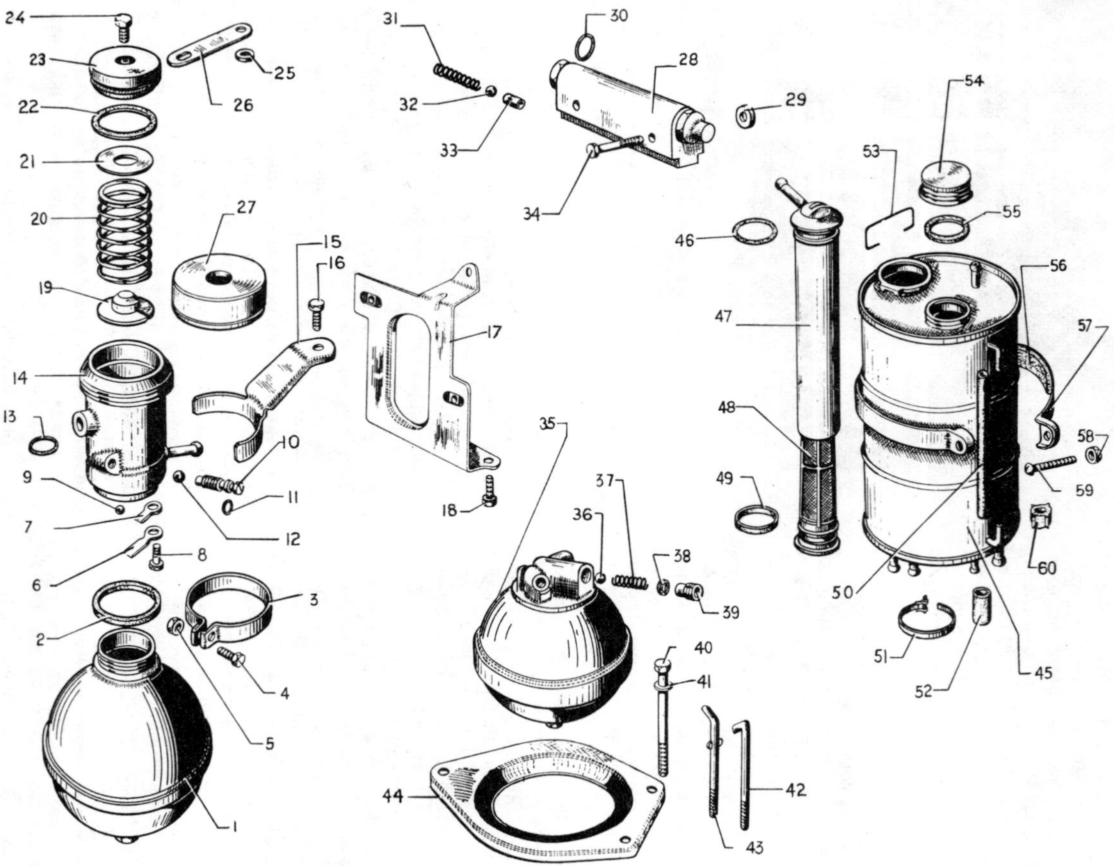

FIG 2:3 An exploded view of the main accumulator, pressure control valve, reservoir and brake accumulator

Key to Fig 2:3 1 Main accumulator 2 Rubber joint for control valve 3 Clip 4 Hexagon-headed screw 5 Nut 6 Ball retaining plate 7 Shim for thrust spring adjustment 8 Retaining plate screw 9 Ball for control valve, fluid passage pump to sphere 10 Bleed screw for pressure control valve 11 Ring seal 12 Ball for bleed screw 13 Ring seal for control valve piston 14 Pressure control valve 15 Valve bracket 16 Retaining screw 17 Valve support (since September, 1962) 18 Retaining screw 19 Cup and ball 20 Spring 21 Washer 22 Rubber joint 23 Cap 24 Retaining screw 25 Distance piece 26 Retaining plate 27 Nut for tightening cap 28 Pressure distribution block 29 Distance piece 30 Cap joint 31 Spring 32 Ball for distribution block 33 Plunger 34 Retaining screw 35 Brake accumulator 36 Ball 37 Spring 38 Thrust washer 39 Screw for thrust spring 40 Flange retaining screw 41 Washer 42 Tie-rod 43 Tie-rod 44 Flange securing brake accumulator 45 Fluid reservoir 46 Ring seal 47 Filter, complete 48 Filter element 49 Sealing washer 50 Gauge tube 51 Clip 52 Rubber cap 53 Retaining spring 54 Reservoir cap 55 Joint 56 Felt packing 57 Strap 58 Nut 59 Retaining screw 60 Gauge tube joint and check all unions for leaks. Check the fluid level in the reservoir, with the engine running and the car raised to the high position. Bleed the brakes (see **Chapter 10**) and refer to **Chapter 12** for refitting the mechanical control for the headlamps.

2:3 Pressure spheres

The basic features of the power distribution system are the hydro-pneumatic pressure spheres used as accumulators and incorporated with hydraulic cylinders to act as pneumatic springs for the suspension system. The principle of their operation is that a variable flow of fluid, which is incompressible, is used to compress a volume of gas. As shown by the diagram of the main accumulator in **FIG 2:1**, the pressure sphere contains a flexible diaphragm which separates an inert gas in one part from hydraulic fluid acting under pressure on the other side of the diaphragm. The gas thus compressed so maintains a continuous reserve of fluid under similar pressure for the various purposes of each accumulator, used fluid being in each case ultimately returned to the reservoir for further pressurization via the fluid pump and the main accumulator. A main accumulator and a brake accumulator sphere are shown in **FIG 2:3** and the suspension spheres in **FIGS 2:5** and **2:6**.

2:4 Main accumulator and pressure regulator

Details of the main accumulator 1 and the pressure control valve 14 are shown in **FIG 2:3.** Any work on the assembly must be accompanied by a strict observance of the need for cleanliness and the plugging of pipe openings as set out in **Chapter 1.** To remove the accumulator, release the pressure in all the circuits, put the manual height control in the low position and continue as follows:

1 Disconnect the cable from the negative terminal of the battery.
2 Remove the lefthand front suspension sphere, using a strap wrench; also the fuel pump.
3 Disconnect from the pressure regulator the outlet pipe and the overflow return pipe to the reservoir.
4 Disengage the regulator retaining clip and its support to obtain access to disconnect the pipe between the regulator and the high pressure pump.
5 Pivot the body of the regulator towards the front and the accumulator towards the rear. Withdraw the regulator/accumulator assembly from underneath the car. Disconnect the regulator from the accumulator.

Dismantling and reassembly of the regulator requires the use of a press to control the spring 20, which exerts a considerable thrust. This precaution is essential to avoid stripping the threads of the cap and it is therefore advisable that the operations should be undertaken by a service agent. In addition it is necessary for various pressure checks to be made, e.g., the initial pressure of the accumulator, the pressure of the assembly, the cutting-in and cutting-out pressures and for leakages. For these purposes service agents use the specially designed test bench (see **FIG 1:3**) complete with the necessary pipes and unions for connecting the units to be tested.

Operations for refitting the accumulator assembly are the reverse of those employed for removal, tightening

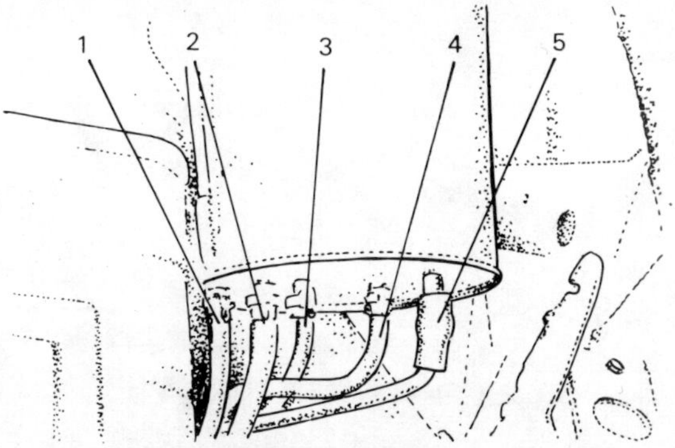

FIG 2:4 Reservoir return pipes. Numbers are identified in text

the accumulator on the regulator by hand. Ensure that the rubber return pipe to the reservoir is not chafing on the brake accumulator outlet pipes. Finally unscrew the bleed screw 10, start the engine, let it run for a few minutes, retighten the bleed screw and put the systems under pressure. Check the unions for leakage and if necessary top up the level of the fluid in the reservoir.

2:5 Hydraulic pump

The hydraulic system is put under pressure by a belt-driven hydraulic pump, in which the pressure is maintained by pistons acting in cylinders and operated by an inclined swashplate. A typical sectional view of the pump is shown in **FIG 2:7.** Later models may differ in constructional details but the general principles remain the same. The operations entailed in the removal and dismantling of the pump are as follows:

1 Release the pressure. Remove the tie-rod between the high pressure pump and the centrifugal regulator and the regulator belt.
2 Disconnect the pipe 5 (see **FIG 2:8**) connecting the pressure regulator to the pump, also the pump tie-rod 2 and the suction pipe 1 from the pump.
3 Remove the nut 3 from the pump fulcrum pin with a 16 mm ring spanner. Free the belts from the pump pulley and withdraw the pump. Do not lose the adjusting shims 4.
4 Drain all fluid from the pump. Hold the pulley in a vice with lead jaws. Remove the retaining nut and its lockwasher to remove the pulley and its key.
5 Hold the pump in the vice as shown in **FIG 2:9.** Detach the closing cup 1, the pump deflector 2, the ring seal 3, the nut 4 and the screws 6 securing the front end plate. Remove the plate 5 for the pump belt tie-rod.
6 Referring to **FIG 2:7,** remove the pump housing, for which service agents use an extractor 2282.T, and remove the seal ring 6 from the pump body.
7 Extract the shaft from the end plate bearing. Note that if the shaft is to be renewed it is also necessary to renew the needle bearings 11.
8 Hold the pump vertically, the swashplate towards the top, and remove the shaft.
9 Disengage the pistons. Note that the pistons and cylinders are paired on assembly and must be kept

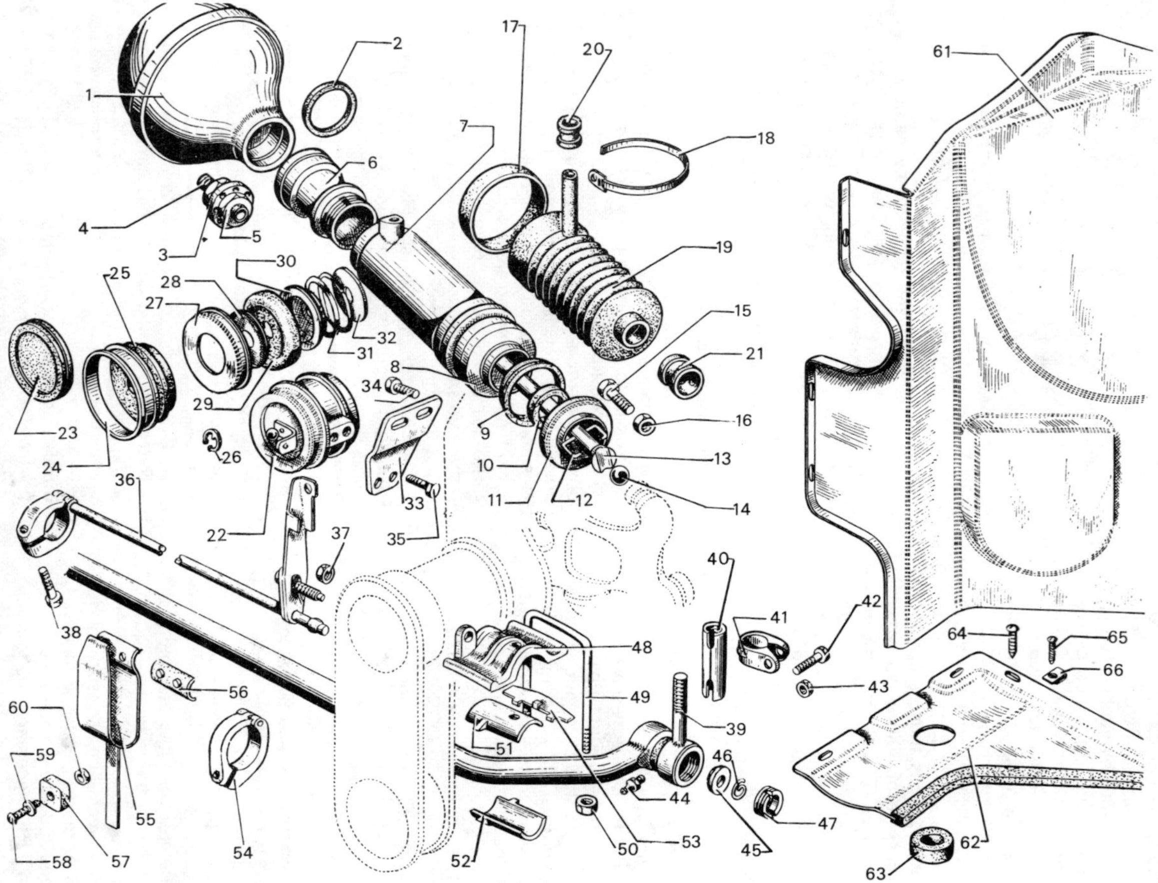

FIG 2:5 An exploded view of the front suspension pressure sphere and cylinder, height corrector and anti-roll bar

Key to Fig 2:5 1 Suspension sphere 2 Rubber joint 3 Damper 4 Stud 5 Nut 6 Sleeve for sphere 7 Suspension cylinder 8 Cylinder nut with cup and joint 9 Cylinder sealing joint 10 Felt sealing washer 11 Cup 12 Pin connecting piston rod with lever 13 Piston rod 14 Ball for piston rod 15 Screw securing cylinder 16 Nut 17 Protective ring under clip 18 Clip for dust cover 19 Rubber dust cover 20 Protective ring under return pipe clip 21 Protective ring under dust cover clip 22 Height corrector 23 Rubber cover for corrector adjustment hole 24 Retaining sleeve 25 Sealing cup 26 Circlip for corrector valve 27 Interior cup for tightening corrector diaphragm 28 Cup 29 Diaphragm 30 Cup 31 Spring 32 Corrector valve 33 Corrector bracket 34 Screw 35 Screw 36 Corrector control rod 37 Nut for eccentric pin operating corrector 38 Screw for corrector control rod 39 Anti-roll bar 40 Coupling sleeve 41 Clip 42 Screw 43 Nut 44 Grease nipple 45 Thrust cup and ball pin 46 Spring for ball pin 47 Ball pin cup nut 48 Bearing cap 49 U-bolt 50 Nut 51 Nylon half bearing 52 Nylon half bearing 53 Adjusting shim 54 Thrust collar 55 Anti-rattle spring 56 Nylon bearing 57 Rubber stop 58 Screw 59 Washer 60 Nut 61 Lateral shield for suspension mechanism 62 Lower shield for suspension mechanism 63 Rubber washer 64 Screw 65 Screw 66 Retaining nut

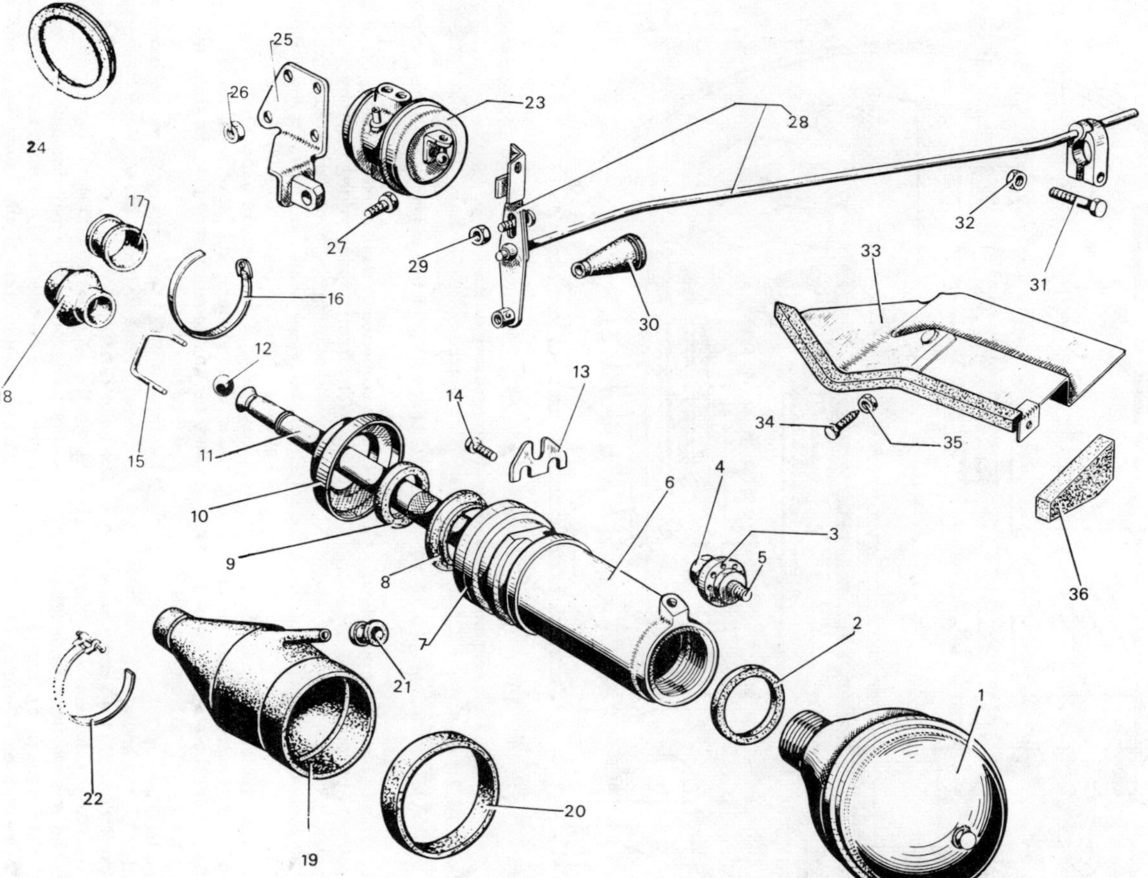

FIG 2:6 An exploded view of the rear suspension pressure sphere, cylinder and height corrector

Key to Fig 2:6 1 Suspension sphere 2 Rubber joint 3 Damper 4 Nut 5 Stud 6 Suspension cylinder 7 Nut with cup and joint 8 Sealing joint 9 Felt sealing washer 10 Cup 11 Piston rod 12 Ball 13 Retaining plate for cylinder 14 Screw 15 Pin, piston rod to lever 16 Clip for piston rod dust cover 17 Protective ring under clip 18 Piston rod dust cover 19 Cylinder dust cover 20 Protective ring under dust cover clip 21 Protective ring under clip securing return from cylinder to reservoir 22 Clip for cylinder dust cover 23 Height corrector 24 Rubber cover for corrector adjustment control passage 25 Corrector bracket with bearing 26 Retaining nut 27 Screw 28 Control rod for rear corrector 29 Retaining nut 30 Sealing sleeve on corrector control 31 Screw 32 Nut 33 Corrector protection panel 34 Screw 35 Retaining nut 36 Rubber sealing pad, body to corrector panel

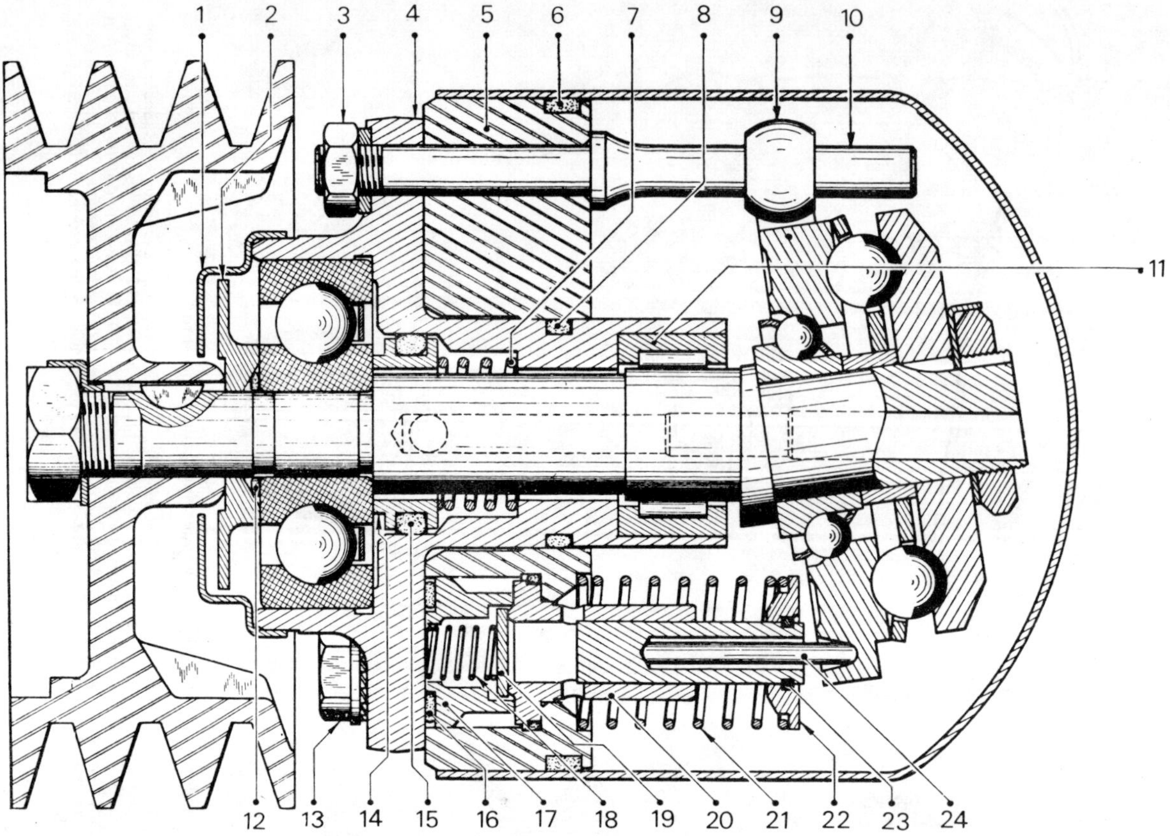

FIG 2:7 A sectional view of the high pressure pump

Key to Fig 2:7 1 Dust cover 2 Thrust washer 3 Nut 4 End plate 5 Pump body 6 Seal ring 7 Springs 8 Seal ring, end plate 9 Olive 10 Rods 11 Needle bearings 12 Seal ring 13 Screws 14 Distance piece and seal assembly 15 Seal ring 16 Seal rings 17 Valve guides 18 Springs 19 Valves 20 Cylinders 21 Return springs 22 Cups 23 Circlips 24 Pushrods

in their correct order for reassembly. Use a numbered rack and commence with the piston nearest the rod supporting the swashplate. Remove the cups and springs. The pushrods, the spring cups and the springs are not matched.

10 Using a mallet, drive out the end plate 4 from the body of the pump 5, steadying the assembly by hand. When the end plate is free, turn the assembly over in order to avoid dropping the cylinders. Note the order of disassembly of the parts.

11 Remove the valve guides 17, the springs 18 and the valves 19. Remove the cylinders 20 in the same order as for the pistons. Keep the cylinders with their corresponding pistons and remove the cylinder seal rings. Drive out the rod 10 from the pump body.

12 Drive out the distance piece and seal assembly 14 and the end plate bearing, by using a mandrel of 17 mm diameter. A new bearing must be fitted on reassembly. Disengage the seal ring 8 from the end plate and the seal 15 from the distance piece.

13 Remove the thrust bearing and the swashplate. With a magnifying glass make sure that there is no pitting or coppering of the thrust plates and ballbearings. Clean the parts with alcohol. A new thrust bearing should be fitted if there is any trace of defect.

Unless otherwise mentioned all parts should be dipped in hydraulic fluid before reassembly. The reassembly and refitting operations are as follows:

1 Grind the valve seats on the cylinders by rubbing lightly on abrasive paper No. 600 dipped in alcohol, if possible with the abrasive paper on a surface plate. Clean with alcohol and blow with compressed air. Carry out the same operation on the front face of the distance piece 14.

2 Refit the rod 10, using a press. Fit the seal rings in the grooves of the cylinder bores. Press the seals in position if necessary.

3 Locate the cylinders 20 in position in the pump body 5 in the same order as when dismantling. Smear the collar of the cylinder with hydraulic fluid. Offer up the cylinder in the bore of the pump body and press sufficiently strongly by means of a mandrel up to the moment when it becomes locked (seal in the collar).

4 Fit the new valves 19 and the valve guides 17. The guides are only in position when they are below the level of the pump, otherwise the guides are bearing on the valves. Fit the ring seals 16 on the guides and fit the valve springs 18.

5 Fit the end plate seal ring 8 on the hub of the front end plate. Carefully position the end plate 4 in the

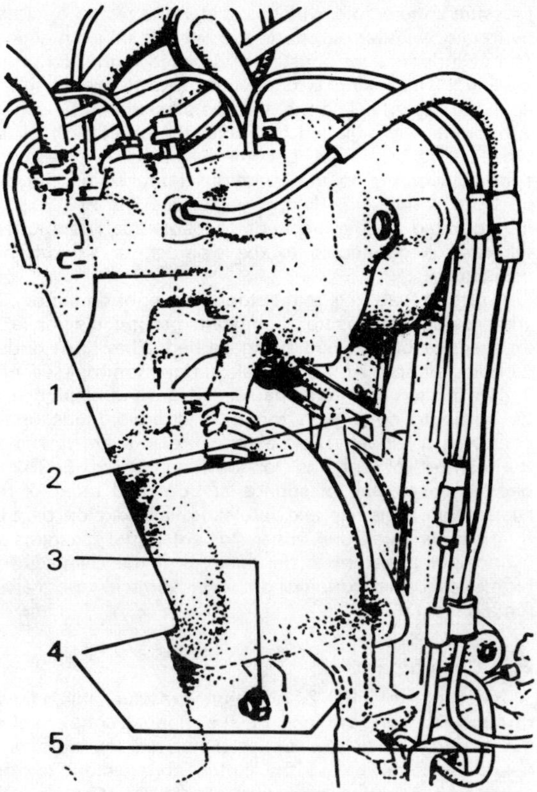

FIG 2:8 Removing the high pressure pump, showing items to be disconnected

Key to Fig 2:8 1 Suction pipe 2 Pump tie-rod 3 Pump fulcrum pin nut 4 Adjusting shims 5 Connecting pipe to pressure regulator

pump body and fit by hand. Fit the screw 13 with serrated washer. Fit the tie-rod fixing plate. Insert the serrated washer between the fixing plate and the end plate, not under the heads of the screws. Tighten the tie-rod screws to a torque of 25$\frac{1}{4}$ lb ft. Provision is made for checking the valves for leakage on the test bench mentioned in **Chapter 1**.

6 Fit the seal ring 15 soaked in castor oil on the distance piece 14. Fit the spring 7 and the distance piece in the pump.

7 Check the condition of the surface of the inner cage of the bearing in the end plate. This face should show no signs of scratches, blows or markings. If grinding the face has left criss-cross marks, the bearing should be renewed. Grease this face with castor oil and offer up the bearing in the end plate with the nylon bush towards the interior of the pump. Insert the bearing in position with the aid of a press. Position the distance piece with a mandrel MR.3436.110.

8 Fit the cups 22 on the pistons, ensuring that the circlips 23 are in position. Dip the pistons in hydraulic fluid and fit the return springs 21. Engage the pistons in their corresponding cylinders in the order of their removal, using the clips 2284.T to hold the pistons as shown in **FIG 2:10.**

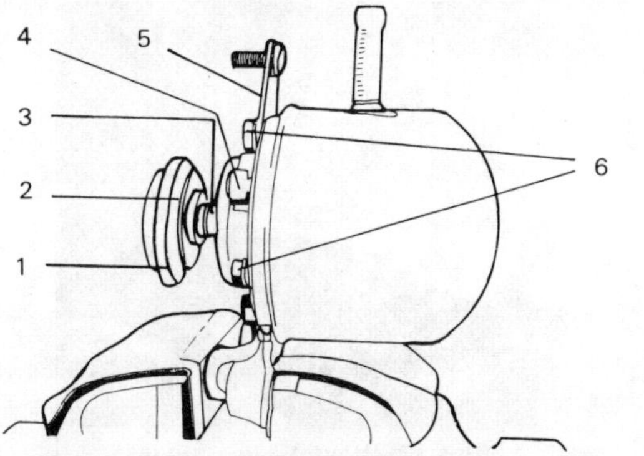

FIG 2:9 Dismantling the high pressure pump

Key to Fig 2:9 1 Closing cup 2 Pump deflector 3 Ring seal 4 Nut 5 Plate for belt tie-rod 6 Screws

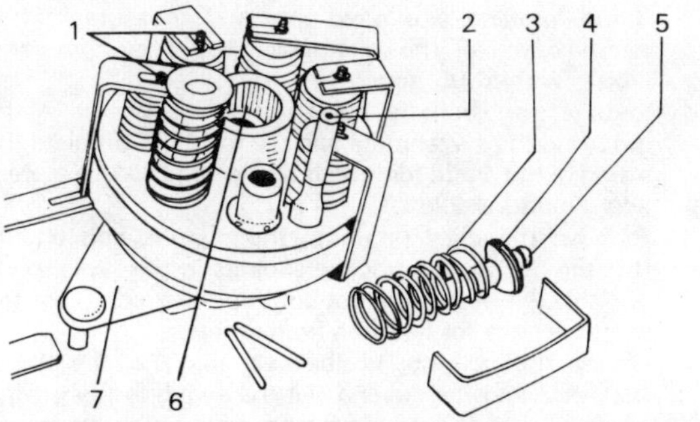

FIG 2:10 Assembling the high pressure pump

Key to Fig 2:10 1 Piston pushrods 2 Olive stem 3 Piston spring 4 Cup 5 Piston 6 Needle bearing cage 7 Plate

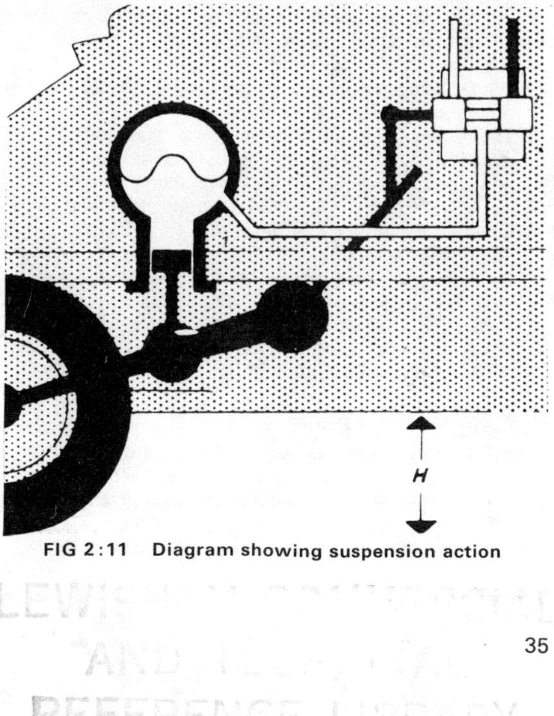

FIG 2:11 Diagram showing suspension action

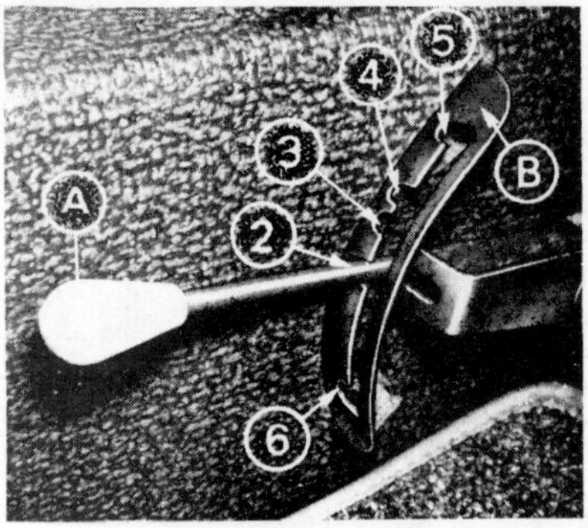

FIG 2:12 **Height adjusting lever**

Key to Fig 2:12 2 Normal driving setting 3, 4 Alternative driving settings 5 Extreme top setting 6 Extreme lower setting **A** Control lever **B** Plate

9 Fit the pushrods 24. Select a pushrod in good condition, preferably a new one, and measure with a micrometer. All the pushrods should be the same length within .05 mm.

10 Engage the shaft by hand. Fit the olive 9 in the groove in the swashplate and the rod 10. Complete the fitting of the shaft, for which service agents use a press and a mandrel 2286.T.

11 Remove the clips retaining the pistons and ensure that the pushrods enter the sockets in the swashplate and that the olive does not bind on the guide. Turn the shaft to check for freedom from stiffness.

12 Grease the bearing, fit the seal ring 12, the thrust washer 2 and the cover 1. Fit the seal 6 in the groove of the pump body. Coat the body with hydraulic fluid and locate the pump casing in position in a press.

13 Fit the key, the pulley and the lockwasher. Hold the pulley with a 19 mm box spanner and tighten the nut to a torque of 28 lb ft (4 kg m). To test the output of the pump it is necessary to employ the test bench shown in **FIG 1:3**.

For refitting the pump, operations in general are those undertaken in removal and carried out in reverse, with regard given to the following:

1 When fitting the pump on the fixing spindle the flat on the spindle faces the pulley.

2 The pulley belt must be correctly tensioned (see **Section 2:11**). Tighten the tie-rod nut using plain and spring washers, and the pump fixing spindle.

3 Refill the pump with fluid through the feed pipe. Connect the pipe to the reservoir, fit a flexible sleeve and tighten the clip.

4 Unscrew the bleed screw on the pressure regulator, start the engine and let it idle for a few minutes. Tighten the bleed screw to put the system under pressure and check for leaks. Also check the level of the fluid in the reservoir.

2:6 Suspension system

Suspension of each of the four independently sprung wheels is by hydro-pneumatic means instead of the conventional coil or laminated spring arrangements. The hydro-pneumatic principle is illustrated diagrammatically in **FIG 2:11**. Referring also to **FIG 2:5**, a pressure sphere, into which is screwed a piston operated hydraulic cylinder, supports the weight of each wheel. The cylinder is kept constantly supplied with fluid under pressure. The piston is connected to a suspension arm linked to the wheel so that the gas pressure in the sphere is hydraulically adjusted following the movement of the wheel, and in effect becomes a flexible pneumatic spring according to the variations imposed on the gas pressure. A two-way damper valve (see 3 in **FIG 2:5**) is incorporated in the neck of the spherical component where it is connected to the cylinder, to smooth out oscillations.

A further feature is that automatic height correctors 22 are provided to ensure a constant ground clearance H irrespective of the load being carried. They give added damping action. An additional manual control (see **FIG 2:12**) of the correctors enables the ground clearance to be raised to cope with rough or flooded roads or for changing a wheel. The height correctors are linked to the centres of anti-roll torsion bars 39 in **FIG 2:5** between each pair of springs at front and rear. As the suspension arms rise and fall, slide valve action permits fluid under pressure either to enter the suspension cylinder or to return to the reservoir if the car rises too high. In normal running on level surfaces the valves remain closed.

2:7 Clutch control

Referring to **FIG 2:13**, high pressure fluid flows through the control block via the manual control valve, the starting valve, the upper piston of the automatic gearchange valve, and the clutch engagement control valve to the clutch operating or control cylinder. The starting valve restricts flow and reduces pressure in the clutch circuit for progressive clutch engagement. A piston in the unit controls the position of the starting valve.

At idling speed the low pressure flow in the circuit passes through a calibrated port in the piston without any pressure rise. The starting valve remains static, allowing the reduced high pressure flow to the clutch operating cylinder to maintain the clutch out of engagement.

Acceleration increases pressure in the low pressure system and the calibrated port in the piston cannot pass the increased flow. Hence the pressure rises, and the piston moves against spring pressure to move the starting valve gradually into a position to cut out the high pressure flow to the clutch. Through interaction with the clutch control valve this ensures the progressive engagement of the clutch. The piston, moving against the spring, uncovers a bypass port back to the reservoir to limit the pressure. The pressure is adjustable through an adjusting screw acting on the spring and a back-pressure valve in the return line stabilizes operation.

The centrifugal clutch control drive is by pulley and belt from the engine to the shaft 2 to which the centrifugal weight carrier 1 is attached. The sliding hollow shaft 3 is linked to the centrifugal weights by the links 4 and to the centrifugal weight carrier by the links 5. Movement outwards, under centrifugal force, of the weights will force the hollow shaft 3 against spring pressure to allow movement of the valve 7. Adjustment of pull-away is by the adjusting screw acting on the spring.

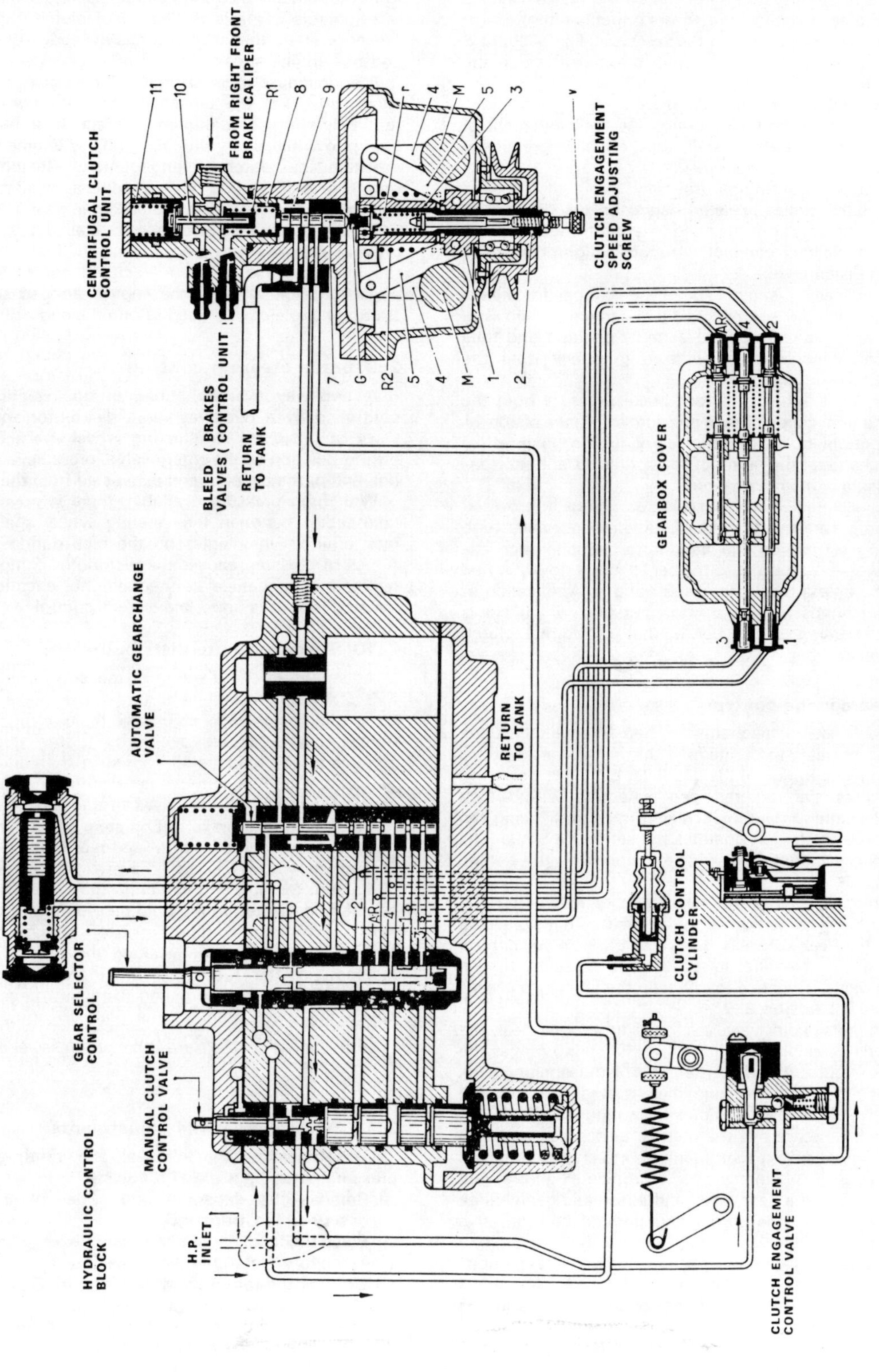

FIG 2:13 A diagrammatic view of the hydraulic gearchange system with centrifugal clutch control unit

The valve 7 under control of the sliding hollow shaft 3 either isolates the clutch circuit, or connects it to the high pressure side or returns it to the reservoir. The dashpot 8 communicates with clutch system pressure through the passage 9.

The valve 7 is in equilibrium under:

1 The action of the three springs. As the movement of these springs is very small, their effect is practically constant.
2 The variable centrifugal assembly.
3 The clutch circuit pressure acting on the dashpot 8.

When the engine is stopped, the centrifugal force is nil, and the valve 7 connects a reduced high pressure to the clutch circuit.

With increasing engine speed, centrifugal force acts on the weights M and moves them outwards, allowing valve 7 to move towards the exhaust position and thus decreasing clutch circuit pressure gradually until the clutch is fully engaged.

Piston 11 is subject to front brake pressure from the righthand front caliper. Brake pressure forces the piston 11 to the bottom of its cylinder, carrying the pushrod 10 with it, changing the rating of the spring R1 and increasing pressure in the clutch circuit.

An accelerated idling speed is automatically provided for smooth take-up. It consists of an abnormally high fast-idling setting on the carburetter which, once the engine is started, will cause the car to move slowly in first or reverse unless the footbrake is applied. Application of the brake brings a linkage into operation which slows down the idling speed below that of normal clutch engagement.

2:8 Gearchange control

Hydraulic servo mechanism when fitted enables the selection of gears to be made with a minimum of effort. Light finger operation of the gearlever behind the steering wheel gives the required gear selection with which clutch operation is automatically combined. Moving the gearlever to the far left operates the starter switch, a lock preventing accidental use of the starter with the engine running.

Referring to **FIG 2:13**, when first or reverse gear is selected the gear selector control releases high pressure fluid to the gear servo. The valve in the selector control moves under pressure to pass high pressure to the starting valve. Clutch engagement then takes place as described in **Section 2:7**.

When the selector valve is moved to another gear, the previously used circuit exhausts, and a spring moves the gearbox selector rod to neutral. The piston operating the automatic gearchange valve then moves to allow the latter valve to pass reduced pressure to the clutch.

A stack of pistons in the manual clutch control valve and the lower spring temporarily limit servo pressure to allow the gearbox pinions to synchronize. High pressure then passes to the gear servo and automatic gearchange valve to connect the clutch engagement control valve with the control block.

The clutch engagement control valve is in effect a non-return valve, with a controlled leak-back. A mechanical connection between the clutch control valve and the accelerator through a spring actuates a lever acting on a ball valve in the clutch control valve, to exhaust pressure from the clutch operating cylinder. Spring tension which is adjustable controls the speed of clutch engagement. The accelerator therefore controls the action of the clutch and not engine speed.

A short pause must be made during gearchanging, to allow time for the selected gear to engage, before re-accelerating. The engine can act as a brake when going downhill, even with 'foot-off', as engine speed will maintain the clutch in engagement. Gearchange can only take place when high pressure is available for the servos, and the car cannot be parked in gear.

To avoid clutch slip or engine stall during energetic braking, a small servo cylinder links the brake circuit with the throttle valve. A manual clutch control valve will engage the clutch with the engine stopped so that the starting handle can be used to turn the engine.

2:9 Servo steering control

A two-way cylinder acting on the steering rack is controlled by a two-way valve distributor and a rotary valve operated by the steering wheel shaft. Depending on the position of the rotary valve, pressure is applied to one end of the cylinder and exhausted from the other.

With high pressure available, there is no mechanical connection between the steering wheel shaft and the rack pinion, which idles on the rack during operation. A loss of pressure causes the distributor compensator to restore the mechanical connection, thus ensuring that the steering is always under the driver's control.

2:10 Brake pressure distributor

As shown in the diagram of the brake control unit in **FIG 2:1**, an arrangement under the brake pedal, or button, is designed to adjust the brake effort applied to front and rear brakes according to the position and amount of the load being carried in the car. The brake button has very small movement, sufficient only to open spring-loaded hydraulic valves to transmit fluid pressure to the brakes. The brake button stem movement is transmitted to the valves for front and rear braking through a carriage moving on rollers on a pivoted blade or balance beam surmounting and actuating the valves. A hydraulic cylinder connected to the fluid pressure in a rear suspension accumulator contains a piston which controls the movement of the carriage along the pivoted plate. An increase in the rear load, therefore, such as extra passengers, causes the piston to move the carriage and hence the pivot point of the plate to apply a greater proportion of the braking effort to the rear wheels. Under other conditions more braking effort can be received by the front wheels.

2:11 Belt renewal and adjustments

Operations for the removal and refitting of high pressure pump belts are as follows:

1 Remove the generator and water pump belts as described in **Chapter 5**.
2 Place the auxiliary clutch control lever under the dash in the forward and upward position.
3 Unhook the return spring 2 (see **FIG 2:14**) from the clutch fork. Unscrew to the maximum the screw 1 for adjusting the clutch clearance and free the rubber seal of the clutch cylinder from the screw.

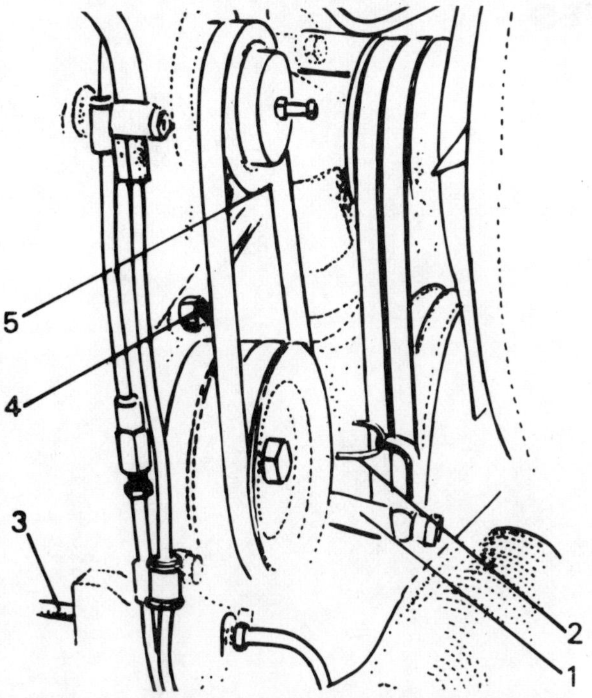

FIG 2:14 The high pressure pump belts, showing (1) the screw for adjusting the clutch clearance, (2) the clutch fork return spring, (3) the fixing screw of the high pressure pump, (4) tie-rod securing nut, (5) belt

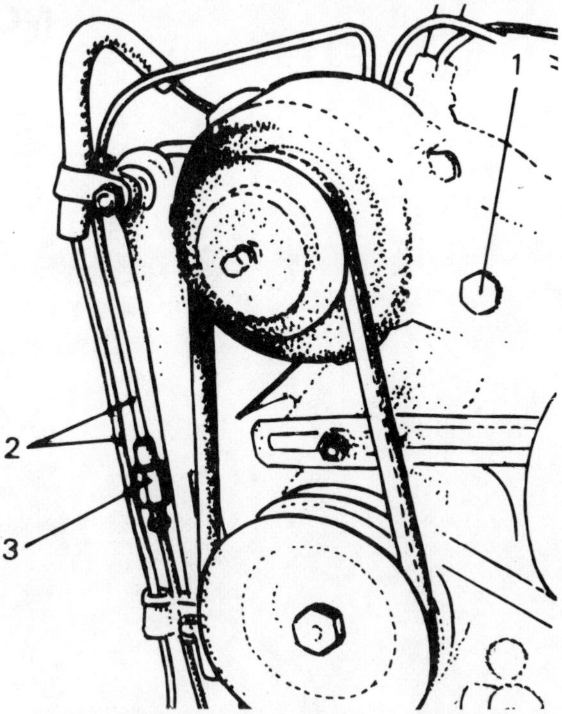

FIG 2:15 The centrifugal regulator belt, showing (1) the regulator fulcrum pin, (2) tubes held by clips and (3) the high pressure pump tie-rod

4 Remove the tie-rod between the high pressure pump and the centrifugal regulator, then remove the belt from the centrifugal regulator as described later in this Section.

5 Loosen the nut on the fixing screw 3 of the high pressure pump using a 16 mm ring spanner. Loosen the tie-rod securing nuts on the high pressure pump and on the water pump and withdraw the belts. New belts are supplied in sets of two of identical dimensions and for this reason it is necessary to renew both belts even if one is in good condition.

6 Fit the belts on the driving pulley and then on the high pressure pump pulley, passing the belts between the clutch fork and the clutch housing. Tension the belts as described later and continue refitting operations in the reverse order to that described for dismantling.

Removal and refitting of the belt for a centrifugal regulator, where fitted, is as follows:

1 Referring to **FIG 2:15**, remove the clips holding the pipes 2.

2 Loosen the nut securing the tie-rod 3 on the HP pump.

3 Loosen the nut 1 on the fulcrum pin of the regulator, pivot the regulator downwards and withdraw the belt.

4 To refit, locate the belt on the pulleys and tension the belt as described later. Tighten the nuts loosened during removal and fit the clips holding the tubes 2.

Tensioning of the various belts is precisely undertaken in service workshops by a specially dimensioned lever, or a hook in the case of the centrifugal regulator belt, appropriately situated with a spring gauge attached to one end, on which a specified pull must be registered to obtain the correct belt tension. In the absence of this equipment the twin belts of the high pressure pump and the centrifugal regulator belt should be adjusted to have $\frac{1}{4}$ inch (6 mm) free play. Adjustment of the former is made by loosening and retightening the tie-rod to the pump and the pump bearing spindle nut, and of the latter by similar operations on the tie-rod fixing nuts and the regulator swivelling nut.

2:12 Fault diagnosis

If any irregularity of working occurs, first check that the hydraulic system is under pressure as follows:

1 With engine idling, unscrew the pressure regulator bleed screw about 1 to $1\frac{1}{2}$ turns, when the release of pressure in the control valve should be heard.

2 Screw up the bleed screw, when the valve should cut-out in less than 20 seconds. The point of cut-out is indicated by a reduction in the noise of operation.

Further checks to be made if the preliminary tests are unsatisfactory are to ensure that:

1 There is sufficient hydraulic fluid in the reservoir.

2 The filter in the reservoir is perfectly clean and in good condition.

3 Air is not being sucked in through the pump inlet pipe.

4 The belt of the high pressure pump is not slipping.

5 The bleed screw is tightened.

A complete hydraulic test of the system can be undertaken if required by a service agent using the test bench equipment described in **Chapter 1**.

NOTES

CHAPTER 3

THE FUEL SYSTEM

3:1 General description

Fuel is supplied from a tank of 14.3 gallons (65 litre) capacity to a mechanical diaphragm operated pump of either SEV or AC type, a sectional view of the latter being shown in **FIG 3:1.** The principles of operation of each are similar. A rocker arm or lever is actuated by a cam and operates a flexible diaphragm against a spring to create a partial vacuum in the pump, which enables the atmospheric pressure in the tank to send fuel through the connecting pipe to the pump. The return action of the spring then pushes the diaphragm upwards to deliver the fuel to the carburetter float chamber. When the bowl is full the float closes a needle valve, preventing further petrol supply from the pump until the carburetter requires more fuel and the needle valve opens. In the meantime the pump rocker arm is given an idling movement.

A number of different carburetter types have been used on the cars covered in this manual of either Weber or Solex manufacture. A description of each type will be given in this chapter and full specifications and jet sizes are in **Technical Data** in the Appendix. Codes as shown

Model	*Makers' code*	*Gearchange*	*Carburetter type*
DS21	DX	H	Weber 28/36 DDE or DLE
DS21	DJ	M	Weber 28/36 DDE.A1 or DLE.A1
DS19A	DY	H	Weber 28/36 DDE.2
DS19A	DL	M	Weber 28/36 DDE.A2
DS20	DY	H	Weber 28/36 DLE.2
DS20	DL	M	Weber 28/36 DLE.A2
D Special	DV	M	Solex 34 PBIC.3 or Weber 28/36 DMA.3
D Super	DT	M	Weber 28/36 DLE.A2 or Solex 28/36 SFIF or Weber 28/36 DMA.3
D Super 5	DP	M	Weber 28/36 DMA.2

H=hydraulic M=manual

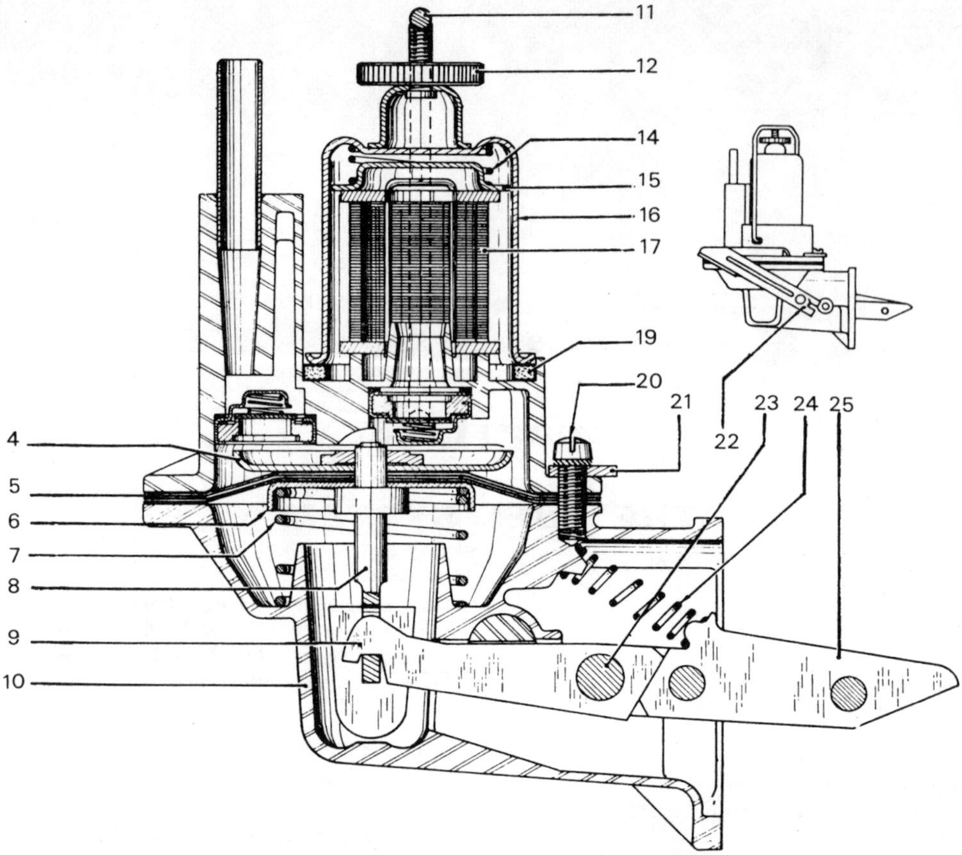

FIG 3 : 1 A typical sectional view of an AC fuel pump

Key to Fig 3 : 1 4 Cup 5 Diaphragm assembly 6 Cup 7 Spring 8 Spindle 9 Relay lever 10 Lower body 11 U-clip 12 Nut 14 Spring 15 Cup 16 Bowl 17 Filter 19 Joint 20 Screws 21 Clip 22 Lever stop 23 Spindle 24 Spring 25 Lever

Note: The valves are incorporated in the pump cover

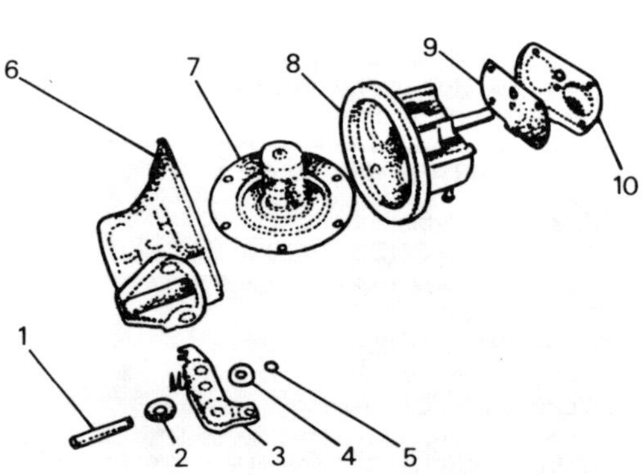

FIG 3 : 2 SEV fuel pump components

Key to Fig 3 : 2 1 Spindle 2 Washer 3 Control lever and spring 4 Washer 5 Circlip 6 Lower body 7 Diaphragm and pushrod assembly 8 Upper body 9 Gasket 10 Cover

in the following tables are used to indicate the characteristics of the carburetters in various models. The DDE code was changed to DLE when a higher-powered DS21 was introduced and when the DS19 of 1968 was replaced by a DS20 with the same engine as the ID20.

FUEL PUMP:

3 : 2 Maintenance and testing

Action of the pump is automatic and normally no maintenance is required. If trouble is experienced with the fuel supply the first approach should be to ensure that there are no leaks or obstructions in the fuel line. Should the pump then become suspect, a quick check can be made by disconnecting the pipe at the pump outlet, engaging the auxiliary clutch control if fitted and turning the engine by the starter motor, when fuel should spurt from the outlet. Another test is to disconnect the inlet union and hold a finger over it whilst again turning the engine by the starter motor, when suction should be felt. With the pump removed from the engine it can be

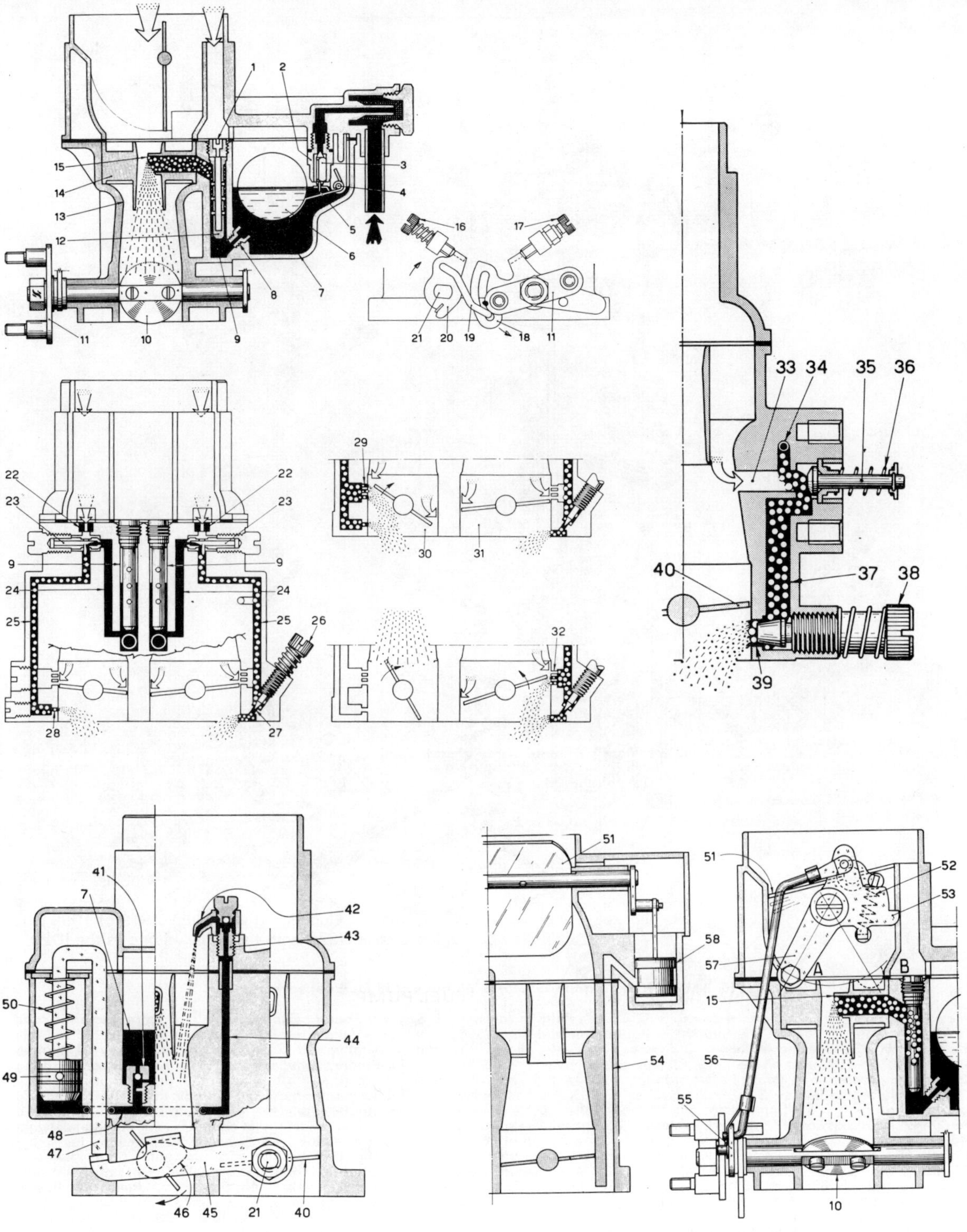

FIG 3:3 Diagrams showing operation of Weber carburetter. The numbered items are identified in the text

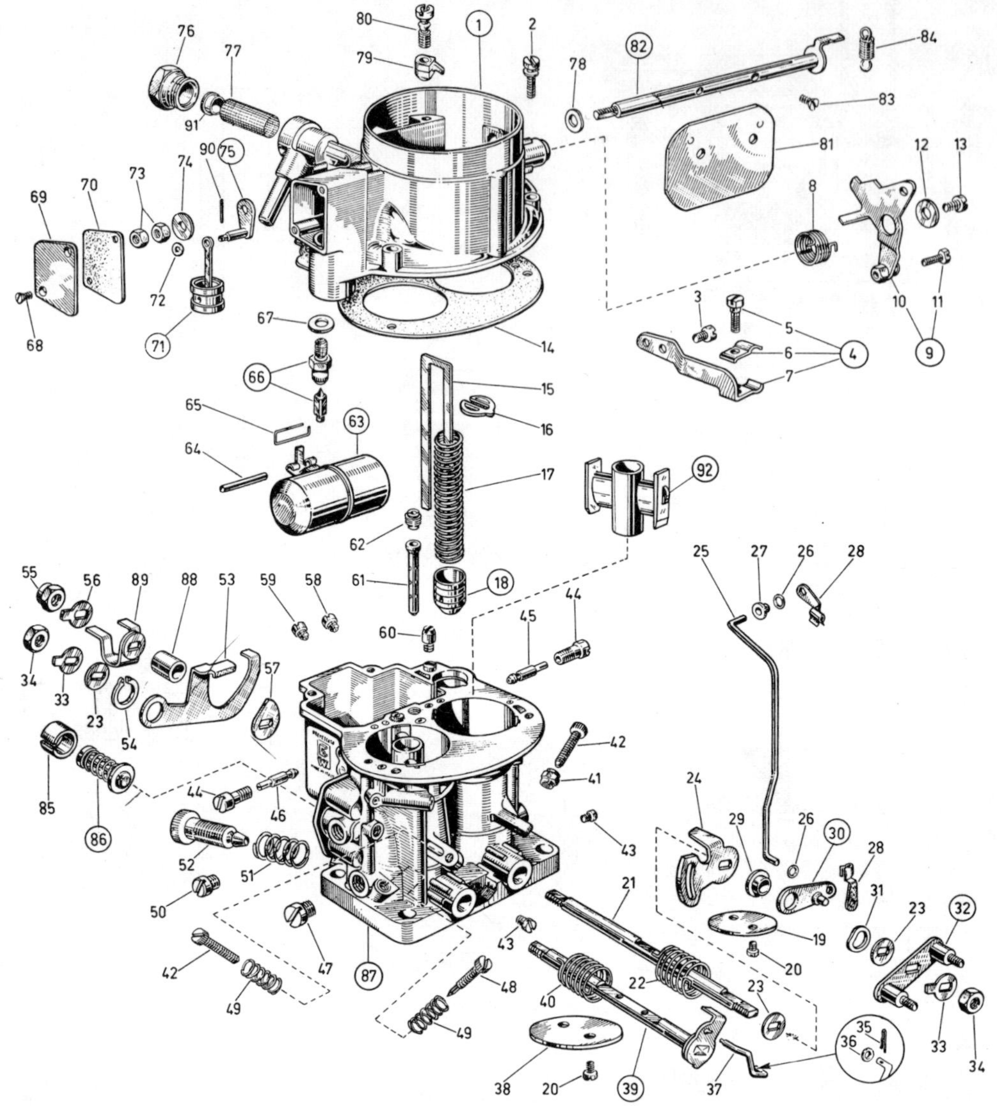

FIG 3:4 An exploded view of a Weber 28/36 DLE carburetter

Key to Fig 3:4 1 Carburetter cover 2 Cover retaining screw 3 Screw for outer cable support 4 Outer cable supports 5 Fixing screw 6 Clamp 7 Support 8 Starter lever return spring 9 Starter lever assembly 10 Control lever 11 Cable fixing screw 12 Spacing washer 13 Screw 14 Cover gasket 15 Pump operating rod 16 Spring retainer plate 17 Pump piston spring 18 Pump piston 19 Primary butterfly valve 20 Screw 21 Primary spindle 22 Primary spindle return spring 23 Spacing washer 24 Primary valve stop lug 25 Fast idle rod 26 Washer 27 Bush 28 Spring 29 Bush for fast idle lever 30 Fast idle control lever 31 Friction washer 32 Valve control lever 33 Locking washer 34 Spindle nut 35 Spring clip 36 Washer for rod 37 Connecting rod 38 Secondary butterfly valve 39 Secondary spindle 40 Return spring 41 Locking nut 42 Adjusting screw for butterfly valves 43 Inspection screw for idling orifice 44 Idling jet carriers 45 Primary idling jet 46 Secondary idling jet 47 Inspection screw for progression orifice 48 Adjustment screw 49 Spring 50 Screw for fast idling orifice 51 Spring 52 Fast idling adjustment screw 53 Pump control lever 54 Lockwasher 55 Cam nut 56 Lockwasher 57 Pump control cam 58 Main primary jet 59 Main secondary jet 60 Pump suction and return valve 61 Emulsion tube 62 Air control jet 63 Float 64 Float spindle 65 Float toggle 66 Needle valve 67 Gasket 68 Screw 69 Plate 70 Gasket 71 Starter piston 72 Washer for lever spindle 73 Starter lever nuts 74 Washer 75 Starter piston lever 76 Filter inspection plug 77 Filter 78 Washer 79 Pump jet 80 Pump return valve 81 Choke plate 82 Spindle 83 Choke plate screw 84 Choke return spring 85 Split bush, valve retaining 86 Conical valve 87 Carburetter body 88 Spacing bush 89 Control lever 90 Pin 91 Filter gauze plug 92 Secondary venturi Items 50, 51, 52, 55, 56, 57, 85, 86, 88 and 89 are not applicable to DLE.A1 carburetters tested for leaks by closing the outlet to the carburetter with a plug, fitting a rubber hose on the inlet opening and immersing the whole pump in a container filled with clean petrol. Compressed air is then blown through the rubber hose at a low pressure, when bubbles of escaping air will indicate either a defective diaphragm or leaking gaskets.

3:3 Removal, servicing and refitting

To remove a fuel pump, set the manual height control in the low position and remove the front lefthand suspension sphere. Disconnect the inlet and outlet connections at the pump and remove the pump retaining nuts. Withdraw the pump together with an insulating spacer, the pushrod and guide and a paper gasket.

Operations for overhauling the SEV fuel pump are as follows:

1 Remove the cover and gasket from the upper body and disconnect the upper body from the lower body.

2 Remove the circlip 5 (see **FIG 3:2**) and tap out the spindle 1 from the control lever. Remove the control lever 3 and its spring, the washers 2 and 4 and the diaphragm-pushrod assembly 7.

3 Remove from the diaphragm-pushrod assembly the rubber cup, the metal cup and the spring. Clean all the parts.

4 Note that the valves are clinched in the upper pump body. If the valves are unserviceable it is necessary to replace the upper body.

5 Reassemble and refit the pump in the reverse order of removal. In cars before April, 1966, apply grease (special bearing grease) to the pump operating lever. In cars since April, 1966, the pump end of the pushrod is oiled from the engine oil circuit. **Do not put grease in the pump.** Apply non-setting sealing compound to the pump flange face and to the face of the pushrod guide in contact with the spacer. Tighten the retaining nuts to a torque of 16 to 20 lb ft (21 to 28 kg m). Connect the inlet and outlet pipes, prime the pump with the lever and check for leaks as previously described.

CARBURETTERS:

3:4 Operating principles

The operation of the Weber 28/36 carburetter is shown by the diagrams in **FIG 3:3** and the relative assembly of the components is given in the exploded view of a DLE type carburetter in **FIG 3:4.**

Referring to the former illustration, fuel is drawn through the needle valve 2 into the float chamber 7, where the float 6 pivots on the spindle 4 to regulate the opening of the needle valve 3, thus keeping a constant level of fuel in the chamber. A toggle 5 connects the needle valve 3 to the float. From the float chamber the fuel is drawn through the main jets 8 into the wells 9. The fuel mixes with the air supplied by the emulsion air jets 1 through the emulsion tubes 12 and is injected by atomisers 15 into the carburation zone formed by the venturis 14 and the choke tubes 13. This diagram also shows the control device for the differentiated opening of the butterfly valves. When the lever 11 operates, the butterfly valve 10 opens at an angle which is proportional to the sliding movement allowed by the lever 18

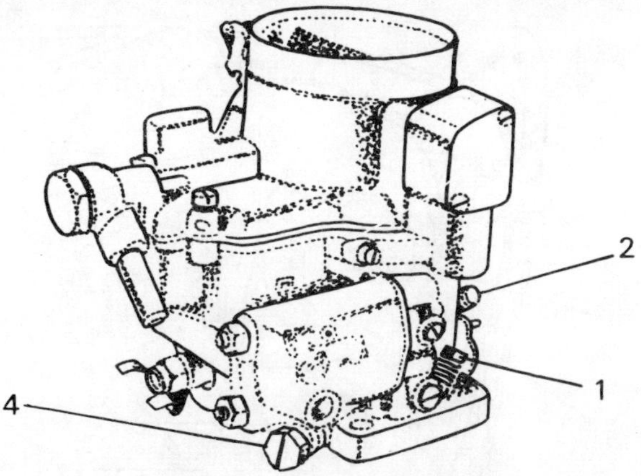

FIG 3:5 Carburetter controls

Key to Fig 3:5 1 Mixture screw 2 Stop screw 4 Accelerated idling adjusting screw

which is integral with lever 11, whilst the secondary butterfly mounted on the spindle 21 remains closed. The lever 20 is then actuated by the lever 18 through the lever rod 19 and causes the rotation of the secondary spindle 21 to effect the complete and simultaneous opening of both butterfly valves. The adjusting screw 16 mounted on the secondary arm regulates the opening of the secondary butterfly valve. On the primary arm the adjusting screw 17 regulates the opening of the primary butterfly valve.

From the emulsion wells 9 fuel is drawn through the ducts 24 to the idling jets 23, where it emulsifies with the air supplied from calibrated holes 22, passing through ducts 25 and idling orifices 28 and 27 and reaching the carburetter ducts below the butterflies. The orifice 27 is fitted with a pointed conical regulating screw. Mixture also reaches the primary and secondary barrels 30 and 31 through the progression holes 29 and 32 to ensure a progressive increase of the engine speed as the butterfly valves open.

For fast idling, by means of an appropriate control the conical valve 35 is lifted off its seat by the return spring 36. The mixture from the passage 34 is further emulsified by the air drawn through the hole 33 in the secondary duct and reaches, through the passage 37, the fast idling orifice 39 regulated by the screw 38 below the secondary butterfly 40.

On closing the butterfly valves the free lever 45 is operated through the cam 46, the rod 47 and the piston 49. Fuel is drawn from the chamber 7 into the pump cylinder through the passage 48 and the inlet valve 41. When the butterfly valves open, the primary spindle rotates first and its cam 46 depresses the free lever 45 mounted on the secondary spindle 21 so that the lever remains in the closed position. In this way the rod 47 and the piston 49 will be displaced by the action of the spring 50. An equivalent quantity of fuel will then be drawn through the passage 44, the valve 43 and the calibrated jet 42 into the primary duct of the carburetter. Then the secondary spindle 21 will rotate and cause a further movement of the piston 49, so that the pump will also supply a certain quantity of fuel during the opening

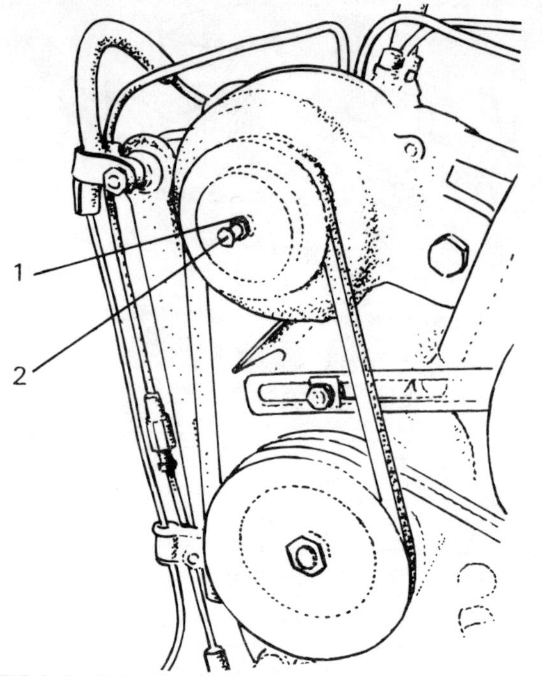

FIG 3:6 Adjusting screw 2 and locknut 1 on the centrifugal regulator

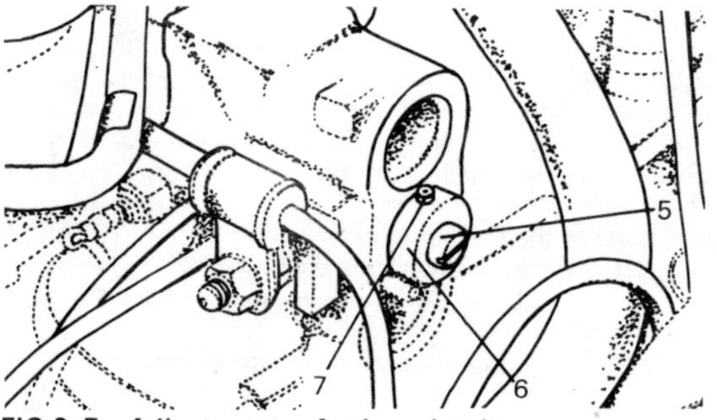

FIG 3:7 Adjustment of the clutch re-engagement control

Key to Fig 3:7 5 Adjusting screw 6 Locking ring 7 Pin

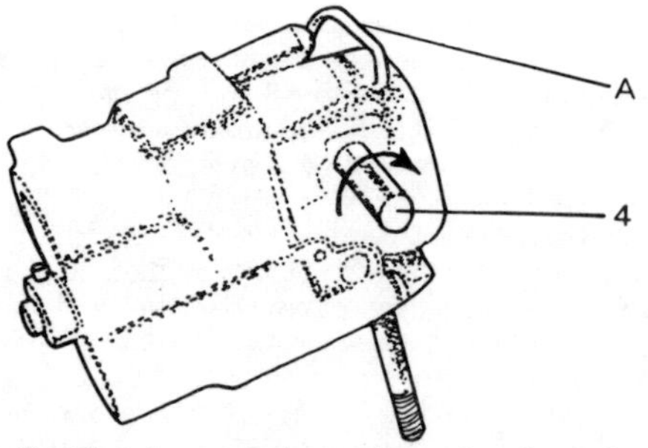

FIG 3:8 Clutch control setting pin A and clutch engagement spindle 4

of the secondary butterfly valve 40. The inlet valve 41 may be provided with a calibrated hole to discharge any excess fuel back into the chamber.

Starting arrangements are that when the lever 57 is in the position A the choke valve 51 will close the air intake, while with the aid of the rod 56 and the lever 55 the primary butterfly valve 10 is partially opened. A very rich mixture is then drawn through the atomizer tube 15 to facilitate starting of the engine. As soon as the engine starts, the vacuum created below the butterfly valves is transmitted through the passage 54 to the piston 58, which moves downwards opening partially the choke plate 51 against the pressure of the spring 52. The atomizer tube 15 then supplies a suitably rich mixture for warming up the engine. If when the starter is connected the accelerator pedal is depressed, this will reduce the vacuum below the valves and consequently neutralize the action of the piston 58. The opening of the choke 51 is hence determined by the air suction from the engine against the action of the spring 52. Whilst the engine is warming up the choke 51 must be progressively opened. When the engine reaches its running temperature, the starter device is completely disconnected (position B) and the choke 51 will be kept completely open by the stop lug 53 whilst the primary butterfly valve 10 is brought to the idling position.

3:5 Routine maintenance, tuning for slow-running

Ordinary maintenance work necessary to keep the carburetters in good working order is mainly concerned with the periodic cleaning of jets and float chambers which can be performed without extensive dismantling and which is described in the general instructions given later for dismantling and reassembly.

To adjust the slow-running it is essential that certain conditions must first be observed. The engine must be hot. Any adjustment made with the engine cold may be incorrect when the engine is hot. Proceed to run the engine at idling speed, then put the starting handle extension in position. Unscrew the adjusting screw of the clutch fork by fractions of a turn at a time until the starter handle extension just begins to turn but may be stopped by hand. Then tighten the screw two turns.

The adjustments to be made are critical with relation to the automatic control of clutch and gearchange operation where provided, and it is essential that a revolution counter is employed which may be either mechanical or electrical. Service agents use a mechanical instrument 2434.T with drive 2423.T driven by the high pressure pump pulley. Alternatively an electrical revolution counter 2436.T may be used, which is connected to the output (red) terminal of the coil. When using the mechanical revolution counter, to compensate for either belt slip or irregular engine performance the bleed screw of the pressure control valve should be unscrewed or the manual height control lever placed in the low position.

Operations are as follows, referring to **FIG 3:5**:

1 Screw in fully, without forcing, the accelerated idling adjusting screw 4.
2 Turn the secondary butterfly stop screw 2 until a speed of approximately 550 rev/min is obtained or 625 to 675 rev/min in cars after September 1968.

3 Turn the mixture screw 1 in one direction or the other, until the point of maximum speed is reached for the butterfly opening as described.

4 Slowly unscrew the stop screw 2 until a speed of 550 rev/min is obtained, or 625 to 675 rev/min in cars after September, 1968.

5 If the running is erratic, readjust the mixture screw 1 very slowly. After each adjustment on the secondary butterfly adjusting screw 2, flip the throttle open slightly, with the manual clutch control in the engaged position to ensure that the butterfly returns fully to the stop screw.

3:6 Adjusting the clutch drag, accelerated idling and clutch re-engagement control

These adjustments must be made with the engine hot and the car standing on level ground. It is to be noted that the required speeds differ in semi-automatic gearchange models produced before and after September, 1968.

For adjusting the speed of clutch drag, start up the engine, engage first gear and accelerate very slowly. Clutch drag should commence between 700 and 750 rev/min or 725 and 775 rev/min in later cars. If otherwise, stop the engine and loosen the locknut 1 of the adjusting screw 2 on the centrifugal regulator (see **FIG 3:6**). If the clutch drags at a speed less than 700 or 725 rev/min, tighten the screw. Unscrew it if clutch drag begins at a speed greater than 750 or 775 rev/min. Finally tighten the locknut 1.

The accelerated idling adjustment is made with the engine idling and the adjusting screw 4 (see **FIG 3:5**) unscrewed until a speed of between 875 and 925 rev/min (850 and 900 rev/min in later cars) is obtained.

For the clutch re-engagement control (see **FIG 3:7**), if the time for re-engagement is too short, unscrew the screw 5 in an anti-clockwise direction. If the time is too long, tighten the screw 5. If the pin 7 contacts its stop before correct adjustment is obtained, slacken the screw locking the ring 6, turn the ring and reposition it so as to give the maximum adjustment in both directions. Then tighten the screw.

3:7 Carburetter removal and refitting

Operations to remove and refit a carburetter are undertaken as follows:

1 Release the pressure in the brake circuit. To avoid having subsequently to set the clutch re-engagement control, remove the plug from the setting hole position as shown in **FIG 3:8** and insert the pin A.

2 Referring to **FIG 3:9**, disconnect the petrol feed pipe 4, the air intake elbow 1, the choke control 2, the feed pipe union 3 from the accelerated idling device where fitted and the drive flange 5 for the clutch re-engagement control on the carburetter spindle.

3 Disconnect the throttle relay from the carburetter, then remove the four nuts securing the carburetter on the manifold.

4 Remove the carburetter, the cruciform control trunnion for the clutch re-engagement control, the distance piece and the flector.

To refit the carburetter, proceed as follows:

1 Pull back fully the control lever of the clutch re-engagement control and fit the flector on the control lever.

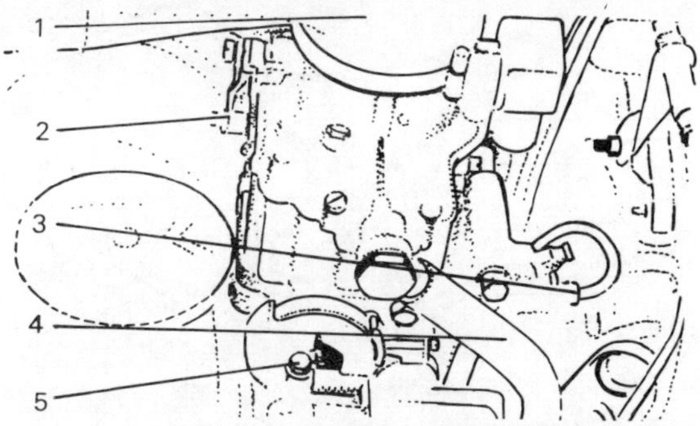

FIG 3:9 Carburetter connections

Key to Fig 3:9 1 Air intake elbow 2 Choke control 3 Feed pipe union from accelerated idling device 4 Fuel inlet 5 Drive flange for the clutch re-engagement control

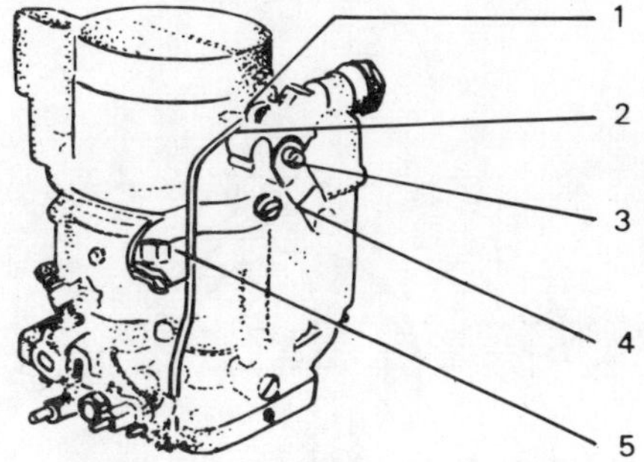

FIG 3:10 Carburetter components

Key to Fig 3:10 1 Ring seals 2 Clips 3 Screw 4 Choke control lever 5 Connecting link

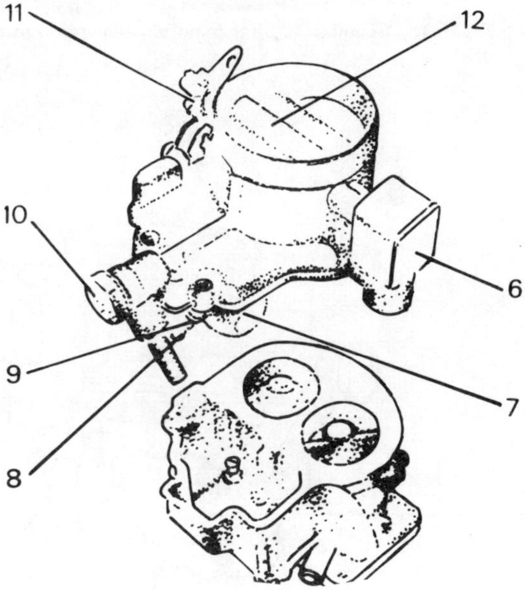

FIG 3:11 Carburetter components

Key to Fig 3:11 6 Plate 7 Float 8 Float spindle 9 Clip 10 Plug 11 Return spring 12 Choke plate

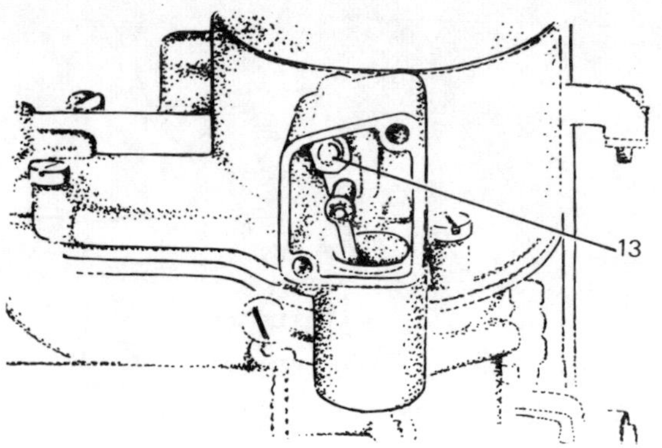

FIG 3:12 Link arm (13) of the starter control piston

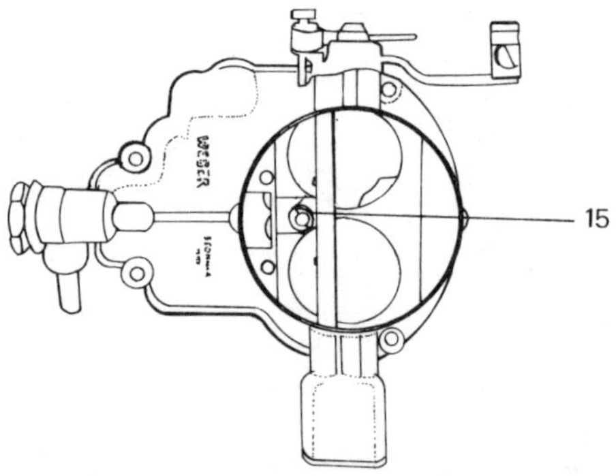

FIG 3:13 The atomizer (15) for the accelerator pump

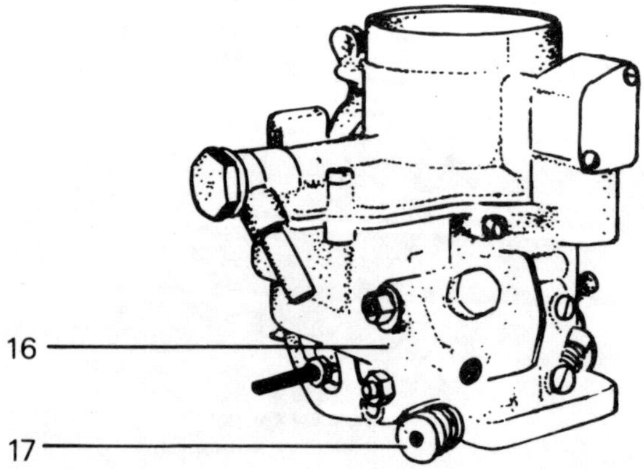

FIG 3:14 The accelerated idling control 16, showing the adjusting screw 17

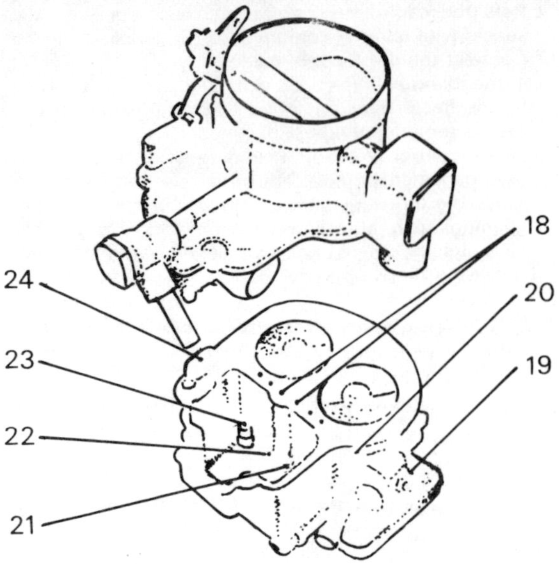

FIG 3:15 Carburetter jets

Key to Fig 3:15 18 Correction jets 19 Mixture control screw 20 Slow-running jets 21, 22 Main jets 23 Accelerator pump non-return valve 24 Accelerator pump piston

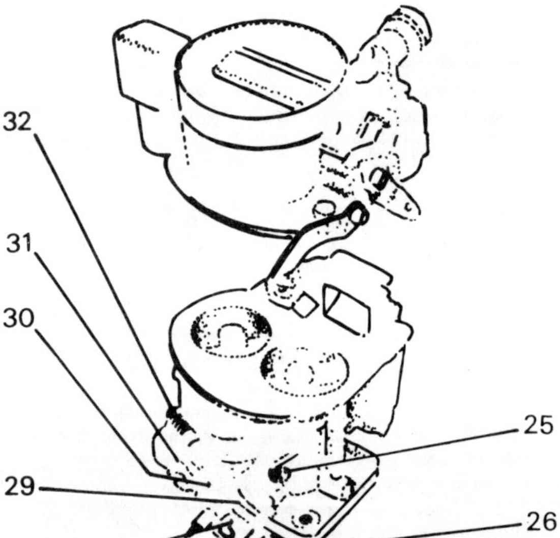

FIG 3:16 Carburetter components

Key to Fig 3:16 25 Stop screw for first (small) butterfly 26 Control lever of connecting link 27 Control lever for butterfly valves 28 Nut 29 Shouldered washer with expansion washer 30 Sector and spring 31 Interlink rod 32 Idling adjusting screw for second (large) butterfly valve

2 Refit the carburetter on the manifold, smearing the spacer with jointing compound.
3 Connect the throttle control relay and set the throttle in the idling position.
4 Fit the flector on the carburetter control lever. Allow the flector an end float of .5 mm, then tighten the clip on the control lever. Withdraw the pin from the clutch re-engagement control and insert the plug.
5 Move the throttle control to the 'maximum permitted opening' so as to engage the clutch re-engagement control spindle and hold the spindle in this position. Releasing the throttle control, the carburetter butterfly valve should return to the idling position. If it does not return, check the alignment in the vertical and horizontal planes of the spindles of the carburetter and the clutch re-engagement control.
6 Connect up the choke control, the feed pipe for the accelerated idling device, the petrol feed hose and the air intake hose. Adjust the idling as previously described.

Note that with the strangler flap in the closed position there must be a clearance of .9 mm between the edge of the primary butterfly and the bore. If this clearance is not obtained, check that the connecting rod is not twisted or that the lug which carries the end of the return spring of the lever controlling the strangler flap is not deformed.

3:8 Weber 28/36 dismantling and reassembly

Referring to **FIG 3:4** and to the details shown in **FIGS 3:10, 3:11** and **3:12,** remove the clips 2, the ring seals 1 and the connecting link 5 with its shouldered washers. Detach the cover and proceed as follows:

1 Remove the spring clip 9 holding the float, the float spindle 8 and the float 7. Remove the paper joint and the needle with its joint.
2 Remove the plug 10 and the filter, the plate 6 covering the strangler control piston and the paper joint.
3 Remove the locknut 13, the nut and flat washer securing the link arm of the strangler control piston, the screw 3, the return spring 11 of the strangler 12 and the control lever 4 of the strangler, with its return spring.
4 Disconnect the strangler 12, the strangler spindle with its expanding washer and the strangler control piston.
5 Referring to **FIG 3:13,** remove the atomizer 15 for the accelerator pump.
6 Where fitted, remove the accelerated idling control 16 (see **FIG 3:14**) with its valve mechanism, complete, also the accelerated idling speed adjusting screw 17 with its spring.
7 Remove the main jets 22 and 21 (see **FIG 3:15**), the non-return valve 23 for the accelerator pump and the correction jets 18.
8 Withdraw the emulsion tubes under the correction jets and the accelerator pump piston 24 by pulling its elbowed lever.
9 Remove the idling mixture control screw 19 with its spring and the slow-running jets 20.
10 Referring to **FIG 3:16,** remove the idling adjusting screw 32 and its spring for the second (large) butterfly. Note that under no circumstances must anything be done to the stop screw 25 for the first

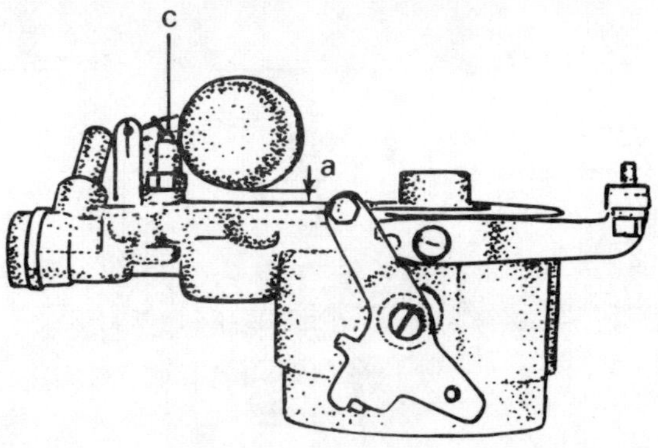

FIG 3:17 **Adjusting the float level. For dimensions see text**

(small) butterfly, individual adjustment of this screw having been carried out by the makers on each carburetter.
11 Unlock the nut 28 and remove the control lever 27 of the butterflies, the control lever 26 of the connecting link, the shouldered washer 29 with its expanding washer, the pin and the interlink rod 31 and the sector 30 with its spring.
12 Remove the pump control lever 53 (see **FIG 3:4**) and the accelerator pump control cam 57.
13 Any dismantling of the carburetter must be limited to the foregoing operations, otherwise it may be rendered unusable.
14 Remove the plugs, clean the parts in petrol and blow out very thoroughly with compressed air the passages in the carburetter and the various jets. Never use wire or anything which may enlarge the jets.
15 Before assembling the carburetter, check (a) the state of the needle of the idling mixture screw, (b) the accelerator pump non-return valves for leaks, (c) the needle valve for leaks and (d) the float.

Reassemble the carburetter by following the dismantling operations in reverse. Check the float level and adjust if required as follows:

1 With the needle valve closed, turn the cover over, when the distance 'a' (see **FIG 3:17**) between the float and the cover gasket must be 4.75$\pm$.1 mm. If otherwise, adjust the tongue 'c', which should be parallel to

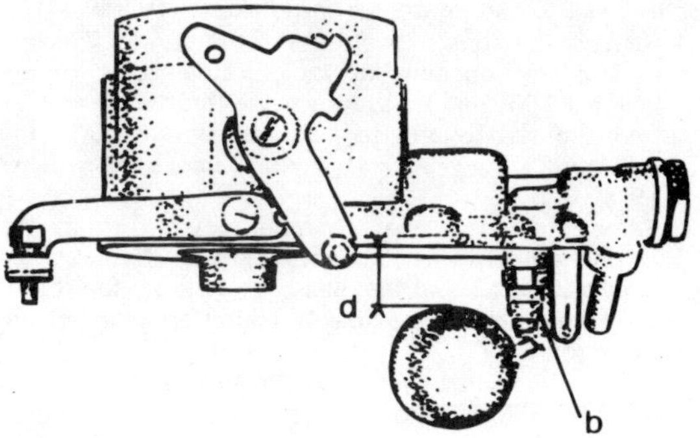

FIG 3:18 **Adjusting the float level. For dimensions see text**

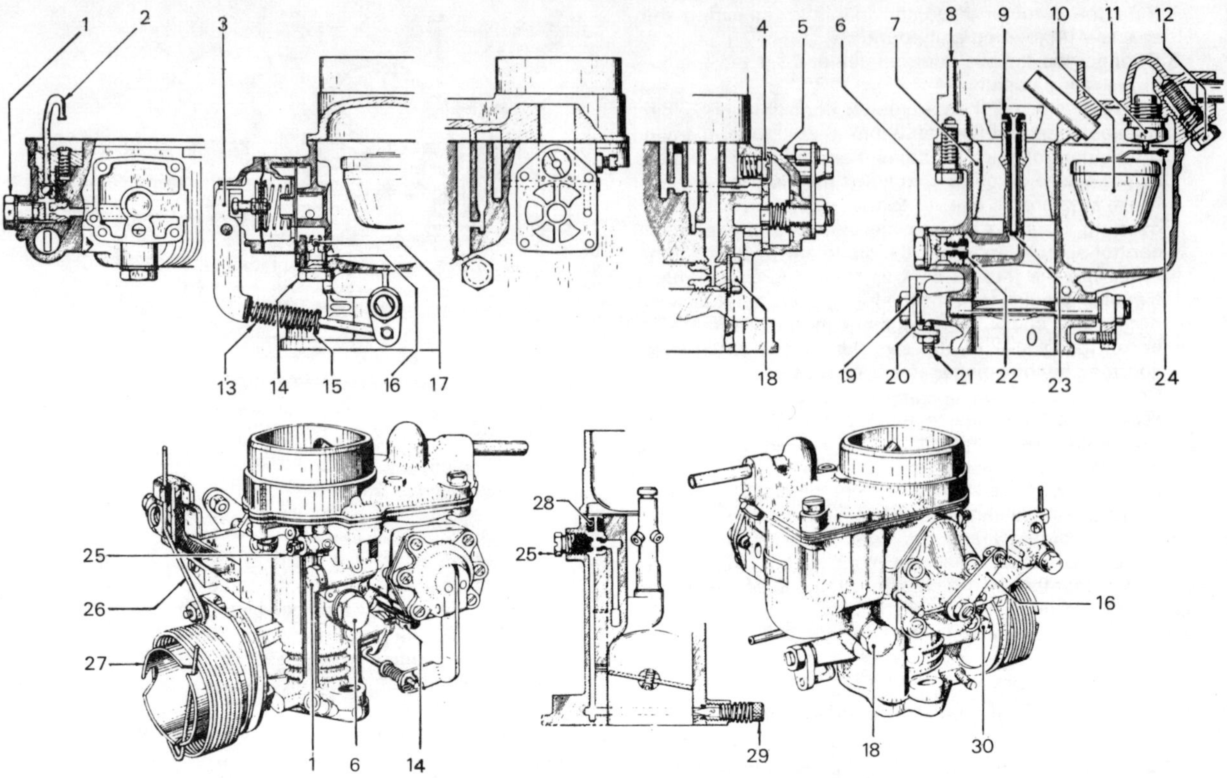

FIG 3:19 Details of the Solex 34 PBIC carburetter

Key to Fig 3:19 1 Pump jet 2 Injector 3 Pump lever 4 Starter air jet 5 Accelerator pump 6 Main jet carrier 7 Choke tube 8 Float chamber cover 9 Air correction jet 10 Float 11 Needle valve 12 Filter plug 13 Spring 14 Non-return valve 15 Spring seat 16 Filter 17 Steel ball 18 Starter fuel jet 19 Washer 20 Support 21 Butterfly regulating screw 22 Main jet 23 Emulsion tube 24 Float spindle 25 Slow-running jet 26 Spring 27 Throttle control 28 Idling air bleed 29 Volume control screw 30 Throttle stop screw

the cover joint face and at a distance of 19.75 mm from the paper joint.

2 With the needle valve in the fully-open position, place the cover as shown in **FIG 3:18,** when the distance 'd' between the float and the cover joint should be 11.5±.1 mm. If not, adjust the tongue 'b'.

3:9 Solex 34 PBIC dismantling and reassembly

Referring to **FIG 3:19,** dismantling operations on the Solex 34 PBIC carburetter are undertaken as follows:

1 Remove the spring 26 of the throttle control 27 controlling the opening of the throttle (cars before October 1960) and disconnect the throttle control 27 from the carburetter. Remove the support 20 of the regulating screws 21 and 30 and remove the washer 19.

2 Remove the top float chamber cover 8 from the carburetter. Remove the paper gasket. Remove the needle valve 11 and the filter plug 12 from the top of the cover. Remove the float 10 and its spindle 24 from the carburetter.

3 Remove the screws retaining the injector 2 and paper gasket. Remove the air correction jet 9 and withdraw the emulsion tube 23. Remove the choke tube locking screw and the choke tube 7.

4 Remove the accelerator pump 5 from the carburetter body. Remove the pump lever pin 3, the spring 13 and the washer 15. Disconnect the accelerator pump (secured by four screws) from the carburetter and withdraw the gasket. Note that if a pump diaphragm is damaged, a new pump must be fitted. Never remove the diaphragm.

5 Remove the main jet carrier 6 and remove the main jet 22 from the carrier 6. Remove the starter petrol jet 18 and the starter air jet 4. Remove the pump jet 1, the pilot jet 25 and the idling air bleed 28. Remove the seat 14 of the pump inlet valve ball 17 and the volume control screw 29.

6 Clean the parts and blow compressed air through the ducts and the jets. Thoroughly clean the filter plug 12 and the filter 16 of the pump valves 17. Do not use wire to clean the jets.

Reassembly operations are in general the same as those applied to dismantling but in reverse order. New copper gaskets should be fitted to the needle valve 11, pump inlet valve 17, the pump jet 1 and the starter jets 18 and 4. New paper gaskets are required for the accelerator pump 5, the pump injector 2 and the float chamber cover 8, also a new fibre washer for the main jet carrier 6.

Idle adjustment:

This is carried out with the engine hot, but the procedure is a little different from that detailed for the Weber carburetter in **Section 3:5** as only two adjusting screws are used, namely the throttle stop screw and the volume control screw, items 29 and 30 in **FIG 3:19**.

Using the throttle stop screw, obtain an engine speed of about 550 rev/min.

Turn the volume control screw in one direction or the other to obtain the fastest possible engine speed at the throttle opening just set.

Slowly turn the stop screw until the engine speed is between 625 and 675 rev/min.

If the running of the engine is uneven at this speed, carefully rotate the volume control screw to obtain the desired quality of running.

3:10 Removing and refitting inlet and exhaust manifolds

An inlet manifold is removed and refitted as follows:

1 Drain the water from the radiator and cylinder block and disconnect the negative terminal of the battery.
2 Remove the clutch re-engagement control (see **Chapter 6**) and the carburetter (see **Section 2:7**).
3 Remove the accelerator control relay from its mounting on the scuttle and turn it round sideways. Remove the oil dipstick and its guide 1 (see **FIG 3:20**).
4 Remove the eight nuts securing the manifold and separate the manifold from the head as far as possible. Remove the two studs 2 and withdraw the manifold.
5 Disconnect the hot-spot hose 3 from the manifold and remove the gaskets.
6 Refit in the reverse order of removal, coating the studs 2 with hermetic compound. If there is any stiffness in the accelerator control, check the alignment of the carburetter with the clutch re-engagement control (see **Chapter 6**). Adjust the idling as previously described.

To remove and refit an exhaust manifold proceed as follows:

1 Remove the air filter assembly and its bracket and the shield for the exhaust manifolds.
2 Remove the nuts holding the downpipes, which are accessible from the underside of the vehicle, using spanner 2431.T. Remove the screw holding the clamp on the bracket under the engine.
3 Free the flanges from the studs on the manifolds, then remove the two manifolds and the copper asbestos gaskets.
4 When reassembling, if the manifolds have been replaced fit the downpipe mounting studs before setting the manifolds. Note that the flanges fixing the manifolds on the cylinder head should never be refaced.
5 Fit the copper asbestos gaskets and the manifold 2 then the manifold 3 (see **FIG 3:21**). Fit the nuts and flat washers but do not tighten them.
6 Connect the manifold downpipes. Insert the copper asbestos gaskets and the downpipes. Tighten the nuts from the underside of the vehicle. Tighten the nuts securing the manifolds.
7 Fit the shield for the exhaust manifolds, the air filter and its bracket and the collar securing the pipe to the bracket under the engine with flat and shakeproof washers.

AIR CLEANERS:

3:11 Routine maintenance

Removal of the air cleaner shown in **FIG 3:21** is undertaken by disconnecting the air hose after removing the clips and then detaching the two nuts securing the air filter on the exhaust manifold. When refitting, connect the oil vapour intake to the cylinder head cover and tighten the nuts. Connect the air hose on the filter, and then on the carburetter. Tighten the clips.

The filter element must be cleaned every 6000 miles or 10,000 km. Release the three catches, raise the upper cover and remove the filter element. Clean the parts in

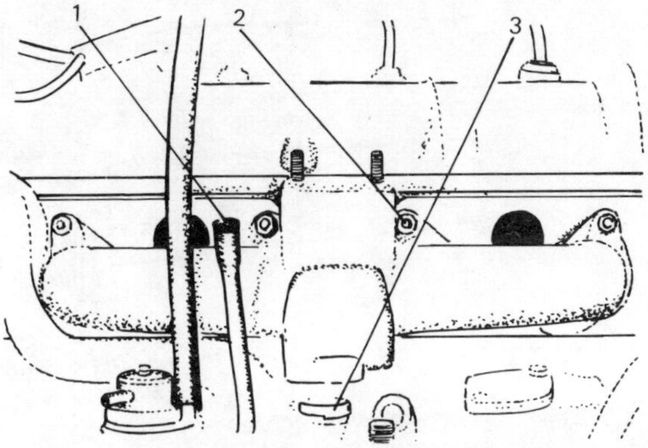

FIG 3:20 Inlet manifold

Key to Fig 3:20 1 Dipstick guide 2 Studs 3 Hot spot hose

FIG 3:21 Exhaust manifolds, indicated by 2 and 3

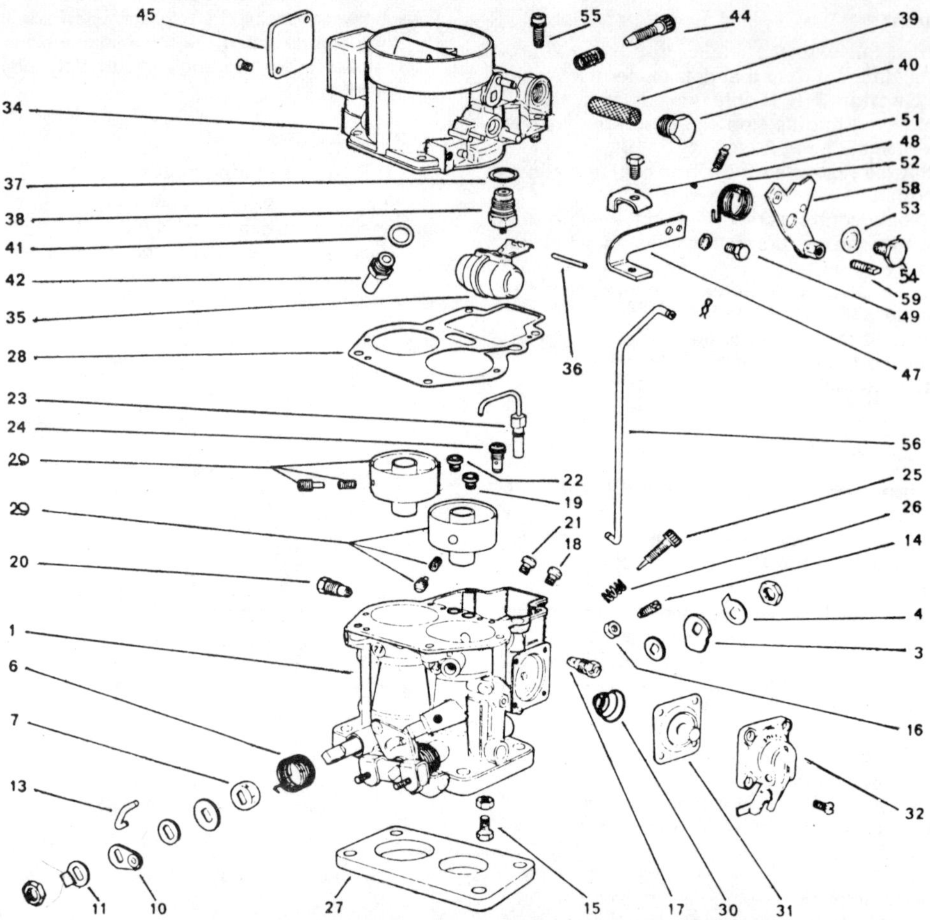

FIG 3:22 Components of Solex carburetter type 28/36 SFIF

Key to Fig 3:22 1 Body and float chamber 3 Pump operating cam 4 Lockwasher 6 Return spring 7 Cover 10 Secondary throttle operating lever 11 Lockwasher 13 Connecting rod 14 Idle screw 15 Stop screw 17 Idle jet 18 Main jet (primary) 19 Compensating jet (primary) 20 Idle jet 21 Main jet (secondary) 22 Compensating jet (secondary) 23 Pump injector 24 Ball valve 25 Mixture control screw 26 Spring 27 Insulator plate 28 Copper gasket 29 Diffuser 30 Spring 31 Diaphragm assembly 34 Upper body 35 Float 36 Float pivot pin 37 Washer 38 Needle valve 39 Filter 40 Plug 44 Air screw 45 Cover 47 Bracket 51 Choke return spring 52 Spring 54 Pivot 56 Connecting rod 58 Choke operating lever 59 Cable securing screw

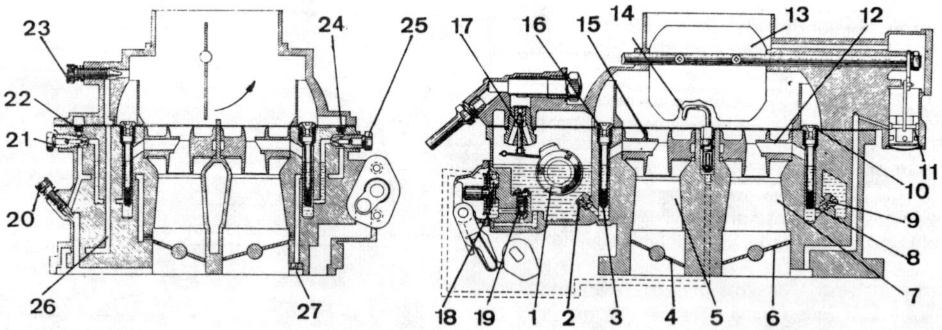

FIG 3:23 Transverse and longitudinal sections of 28/36 SFIF carburetter

Key to Fig 3:23 1 Float 2 and 9 Main jets 3 and 8 Emulsion tubes 4 and 6 Throttle butterflies 5 and 7 Diffusers 10 and 16 Compensating jets 11 Piston 12 and 15 Venturis 13 Choke plate 14 Pump injector 17 Needle valve 18 Pump diaphragm 19 Ball valve 20 Mixture control screw 21 and 25 Idle jets 22 and 24 Air jets 23 Air control screw 26 and 27 Slow-running air passages petrol, then blow out the filter element with compressed air, immerse it in engine oil and allow it to drain. When reassembling make quite sure that the gasket is correctly located on the filter element. Put the filter element in the lower part of the filter and fit the cover placing the notch in line with the clip. Finally make quite sure that the gasket is properly embedded all round the circumference of the filter body.

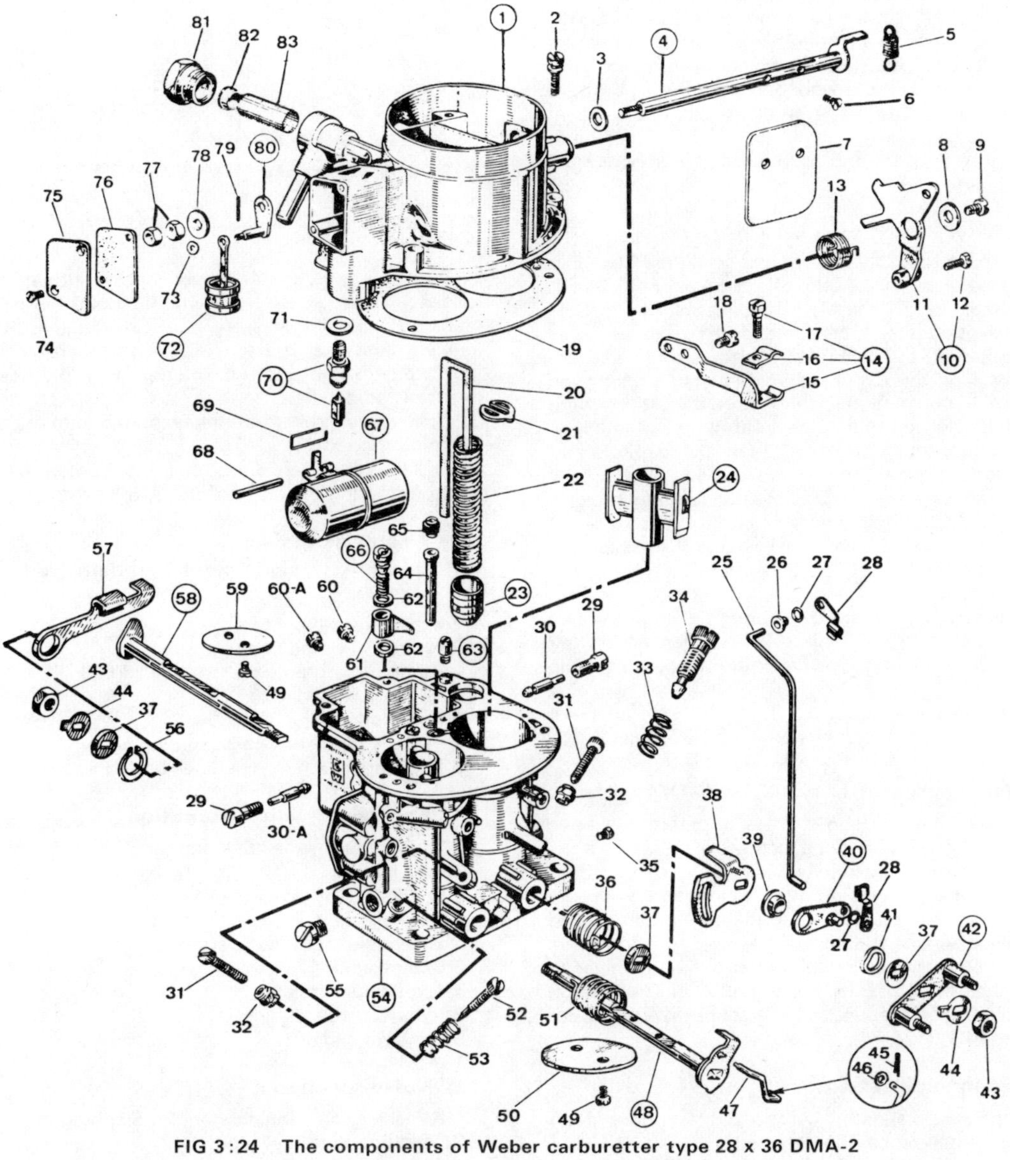

FIG 3:24 The components of Weber carburetter type 28 x 36 DMA-2

Key to Fig 3:24 1 Top cover 2 Screw 3 Washer 4 Choke spindle 5 Spring 6 Screw 7 Choke plate 8 Spacer 9 Screw 10 Choke operating lever 13 Return spring 14 Cable bracket 19 Gasket 20 Pump operating rod 21 Retainer 22 Spring 23 Pump piston 24 Secondary venturi 25 Fast idle rod 26 Bush 27 Washer 28 Spring 29 Idle jet carrier 30 Primary idle jet 30A Secondary idle jet 31 Throttle stop screw 33 Spring 34 Idle mixture control screw 35 Inspection screw 36 Throttle return spring (P) 38 Primary stop lever 39 Bush 40 Fast idle lever 41 Friction washer 42 Throttle lever 47 Connecting rod 48 Throttle spindle (S) 50 Throttle plate (S) 51 Return spring 52 Volume control screw 54 Body 55 Progression hole inspection screw 56 Locking ring 57 Pump operating lever 58 Throttle spindle (P) 59 Throttle plate (P) 60 Main jet (P) 60A Main jet (S) 61 Pump jet 62 Washer 63 Pump valve 64 Emulsion tube (P) 64A Emulsion tube (S) 65 Air control jet 66 Pump valve 67 Float 68 Float spindle 69 Needle clip 70 Needle valve 72 Choke piston 75 Plate 77 Nuts 80 Piston lever 81 Filter inspection plug 82 Filter plug 83 Filter

3:12 Solex carburetter type 28/36 SFIF

After February 1970 some D Super models were equipped with the above type of Solex carburetter in place of the double-barrelled Weber described earlier in this chapter and with which it is interchangeable. An exploded view of the components of the carburetter is given in **FIG 3:22** and sectional views in **FIG 3:23**. Details of jet sizes, etc. will be found in **Technical Data.**

The operation of this carburetter in normal running is similar to that of other double-barrel instruments with the butterfly throttle of the secondary barrel being brought into action when the first throttle is two-thirds open. This arrangement gives good acceleration, maximum power at full throttle and good economy at moderate cruising speeds.

Slow-running:

It is in this respect that the operation differs from that described earlier as will be seen by reference to **FIG 3:23.** The fuel required for the slow-running mixture is provided by the two jets 21 and 25 and the necessary air is admitted through the calibrated apertures at 22 and 24. The screw 23 at the top of the float chamber, taking the place of the conventional throttle stop screw which remains fully closed at this time, controls the quantity of air flowing through the passage 27 into the manifold and so regulates the slow-running mixture and thereby the speed of the engine. The basic slow-running mixture strength is adjusted by the mixture control screw 20.

To adjust the idle speed of the engine it is necessary first to obtain the fastest speed possible by turning the mixture control screw 20 as necessary.

Turn the air control screw 23 to bring the engine speed to between 600 and 650 rev/min and then adjust the mixture screw again to achieve the fastest possible running.

Repeat these operations until the maximum speed obtained with smooth running is 600 to 650 rev/min.

3:13 Weber carburetter type 28 x 36 DMA-2 or -3

From July 1972 the above types of carburetter have been available on cars intended for those areas where anti-pollution regulations are in force. As with all such installations the owner is warned not to interfere with the adjustment screws, but to entrust the carburetter setting to a qualified service station.

The components of the carburetter are very similar to those of the 28/36 DLE described earlier in this chapter and detailed specifications will be found in **Technical Data**. See **FIG 3:24**.

Slow running adjustment:

This operation is easily carried out at home if an exhaust gas analyzer can be obtained.

Proceed as described for the Solex SFIF carburetter described in **Section 3:12** using the mixture control screw 34 and the volume control screw 52 to obtain an idle speed of 950±25 rev/min, with readings of 1.8 to 3.6% CO and not more than 8.7% CO_2.

Float level adjustment (see **FIG 3:25**):

Check first that the float and its operation are correct and the needle valve in good condition.

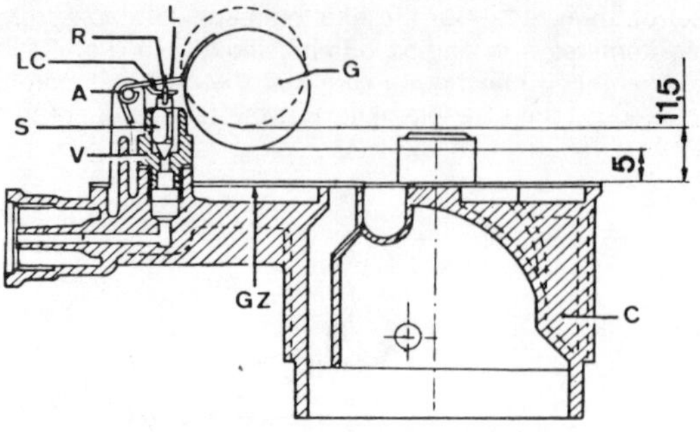

FIG 3:25 Float level adjustment

Key to Fig 3:25 **A** Float travel tag **C** Carburetter cover **G** Float **GZ** Gasket **LC** Needle operating tag **L** Float link **R** Return clip **S** Needle **V** Needle valve

Turn the carburetter cover upside down and the distance between the top of the float and the gasket GZ must be 5 mm. If necessary, adjust by bending the link L, making sure that the tag LC remains perpendicular to the needle S and does not interfere with the free movement of the needle.

Now check the float travel at 6.5 mm by suitably bending the tag A.

Fit the cover, ensuring that the float moves freely without fouling the sides of the float chamber.

3:14 Fault diagnosis

(a) Leakage or insufficient fuel delivered

1 Air vent in tank restricted
2 Petrol pipes blocked
3 Air leaks at pipe connections
4 Pump or carburetter filters blocked
5 Pump gaskets faulty
6 Pump diaphragm defective
7 Pump valves sticking or seating badly
8 Fuel vaporizing in pipe lines due to heat

(b) Excessive fuel consumption

1 Carburetter needs adjusting
2 Fuel leakage
3 Sticking controls or choke device
4 Dirty air cleaner
5 Excessive engine temperature
6 Brakes binding
7 Tyres under-inflated
8 Idling speed too high
9 Car overloaded

(c) Noisy fuel pump

1 Air leak on suction side and at diaphragm
2 Obstruction in fuel pipe
3 Clogged pump filter

(d) No fuel delivery

1 Float needle stuck
2 Vent in tank blocked
3 Pipe line obstructed
4 Pump diaphragm stiff or damaged
5 Inlet valve in pump stuck open
6 Bad air leak on suction side of pump

CHAPTER 4

THE IGNITION SYSTEM

4:1 Operating principles

The main elements in the ignition system providing high tension current to the sparking plugs are the battery, the ignition coil, the contact breaker and the distributor, which may be of either Ducellier or SEV-Marchal manufacture. Different characteristics are incorporated in these distributors for the range of engines produced and for changes in engine design and performance, but their general principles of operation remain unchanged. The various types are identified by a reference number and letter carried by each distributor, which should always be quoted in full if the necessity for spare parts should arise.

The distributor in DX (DS21) engines is housed in a drive tower (see **FIG 4:1**) mounted on the crankcase and is driven by a pinion which engages with a skew gear on the front end of the camshaft. In DY (DS19A) engines (see **FIG 4:2**) the distributor shaft is engaged at its lower end with the oil pump spindle driven in both models by a skew gear at the rear end of the camshaft. In all D-type engines since October, 1968, however, the distributor is incorporated at the front of the engine. Ignition advance is mechanically controlled according to engine speed by governor weights inside the distributor body. The two weights are pivoted so that they move outwards from the distributor shaft as the engine speed increases, turning the cam on the shaft and so advancing the firing point. The weights are restrained by springs to give a progressive advance action.

4:2 Distributor maintenance, contact point adjustment

Maintenance of the distributor is chiefly concerned with occasional lubrication of the moving parts. Referring to **FIG 4:3**, lift out the rotor B and apply two drops of engine oil to the felt pad 28 in the centre of the cam. The cam faces on the assembly H should be very lightly smeared with petroleum jelly. Only a film of oil should be applied to the breaker arm pivot, ensuring that none contaminates the distributor points. Be careful not to over-lubricate, otherwise lubricant may reach the contact breaker points, resulting in burning and difficult starting.

To adjust the contact breaker points in a Ducellier or SEV distributor, remove the cap and rotor arm and turn the engine with the starting handle so that the heel of the moving contact breaker arm is on the highest point of the cam. Slacken the adjusting screw 6 in the Ducellier unit (see **FIG 4:5**)or its counterpart in an SEV unit, then

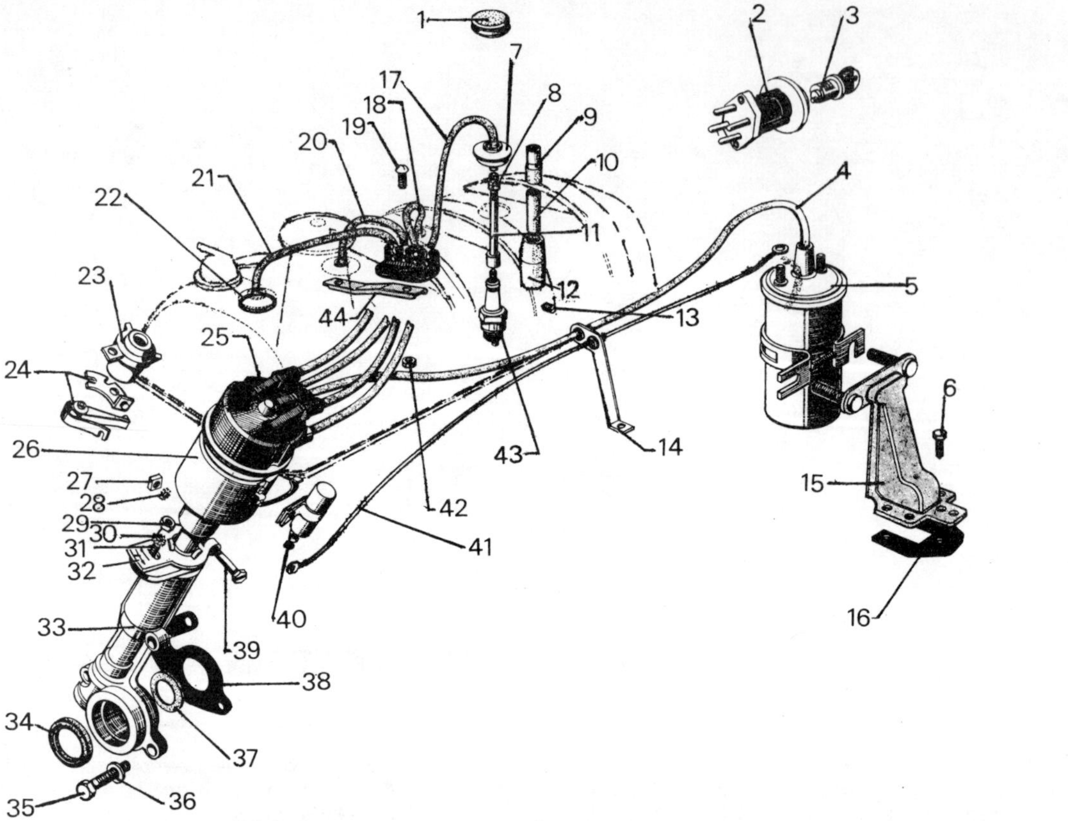

FIG 4:1 Details of ignition system on DX engines

Key to Fig 4:1 1 Cap 2 Connector 3 Ignition switch 4 Lead 5 Coil 6 Screw 7 Cap 8 Connector 9 Insulating tube 10 Insulating tube 11 Plug extension 12 Insulator 13 Screw 14 Bracket 15 Bracket 16 Joint 17 Plug lead 18 Plug lead 19 Screw 20 Plug lead 21 Plug lead 22 Joint 23 Rotor housing 24 Contact breaker assembly 25 Distributor cap 26 Distributor 27 Nut 28 Washer 29 Nut 30 Washer 31 Screw 32 Clamp plate 33 Drive tower 34 Ring 35 Bolt 36 Washer 37 Joint 38 Brackets 39 Clamp screw 40 Capacitor 41 Lead 42 Nut 43 Sparking plug 44 Bracket

in the former insert a screwdriver into the slot in the contact carrying plate 10 and move the plate as necessary to obtain a contact gap of $.45 \pm .05$ mm. An adjusting screw 27 (see **FIG 4:7**) is provided in the SEV unit to carry out the same operation. Tighten the locking screw and recheck the gap. In each case refit the rotor arm squarely, press it firmly down and refit the cap.

4:3 Distributor removal and refitting

To remove the distributor on DX engines, disconnect the leads to the plugs, the coil and to earth. Then remove the screw 1 (see **FIG 4:12**) fixing the distributor and withdraw the latter from its housing. Refit by following the same procedure in reverse.

On DY engines, similarly remove the HT leads and the primary lead to the distributor. Remove the retaining clip securing the earth lead, then unscrew a few turns the two nuts 2 (see **FIG 4:4**) holding the clamp plate 3. Turn the distributor clockwise, about one-third of a turn, to free and remove it from the clamp plate. To refit, remove the distributor head and locate the distributor in its housing. The flats on the distributor must correspond with those on the housing. Turn the rotor to ensure that the distributor drive dog is correctly engaged with its drive slot. Then secure the distributor under the clamp plate by turning it back by the same amount as in removal. **The capacitor must be towards the rear of the engine.** Connect the earth terminal under the clip and the leads originally removed, tighten the nuts on the clamp plate and adjust the ignition setting as described later.

4:4 Distributor dismantling and reassembly

For the overhaul of a Ducellier distributor, remove the distributor head with the leads and proceed as follows:

1 Remove the rotor arm 1 (see **FIG 4:5**), then free the capacitor connection 7, unscrew the nut 4 and withdraw the steel washers and the insulating washer 3. Remove the securing clip 8 and the capacitor 7.

2 Remove the circlip 13 and the insulating washer 14 from the moving contact pivot.

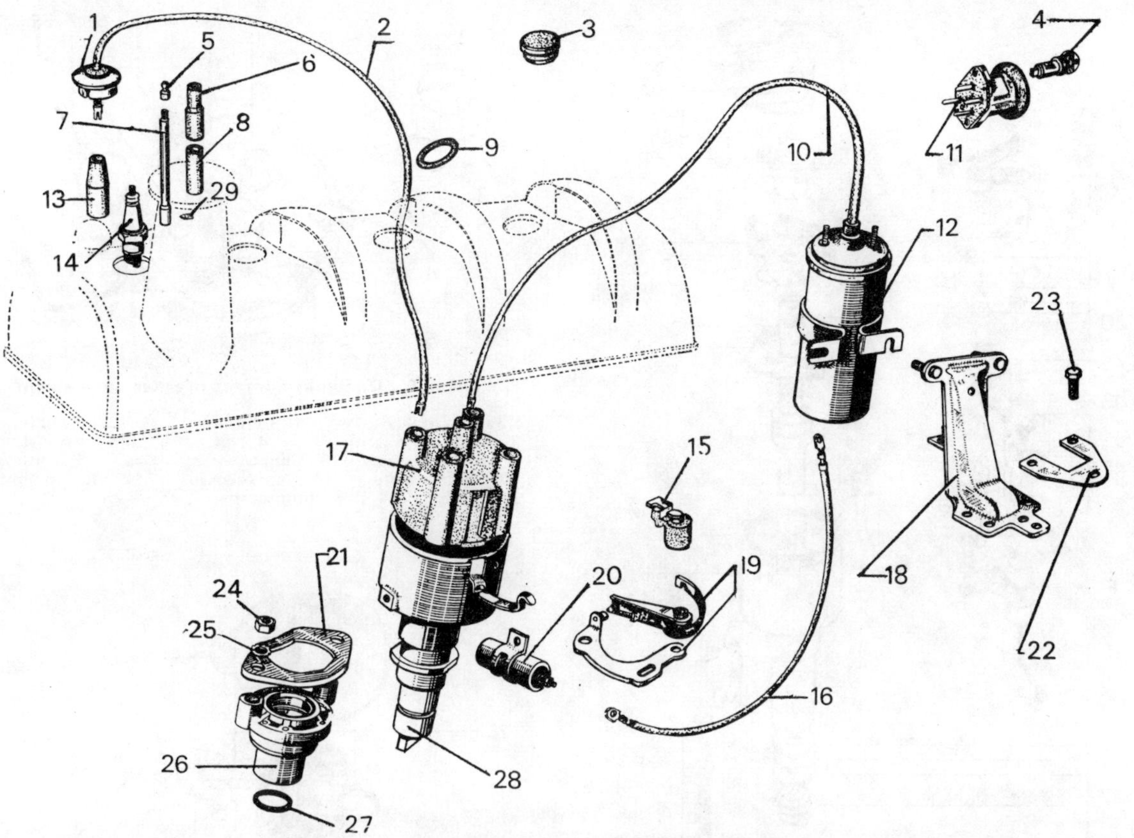

FIG 4:2 Details of ignition system on DY engines

Key to Fig 4:2 1 Cap 2 Plug lead 3 Cap 4 Ignition switch 5 Connector 6 Insulating tube 7 Plug extension 8 Insulating tube 9 Ring 10 Lead 11 Connector 12 Coil 13 Insulator 14 Sparking plug 15 Rotor 16 Lead 17 Distributor cap 18 Bracket 19 Contact breaker 20 Capacitor 21 Contact plate 22 Joint 23 Screw 24 Nut 25 Washer 26 Bearing sleeve 27 Ring 28 Driving collar 29 Screw

3 Withdraw the moving contact 12 and the primary terminal 5 with its insulating pad 2.

4 Withdraw the contact carrying plate 10 holding the cam follower 11 away from the cam.

5 Tap out the pin 17 (see **FIG 4:6**) from the driving head 18. Remove the head, the steel washer 19, the celeron washer 20 and the steel washer 21.

6 Withdraw the drive spindle 26 from the body of the distributor 15 together with the steel washer 19, the celeron washer 20 and the steel washer 21. Remove the circlips 23 unhook the springs 24 and free the advance weights 22.

7 Remove the felt, the screw limiting cam end float and the cam 25.

8 Clean all the parts. Renew the weights if they show abnormal clearance on their pivots. Clean with fine emery the end of the rotor and the inside of the contacts in the distributor head. Renew the contacts if the points are defective.

9 Reassemble by locating the weights in position after lightly oiling their pivots.

10 Engage the cam 25 on the spindle 26. Hook up the springs 24 and fit the circlips 23. Fit the screw limiting cam end float with flat and shakeproof washers. Fit the felt, soaked in oil.

11 Oil and reassemble the spindle and its components and insert the assembly in the distributor body.

12 Provisionally fit the drive sleeve 18 and the pin 17 and check that the spindle turns freely without end float. If not change the number of adjusting washers 21.

13 Engage the drive sleeve on the drive spindle with the offset portion towards the slot into which the rotor engages on the cam. Insert the pin 17 and spread the ends.

14 Fit the plate 10, guiding the cam follower 11. Make sure that the cam follower is correctly positioned in relation to the plate after fitting.

15 Fit the insulating sleeve 2 on the primary terminal 5.

16 Fit the moving contact 12, compressing its spring. Insert the primary terminal thus prepared in the body of the distributor. Fit the insulating washer 3, a steel

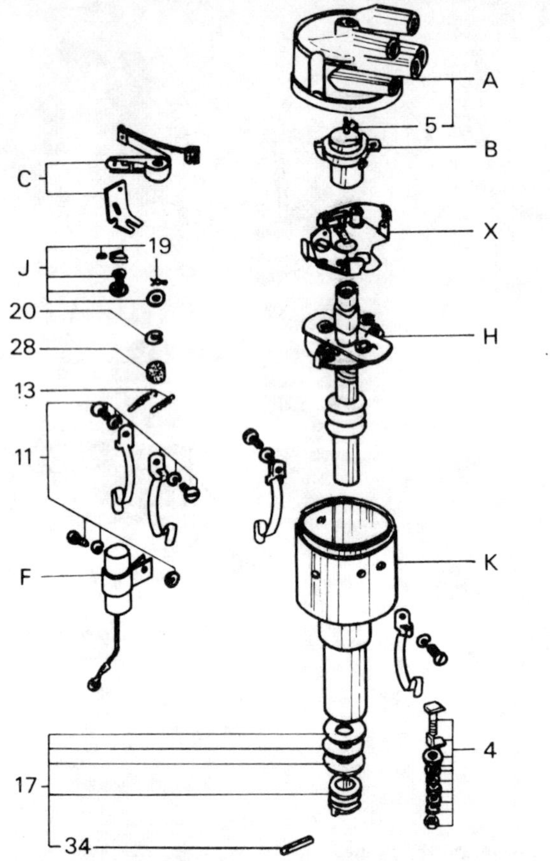

FIG 4:3 An exploded view of a Ducellier distributor (Types 4253A and 4254A)

Key to Fig 4:3 **A** Cover **B** Rotor **C** Contact assembly **X** Breaker assembly **F** Capacitor **H** Shaft assembly **J** Contact breaker mounting assembly **K** Casing 4 Terminal set 5 Carbon brush assembly 11 Retaining clips 13 Advance springs 17 Drive dog assembly 19 Clip 20 Ring 28 Cam felt 34 Pin

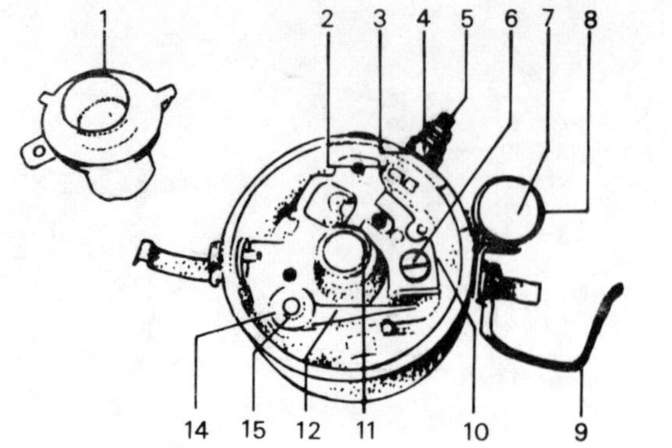

FIG 4:5 Ducellier contact breaker mechanism

Key to Fig 4:5 1 Rotor arm 2 Insulating pad 3 Insulating washer 4 Nut 5 Primary terminal 6 Adjusting screw 7 Capacitor 8 Clip 9 Earth lead 10 Contact plate 11 Cam follower 12 Moving contact 13 Circlip 14 Insulating washer 15 Pivot

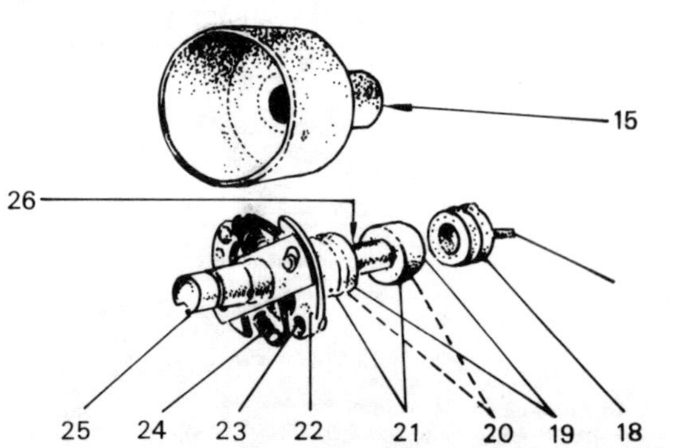

FIG 4:6 Ducellier shaft assembly

Key to Fig 4:6 15 Distributor body 17 Pin 18 Driving dog 19 Washer 20 Celeron washer 21 Washer 22 Advance weights 23 Circlips 24 Springs 25 Cam 26 Shaft

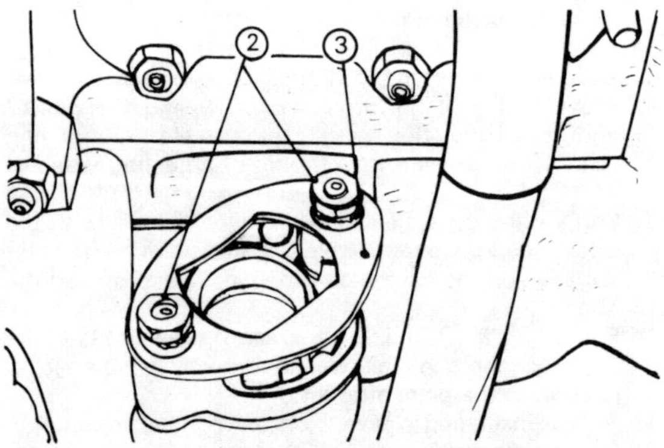

FIG 4:4 SEV distributor on DY engines

Key to Fig 4:4 2 Securing nuts 3 Clamp plate

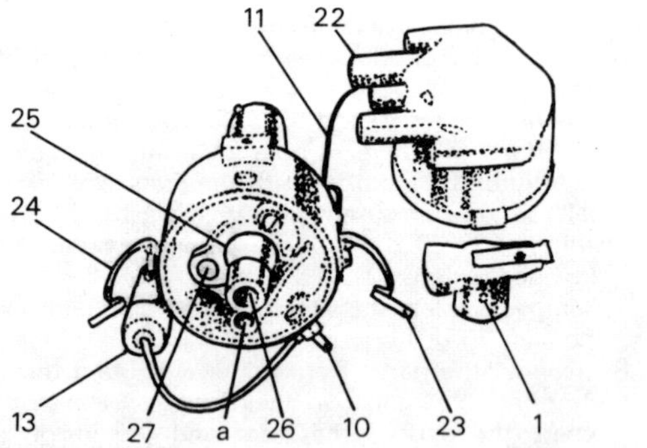

FIG 4:7 SEV contact breaker mechanism

Key to Fig 4:7 1 Rotor arm 10 Primary terminal 11 Earth lead 13 Capacitor 22 Cap 23 Clip 24 Clip 25 Fixed contact 26 Cam felt 27 Adjusting screw washer, and tighten the nut 4. Fit the insulating washer 14 and then the circlip 13.

17 Fit the securing clips, the capacitor and the earth lead 9. Connect up the capacitor and the capacitor lead 7 to the primary terminal 5.

18 Adjust the contact gap to .45±.05 mm by means of the adjusting screw 6. Fit the rotor and then the distributor head with its leads.

Similar operations for an SEV distributor are as follows:

1 Referring to **FIGS 4:7, 4:8** and **4:9,** remove the distributor head 22 and the rotor arm 1. Disconnect the capacitor lead 13, then remove the plain steel washers 5 and the insulating washers 6. Remove the primary terminal 10, the insulating washer 9, the insulating strip 8 and the two insulating washers 7.

2 Withdraw the moving contact 2 and the insulating washer 4.

3 Remove the clips 23 and 24 holding the distributor head with its earth lead 11 and the capacitor 13. Withdraw the plate 3 with the fixed contact 25.

4 Tap out the pin 14 and free the driving head 15 and steel washer 16. Withdraw the driving spindle 17 from the body 12 and remove the steel washer 18.

5 Remove the two springs 20 and the two circlips holding the weights 19. Remove the weights and the cam 21.

6 Clean all the parts as described in the preceding Operation 8. Renew the weights if showing abnormal wear in the bores.

7 To reassemble, fit the cam 21 on the driving spindle 17 lubricating it very lightly. Assemble the weights, lightly lubricating their bearing surfaces, fit the circlips, attach the springs 20 and fit the felt 26 soaked in oil.

8 Further reassembly is undertaken in the reverse order of dismantling, following closely the detailed instructions given for the Ducellier distributor in Operations 11 to 18.

4:5 Distributor drive tower

Instructions for removing and refitting a distributor drive tower on DX engines were given in **Chapter 1.** Operations for the dismantling and reassembly of this unit are as follows, referring to **FIG 4:10**:

1 Press out the spindle 1 from the distributor drive housing, and the cup 2 using a piece of 9 mm diameter steel about 100 mm long, under a press.

2 Remove the oil seals 3 and 4, both of which should be renewed.

3 To reassemble, offer up the oil seal 3 previously oiled in the position shown in the sketch, making it seat at the bottom of its recess.

4 Oil the distributor drive spindle 1 with engine oil and fit it in position. Press the distributor drive socket on the spindle, using a press and a shouldered mandrel MR 3436-210.

5 Press in the pad 2. Leave a clearance 'a' of .15 to .30 mm by inserting a feeler at 'b', between the pinion and the distributor drive spindle bearing, before bringing the cup 2 into contact with the spindle 1.

6 Fit the oil seal 4, previously oiled, in the way shown on the sketch, and ensure that it seats at the bottom of its recess.

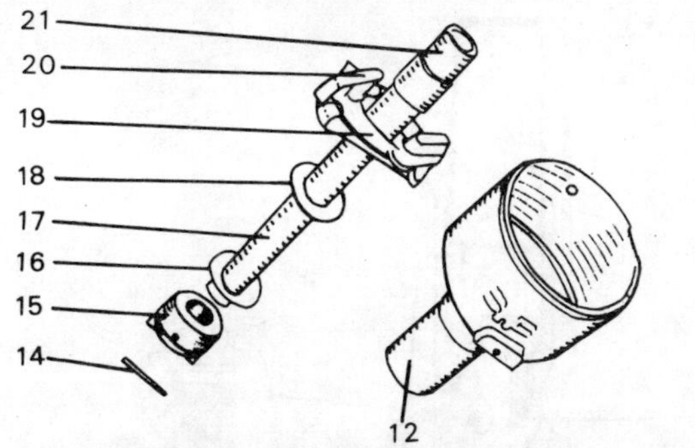

FIG 4:8 SEV shaft assembly

Key to Fig 4:8 12 Distributor body 14 Pin 15 Driving dog 16 Washer 17 Shaft 18 Washer 19 Weights 20 Springs 21 Cam

4:6 Retiming the ignition

To adjust the initial ignition advance setting on DX engines proceed as follows:

1 Remove the distributor head and adjust the gap at the contact breaker points to between .4 and .5 mm if necessary.

2 To find the position of initial advance on the engine, release the pressure in the suspension circuit by moving the manual height control lever to the low position. Make sure that the suspension sphere is free. Remove the front lefthand suspension sphere and screw a plug into the suspension cylinder.

3 Bring No. 1 cylinder to the end of the compression stroke. Insert a 6 mm diameter locating pin P (see **FIG 4:11**) into the hole provided in the clutch bell-housing under the dynamo. Slowly turn the engine until the locating pin falls into the hole in the fly-wheel. In this position the engine is at the firing point of No. 1 cylinder, at 12 deg. before TDC in engines up to 1968. Withdraw the locating pin.

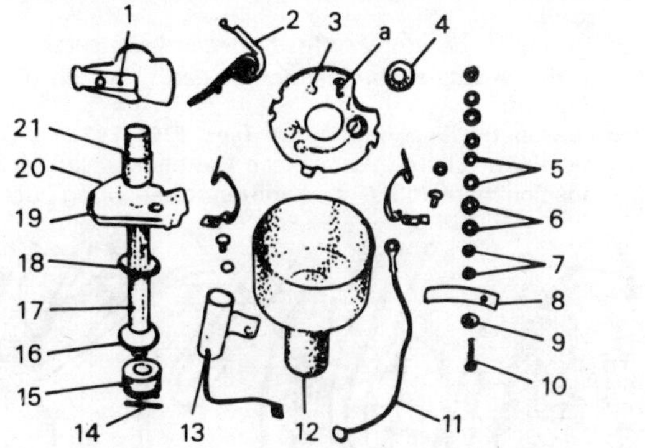

FIG 4:9 An exploded view of the components of an SEV distributor

Key to Fig 4:9 2 Moving contact 3 Breaker plate 4 Insulating washer 5 Plain washers 6 Insulating washers 7 Insulating washers 8 Insulating strip 9 Insulating washer 10 Primary terminal 11 Earth lead 12 Distributor body 13 Capacitor 14 Pin 15 Driving dog 16 Washer 17 Spindle 18 Adjusting washers 19 Weights 20 Springs 21 Cam

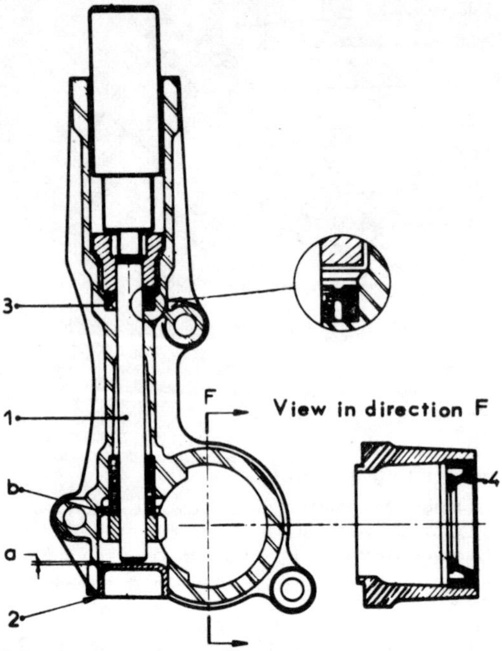

FIG 4:10 A sectional view of the distributor drive tower

Key to Fig 4:10 1 Spindle 2 Cup 3 Oil seal 4 Oil seal a .15 to .30 mm b Point of measurement of a

From July 1971 a modified flywheel is fitted. The hole provided for the setting of the ignition point now corresponds to TDC.

An engraved scale is attached to the body of the water pump on which each division corresponds to 2 deg. on the crankshaft or 1 deg. on the distributor.

The crankshaft pulley carries a yellow mark which, when the locating pin inserted through the aperture in the bellhousing is in the hole in the flywheel, should be opposite the 0 mark on the graduated scale.

4 To adjust the ignition, fit the leads from a test lamp to the capacitor terminal and to earth. Switch on the ignition.

5 Loosen the securing nut 1 (see **FIG 4:12**) of the distributor clamp plate. Place the clamp plate at the position marked SUP and tighten the securing nut.

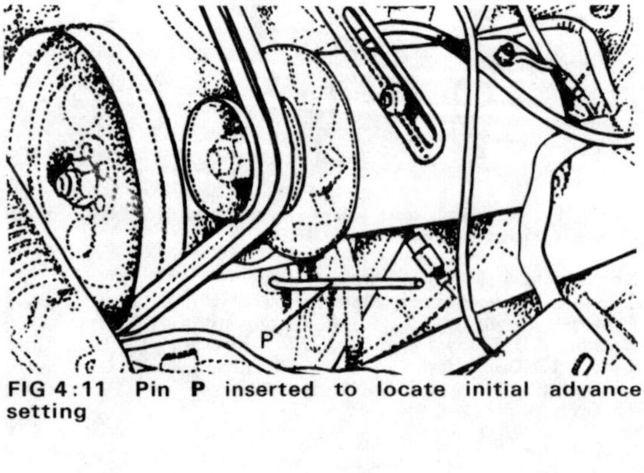

FIG 4:11 Pin **P** inserted to locate initial advance setting

6 Slacken the nut of the fixing screw at the split end of the clamp plate behind the distributor. Slowly turn the body of the distributor in an anti-clockwise direction. Stop the moment the lamp lights, which is the point at which the contacts just open.

7 Tighten the screw 1 behind the distributor and switch off the ignition.

Ignition advance is set on DY engines by undertaking the preceding operations 1 to 4 and then proceeding as follows:

1 Loosen the two securing nuts 1 (see **FIG 4:4**) of the distributor clamp plate 2. Then slowly turn the body of the distributor in an anticlockwise direction until the lamp lights, as in Operation 6.

2 Tighten the two securing nuts, switch off and recheck the points gap.

If the ignition remains unsatisfactory, checks may be made by a service agent on a test bench of the secondary winding insulation, the spark grouping, the closing angles of the breaker, the automatic ignition advance curve relative to the distributor under test and the primary circuit insulation. The capacitance of the condenser or capacitor must be between .21 and .23 microfarad, but the best test is by substitution.

4:7 Sparking plugs

The sparking plugs type are shown in **Technical Data**. The plugs should be removed every 3000 miles or 5000 km or so to check the gaps, also the insulators for cracks and the electrodes for excessive burning. Remove as far as possible all deposits of carbon and oil from the insulation and electrodes, using only a hard wood spatula and nothing metallic for this job. The sparking plug gaps should be set to a gap of .6 mm (.024 inch) by bending only the side electrode. Use new gaskets when refitting the plugs and remember to refit the cap on the scuttle hole.

Plugs can be cleaned and tested under working pressure on a blasting machine used by most service agents. A deposit of brown to greyish tan colour is the normal condition of a plug used for a mixed period of high and low speed driving. Wet black deposits indicate oil fouling and dry fluffy black deposits are caused by too rich a mixture or misfiring. Badly eroded electrodes will be a sign of overheating. Excessive idling or low speeds may keep temperatures so low that normal deposits are not burned off.

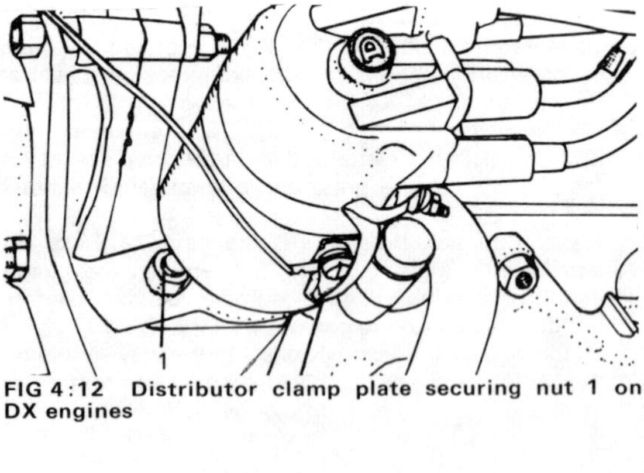

FIG 4:12 Distributor clamp plate securing nut 1 on DX engines

4:8 Fault diagnosis

(a) Engine will not fire

1 Battery discharged
2 Contact breaker points dirty, pitted or out of adjustment
3 Distributor cap dirty, cracked or 'tracking'
4 Carbon brush inside distributor cap not in contact with rotor
5 Faulty cable or loose connection in low-tension circuit
6 Distributor rotor arm cracked
7 Faulty coil
8 Broken contact breaker spring
9 Contact points stuck open

(b) Engine misfires

1 Check 2, 3, 5 and 7 in (a)
2 Weak contact spring
3 High-tension plug and coil leads cracked or perished
4 Sparking plug loose
5 Sparking plug insulation cracked
6 Sparking plug gap incorrect
7 Ignition timing too far advanced

NOTES

CHAPTER 5

THE COOLING SYSTEM

5:1 Principle of system

The engine is watercooled by water circulating through the radiator and through water passages in the cylinder block. The cooling system is thermostatically controlled and works under slight pressure, maintained by the spring-loading of the radiator cap, which enables a higher temperature to prevail before the water boils. Circulation of the water is by thermosyphon action assisted by a centrifugal water pump bolted to the front face of the cylinder block. A belt drive from a pulley on the end of the camshaft serves the generator and water pump, on the end of which is an eight-bladed nylon fan running in a ducted cowl behind the radiator.

5:2 Maintenance, flushing, antifreeze, belt tension

Service attention is directed mainly to ensure that the radiator is kept clear of sediment and that the coolant level is topped up as necessary. When checking the water level, **do not remove the radiator cap immediately after stopping the engine when it is hot,** when the radiator will be slightly under pressure. Start by turning the cap a quarter of a turn so as to bring the cap onto its safety catch and wait while the pressure falls before removing it completely. If the engine is very hot it is advisable to wait until it has cooled down. Radiator hoses and clamps should be periodically inspected for signs of leakage and the radiator cleaned externally to remove dirt, leaves or insects. The fan belt tension should be checked every 3000 miles or 5000 km. Renewal of the belts is advised every 30,000 miles or 50,000 km.

The system should occasionally be flushed out. To drain the system the car should be standing on level ground, the radiator cap removed and the drain taps in the radiator and cylinder block opened. Retain the coolant with its antifreeze content. Insert a hose from a fresh-water tap into the filler neck and allow water to flush through the system with the drain taps open, continuing the operation until the water comes out clear.

In extreme cases the radiator may be removed for reverse flushing under pressure through the bottom hose connection. To remove the radiator after draining the system, first remove the spare wheel and then disengage the air duct from the radiator by removing the two righthand screws and slackening the two lefthand ones. Disconnect the upper hose from the radiator and the lower hose from the steel pipe. Disengage the tie-rod, remove the screws, the metal cups and the rubber blocks fixing the radiator to the front crossmember and withdraw the radiator. When the cleaning operations are completed, refit the radiator in the reverse manner of its

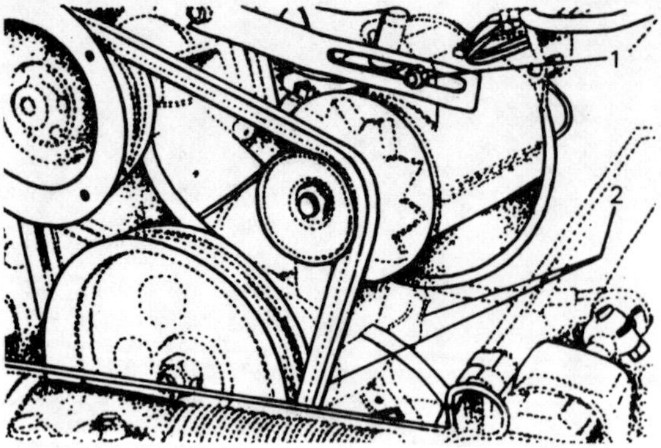

FIG 5:1 Water pump and generator driving belts

Key to Fig 5:1 1 Nut securing generator tie-rod 2 Generator securing screws on clutch housing

removal, making sure that it is centred so that the fan blades do not touch the cowl. The hoses should be renewed if they show any signs of cracking or interior fouling.

When refilling the system close the two drain taps and add the coolant slowly to avoid the possibility of air locks. Check that the main heater control under the facia is on its fully open stop. Start the engine and give a few bursts on the accelerator to ensure that all ducts are full. When returning an antifreeze solution formerly in the cooling system, the available amount may not be sufficient to fill the system. Do not add plain water, otherwise the solution will be weakened and the freezing point raised. Add additional antifreeze liquid as required. A test may be made with a hydrometer, a 20 per cent solution at 15.6°C (60°F) normally having a specific gravity of 1.032 and a 25 per cent solution a specific gravity of 1.040.

The capacity of the cooling system and heater is 11.3 litre (20 pints) of liquid including antifreeze solution, which it is advised should be retained during all seasons whatever its concentration. Cars leaving production normally contain sufficient antifreeze in the cooling system to protect the radiator and cylinder block down to a temperature of —5°C or —15°C, shown on a label on the air duct behind the radiator. To increase protection from the —5°C level down to —15°C, the proportion is 3 litre (5.25 pints) of concentrated antifreeze with 10 litre (18.5 pints) of water. This is obtained by draining 2.2 litre (4 pints) of the original coolant and adding the same quantity of Antifreeze. The makers recommend that renewal of coolant should be carried out by an official service agent who is kept up-to-date with procedures and products to be used. Glycerine and ethylene glycol are solutions which are satisfactory for antifreeze purposes, but these inorganic compounds do not contain an anti-rust inhibitor. The makers advise the use of TOTAL antifreeze solution, which contains a suitable inhibitor to reduce rust formation and corrosion in the cooling system to a minimum.

Renewal of the belts (see **FIG 5:1**) is undertaken by unscrewing the nut 1 of the generator tie-rod, loosening

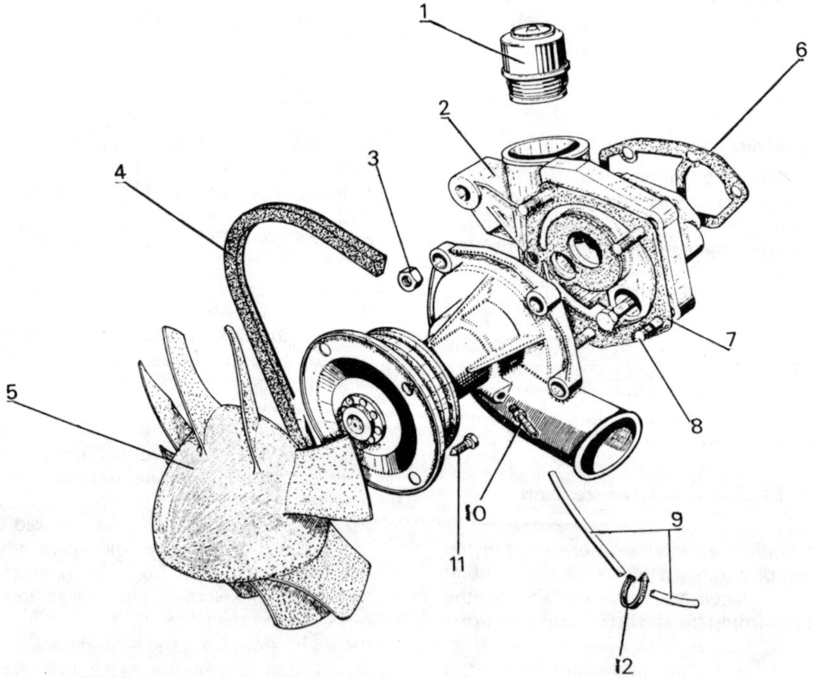

FIG 5:2 An exploded view of the water pump, fan and thermostat

Key to Fig 5:2 1 Thermostat 2 Water pump cover 3 Nut 4 Belt 5 Fan 6 Cover joint 7 Cover joint 8 Securing stud 9 Overflow pipe 10 Union 11 Screw securing fan 12 Clip the screws 2 holding the generator on the clutch housing and then moving the generator as far as possible towards the engine. Disengage the first belt by passing it between the blades of the fan. Bend one fan blade slightly, but take special care in cold weather when the fan is more fragile. Disengage the second belt by first passing it into the front groove of the pulley. New belts are provided in sets of two, because the belts are paired with identical dimensions and it is therefore necessary to renew both belts even if one is in good condition. Fitting is undertaken as in removal, except in reverse order of operations.

Adjustment of a belt to its correct tension is important, as a loose fan belt will cause it to slip on the pulleys, resulting in engine overheating and the failure of the generator to charge the battery. If the belt is too tight, excessive wear may occur on the generator and water pump bearings and the belt itself may be damaged. Adjustment is made by moving the generator on its mountings. Generally the belt tension should be such as to allow it to be depressed $\frac{1}{2}$ inch midway between the water pump and generator pulleys. More precise tensioning can be obtained by using the service lever MR.4208 to press on the boss between the two securing clips of the generator and the generator body. Using a spring balance, exert an effort of 5 kg on the end of the lever, which corresponds to a tension of 28 kg on the belt. Maintain this tension and tighten the fasteners securing the generator and tie-rod.

5:3 Water pump removal and refitting

A part-exploded view of the water pump is shown in **FIG 5:2.** Operations for removing and refitting a water pump commence by draining the cooling system and then proceeding as follows:

1 Remove the fan, but without removing it from inside the fan cowl.
2 Disconnect the tie-rods of the generator and high pressure pump from the water pump and disconnect the distributor earth lead.
3 Loosen the screws securing the generator and the high pressure pump on the clutch bellhousing, and the nuts securing the tie-rods. Free the belts as previously described.
4 Disconnect the lower hose from the water pump. Remove the securing screws for the water pump on the cover and cylinder head, when the water pump and its gasket may be withdrawn.
5 To remove the water pump cover, remove the engine sling bracket and disconnect the battery earth lead. Remove also the radiator tie-rod, and the clip securing the distributor feed lead.
6 Disconnect the hose from the carburetter hot spot, the upper radiator hose and the feed lead from the thermometer transmitter 4 (see **FIG 5:3**).
7 Remove the centrifugal regulator where fitted. Then remove the nuts 3 and 5 securing the pump backplate on the cylinder head and withdraw the cover and its gasket.
8 When reassembling, smear with hermetic compound the gasket between the pump backplate and the cylinder head (see **FIG 5:4**).
9 Fit the gasket positioned as illustrated. Note that in later cars the top corner adjacent to 'a' has been squared off and it is necessary that this portion should appear at the top and to the left of the pump cover when viewed from the front. Any other position of the joint will entail a risk of leakage.
10 Refit the pump backplate and continue further operations in the reverse order of dismantling.
11 If the pump backplate has been renewed the pulley alignment should be checked. This is done as shown in **FIG 5:5.** Place the tool 3082.T in one of the grooves of the water pump pulley, when the rod must centralize in the corresponding groove of the generator

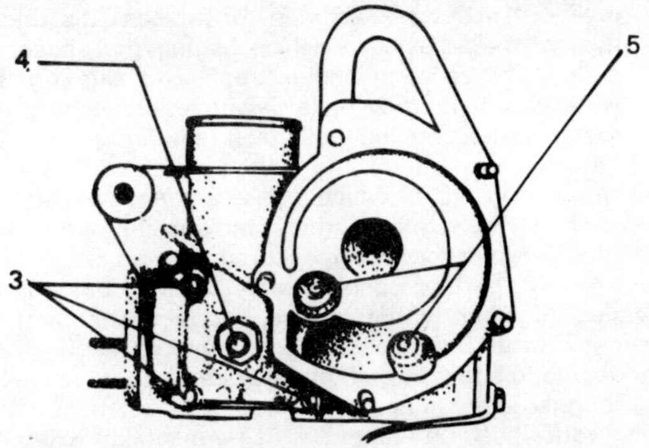

FIG 5:3 Water pump with cover removed

Key to Fig 5:3 3, 5 Nuts securing backplate on cylinder head 4 Thermometer transmitter

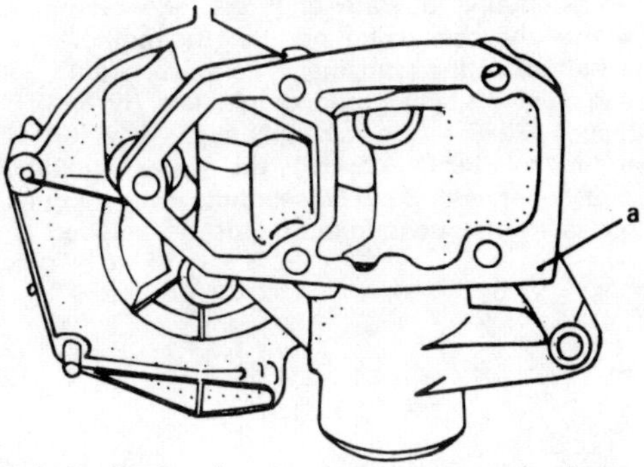

FIG 5:4 Gasket between water pump backplate and cylinder head

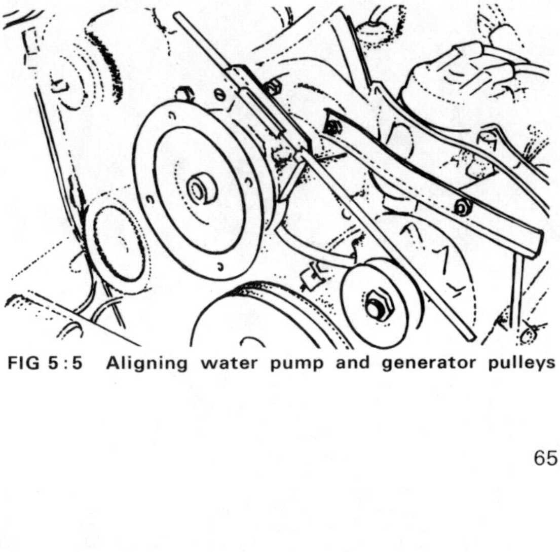

FIG 5:5 Aligning water pump and generator pulleys

pulley. If necessary, decrease or increase the thickness of the adjusting washers behind the generator pulley. The same procedure applies to aligning the water pump and drive pulleys, with adjustments made to the washers behind the latter if required.

For the overhaul of the unit a press and special mandrels are used, for which a service agent's assistance will normally be required. After removing the pulley, the spindle and impeller are removed by tapping out with a bronze drift. Further operations are to drive out a ball-bearing together with the pump body bush made of porous bronze. Before assembling, immerse this bushing in engine oil for several minutes until the bronze is thoroughly impregnated. Under no circumstances must this bronze bush be rebored as its permeability will then deteriorate. Make sure that the bearing face of the packing gland on the pump is neither pitted nor scored. Located on the pump shaft is a seal, which should be renewed and moistened with castor oil. The remaining reassembly operations are carried out in the reverse order of dismantling.

5:4 Thermostat removal and testing

To remove the thermostat open the radiator drain tap and partially drain off the water to a level below the bottom of the thermostat housing. Keep the water with an antifreeze content in a clean receptacle. Loosen the retaining clip and free the flexible hose containing the thermostat from the water pump cover. Remove the thermostat after detaching its securing clip.

In order to test a thermostat, suspend it and a thermometer in a container of water and heat the water. Ensure that neither the thermostat nor the thermometer rests on the bottom of the container. The valve should commence to open at a temperature of between 75° and 78°C (167° and 172°F). Also when shaken in water at a temperature of 90°C (194°F) the valve should be completely open with 20 to 50 seconds. If the thermostat does not satisfy these conditions it must be renewed.

Finally relocate the thermostat in the flexible hose, with the flanged edge of the thermostat body in contact with the shoulder in the hose, and tighten the securing clip. Refit the hose and fill up the cooling system, maintaining an antifreeze solution if employed at its required level of concentration.

5:5 Fault diagnosis

(a) Internal water leakage

1 Cracked cylinder wall
2 Loose cylinder head nuts
3 Faulty head gasket (see **Chapter 1**)

(b) Poor circulation

1 Radiator core blocked
2 Engine water passages restricted
3 Low water level
4 Loose fan belt(s)
5 Defective thermostat
6 Perished or collapsed radiator hoses

(c) Corrosion

1 Impurities in the water
2 Infrequent draining and flushing

(d) Overheating

1 Check (b)
2 Sludge in crankcase
3 Faulty ignition timing (see **Chapter 4**)
4 Low oil level in sump
5 Tight engine
6 Choked exhaust system
7 Binding brakes (see **Chapter 10**)
8 Slipping clutch (see **Chapter 6**)
9 Incorrect valve timing (see **Chapter 1**)
10 Retarded ignition (see **Chapter 4**)
11 Mixture too weak (see **Chapter 3**)

CHAPTER 6

THE CLUTCH

6:1 Construction and operation

The clutches fitted to all engines are of the single dry plate type bolted to the flywheel and enclosed in a housing attached to the cylinder block and crankcase. As shown in **FIGS 6:1** and **6:2,** the clutch assembly consists of two main units, a pressure plate assembly and the clutch disc. The disc plate has riveted friction facings and incorporates coil-type cushioning springs.

In cars with semi-automatic gearchange the operation of the clutch is performed hydraulically along with gearchanging and there is no clutch pedal. In other cars, depression of the clutch pedal operates a mechanical linkage and cable (see **FIG 6:3**) by which the clutch withdrawal fork shown in **FIG 6:1** moves the release collar and its ballbearing towards the flywheel to apply pressure on the three release levers or toggles. The reverse action of the levers turning on their pivots disengages the clutch, by withdrawing the pressure plate from contact with the clutch disc against the pressure of the springs.

6:2 Adjustments of mechanical linkage

Correct adjustments of pedal travel where employed and the clearance of the fork control rod from the clutch housing are essential to be maintained in order to ensure the required clearance between the clutch release levers and the release bearing. Referring to **FIG 6:3,** the height of the pedal as shown at 'a' should be 137 to 142 mm in lefthand drive cars or 162 to 167 mm in righthand drive cars, from the underside of the pedal pad with the cover removed to the floor panel. Note, however, that due to design changes in early 1967, this dimension is modified in later lefthand drive cars without pedal rubbers to 141 to 143 mm and on the Pallas versions with pedal rubbers to 136 to 138 mm. To alter the height of the pedal, unscrew the locknut, turn the stop screw 13 as required and then retighten the locknut.

The clearance between the end of the connecting rod 2 (or 5 in **FIG 6:4**) and the clutch housing must be 3.5 to 4.5 mm in lefthand drive cars as shown by 'j', or 2.5 to 3.5 mm in righthand drive cars between the pushrod and the bracket on the bellhousing. In later lefthand drive cars the specified clearance is reduced to 2.5 to 3.5 mm. On 1972 cars this dimension is 3-4 mm. To obtain these dimensions move the threaded sleeve 9 by adjusting the nuts 8.

To adjust the clutch clearance, measure exactly the clearance 'j'. Now obtain an assistant to depress the clutch pedal by hand until it is felt that the thrust comes into contact with the toggles. Measure the new clearance. The difference between the two dimensions should be between 1.6 to 2.4 mm. If otherwise, adjust the screw 6 in **FIG 6:4**.

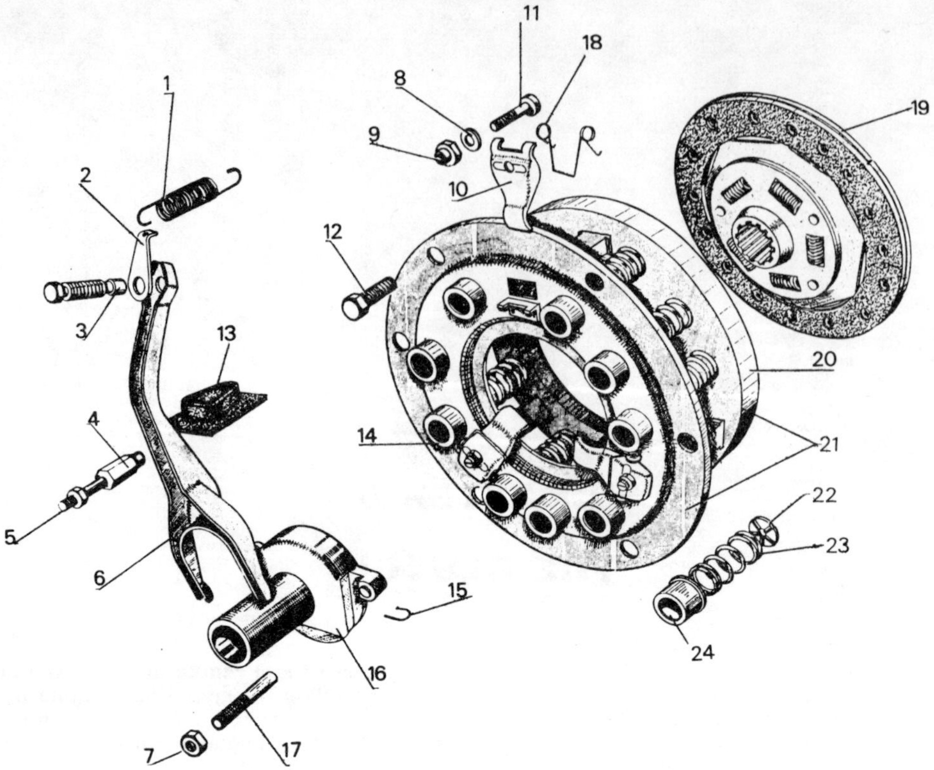

FIG 6:1 An exploded view of the clutch

Key to Fig 6:1 1 Spring 2 Lever 3 Bush 4 Adjusting sleeve 5 Spindle and nut 6 Withdrawal fork 7 Nut 8 Washer 9 Nut 10 Clutch toggle 11 Bolt 12 Bolt 13 Dust cover 14 Spring cup 15 Spring pin 16 Release collar 17 Guide pin 18 Toggle return spring 19 Clutch disc 20 Pressure plate 21 Carrier plate 22 Spring seat 23 Spring 24 Spring cup

6:3 Adjustments of hydraulic components

The elements of the clutch hydraulic system in semi-automatic gearchange cars on which adjustment checks may be necessary to ensure the continued effective operation of the system include the idling or slow-running, clutch clearance, clutch drag and also the clutch engagement control. For the adjustment of slow-running and accelerated idling reference should be made to **Chapter 3.** Adjustment of the clutch clearance is made as follows:

1 The engine must be hot, as any adjustment carried out with the engine cold may be incorrect with the engine hot.

2 Run the engine at idling speed and put the starting handle extension in position.

3 Unscrew the adjusting screw 1 (see **FIG 6:5**) of the clutch fork by a fraction of a turn at a time, until the starting handle extension just begins to turn but may be stopped by hand.

4 Adjust by tightening the screw 1 two turns.

5 Release the pressure in the clutch system by operating the auxiliary clutch control and check that the clutch fork is free. If it is not free, carry out the adjustment operation for clutch clearance again, which is probably excessive.

The operations for the adjustment of the clutch drag and of the clutch re-engagement control have been described in **Chapter 3, Section 3:6.**

6:4 Clutch removal and refitting

Before the clutch can be removed a considerable amount of work is required to remove the gearbox, necessitating taking the engine out of the car as described in **Section 1:10, Chapter 1.** Removal operations among other matters include the removal of the radiator, the steering assembly, the generator, the front wheels and the flexible couplings, as well as various hydraulic details in cars with semi-automatic gearchange. The clutch is then withdrawn by disconnecting it from the engine flywheel as described in **Chapter 1** with details of inspection requirements for the flywheel.

The clutch disc or driven plate should be examined for excessive wear and signs of overheating. Check that the friction linings are secure and free from oil. A polished glaze on the linings is normal, but they should be light in colour with the grain clearly visible. A much darker colour obliterating the grain is a sign of oil on the linings, which can cause clutch slip or possibly difficulty in disengagement. If this condition is found or if the linings are worn down near to the rivet heads, it is advised that the complete disc assembly should be renewed in preference to riveting new linings on the existing assembly. It should be ensured that the damper springs are firmly attached and serviceable, also that the hub splines are not excessively worn. Further dismantling of the pressure plate assembly is not advised, as a special fixture and equipment are necessary for reassembly and it follows that the work is more suitably to be undertaken by a service agent. At the same time, if the driving plate is worn it can under certain circumstances be ground on a lathe. Dimensions are critical, however, because rectification of the surface causes loss of pressure on the clutch disc and if badly worn the plate must be renewed. Refitting the clutch to the flywheel is described in **Chapter 1**.

In pedal-operated clutches, details of the clutch control linkage are shown in **FIG 6:3.** Removal and refitting operations are as follows:

1 Unscrew the nut 1 and disengage the rod 2 from the clutch fork 3 and the lever 4.
2 Remove the screw securing the lever 4 to the clutch housing. Disconnect the lever 4 from the front socket of the cable 5. Remove the lever 4 and the shouldered spindle 6.
3 Disconnect the cable 5 and its sheath from the sheath retaining boss on the clutch housing. Disconnect the rear socket of the cable 5 from the pedal shaft lever 7.
4 Unscrew the nut 8 and remove the threaded sleeve 9 from the support 10. Remove the control cable assembly.
5 When refitting, connect the rear socket of the cable 5 to the pedal shaft lever 7.
6 Place the threaded sleeve 9 in position on the support 10 and screw up the nut 8 without tightening it.
7 Place the cable 5 and sheath in position on the retaining boss on the clutch housing.
8 Connect the lever 4 to the front socket of cable 5 and place the lever 4 and the shouldered spindle 6 in position after first greasing them lightly. Tighten the fixing nut.
9 Connect the rod 2 to the lever 4 and to the clutch fork 3. Screw on the nuts 1 and 11 without tightening them. Adjust the clutch control as described in **Section 6:2.**

6:5 Clutch fork and thrust race removal and refitting

Referring to **FIGS 6:5** and **6:6,** operations to remove and refit the clutch fork and thrust race are as follows:

1 With the gearbox disconnected from the engine as previously described, remove the return spring 3 from the clutch fork 4 and the adjusting screw 1 from the fork.
2 Remove the anchor clip 2 and the rubber dust cover 5 from the fork aperture. Then remove the clutch thrust roll retaining springs 8.
3 Withdraw the thrust race and its sleeve 7, the pin 6 and the fork 4.
4 To reassemble, slide the thrust race and sleeve 7 over its guide-peg 9. Refit the remaining items in the reverse order of their dismantling.

6:6 Clutch cylinder removal, overhaul and refitting

To commence operations, release the pressure by means of the auxiliary clutch control lever under the dash, and disconnect the pressure feedpipe from the clutch cylinder. Proceed as follows:

1 Remove the two screws securing the clutch cylinder, using a 12 mm socket with 125 mm extension and ratchet spanner.
2 Unscrew fully the screw 2 (see **FIG 6:7**) which adjusts the clutch clearance. Wedge the clutch fork, using a bar 1 levering on the pulley.
3 Withdraw the cylinder and clutch fork control rod assembly.
4 Remove the dust cover and control rod assembly from the cylinder.
5 Remove the pin and the nut 3 (see **FIG 6:8**) from the cylinder.

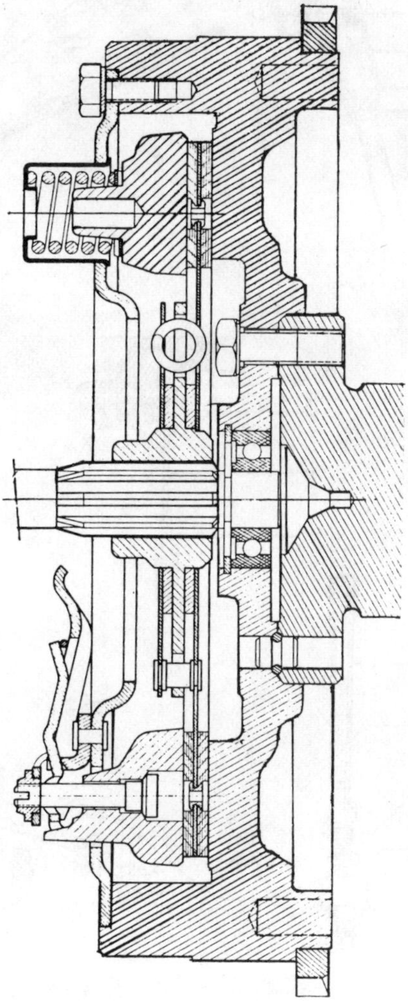

FIG 6:2 A sectional view of the clutch

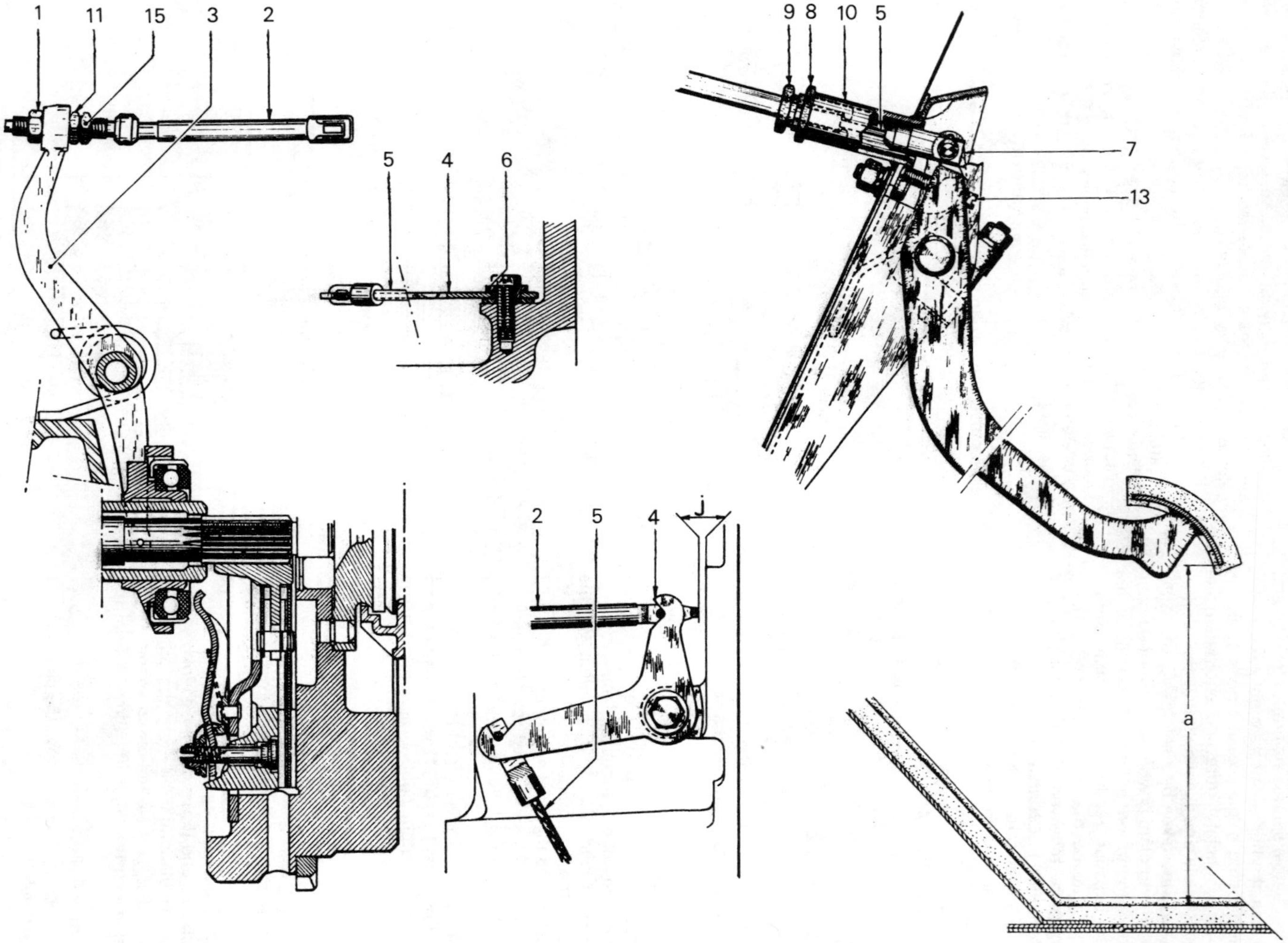

FIG 6:3 Clutch withdrawal linkage for pedal operation

Key to Fig 6:3 1 Adjusting nut 2 Fork control rod 3 Clutch release arm and fork 4 Bell crank 5 Cable 6 Shouldered spindle 7 Pedal shaft lever 8 Adjusting nuts 9 Threaded sleeve 10 Support 11 Adjusting nut 13 Pedal stop screw 15 Locknut **a** Pedal height **j** Fork control rod clearance

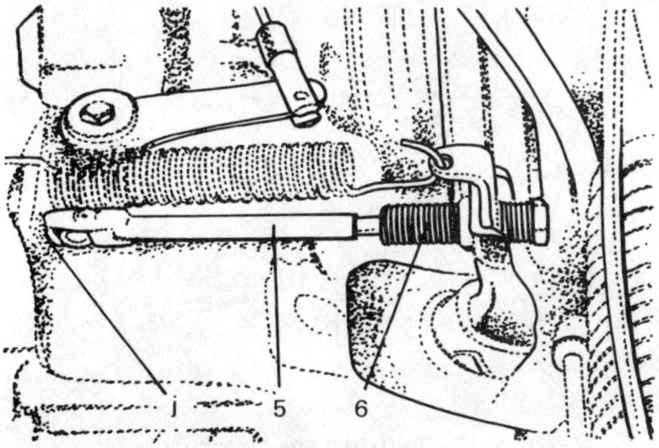

FIG 6:4 Adjustment of clutch clearance for pedal operation

Key to Fig 6:4 5 Connecting rod 6 Adjusting screw j Clearance (see text)

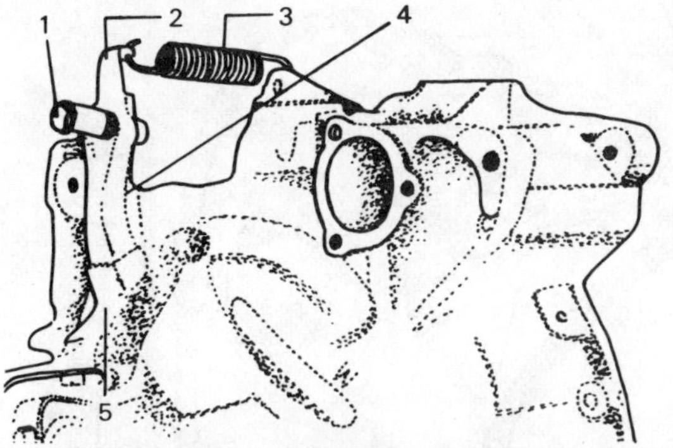

FIG 6:5 Removing the clutch fork

Key to Fig 6:5 1 Adjusting screw 2 Anchor clip 3 Return spring 4 Clutch fork 5 Rubber dust cover

6 Force the piston from the cylinder using compressed air. Alternatively fluid under pressure may be used in conjunction with a test rig 2290.T.
7 Remove the ring seal using a small brass wire hook.
8 Clean all parts thoroughly with alcohol and blow out with compressed air.
9 To reassemble, insert the mandrel MR.3045.60 (see A in **FIG 6:9**) in the cylinder.
10 Moisten the ring seal 5 (see **FIG 6:8**) with special hydraulic fluid. Offer up the ring seal in the bore of the cylinder and obtain its correct position in its groove by pushing it with the piston.
11 Withdraw the piston and the mandrel, using a screw 6 mm diameter x 100.
12 Lubricate the cylinder bore and the piston with special hydraulic fluid. Insert the piston 4 in the cylinder, then screw in the nut 3 until its face 'a' is either flush with or .5 mm maximum under the cylinder face 'b'. Fit a new splitpin and then the dust cover control rod assembly on the cylinder.
13 If required the cylinder may be checked for leaks by a service agent equipped with the test bench mentioned in **Chapter 1.**

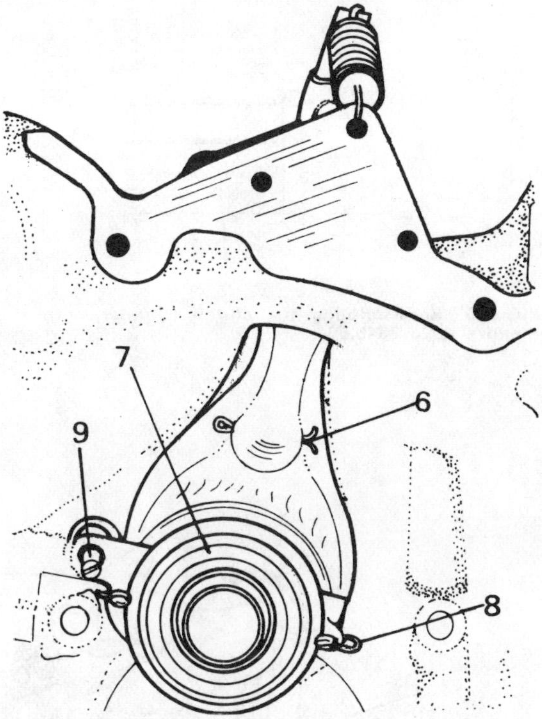

FIG 6:6 Clutch thrust race and sleeve assembly

Key to Fig 6:6 6 Pin retaining springs 7 Sleeve 8 Thrust race 9 Sleeve guide

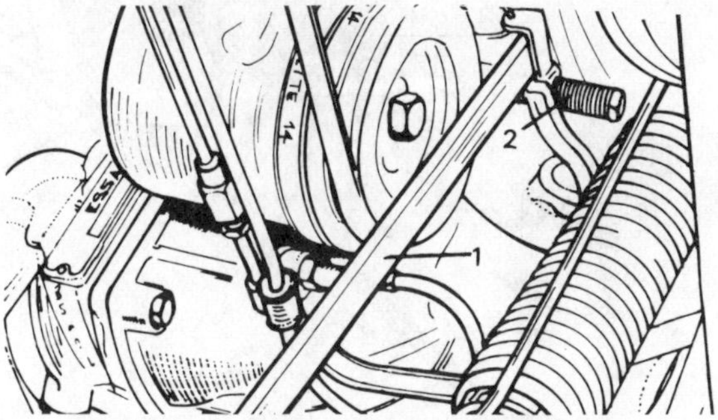

FIG 6:7 Removing the clutch cylinder

Key to Fig 6:7 1 Lever 2 Clutch clearance adjusting screw

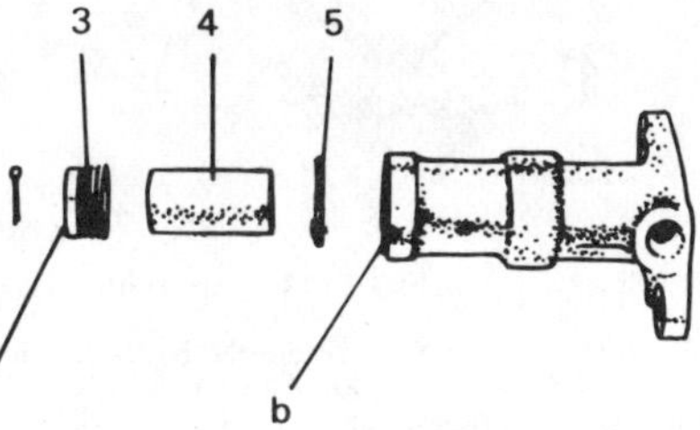

FIG 6:8 An exploded view of the clutch cylinder

Key to Fig 6:8 3 Nut 4 Piston 5 Ring seal **a** Face nut **b** Face of cylinder

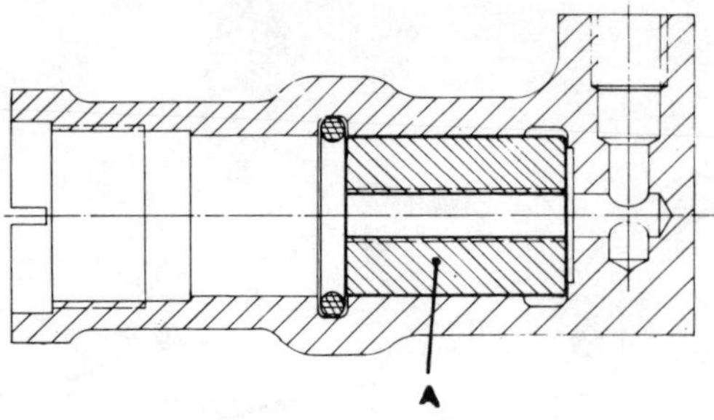

FIG 6:9 Reassembling the clutch cylinder with the mandrel A No. 3045.60

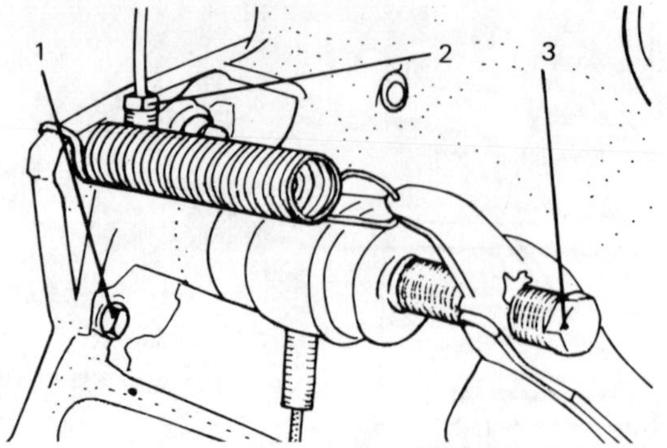

FIG 6:10 Refitting the clutch cylinder

Key to Fig 6:10 1 Retaining screws 2 Pressure feed pipe 3 Adjusting screw

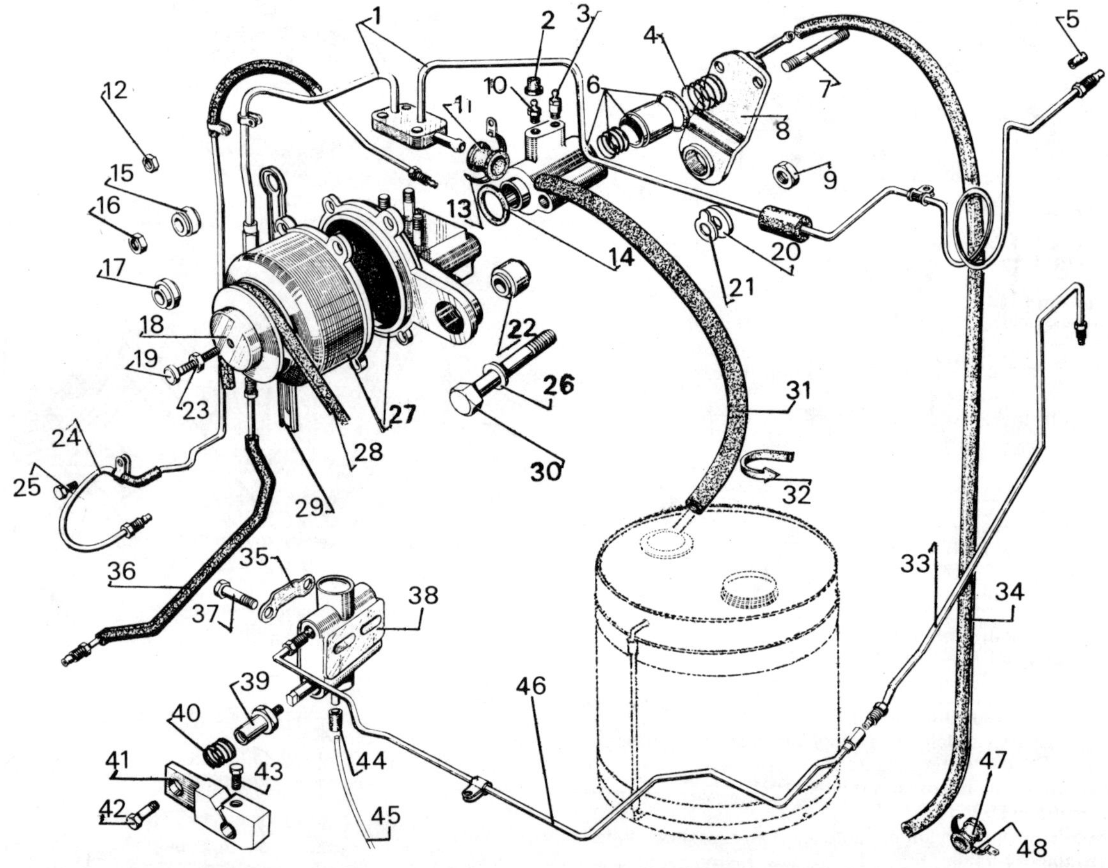

FIG 6:11 An exploded view of the centrifugal regulator and clutch lock

Key to Fig 6:11 1 Pipe assembly, hydraulic gear selector, clutch lock and centrifugal regulator 2 Cap 3 Bleed screw 4 Spring 5 Adaptor 6 Control unit 7 Stud 8 Bracket 9 Nut 10 Bleed screw 11 Grommet 12 Nut 13 Clip 14 O-ring 15 Distance piece 16 Nut 17 Distance piece 18 Drive pulley 19 Adjusting screw 20 Washer 21 Tabwasher 22 Distance piece 23 Locknut 24 Pipe to front brake unit 25 Screw 26 Washer 27 Centrifugal regulator 28 Drive belt 29 Tie rod 30 Fulcrum pin 31 Return hose 32 Clip 33 Pipe, clutch lock to hydraulic gear selector 34 Return hose 35 Bracket 36 Flexible hose 37 Bolt 38 Clutch lock 39 End piece 40 Spring 41 Operating plate 42 Bolt 43 Clamp screw 44 Rubber connection 45 Spill pipe 46 Pipe, clutch lock to hydraulic gear selector 47 Grommet 48 Clip

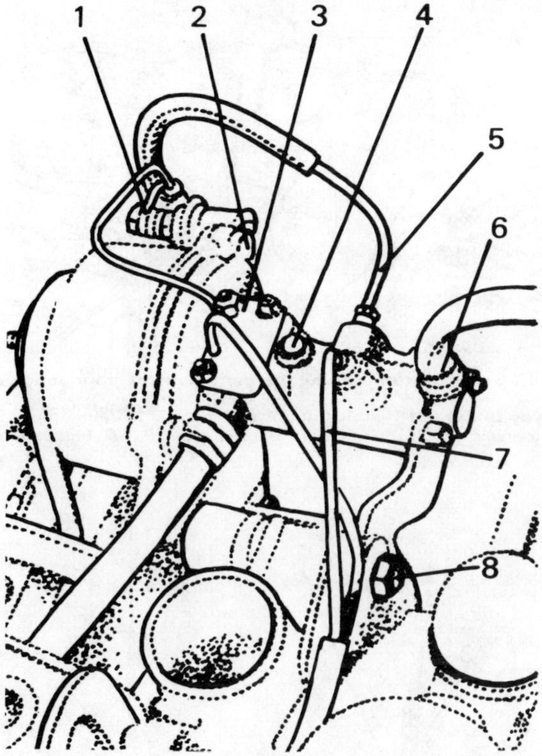

FIG 6:12 Centrifugal regulator connections

Key to Fig 6:12 1 Pipe clips 2 Tie-rod screw 3 Pipe assembly flange 4 Bleed screw 5 Pipe to righthand brake unit 6 Return pipe to reservoir 7 Pipe to accelerated idling device 8 Spindle nut

14 To refit the cylinder, place the clutch fork pushrod in position with the shouldered part towards the adjusting screw, and the dust cover on the cylinder, with the nylon overflow tube pointing downwards and to the right.

15 Offer up the cylinder. Referring to **FIG 6:10,** tighten the screws 1 and place the control rod in the bore of the adjusting screw 3. Locate the dust cover on the adjusting screw 3.

16 Couple up the pressure feedpipe 2, which must be free and not strained. Place the nylon overflow tube against the clutch housing.

17 Put the circuit under pressure following the procedure described in **Chapter 1.** Adjust the clutch clearance as in **Section 6:2.**

6:7 Centrifugal regulator removal and refitting

Details of the centrifugal regulator and the clutch lock are shown in **FIG 6:11.** The regulator operates according to engine speed to control the clutch engagement or disengagement when the car either starts to move or stops with a gear still engaged. Operations to remove and refit the regulator are as follows:

1 Referring to **FIG 6:12,** slacken the bleed screw on the pressure regulator and the bleed screw 4 on the centrifugal regulator.

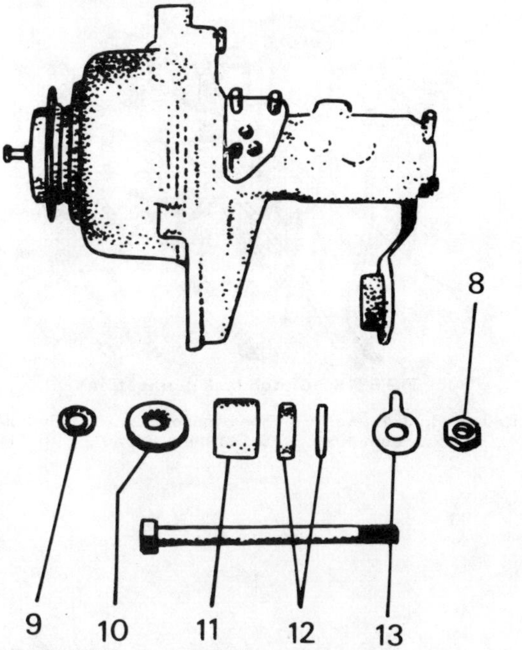

FIG 6:13 Centrifugal regulator components

Key to Fig 6:13 8 Spindle nut 9 Washer 10 Shouldered washer 11 Distance piece 12 Alignment adjusting washers 13 End float washer

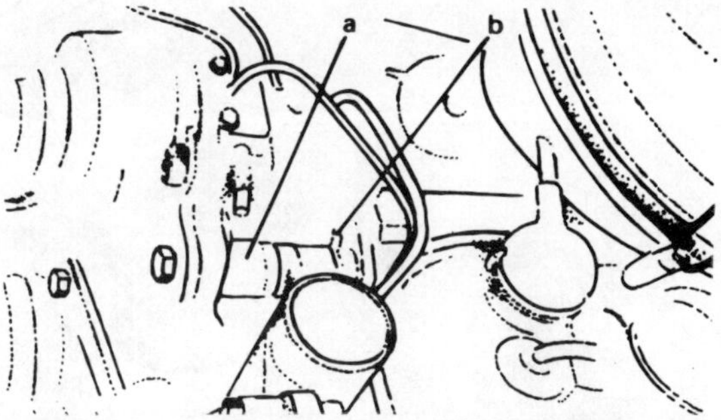

FIG 6:14 Packing pieces at a and b for alignment of the centrifugal regulator pulley

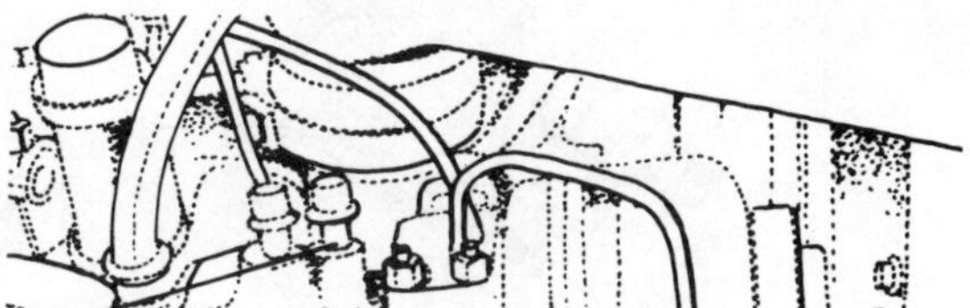

FIG 6:15 Centrifugal regulator bleed screw (1)

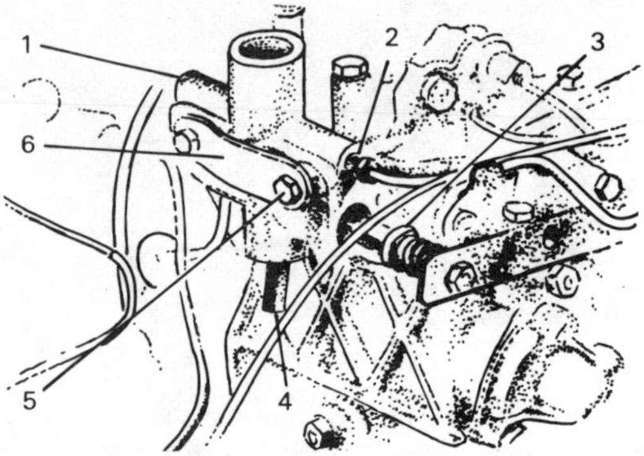

FIG 6:16 Clutch lock connections

Key to Fig 6:16 1, 2 Pipe connections 3 End piece 4 Overflow return pipe 5 Retaining screws 6 Plates

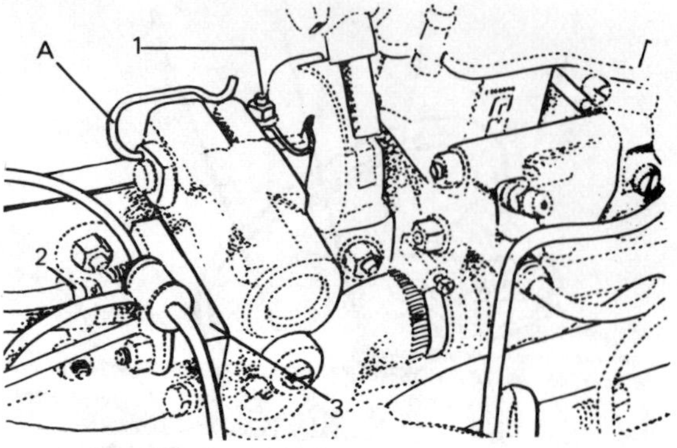

FIG 6:18 Clutch re-engagement control connections

Key to Fig 6:18 1 Control lever nut 2 Return pipe to reservoir 3 Union flange and seal plate **A** Setting pin

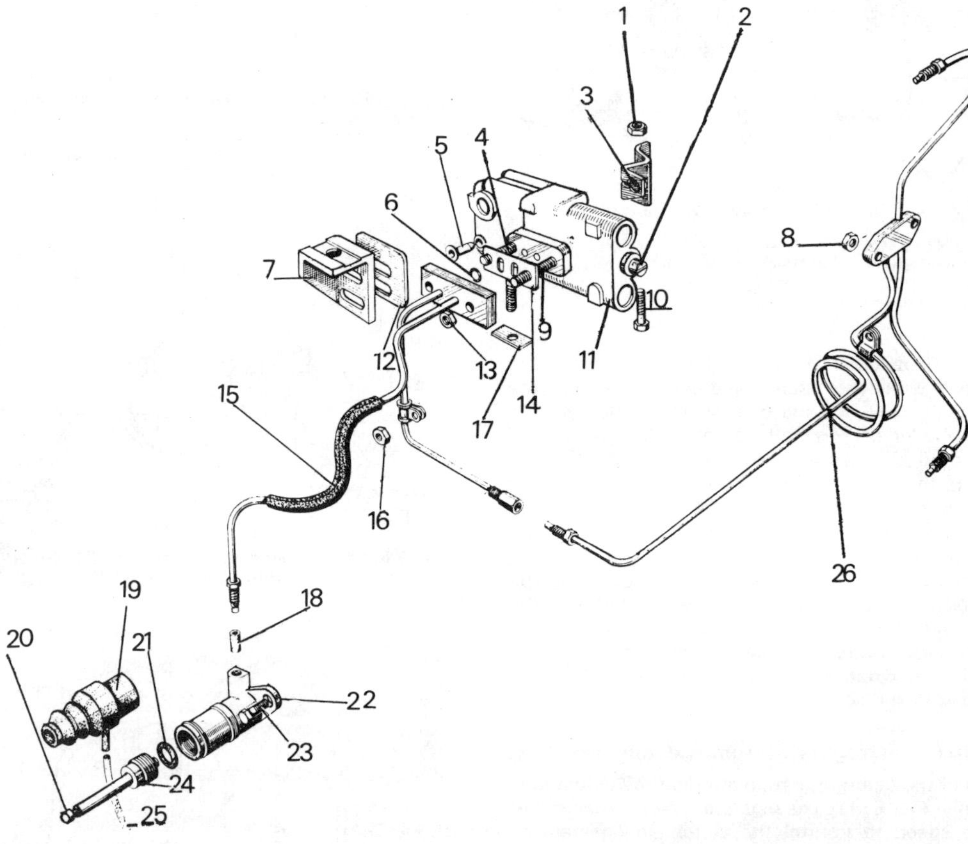

FIG 6:17 An exploded view of the clutch re-engagement control

Key to Fig 6:17 1 Nut 2 Clutch re-engagement adjustment 3 Clip 4 Stud 5 Plug 6 O-ring 7 Bracket 8 Nut 9 Stud 10 Bolt 11 Casing 12 Gasket 13 Nut 14 Gasket 15 Union flange and pipe assembly 16 Nut 17 Plate 18 Adaptor 19 Boot 20 Pushrod 21 O-ring 22 Clutch cylinder 23 Bolt 24 Seal 25 Drain pipe 26 Pipe assembly

2 Disconnect from the regulator the pipe 5 leading to the righthand brake unit and the pipe 7 between the regulator and the accelerated idling device. Also disconnect the return pipe 6 to the reservoir and the pipe assembly flange 3.
3 Remove the two pipe retaining clips 1, the screw 2 securing the tie-rod on the regulator and the mounting spindle 8 of the regulator on the water pump backplate.
4 Remove the belt and then remove the regulator. Do not lose the packing pieces for adjusting the alignment of the regulator.
5 To refit the regulator, assemble the parts on the spindle in the order of the flat washer 9 (see **FIG 6:13**), the front lug of the regulator, the shouldered washer 10, the distance piece 11 and the alignment adjusting washers 12.
6 Offer up this assembly on the water pump backplate, engage the spindle, then fit the washer 13 for adjusting the end float and tighten the nut 8 (see **FIG 6:12**) moderately.
7 At this stage the pulley alignment must be checked. Place the tool 3082.T (see **Chapter 5, Section 5:3**) in the groove of the regulator pulley, when the rod must centralize in the first groove of the high pressure pump pulley. To obtain correct alignment adjust the thickness of the packing pieces at 'a' in **FIG 6:14**, then modify the packing pieces at 'b' so that before tightening there is a maximum clearance of 1 mm between the support clip and the housing. This clearance will be taken up on tightening the securing nut.
8 Connect the union flange of the pipe assembly 3 to the centrifugal regulator, inserting the sealing plate with new ring seals.
9 Referring to **FIG 6:12**, assemble the pipe 5, the pipe 7 and the pipe 6 for return to reservoir.
10 Fit the screw 2 securing the tie-rod and the two pipe-clips 1. Then fit and tension the belt as described in **Chapter 5, Section 5:2.**
11 Put the circuits under pressure and check all the unions for leaks. Bleed the centrifugal regulator (see **Section 6:8**) and adjust the clutch drag as described in **Chapter 3.**

6:8 Bleeding the centrifugal regulator

Bleeding the centrifugal regulator is undertaken by fitting a flexible pipe (preferably transparent) on the forward bleed screw 1 (see **FIG 6:15**) of the regulator and inserting the other end of the pipe into the filler hole of the hydraulic reservoir. Make sure that the bleed screw on the pressure regulator, and both bleed screws on the centrifugal regulator, are tight.

Start the engine and run it at between 1500 and 2000 rev/min by unscrewing the accelerated idling adjusting screw on the carburetter. Slacken the centrifugal regulator bleed screw 1 and very slowly adjust the accelerated idling adjusting screw to bring the engine speed down to 500 to 600 rev/min.

Let the engine idle for about two minutes, then tighten the bleed screw. Remove the flexible pipe and refit the rubber cap on the bleed screw. Then adjust the accelerated idling as described in **Chapter 3.**

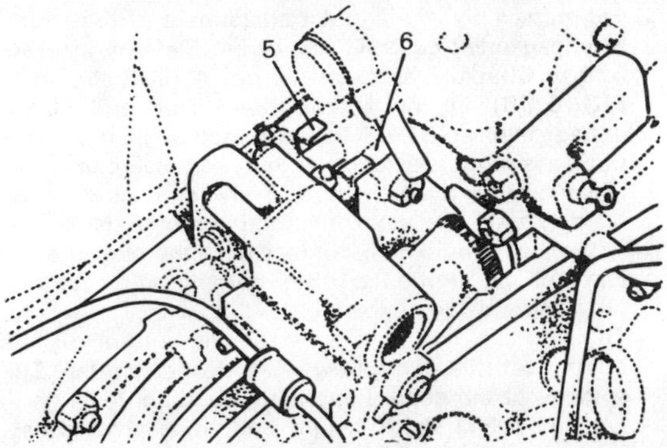

FIG 6:19 Aligning the clutch re-engagement control, showing the re-engagement control lever 5 and the lugs 6

6:9 Clutch lock removal and refitting

The clutch lock is a safety device to prevent the clutch re-engaging during changes to and from first and second gears if either of the gears is not fully engaged. To remove the unit, referring to **FIGS 6:11** and **6:16**, remove the spare wheel and the spare wheel support crossmember with the radiator air intake duct. Release the pressure and proceed as follows:

1 Disconnect the pipes 1 and 2 from the lock and the overflow return pipe 4.
2 Remove the end piece 3 securing the clutch lock spindle to its operating plate, holding the spindle still with an 8 mm spanner. Withdraw the lock after removing the screws 5 securing it on the gearbox.
3 To reassemble, place the lock in position and fit the screws 5 through the plates 6 without tightening.
4 Connect the lock control spindle to its operating plate. The lock spindle has three grooves, with a spring-loaded ball engaging in one or other of the grooves. Move the lock in its slots so that the ball engages in the central groove, then tighten the screws 5.
5 Connect up the pipes 1 and 2 and the overflow return pipe 4. Put the circuit under pressure, check all unions for leaks and check that the gearchange operates correctly. Refit the remaining items removed for access.

6:10 Clutch re-engagement control removal and refitting

Details of the clutch re-engagement control are shown in **FIG 6:17.** To remove the control, first release the pressure and remove the front lefthand sphere. Further operations are as follows:

1 Referring to **FIG 6:18**, disconnect the union flange 3, and remove the sealing plate. Then remove the return pipe 2 to the reservoir and the nut 1 from the control lever. Withdraw the lever towards the re-engagement control and the petrol feedpipe from the carburetter.
2 Remove the fixing nut under the inlet manifold, using a spanner 3107.T and withdraw the clutch re-engagement control. Do not lose the packing washer(s) between the control and the manifold, if fitted.

3 For reassembly, the angular adjustment of the clutch re-engagement control must be set. Referring to **FIG 3:8** in **Chapter 3,** insert the pin A (also shown in **FIG 6:18**) in the setting hole. Turn the clutch engagement spindle 4 in the direction of the arrow until a spring resistance is felt and overcome this resistance to reach a stop. Turn back now about 30 deg. until the pin enters and bottoms. Note that when the spindle is in contact with the stop the pin can still be introduced but correct adjustment is not achieved.

4 To align the clutch re-engagement control, fit the control with its control lever but do not tighten. The spindles of the control and the carburetter must be in line, for which both height and transverse adjustments are necessary.

5 To make the height adjustment, turn the carburetter spindle to bring the control lever legs 6 (see **FIG 6:19**) together in the horizontal plane. Do the same with the re-engagement control, turning the lever on the spindle. Introduce packing washers between the control and the inlet manifold so that the lugs on the levers are in the same plane.

6 For the transverse adjustment, turn the carburetter spindle and the clutch re-engagement control lever 5 so that the lugs are vertical. Move the re-engagement unit towards or away from the engine in the slot in the manifold so that the lever lugs are in one plane. Finally fit and tighten the fixing nut.

7 Refer to **Chapter 3, Section 3:7,** Operations 4 and 5 for the correct fitting and adjustment of the flector on the carburetter control lever and refit the items removed for access.

8 Start the engine and check for leaks. Check also the adjustment of the clutch re-engagement control as described in **Chapter 3.**

6:11 Fault diagnosis

(a) Clutch drag or spin

1 Excessive play at clutch fork
2 Oil or grease on linings
3 Flywheel face not running true
4 Misalignment between engine and gearbox
5 Clutch disc hub binding on splines
6 Clutch disc distorted
7 Pressure plate distorted
8 Disc linings broken
9 Foreign matter in clutch

(b) Fierceness or snatch

1 Check 2, 3, 4, 6 in (a)
2 Worn clutch linings

(c) Clutch slip

1 Check 2 and 3 in (a)
2 Check 2 in (b)
3 Weak pressure springs
4 Insufficient clearance at clutch fork

(d) Judder

1 Check 2, 3 and 6 in (a)
2 Pressure plate not parallel with flywheel face
3 Contact area of friction linings not evenly distributed

(e) Rattles and knocks

1 Broken damper springs in clutch disc
2 Badly worn splines in disc hub
3 Worn release bearing
4 Loose flywheel

CHAPTER 7

THE TRANSMISSION AND DRIVE SHAFTS

7:1 General description

One of the main features of the front wheel drive system is that the engine, gearbox, differential and final drive gearing are assembled as a complete unit. Power generated by the engine is transmitted to the gearbox through the flywheel and clutch at the front end of the crankshaft. From the clutch the drive is taken up by the upper of the two parallel shafts in the gearbox shown in **FIG 7:1** which carry the gearwheels providing changes of engine speed and power according to driving requirements. There is also an intermediate reverse gear layshaft which is brought into operation to reverse the drive when necessary. A final drive pinion is located on the rearward end of the lower shaft, continuing the drive through the crownwheel and differential assembly to the differential and drive shafts and the front wheels.

The gearbox has four forward ratios and one reverse, with synchromesh engagement of the forward gears. With semi-automatic operation a light touch on the gearlever behind the steering wheel gives selection of gears by hydraulic servos directing fluid under pressure into any one of five hydraulic cylinders in the gearbox cover. The lever engages first or reverse if pushed away from the driver, reverse being to the right of the first gear position after forcing the lever through a stop. The lever is pulled back to engage second, third and top gears in the plane closest to the driver. The positions are marked on the dashboard and notching rollers with a light but perceptible action enable the driver to feel the various gear positions. Engagement is effected by three selector forks and shafts in the gearbox for first and second gears, third and fourth gears and also the reverse gear. The principles governing the operation of hydraulic gear selection are described in **Chapter 2.** It should be noted that when the car is at rest a gear should never be engaged when the engine is running on the choke, as the relatively high engine speed will then cause sudden engagement of the clutch

For manual gearchange the gearbox arrangements are similar to those shown in **FIG 7:1** except for a selector mechanism which replaces the hydraulic cylinders in the cover. This mechanism is operated by a cable control from the gearlever behind the steering wheel after depression of the clutch pedal. First and second gears are engaged when the lever is positioned closest to the driver, third and fourth gears are engaged in an intermediate plane and reverse gear in the plane furthest from the driver.

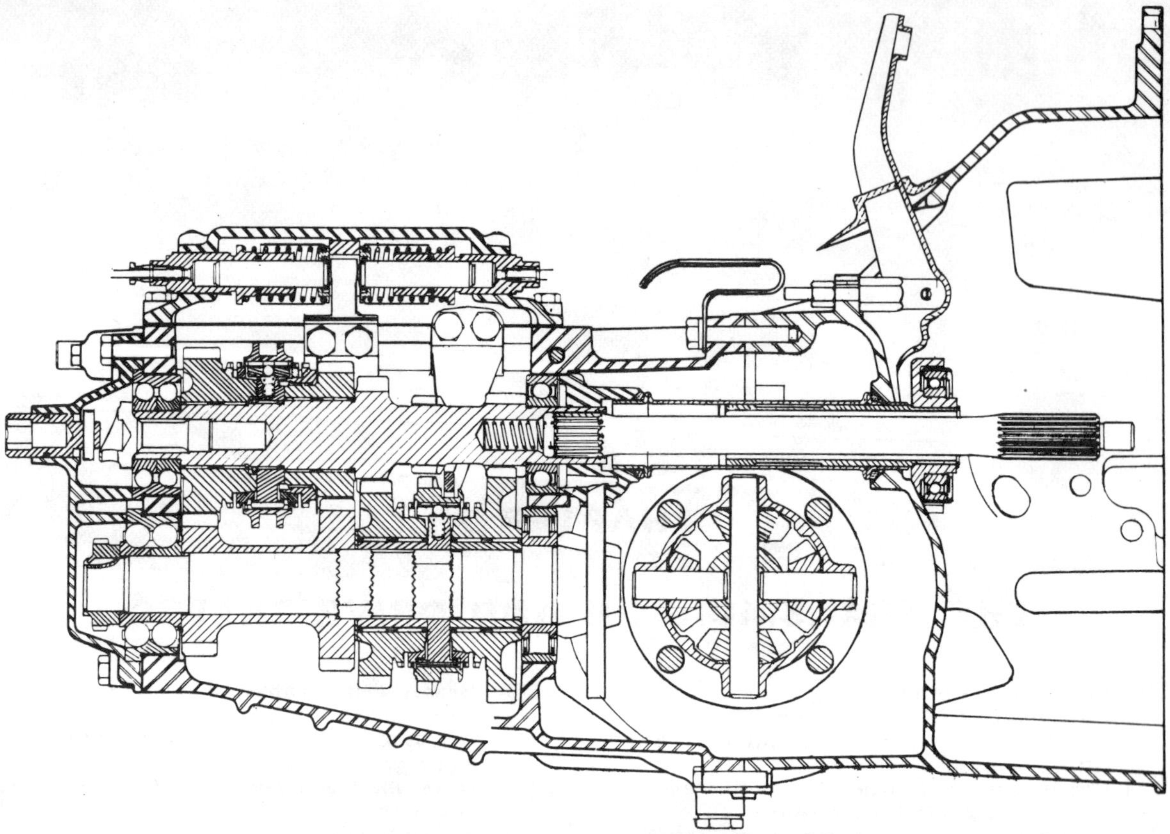

FIG 7:1 A sectional view of the gearbox fitted with cover for hydraulic gear selection

In both types of car the differential gear transmits the drive from each side of the transmission casing through universal joints to the constant velocity joints at the front road wheels. The constant velocity joints are specially designed to transmit uniform rotary movement over the wide angle of movement of the front wheels and are sometimes considered analagous to three-dimensional ballbearings.

7:2 Gearbox removal and refitting

Considerable work is entailed in removing the gearbox as it is necessary first to remove the complete engine and gearbox assembly from the car, for which the operations were described in **Chapter 1.** The gearbox may then be disconnected from the engine by removing the clutch housing fixing screws. After such servicing operations as may need attention the gearbox is refitted to the engine and the whole assembly re-installed in the car, again as described in **Chapter 1.** In cars with semi-automatic gear selection, however, if difficulty is experienced in operating the gears it should be ensured before removing the gearbox or the hydraulic gear selector that the pressure distribution is correct for each gear by first raising the front of the car with the engine running at accelerated idling. Then with the aid of an assistant engage first gear and observe the movement of the clutch fork, which should move slowly towards the rear (engaged position). Proceed similarly for the remaining four gears. If the fork remains in the de-clutched position, checks must be made on the operating pressures, the hydraulic gear selector and the gear control cylinders with the aid of the test bench shown in **FIG 1:3** in **Chapter 1,** for which the assistance of a service agent should be obtained. Also check the adjustment of the slow-running, as in **Chapter 3,** as well as the clutch clearance, the clutch drag and the clutch re-engagement control, all as described in **Chapter 6.**

The internal components of the gearbox are shown in **FIG 7:2.** Servicing operations on the mechanism are necessarily limited by the facilities available for precise reassembly after dismantling and which are only ordinarily to be found in a well-equipped service workshop. Dismantling operations present no serious difficulties but reassembly needs observance of very precise limits for clearances and fits in both differential gear (see **FIG 7:3**) and final drive. The precise adjustment of the final drive bevel pinion, for example, is of very great importance because an incorrect setting of the gear teeth will result in noisy operation and reducing the life of the gear. The setting dimension is specified between the centre line of the differential shaft and the ground end of

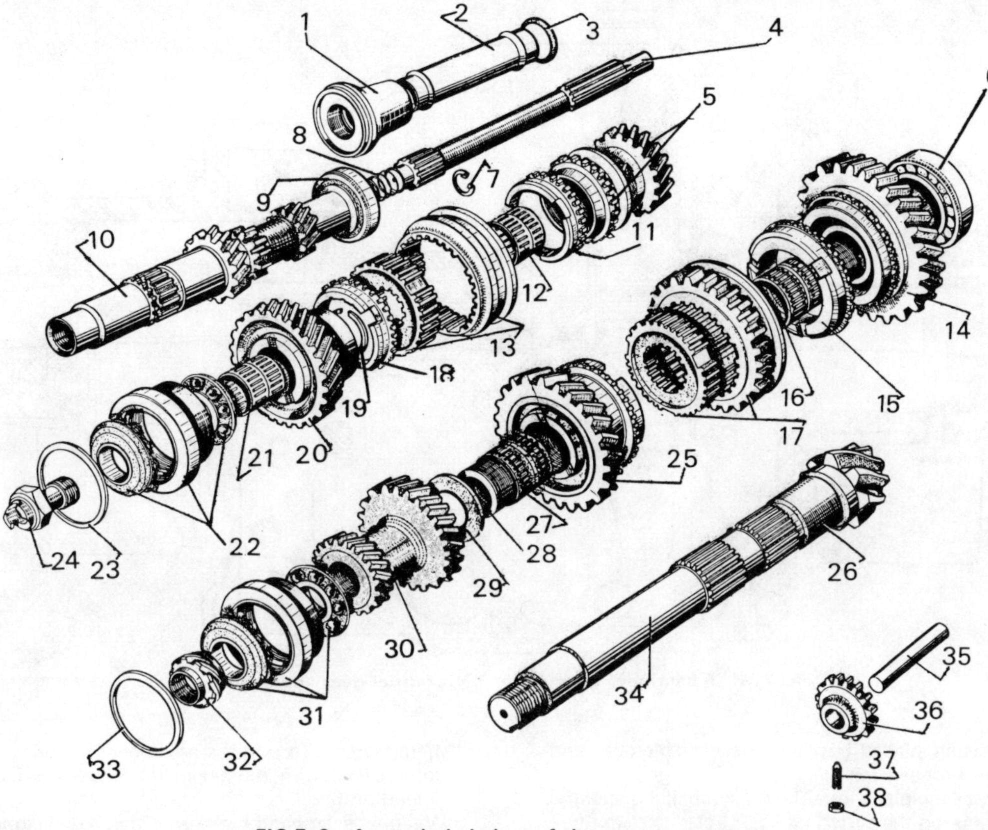

FIG 7:2 An exploded view of the gear components

Key to Fig 7:2 1 Clutch shaft sealing tube support 2 Sealing tube 3 Seal 4 Clutch shaft 5 3rd speed gear and synchromesh ring 6 Bearing 7 Circlip 8 Spring 9 Bearing 10 Main shaft 11 Synchromesh ring, 3rd speed gear 12 Needle roller bearing 13 3rd/4th speed selector ring 14 1st speed gear 15 Synchromesh ring 16 Needle roller bearing 17 1st/2nd selector ring and reverse gear 18 Synchromesh ring, 4th speed 19 Circlip 20 4th speed gear 21 Needle roller bearing 22 Double ballbearing 23 Shim 24 Starting dog 25 2nd speed gear 26 Distance piece 27 Needle roller bearing 28 Distance piece 29 Shim 30 3rd/4th speed gear train 31 Double ballbearing 32 Drive shaft nut and tachometer gear 33 Shim 34 Drive pinion and shaft 35 Reverse idler pinion shaft 36 Reverse idler 37 Grub screw 38 Locknut

the pinion and varies with each crownwheel and pinion. Its significance is shown by its being engraved by the makers in millimetres and hundredths of millimetres on each pinion. In addition there have been a number of changes of design of gearwheels made from time to time, which have to be taken into account if renewal of gears becomes necessary. All of this requires special tools and workshop equipment as well as practical experience and it follows that the complete stripping and reassembly of a gearbox should be undertaken only by a qualified service agent. Alternatively a replacement unit on an exchange basis is advised, as an overhaul usually requires the renewal of all the parts.

Operations which can be undertaken without serious difficulty and which are described later in this Chapter include the dismantling and reassembly of gearbox covers and selector assemblies, also the various hydraulic units where fitted contributing to the general gearbox and clutch system. Where special tools are mentioned it is useful to note that individual items may be obtained under hiring arrangements provided by the manufacturers.

7:3 Gearbox cover removal, dismantling and refitting (hydraulic gearchange)

If the engine-gearbox assembly has not been removed from the car, preliminary operations to remove the gearbox cover, referring to **FIG 7:4,** are to remove the spare wheel, the headlamp beam level control 3, the crossmember assembly 2 for the spare wheel support, the air cowl 1, the battery with its tray and the radiator. Disconnect the electrical cable assemblies and free the cables 4 for the bonnet lock control. Removal of the wings is not essential but makes the work easier. Release the pressure in the circuits and unscrew the bleed screw of the pressure regulator about 1 turn. Move the manual height control to the low position. Connect a flexible pipe on the screw A (see **FIG 7:5**) to bleed the accelerated idling device, placing the other end of the pipe in the reservoir of the liquid. Press on the brake pedal and loosen the bleed screw.

Support the engine-gearbox assembly by means of a sling, then remove securing screws (see **FIG 7:6**) and the front crossmember support for the gearbox. Do not

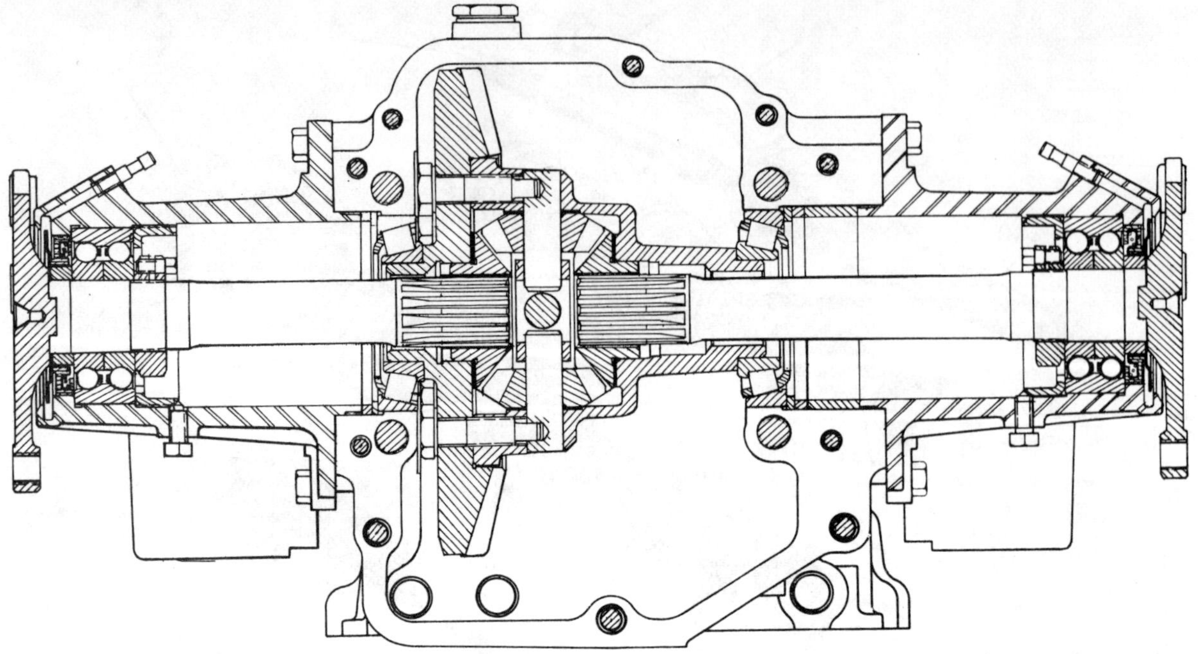

FIG 7:3 A sectional view of the differential gear and shafts

lose the packing placed between the crossmember and sidemember. Proceed to:

1 Disconnect the pipes from the clutch lock. Loosen the screw securing the clutch lock control clamp and free this clamp from the first and second speed selector fork shaft.

2 Disconnect the five-tube pipe assembly 9 (see **FIG 7:7**) also the leads 8 for the brake pad wear tell-tale light. Remove the pipe 7 connecting the brake units and the rubber clips 6.

3 Remove the gearbox cover, using spanner 1677.T for the screws with flat heads.

4 Remove the cover 10 over the end of the reverse gear fork spindle and the cover over the end of third and fourth gear selector fork shaft.

5 To dismantle the cover, remove the cylinder feedpipe assemblies shown in **FIG 7:8.**

6 Compress the return springs of the gearchange control pistons, for which a tool 3171.T is available. Alternatively use a screw B of 4 mm dia. x 80 mm long under the head, with a nut and plain washer as shown in **FIG 7:8.**

7 Remove the screw 2 and the neutral position stop block 3 shown in **FIG 7:10.** Remove the stop screws 1 from the cylinders and withdraw the cylinder piston assemblies via the inside of the cover. Note that the cylinder piston assembly for the reverse gear has no return spring.

8 If it is required to renew the ring seals in the gearchange control cylinders, details of which are shown in **FIG 7:9,** they may be dismantled by hand and the ring seals withdrawn by a small brass wire hook. Take care not to score the cylinder and do not mix the cylinder piston assemblies as they are paired in manufacture. To refit the assembly the spring may be compressed with the aid of the screw mentioned in Operation 6.

9 When reassembling make sure that the pistons are at the bottom of their cylinders by means of securing screws C as shown in **FIG 7:10.**

10 Fit the cylinder piston assemblies into the gearbox cover, screwing in fully. Locate the neutral position stop block 3 on the dowels in the cover and tighten the securing screws 2. A gauge 3172.T is available to check and adjust if necessary the gearchange control dogs.

11 Check the various speed positions, noting that with the cover removed the gearbox is not in neutral position, the reverse fork shaft being brought beyond neutral by its return spring. To select a gear it is necessary to bring the reverse gear to neutral, using a screwdriver or a gauge 3183.T.

12 To check the position of first gear, engage first gear with the sliding gear of first and second in contact with the idler of first. Measure the projection of the fork shaft from the face of the housing, for example 34.3 mm.

13 Carry out the same procedures for the second, third and fourth gears with their sliding pinions in contact with their respective idlers, obtaining fork shaft projections of, say, 55.3, 1.3 and 23.9 mm.

14 Check the end play of the reverse fork shaft when in neutral. Engage third or fourth speed and push the reverse fork shaft towards the rear of the gearbox. Using a depth gauge, measure the distance 'a' (see **FIG 7:11**) between the end of the shaft and the front face of the gearbox, say 1.6 mm. Pull the shaft forwards and measure the distance again, say 2.6 mm.

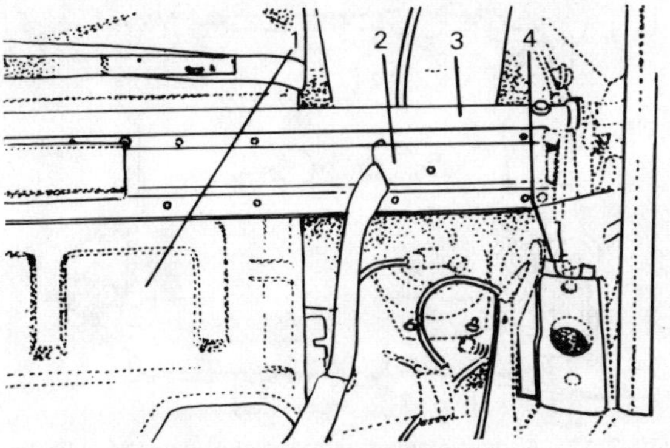

FIG 7:4 Front components

Key to Fig 7:4 1 Air cowl 2 Crossmember assembly 3 Headlamp beam control 4 Bonnet lock control cables

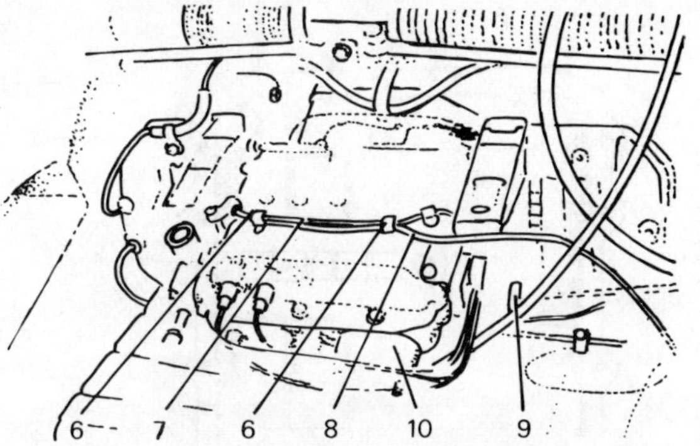

FIG 7:7 Gearbox pipe assembly

Key to Fig 7:7 6 Rubber clips 7 Pipe connecting brake units 8 Brake pad wear leads 9 Five-tube pipe assembly 10 Cover for end of reverse fork spindle

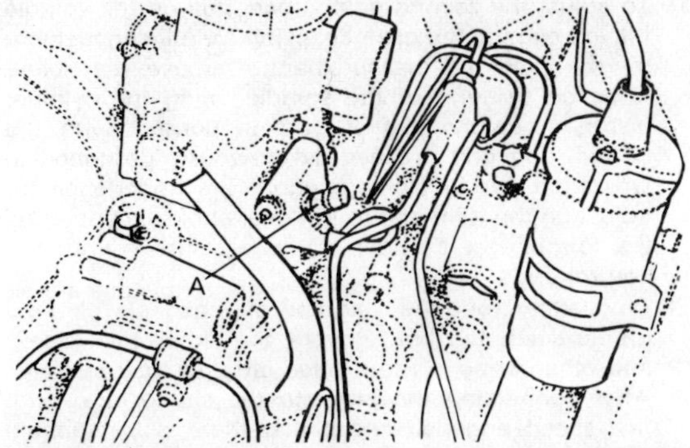

FIG 7:5 Location of accelerated idling bleed screw A

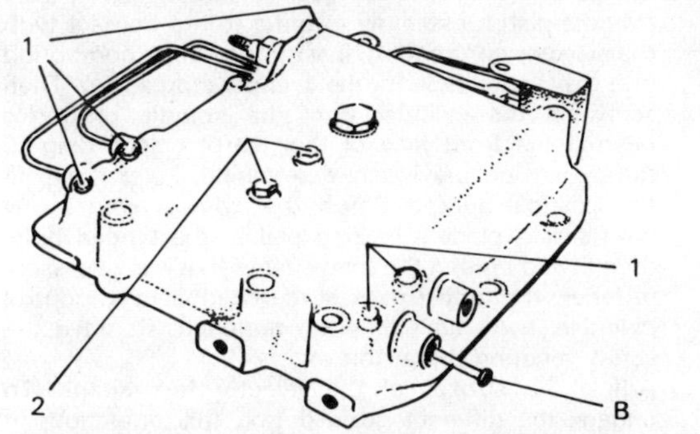

FIG 7:8 External view of gearbox cover for hydraulic selection

Key to Fig 7:8 1 Cylinder stop screws 2 Neutral stop block screws **B** Screw compressing piston springs

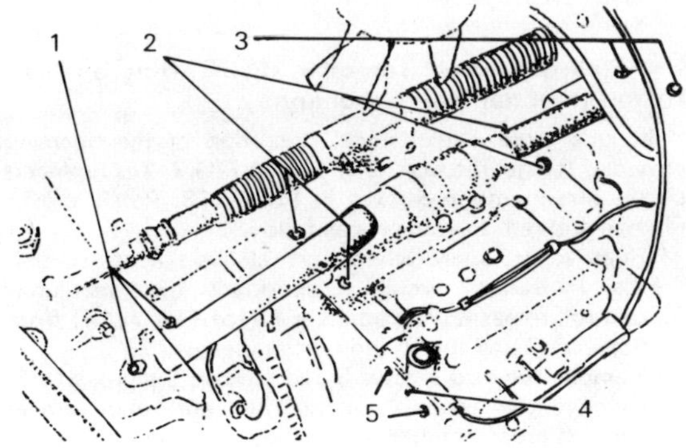

FIG 7:6 Crossmember and clutch lock attachment

Key to Fig 7:6 1, 2, 3 Screws securing crossmember 4 Clutch lock clamp 5 Securing screw

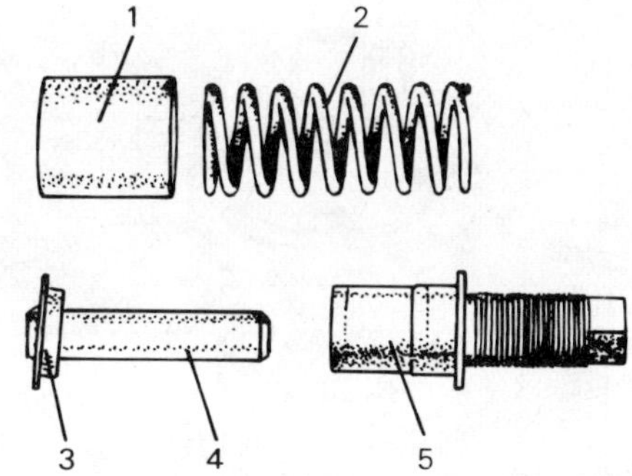

FIG 7:9 An exploded view of a gearchange cylinder

Key to Fig 7:9 1 Sleeve 2 Spring 3 Thrust cup 4 Piston assembly 5 Cylinder

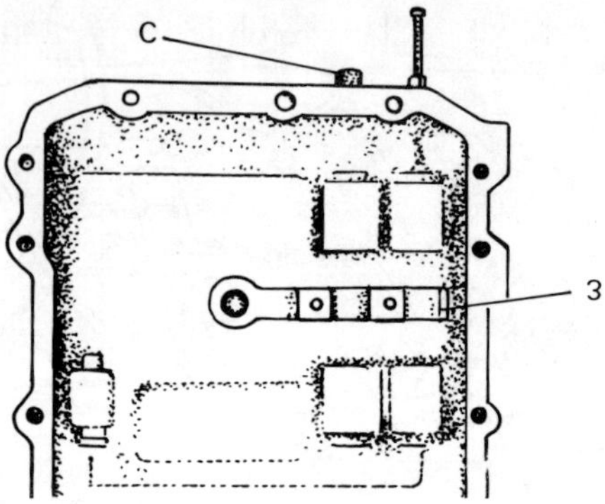

FIG 7:10 Reassembling the cover, showing the neutral position stop block 3 and the piston securing screws C

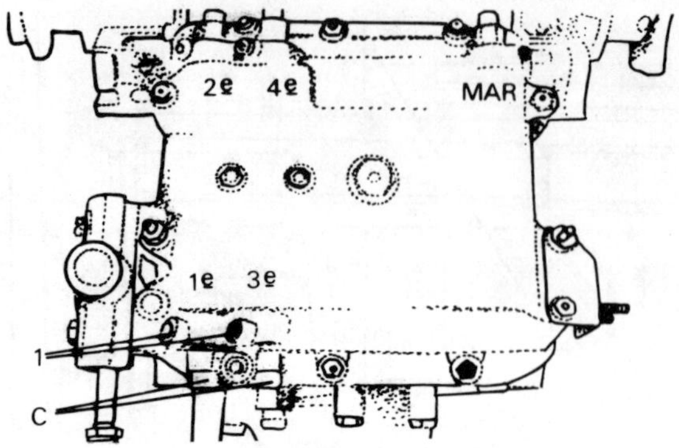

FIG 7:12 Fork shafts adjustment showing the cylinder stop screws 1 and the piston securing screws C

Take the average of these two measurements, i.e. 2.1 mm, which gives the projection to which the shaft is to be adjusted.

15 Fit the cover, coating the joint with sealer and tighten the securing screws.

16 To adjust the reverse gear cylinder, screw the cylinder piston assembly to bring it into contact with the selector control dog, inserting a sealer compound into the tapped hole for the cylinder stop screw. Then screw in the cylinder until the spindle protrudes beyond the front face of the gearbox according to the dimension previously determined, i.e. 2.1 mm in the example quoted. Smear the cylinder stop screw with sealer, place a locking pad in the tapped hole, then fit and tighten the screw. Note that it is necessary to renew the rubber pads of the changespeed control cylinders each time they are removed. Remove the screw securing the piston.

17 Adjust the strokes of the selector fork shafts. To engage the different gears during this operation, fit a screw, 7 mm diameter x 100 mm pitch in the tapped holes in the ends of the shafts.

18 To adjust the stroke for first gear, engage the gear and check for full engagement by measuring the shaft position as determined in Operation 11. Referring to **FIG 7:12,** screw the second gear cylinder piston to bring it in contact with the selector dog, introducing sealer into the tapped hole receiving the screw 1. Then screw the cylinder a further one-third of a turn to obtain a clearance of .4 to .6 mm between the sliding pinion and the loose pinion. Smear the cylinder stop screw 1 with sealer. Locate a rubber pad in the tapped hole and tighten the screw. Remove the screw C holding the piston in the cylinder.

19 To adjust the second gear stroke, pull on the spindle fully to engage the gear, checking for full engagement by the previous measurement. Remove the screw fitted on the end of the spindle, bring the cylinder piston assembly of first gear in contact with the control dog and proceed as previously described in Operation 17. Similar operations are undertaken for adjusting the third and fourth gear strokes, contacting the fourth gear cylinder piston assemblies with the control dogs.

20 Proceed to refit the feedpipe assemblies with new rubber seals, the front covers, the clutch lock clamp and other items in the reverse order of their removal. After connecting the pipes to the clutch lock, with first-speed engaged check that there is a minimum clearance of 1.7 mm between the clamp and the adjacent screw securing the shaft cover. On completion bleed the front brake circuit (see **Chapter 10**) and bleed the gearchange control circuits by operating the gear selector lever and the clutch control by hand. Check all unions for leaks.

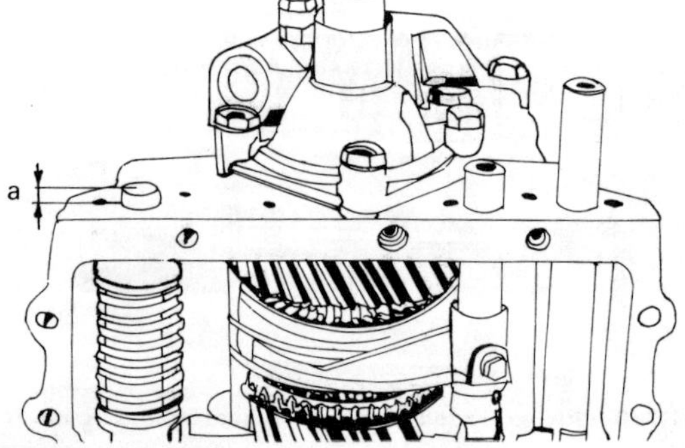

FIG 7:11 Checking the end play of the reverse fork shaft when in neutral

7:4 Gearbox cover removal, dismantling and refitting (mechanical gearchange)

In cars where mechanical operation of the gears is provided the gearbox cover shown in **FIG 7:1** is replaced by the arrangements shown in **FIG 7:13.** Procedure to remove and refit the cover is as follows:

1 Remove the spare wheel and release the pressure in the hydraulic circuit. Disconnect the headlamp control, releasing the adjuster 1 (see **FIG 7:14**) from the lever 2 and the spring 4 from the lever 2.

2 Remove the two screws 5 and remove the crossbar 3. Remove the assembly of air duct and spare wheel support crossmember.

3 Disconnect the gearchange control, releasing the tube 5 (see **FIG 7:15**) from the cover cross shaft and the bracket 3 from the extension on the gearbox cover.

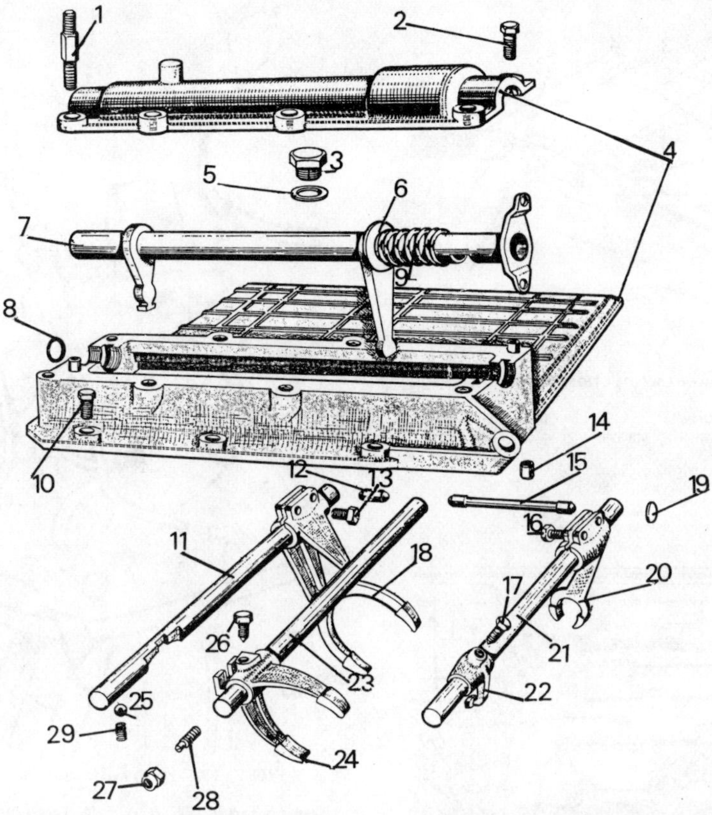

FIG 7:13 An exploded view of the gearbox cover for mechanical gearchange

Key to Fig 7:13 1 Pillar screw for cross shaft cover (two) 2 Bolt 3 Oil filler plug 4 Gearbox cover 5 Washer 6 Washer 7 Cross shaft 8 O-ring 9 Spring 10 Screw 11 1st/2nd gear selector shaft 12 Inter-lock plunger 13 Screw 14 Dowel 15 Inter-lock plunger 16 Screw 17 Lock screw 18 1st/2nd gear shifting fork 19 Closing plug 20 Reverse gear fork 21 Reverse selector shaft 22 Reverse gear operating dog 23 3rd/4th gear selector shaft 24 3rd/4th gear selector fork 25 Detent ball 26 Lock screw 27 Locknut 28 4th gear selector shaft stroke adjuster 29 Spring

4 Disconnect and free the lead for the brake pad wear tell-tale light 2 from the righthand brake unit, also the feedpipe 1 from the righthand brake unit.

5 Remove the securing screws and take off the gearbox cover.

6 Remove the securing screws to detach the gearchange cross shaft cover and then remove the cross shaft.

7 To reassemble the cover, referring to **FIG 7:16**, change the sealing washers 4 and 7 on the change-speed control cross shaft 5 and wrap the flange 8 with sellotape or adhesive paper, passing the seal over it.

8 Fit the changespeed control cross shaft 5 in the cross shaft cover 2. Compress the spring 6 with the aid of the tool No. 3171.T with its distance pieces. The sealing rings fit in the grooves 1 and 3 in the cover. Fit the cross shaft cover on the gearbox cover with sealing compound.

9 Before fitting the gearbox cover smear the joint face lightly with sealing compound, also fit into its hole in the cover the centre screw of the rear row (length under head 35 mm).

10 Position the rear centring dowels on the gearbox housing, then lower the front of the cover holding the fork control dogs in a vertical position. Engage the dowels.

11 If the positioning of the fork control dogs is correct, the cover cross shaft should have an end play of approximately 5 mm and no backlash in rotation. Fit and tighten the securing screws for the gearbox cover.

12 Refit the remaining items in the reverse order of their removal. Start up the engine and check that the gears engage normally. Re-establish the pressure in the hydraulic cicuits and bleed the brakes as described in **Chapter 10.**

7:5 Hydraulic gear selector removal and refitting

Operations to remove and refit the hydraulic gear selector are as follows:

1 Remove the finisher from the facia board adjacent to the gear selector lever, then remove the cover from above the steering column followed by the speedometer surround after detaching the five Phillips-head screws.

2 Release the pressure in all the circuits. Remove the lefthand front suspension sphere 1 (see **FIG 7:17**).

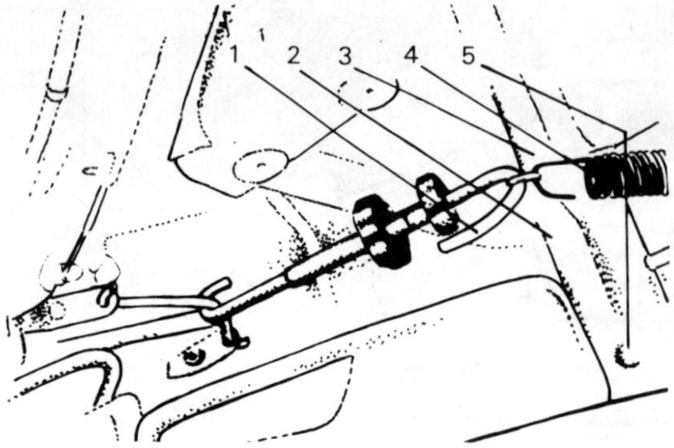

FIG 7:14 Front components (mechanical gearchange)

Key to Fig 7:14 1 Adjuster 2 Lever 3 Crossbar 4 Spring 5 Crossbar retaining screws

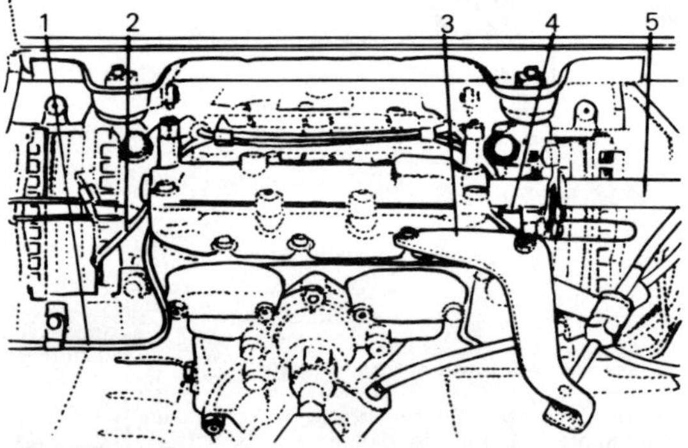

FIG 7:15 Gearchange control assembly, mechanical operation

Key to Fig 7:15 1 Feed pipe 2 Brake pad wear leads 3 Bracket 4 Dog 5 Control tube

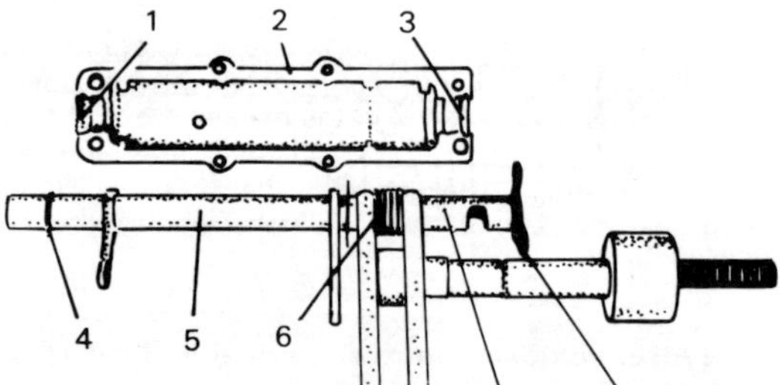

FIG 7:16 Gearbox cover components, mechanical gearchange

Key to Fig 7:16 1 Sealing ring groove 2 Cross-shaft cover 3 Sealing ring groove 4 Sealing washer 5 Changespeed control cross-shaft 6 Spring compressed by tool 3171.T 7 Sealing washer 8 Flange

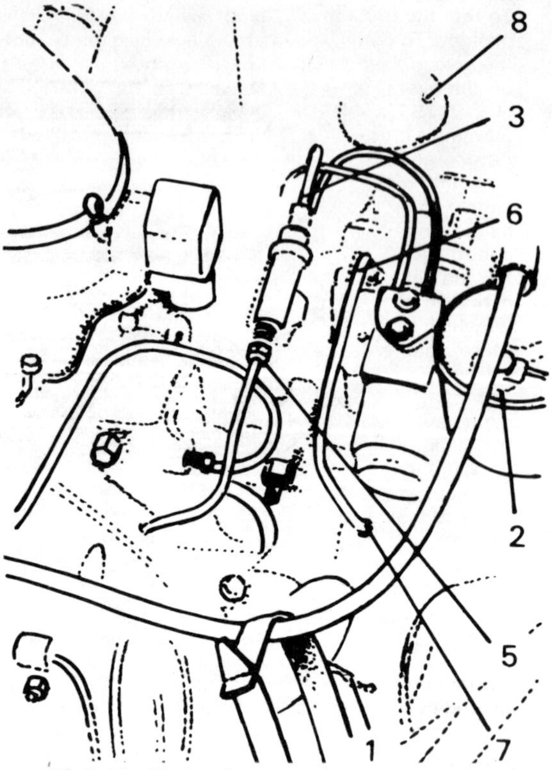

FIG 7:17 Hydraulic gear selector connections

Key to Fig 7:17 1 Lefthand front suspension sphere 2 Coil 3 Screwed union 5 Pipe to centrifugal regulator 6 Pipe to clutch lock 7 Rubber pipe to the four-way union 8 Rubber plug in steering tunnel

3 Remove the coil 2, disconnect the lead from the switch and loosen the two securing screws.

4 Disconnect from the hydraulic gear selector (a) the pressure feedpipe, (b) the screwed union 3, (c) the flange, removing the seal plate, (d) the securing clip, (e) the connecting pipe 5 between the centrifugal regulator and the hydraulic gear selector, (f) the connecting pipe 6 between the hydraulic gear selector and the clutch lock, (g) the rubber pipe 7 from the hydraulic gear selector to the four-way union, (h) the pipe assembly from the selector to the gearbox, removing the seal plate, (j) the Rilsan overflow pipe.

5 Free the speedometer cable from the clip 10 on the hydraulic gear selector after having disconnected the two parts of the cable.

6 Remove the rubber plug 8 from the steering tunnel and loosen the front screw connecting the change-speed lever to the slide valve of the hydraulic gear selector, on the hydraulic gear selector side.

7 Loosen the clamp screw securing the manual clutch control rod.

8 Remove the two nuts from the studs securing the hydraulic gear selector to the mechanical selector assembly for which a spanner 2431.T is available. Free the hydraulic gear selector.

9 To refit the unit, put the slide valve in the first-speed position. To do this pull and turn the sliding valve until the hole in the valve is in line with that in the rear cap on the hydraulic gear selector. Insert the control rod No. 2429.T which must penetrate approximately 30 mm. If it does not, turn the slide valve half a turn.

10 Put the gear selector lever in the first-speed position, then offer up the unit taking care to pass the auxiliary clutch control rod through the hole in the selector flange and in the trunnion of the auxiliary clutch control lever.

11 Fit and tighten the nuts on the studs securing the hydraulic gear selector to the selector lever assembly, for which a spanner No. 2428.T is available.

12 Make sure that the lever is still in the first-speed position, then tighten the screws on the coupling clamp.

13 Withdraw the alignment rod No. 2429.T from the hydraulic gear selector. Refit the rubber plug in the locating hole and also the plug in the steering tunnel.

14 Push the auxiliary clutch control rod as far as possible towards the hydraulic gear selector and pull the lever towards the driver. Then lock the screw of the trunnion.

15 Refit the remaining pipes and components in the reverse order of their removal. Start up the engine, let it idle for a few minutes, then tighten the bleed screw on the pressure regulator. Put the manual height control lever in the normal position and check all unions for leaks. Change into each gear in succession in order to check the sealing of the flanges.

7:6 Hydraulic gear selector dismantling and reassembly

Operations to overhaul the hydraulic gear selector are as follows:

1 Secure the hydraulic gear selector in a vice, gripping the rear cover. Remove the gearchange speed-regulator with its pipe assembly 1 shown in **FIG 7:18** and seal plates.

2 Unscrew the nut and screws of the front cover 2 in turn by one flat each at a time to avoid jamming the cover sideways. Remove the cover, the return springs 9 and 10 (see **FIG 7:19**) for the synchro delay pistons, also the upper and lower thrust washers 8 and 11 for the springs. Remove the gasket.

3 Remove the selector slide valve and withdraw the synchro delay piston 12 for third-speed with its seal. Withdraw the other synchronizing pistons 13 by pushing them with the auxiliary clutch control slide valve and then with a brass drift. Place the pistons in order in a rack immediately after dismantling.

4 Remove the auxiliary manual clutch control slide valve 14, then clean the bores of the hydraulic gear selector with alcohol and blow out with compressed air.

5 Check the diameter of the bore, between the end of the selector and the first groove with the plug gauge 2277.T. Try the gauge in several positions. If the no go end can be inserted, or if there are deep scratches in the bore, the selector is unserviceable.

6 Remove the ring seals from the grooves round the synchro delay pistons. Use a brass wire hook, but be careful not to scratch the bore or damage the groove, the corners of which must be sharp.

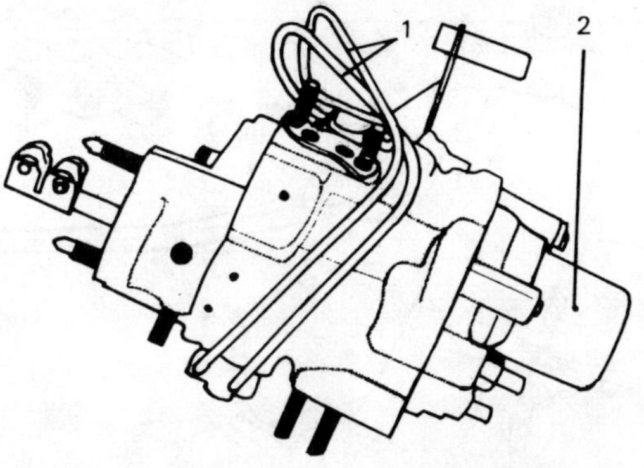

FIG 7:18 A view of the hydraulic gear selector

Key to Fig 7:18 1 Gearchange speed regulator with pipe assembly and seal plates 2 Front cover

7 Remove the rear cover, then remove the automatic gear control pistons 5 by tapping on the automatic gearchange slide valve with a brass drift until the plug 6 is freed. Place the pistons in a rack in their order of

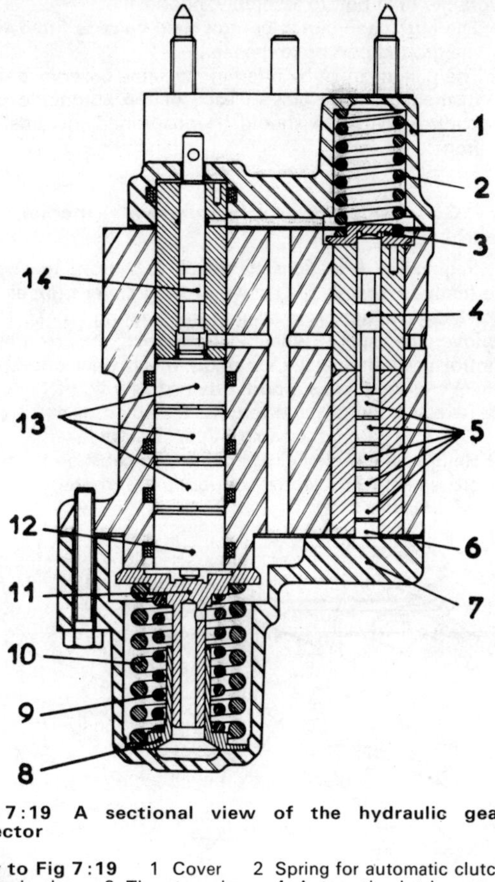

FIG 7:19 A sectional view of the hydraulic gear selector

Key to Fig 7:19 1 Cover 2 Spring for automatic clutch control valve 3 Thrust washer 4 Automatic clutch control slide valve 5 Automatic gear control pistons 6 Plug 7 Front cover 8 Cup 9, 10 Springs for synchro delay pistons 11 Cup 12, 13 Synchro delay pistons 14 Auxiliary manual clutch control slide valve

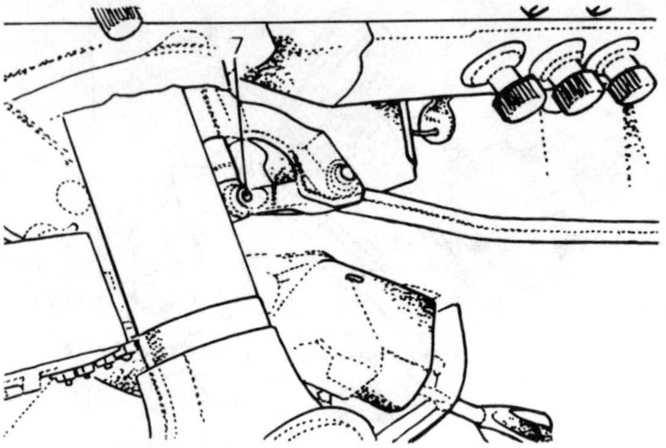

FIG 7:20 Gearchange cable fulcrum pin 7

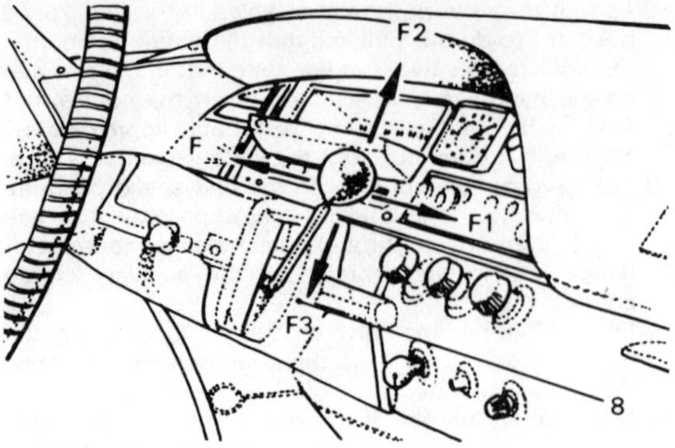

FIG 7:22 Gearlever positions and aperture finisher 8

disassembly. Remove the automatic gearchange slide valve 4. Clean all parts with alcohol and blow out with compressed air.

Refit the elements of the selector in the reverse order of their removal, dipping all parts in the approved hydraulic fluid before assembly, noting that:

1 The automatic clutch control slide valve is fitted with the ground portion to the rear.
2 The pistons must be fitted in the same order as before dismantling. The pips of each of the automatic gear control pistons 5 should be positioned towards the front.

7:7 Gear selector cable renewal (mechanical gearchange)

Preliminary operations to renew a gearchange cable are firstly to remove the upper steering cover from above the electrical controls in front of the steering wheel. Then remove the spare wheel, disconnect the headlamp control and remove the assembly of air duct and spare wheel crossmember support. Proceed as follows:

1 Take out the pin and remove the fulcrum pin 7 (see **FIG 7:20**) from the cable on the selector lever.
2 Remove the rubber clips holding the cable on the front crossmember gearbox support and on the speedometer cable.

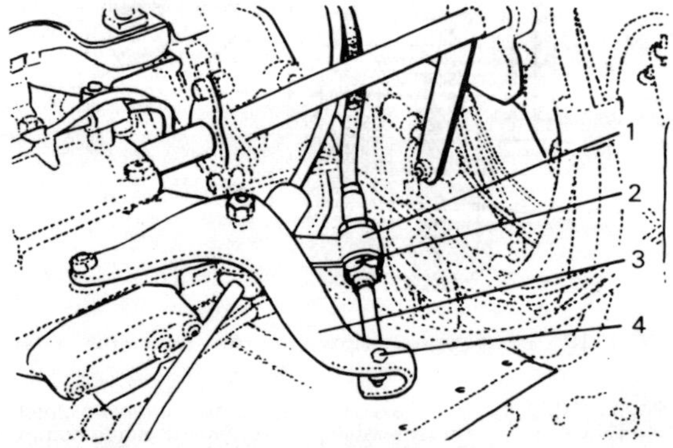

FIG 7:21 Gearchange cable connections

Key to Fig 7:21 1 Relay bracket 2 Nut 3 Bracket on gearbox cover 4 Spindle

3 Take out the pin and remove the spindle 4 (see **FIG 7:21**) securing the cable to the bracket 3 on the gearbox cover.
4 Remove the nut 2 and free the cable from the relay bracket 1, then release the locknut 9 (see **FIG 7:24**), unscrew the adjuster 10 and withdraw the cable towards the front. Remove the locknut.
5 Insert a new cable from the front, passing it along the length of the speedometer cable between the steering and the mechanical brake cable and in the sleeve on the support bracket on the side of the steering centralizer cam.
6 Fit and tighten the locknut 9, then insert the cable in the control shaft and screw up the adjuster 10.
7 Insert the cable in the relay bracket 1 shown in **FIG 7:21.** Fit the nut 2 and ensure that the threaded sleeve protrudes for a minimum of 3 mm. Lock the nut 2.
8 Fit and pin the spindle 4 securing the front end of the cable and the fulcrum pin 7 shown in **FIG 7:20** for the cable on the lever. Adjust the length of the cable as described in **Section 7:8.**
9 Fit the cover over the electrical controls, the rubber clips on the cable and the remaining items removed for access.

7:8 Adjustment of changespeed control (mechanical gearchange)

The directions of gearlever movement for mechanical gearchange are shown in **FIG 7:22.** When changing gear, the lever must not touch the finisher 8 surrounding the aperture for the gearchange lever. Check the alignalignment of the control tube 2 (see **FIG 7:23**), which must lie on the centre line of the control cross shaft of the gear selector forks in the gearbox cover. To adjust, proceed as follows:

1 Disconnect the rod 1 from the lever 5.
2 Loosen the securing screws of the bearing housing 6 and move this housing in its slots to obtain vertical adjustment, and in the slots in the sidemember to move it forwards or backwards.
3 Tighten the securing screws of the bearing housing and connect the rod 1 to the lever 5.

To adjust the gearlever movement in the directions F and F1, the length of the cable must be adjusted so that

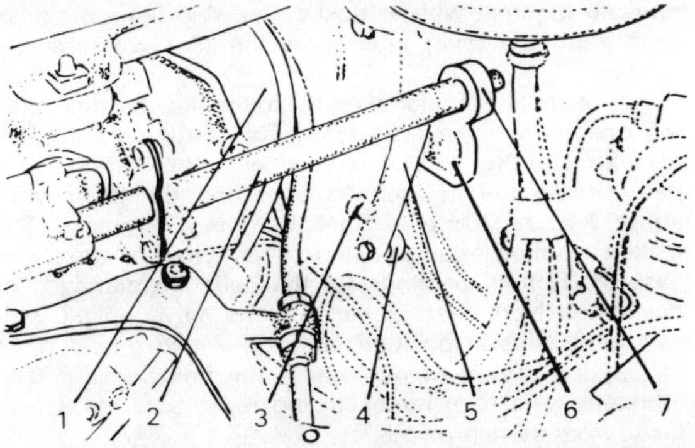

FIG 7:23 Gearchange control, mechanical operation

Key to Fig 7:23 1 Control rod 2 Control tube 3 Nut 4 Union 5 Lever arm 6 Adjusting screws 7 Bearing housing

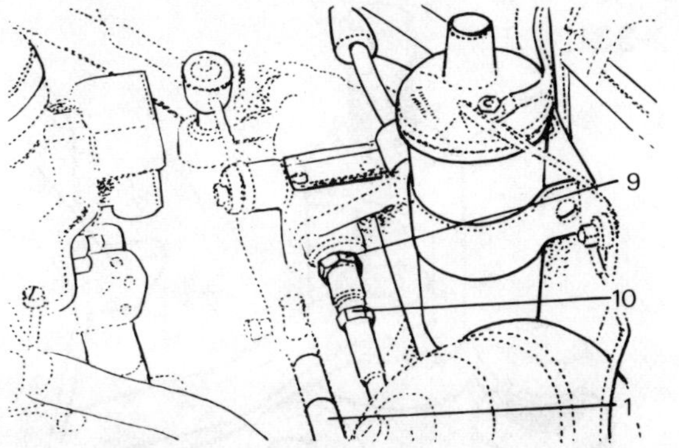

FIG 7:24 Gearchange control adjustment

Key to Fig 7:24 1 Control rod 9 Locknut 10 Adjuster

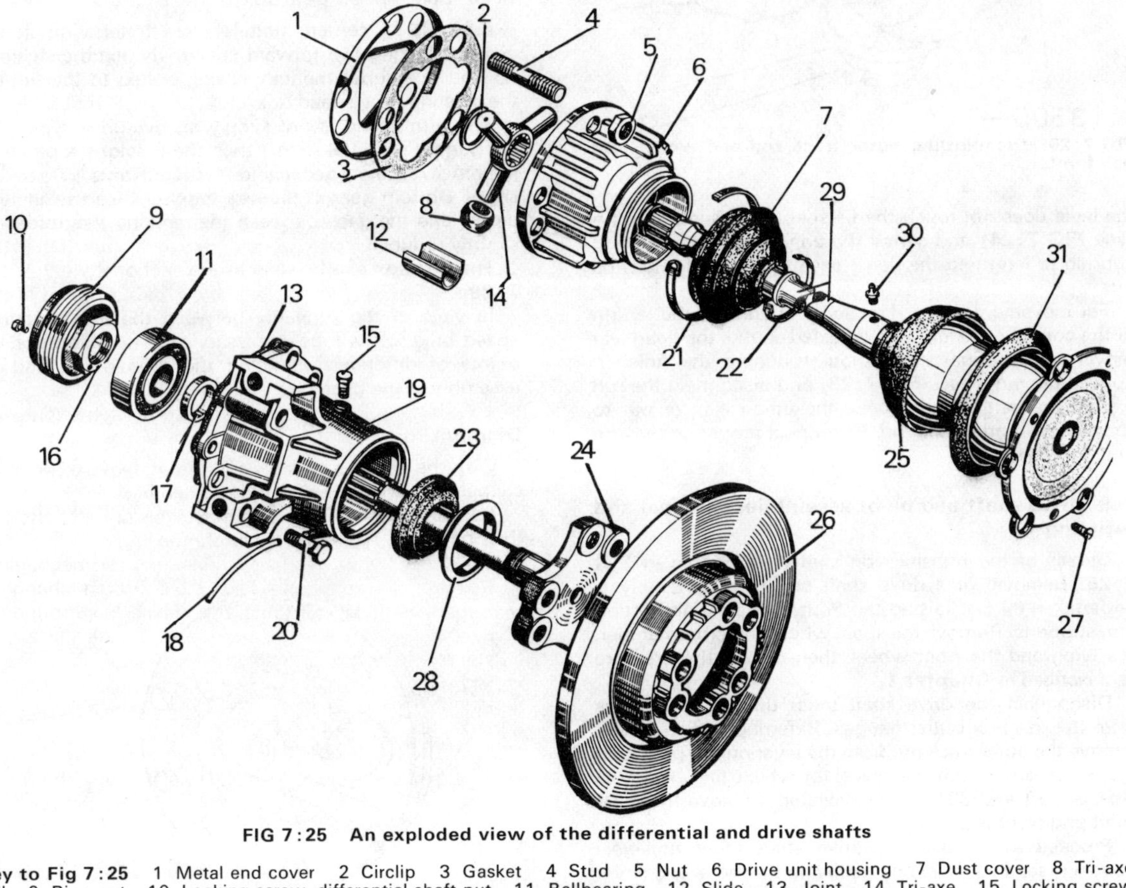

FIG 7:25 An exploded view of the differential and drive shafts

Key to Fig 7:25 1 Metal end cover 2 Circlip 3 Gasket 4 Stud 5 Nut 6 Drive unit housing 7 Dust cover 8 Tri-axe ball 9 Ring nut 10 Locking screw, differential shaft nut 11 Ballbearing 12 Slide 13 Joint 14 Tri-axe 15 Locking screw for ring nut 16 Differential shaft nut 17 Thrust block 18 Oil drain flexible pipe 19 Differential shaft housing 20 Screw 21 Clip 22 Clip 23 Ballbearing sealing ring 24 Flange 25 Rubber cover for drive shaft universal joint 26 Brake disc 27 Screw 28 Oil retaining washer 29 Shaft 30 Grease nipple 31 Sealing ring

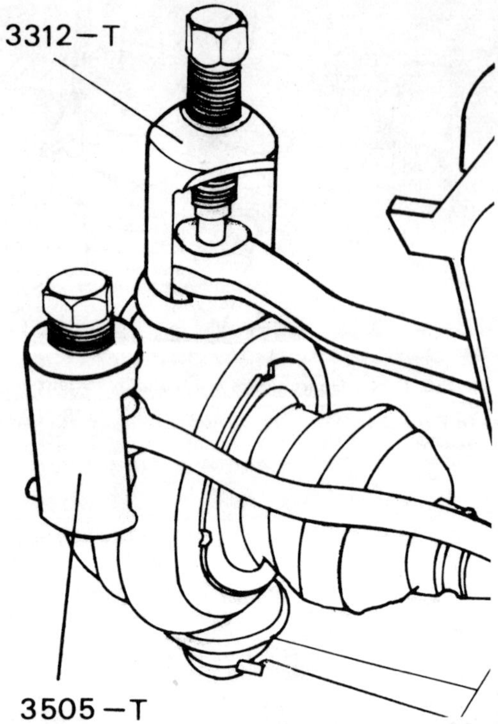

FIG 7:26 Dismantling outer track rod and wheel arm ball joints

the lever does not touch the finisher 8. Loosen the nut 9 (see **FIG 7:24**) and screw the adjuster 10 in or out to shorten or lengthen the cable sheath, then retighten the nut.

For movement in the directions F2 and F3, the length of the control rod 1 must be adjusted so that the gearlever movement is equalized without touching the finisher. Loosen the nut 3 (see **FIG 7:23**) and disconnect the rod 1 from the arm 5, then screw the union 4 in or out to shorten or lengthen the rod. Reconnect the rod to the arm and tighten the nut.

7:9 Drive shaft and pivot assemblies removal and refitting

Details of the transmission shafts are shown in **FIG 7:25.** Removal of a drive shaft and pivot assembly is undertaken by first raising the front of the car and fitting firm supports. Remove the spare wheel and crossmember, the wing and the front wheel, then release the pressure as described in **Chapter 1.**

Disconnect the drive shaft inner universal housings from the gearbox outlet flanges. Referring to **FIG 7:26,** remove the outer track rod from the lever on the pivot and the wheel arms from the pivot, for which the extractors Nos. 3505.T and 3312.T are available. Remove the drive shaft and pivot assembly.

Proceed to remove the drive shaft inner universal housing (see **FIG 7:27**) by removing the metal end cover and the gasket and then the balls 7 from the tri-axe 6 and the circlip 5. Withdraw the tri-axe, for which an extractor No. 1931.T is available, and free the drive unit housing together with its dust cover. Withdraw the drive shaft from the pivot after removing the two retaining screws.

Reassembly is undertaken by following the dismantling operations in reverse order. For refitting the tri-axe, the extractor No. 1931.T is used with the addition of a pad. Grease the tri-axe, the balls and the liners with about 7 oz or 200 g of Shell Retinax AM grease. The makers caution against using other types of grease in case the 'teflon' bearings for the balls are damaged or destroyed. Note that exchange units are supplied with two lubricators in position, through which grease must be applied until it comes out of the ball housing. The lubricators are then removed and replaced with screws taken from the old pivot.

Refit the drive shaft and pivot assembly. Referring to **FIG 7:28,** tigjten the nuts 13 on the ballpins to a torque of 72 lb ft (10 kg m), tighten the nut 12 on the outer track rod ballpin to a torque of 50 lb ft (7 kg m) and tighten the nuts securing the inner universal housing to a torque of between 58 and 80 lb ft (8.5 to 11.0 kg m). Refit the remaining items removed for access and lower the car to the ground.

7:10 Five-speed gearbox

From 1971 certain models were fitted with a new gearbox having five forward speeds the extra gear being housed in a supplementary casing bolted to the front of the existing four-speed box.

The fifth speed is not simply an overdrive type ratio, although it is a little higher than the previous top gear as reference to the specification in **Technical Data** will show. Bottom gear in the new box remains the same as before and the gaps between the remaining ratios are all slightly reduced.

The gearbox can be seen in the sectional view of **FIG 7:29.**

In view of the similarity between the four and five-speed boxes, it will be necessary only to enlarge on the points of difference affecting the dismantling and re-assembly of the gearbox.

Dismantling:

With the gearbox suitably supported, remove the brake calipers, discs and the front crossmember.

Take off the top cover. Remove the drive shafts and their bearings. Remove the clutch housing.

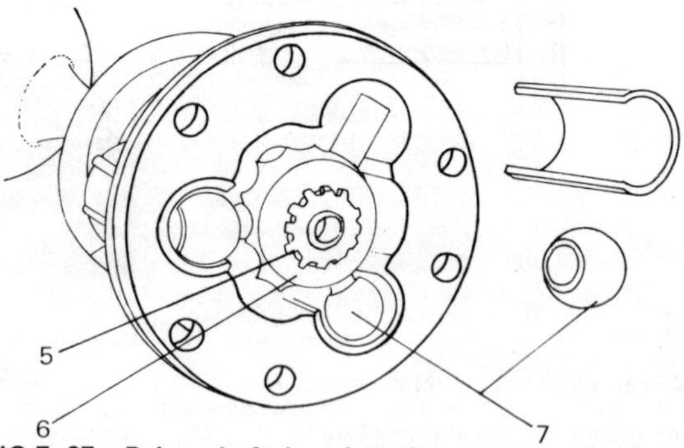

FIG 7:27 Drive shaft housing showing the circlip 5, the tri-axe 6 and the balls 7

Disengage the clutch shaft tube support and the oil return flange and then unscrew the reverse fork securing screw and select two gears together, e.g. first and reverse.

Take off the front cover and remove the securing screw to release the fork and synchro hub for the 5th gear. Remove the 5th speed gear wheel and the cover and spacer.

Unscrew the speedometer gear using as a key the tool 3179-Tbis. Remove the shafts for the reverse and the 5th speed selector forks.

Remove the screws securing the gearchange lever and then disengage the shaft lever, locking ball and spring and take out the shafts for the 3rd/4th and 1st/2nd selector forks.

Remove the drain plugs and the securing screws and then unscrew the locknut and remove the stop screw from the reverse gear idler shaft. Remove the shaft and the gearwheel.

The primary shaft is removed by freeing the front and rear bearings and then taking out the bearing and pushing the drive-pinion assembly towards the rear.

Release the 1st/2nd gear selector fork and take out the drive pinion.

Dismantle the primary shaft and disconnect the drive shaft from the primary shaft, if necessary by removing the snap ring and the spring between the two shafts.

Remove the differential and dismantle the clutch housing and the top cover.

Reassembly:

With reference to **FIG 7:30** reassemble the drive pinion assembly as follows:

Fit the washer 2 onto the pinion shaft as shown and then the ballbearing 1, using for this a tube having an interior diameter of 44 mm and a length of 240 mm.

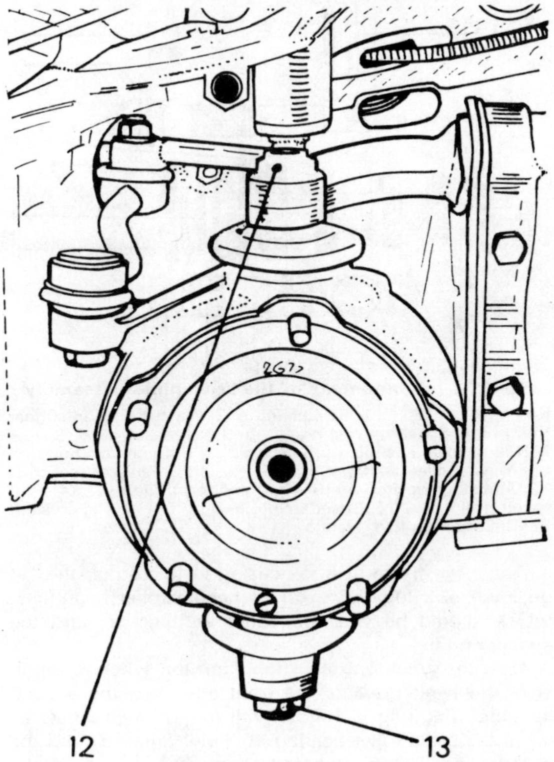

FIG 7:28 Pivot and drive shaft assembly showing the nuts 12 and 13 on the ballpins

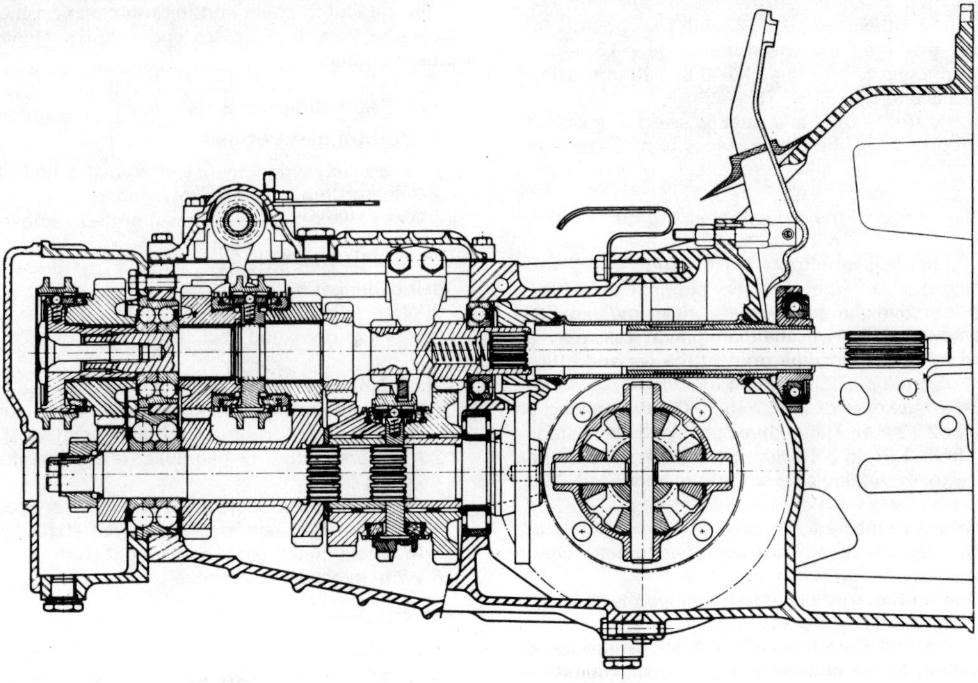

FIG 7:29 Section through the 5-speed gearbox

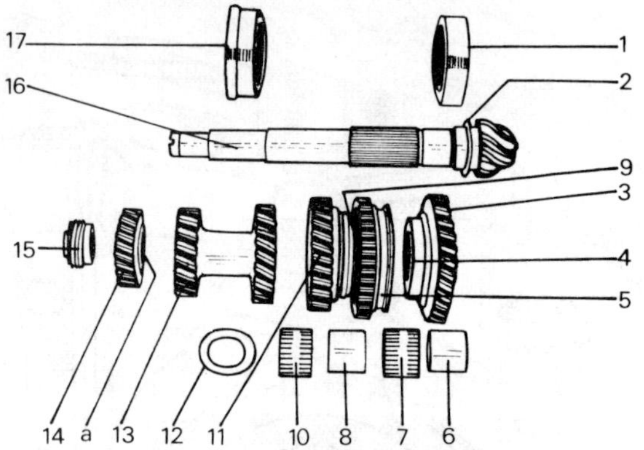

FIG 7:30 Components of the drive pinion assembly

Key to Fig 7:30 1 Ballbearing 2 Washer 3 Idler gear (first) 4 Synchronizing ring 5 Synchro hub 6 Spacer 7 Needle roller bearing 8 Spacer 9 Synchronizing ring 10 Needle roller bearing 11 Idler gear (second) 12 Adjusting washer 13 Third and fourth gear 14 Fifth speed gear 15 Speedometer gear 16 Pinion shaft 17 Ballbearing **a** Flange

Assemble in the gearbox casing in this order; the 1st gear wheel 3 together with its needle roller bearing 7, which should be well lubricated with grease and the spacer ring 6.

Next the synchronizing ring 4, and the synchro hub 5, with the teeth towards the front and then the second synchronizing ring 9. Follow with the 2nd gearwheel 11 with its needle roller bearing 10 (well greased) and the spacer ring 8, the adjustment shim 12, and then the double pinion for the 3rd and 4th gears.

Fit in the shaft of the drive pinion 16 with its roller bearing and then assemble on the end of the shaft the front bearing 17, 5th speed gear 14, with the shoulder 'a' on the inner side, and the speedometer gear 15 which should be tightened to a torque of 146 to 160 lb ft using key 3179-T bis and tool 3181-Tbis.

Position the front cover and spacer using a smear of jointing compound on the mating faces and tighten the securing screws, at the same time checking that all the wheels are able to rotate freely.

Adjust the setting of the crownwheel and pinion drive as follows:

Having set the adjusting tools 3170-T and 2437-T and measured the distance from the drive pinion, take off the front cover, remove the speedometer gear and the 5th speed gear and then pull out the drive pinion and remove the adjusting shim 12 and measure its thickness.

If, as an example it is 2.81 mm, it must be replaced by a shim with a thickness of 2.81 minus .09 mm making a final figure of 2.72 mm. These shims are available in steps of .04 mm from 1.65 to 3.13 mm. Select the shim of the nearest size to that calculated above, in this case 2.73 mm.

Now reassemble the new shim on the drive pinion with the front bearing 5th speed gear and speedometer gear, fit the front cover and check the adjustment.

Again take off the front cover and remove the speedometer and 5th speed gears and also the front bearing. Push back the drive pinions so that the gearwheels drop into the bottom of the box without displacing the shim between the 3rd and 2nd speed wheels, then place the 1st/2nd selector fork in position with the securing screws towards the inside of the box.

Assemble and install the primary shaft and then the drive pinion assembly and reverse idle gear.

Select two gears together, one being reverse, and tighten the speedometer gear to 146 to 160 lb ft. Fit the housing and joint with a little compound and tighten the securing screws.

Assemble the 5th speed gear, synchronizer and selector fork on the primary shaft and tighten the securing screws to 108 to 124 lb ft.

Fit the 1st/2nd gear fork shaft, then the shaft for 3rd/4th and for 5th gear and engage the fork for 5th gear on its shaft, securing it with the locking screw. Fit the shaft into the gearbox housing, together with the locking ball and spring and fit also the 5th gear selector, finally inserting the locking pin.

Fit the reverse gear shaft. Fit and lock the two securing screws on the 5th gear selector shaft.

Check the gear selectors in all positions. Fit the drain plugs. Grease and fit the speedometer pinion. Fit the front cover.

To adjust the 4th gear stop, select 4th and apply a little pressure on the sliding pinion by pressing on the fork. Measure the clearance between the sliding pinion and the 4th speed gearwheel.

Fit between the gearwheel and the sliding pinion a shim with a thickness equal to the measured clearance plus .5 mm. Tighten the stop screw until it contacts the 3rd/4th selector shaft, then secure the locknut and check the clearance.

Assemble the drive shafts and their bearings, noting that the righthand shaft is the shorter of the two. Assemble the differential and fit it carefully noting the pre-loading on the bearings and adjusting the backlash.

Fit the clutch cover and the top cover on the gearbox. Refit the front brake discs and calipers. Refit the front crossmember.

7:11 Fault diagnosis

(a) Jumping out of gear

1 Excessively worn locating slots in striking fork rods
2 Selector fork locking screws loose
3 Worn synchromesh units

(b) Noisy gearbox

1 Insufficient oil
2 Worn or damaged bearings
3 Worn or damaged gear teeth

(c) Difficulty in engaging gear

1 Clutch clearance, clutch drag, clutch engagement control or slow-running out of adjustment (DS)
2 Incorrect setting of hydraulic gear selector and gear-lever (DS)
3 Gearlever selector gate assembly unserviceable (DS)
4 Operating pressure not maintained (DS)
5 Incorrect clutch pedal adjustment (ID)
6 Worn synchromesh cones

(d) Oil leaks

1 Worn or damaged oil seals
2 Loose or distorted front bearing caps or top cover
3 Defective joints

CHAPTER 8

THE FRONT AND REAR SUSPENSION

8:1 General description

Independent suspension of the weight of the car on each wheel is obtained by the use of separate hydro-pneumatic units of pressure spheres and cylinders as described in **Chapter 2.** The front suspension consists of two transverse arms on each side similar to a divided wishbone arrangement. At their front ends the arms are connected by ball joints (see **FIG 8:1**) to the front half-axle and pivot assembly. The rear ends are supported by taper roller bearings in an assembly attached to the chassis. The rear end of the upper arm is connected to a lever which operates the piston rod of the hydraulic cylinder, which is kept constantly supplied with fluid under pressure. The piston then moves in the cylinder according to wheel displacement and provides compensatory pneumatic damping in the pressure sphere. The lever carries two buffer arms and also another projection on which a coupling sleeve is connected and drops down to be attached to one end of the anti-roll or torsion bar.

From the anti-roll bar a rod is connected as shown in **FIG 8:8** to the control valve of the height corrector. This valve, in conjunction with a similar unit on the rear suspension, adjusts the flow of hydraulic fluid into the suspension cylinders so that the static height of the car remains the same irrespective of alterations of load at front or rear. When at rest the car is down at the rear, but when the engine is started the corrector system comes into operation and the rear of the car then rises until it reaches the normal height designed for comfortable travel. A manual control lever (see **FIG 2:12**) is linked by rods to both front and rear units.

The rear suspension consists of a trailing arm pivoting on an articulating arm and bearings on each side and located on the rear half axles as shown in **FIG 8:2.** Levers on the pivots of the arms are connected to the suspension cylinder pistons and an anti-roll bar is attached by coupling flanges to the two pivot bearings. From the centre of the bar a control rod (see **FIG 8:10**) runs to the height corrector, from which feed pipes are provided to each of the hydro-pneumatic units shown in detail in **FIG 2:6** in **Chapter 2.**

8:2 Suspension spheres and cylinders removal, servicing and refitting

When work is undertaken on the hydro-pneumatic suspension units it is essential to observe extreme cleanliness. The units should be washed externally with a hose and the parts wiped dry to avoid water entering the

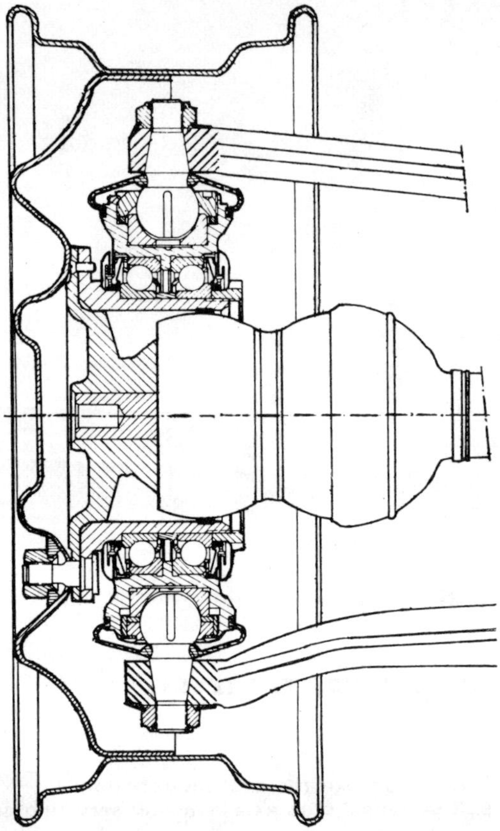

FIG 8:1 A sectional view of the front pivot and ball joints

system when dismantling. After removing the suspension sphere the damper housing in the sphere and cylinder should be cleaned with alcohol with the aid of a syringe. Use very clean plugs and close the openings.

Removal operations for a front suspension sphere and cylinder need firstly the removal of the wing, raising the front of the car, fitting firm supports and removing the wheel and mudshield. Then release the pressure in the suspension system by unscrewing the pressure regulator bleed screw. Put the manual height control lever in the low position. Proceed as follows:

1 Remove the suspension sphere from the suspension cylinder for which a strap wrench 2223.T is available. On a lefthand unit make sure that a distance piece is removed from the sphere. Place a cloth under the cylinder in order to avoid spilling fluid on the side-member and the steering, and seal the openings of the cylinder and sphere.
2 Referring to **FIG 8:3,** disconnect the union on the cylinder feedpipe. Plug the holes in the pipe and in the suspension cylinder. Withdraw the overflow return pipe 4 from the dust cover.
3 Remove the securing clip from the dust cover on the ball thrust cup and withdraw the dust cover.
4 Remove the connecting pin 6, then remove the rod 5 from the piston by pressing down the axle arm to the maximum. Note that the rod can only be disengaged when the holes in the rod and the lever are parallel.
5 Loosen the nuts 3 and the pointed screws 2 and remove the suspension cylinder.
6 To overhaul a suspension cylinder as shown in **FIG 8:4,** release the clip securing the dust cover, then remove the rubber protection sleeve, the dust cover and the suspension piston rod. Remove the piston 1 (see **FIG 8:4**) from the cylinder.
7 Hold the cylinder in a vice by the nut 4. Use wooden jaws and tighten the vice moderately so as not to damage the nut. Unscrew the cylinder with the aid of a pipe wrench bearing on the boss of the feedpipe union 'a' Remove the felt washer 5, the seal 2 and its retaining washer 3.
8 To reassemble, fit the rubber seal 2 previously smeared with special hydraulic fluid, in the seal retaining washer 3.
9 Note that the seal retaining washer is paired with the piston and if one of these parts is renewed the numbers on the edge of the retaining washer and on the head of the piston must be the same.
10 Place the felt washer 5, impregnated with special hydraulic fluid, in the nut 4. The felt washers must be immersed in the special hydraulic fluid for a few hours before being fitted.
11 Fit the joint 2 with the retaining washer 3 on the cylinder and fit the nut 4 without tightening.
12 Lubricate the piston with the approved hydraulic fluid and refit it in the cylinder. Slight scratches may be removed by lightly cleaning with No. 600 abrasive paper smeared with alcohol.
13 With the cylinder in a vice as previously, tighten the cylinder in the nut to a torque of 14 lb ft (2 kg m). Care in obtaining this torque is essential to obtain a good fit. If required, the sealing of the piston cylinder assembly may be given a bench test by a service agent.
14 Check the sliding movement of the piston and refit the dust cover, the suspension piston rod and the rubber protection sleeve.
15 Reassemble the cylinder in its housing with the countersinks on the cylinder in line with the pointed securing screws.
16 Tighten the screws by hand so that the cylinder is fitted without play or strain, then tighten the nuts to a torque of 13.5 lb ft (1.9 kg m).
17 Engage the piston rod in the ball thrust cup by lowering the axle arms to the maximum. Make sure that the ball is in position.
18 Engage the ends of the pin in the holes of the ball thrust cup, then fit the dust cover on the ball thrust cup, the rubber sleeve over the dust cover and the ligarex hose clip using pliers 2483.T. Fit the overflow return pipe and the feedpipe.
19 Remove the damper valve from the sphere and hold it in a vice by the nut at the suspension sphere end. Undo the other nut, then clean the parts with alcohol and blow with compressed air.
20 Note the order of removal of the valve discs, which should be changed each time the damper is dismantled. Sets of discs are obtainable containing the necessary parts for overhauling a damper valve. The valve discs are slightly curved. To mark the convex side, rub the valve lightly on No. 600 abrasive paper

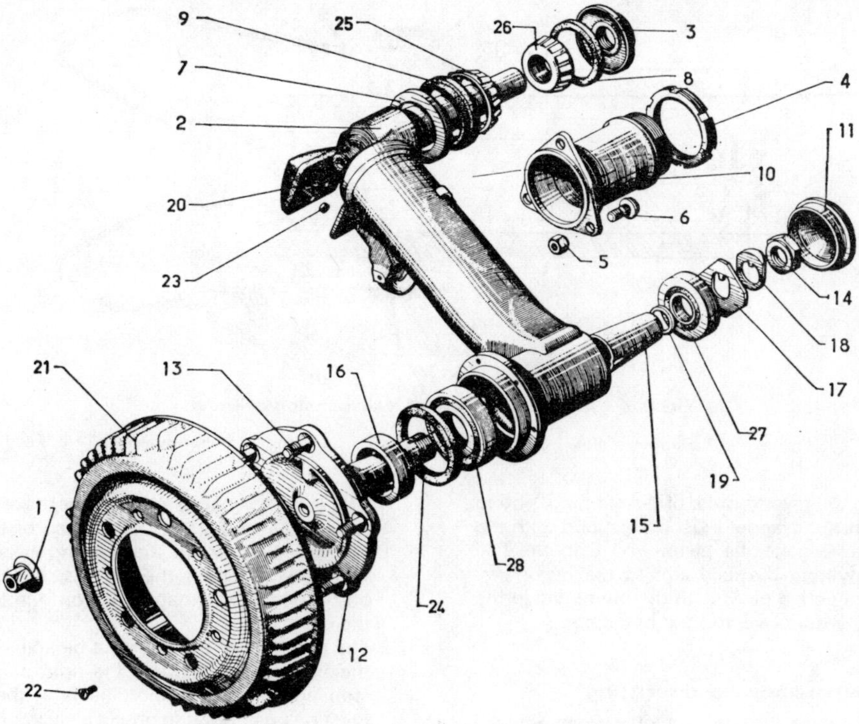

FIG 8 : 2 An exploded view of a rear half-axle

Key to Fig 8 : 2 1 Nut 2 Arm 3 Nut with dished cover 4 Ring nut 5 Nut 6 Screw 7 Seal protector 8 Sealing washer 9 Seal 10 Housing 11 Dust plug 12 Flange 13 Stud 14 Nut 15 Conical distance piece 16 Distance piece 17 Distance washer 18 Lockwasher 19 Shim 20 Stud 21 Brake drum 22 Screw 23 Nut 24 Distance piece 25 Taper roller bearing 26 Taper roller bearing 27 Ballbearing 28 Ballbearing

on a surface-plate, when the convex face of the disc will show a mark near its centre.

21 To reassemble, screw the stud into the short-thread end of the nut until the upper face of the nut reaches the end of the thread on the stud. This prevents the valve discs from being pinched in the threaded part of the stud.

22 Fit the valve discs on cylinder and sphere sides in the correct order of thicknesses as removed. Fit the damper valve body either way up. Screw on the upper nut, taking care not to turn the stud, and tighten it to a torque of 14.5 lb ft (2 kg m) exactly.

23 Fit the suspension sphere and tighten by hand inserting the seal moistened with approved hydraulic fluid. On the lefthand side make sure that the suspension sphere is fitted with its distance piece.

24 Start the engine. Retighten the pressure regulator bleed screw, put the suspension system under pressure and the height control at normal. Check the unions for leakage. Refit the lateral protection panel, the wheel and the wing.

The removal and refitting of a rear suspension unit is preceded by similar operations on the rear of the car as described for the front suspension units. Operations are as follows:

1 Disconnect the suspension cylinder feedpipe and the overflow return pipe. Close the holes in the pipes and the suspension cylinder with plugs.

2 Referring to **FIG 8 : 5**, remove the connecting pin 3 and the clip 4. Pull away the dust cover 5 towards the rear.

3 Disconnect the piston rod 6, lowering the axle arm to the maximum. The piston rod can only be freed when the pin holes in the rod and the lever are parallel.

4 Remove the suspension sphere as previously described.

5 Remove the screw and suspension cylinder stop plate and withdraw the suspension cylinder towards the front.

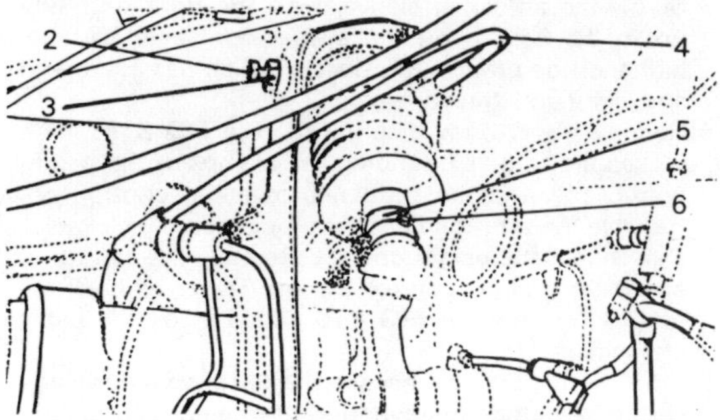

FIG 8 : 3 Details of a front suspension cylinder

Key to Fig 8 : 3 2 Pointed screw 3 Nuts 4 Overflow return pipe 5 Piston rod 6 Connecting pin

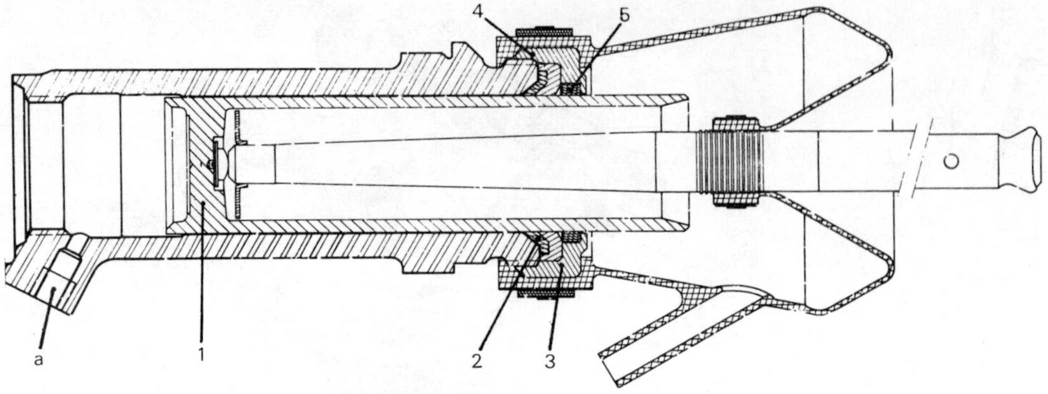

FIG 8:4 A sectional view of a suspension cylinder

Key to Fig 8:4 1 Piston 2 Rubber seal 3 Retaining washer 4 Nut 5 Felt washer a Feed pipe union boss

6 Reassemble in the reverse order of dismantling, noting that the flat on the cylinder must correspond with the securing plate. Engage the piston rod 6 in the ball thrust cup, lowering the axle arm to the maximum, and fit the connecting pin 3 with the longer leg in the ball thrust cup. Knock over the end of the pin.

8:3 Anti-roll bars removal and refitting

Initial operations for the removal of a front anti-roll bar include raising the front of the car and fitting firm supports, removing the front wheels, the spare wheel and its support, the headlamp control rod, the front wings and the lateral and lower protection panels. Release the pressure in the suspension system by unscrewing the pressure regulator bleed screw and put the manual height corrector in the low position. Further operations are as follows:

1 Referring to **FIG 8:6**, disconnect the unions on the height corrector in the order of (a) the overflow return pipe 3, (b) the suspension cylinder feedpipe 5, (c) the return pipe 1 from the corrector and (d) the feedpipe 2 from the corrector. Plug the openings on the corrector and the pipes as the work proceeds.

2 Detach the screws securing the height corrector bracket on the half axle and remove the corrector, of which a sectional view is shown in **FIG 8:7**.

3 Screw the adjusting sleeve 6 on the righthand side up to the ballpin on the suspension lever. On the lefthand side remove the sleeve, which has a lefthand and righthand thread.

4 Remove the anti-rattle springs 8 (see **FIG 8:8**), then loosen the screws 9 holding the clamps of the height control rod and the headlamp levelling control rod. Remove the anti-roll bar bearing clamps.

5 Disconnect the height control. Remove the cap nut 4 and the headlamp control if fitted. Then pull back the tongue A shown in **FIG 8:9** and unhook the cable attachment 10.

6 Remove the anti-roll bar via the lefthand side of the car. If required, remove the headlamp and height corrector controls, also the end stop clamps.

7 When reassembling, the correct position of the righthand stop clamp is so that there is a distance of 110±.5 mm between the inner face of the ballpin securing boss and the outer face of the stop clamp.

8 Fit the rods for the height and headlamp controls without tightening the clamps. Locate the anti-roll bar in position, engaging it from the lefthand side of the car.

9 The end float of the bar must be adjusted so that with the bar pushed towards the right and the righthand stop against the support bearing, the lefthand stop must be positioned to obtain a clearance of .5 to 1 mm between the stop and the lower lefthand bearing.

10 Smear the bearings with graphite grease when refitting the bearing caps. With the nuts of the U-bolts tightened to a torque of 9 lb ft (1.2 kg m) the anti-roll bar should turn under a load of 9 to 13 lb (4 to 6 kg) applied on the ball joint. If not, the thickness of the shims needs adjustment.

11 Engage the hook of the headlamp cable on the lever on the rod and flatten the tongue. Engage the end of the rod in the hole in the righthand bearing cap.

12 Insert the end of the height control rod into the hole in the lefthand bearing cap. Connect the manual control to the lever and fit the nut 4.

13 Refit the height corrector and reassemble the pipe connections in the reverse order of their removal. Grease and fit the anti-rattle springs.

14 Connect the anti-roll bar to the suspension levers as described in **Section 8:4**. A check on the front heights after these operations is desirable, but this requires the use of special gauges MR.1401-30 for which the assistance of a service agent should be obtained.

15 Fit the lower and side mudshields, the front wheels, the spare wheel and the front wings. Fit and adjust the headlamp control rod (see **Chapter 11**).

16 Lower the car to the ground and adjust the headlamps and the automatic levelling arrangements if required.

To remove and refit a rear anti-roll bar, release the pressure and raise the rear of the car on firm supports. Remove the wing, the mudshield and the corrector protection panel. Unhook the return spring for the automatic headlamp control if fitted.

Referring to **FIG 8:10**, disconnect the clamp 3 of the corrector control rod from the anti-roll bar and the clamp

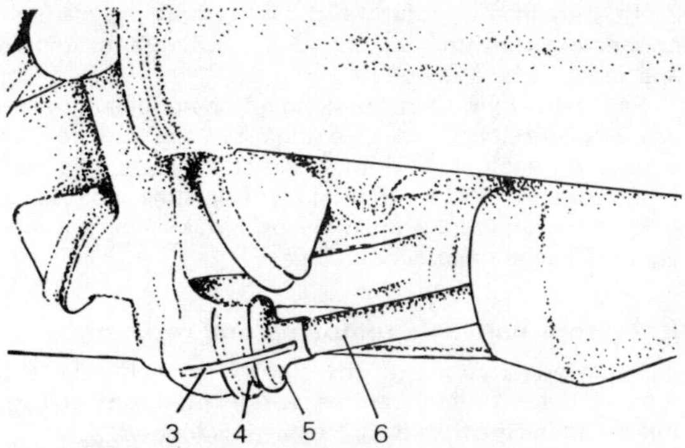

FIG 8:5 Rear suspension cylinder

Key to Fig 8:5 3 Connecting pin 4 Clip 5 Dust cover 6 Piston rod

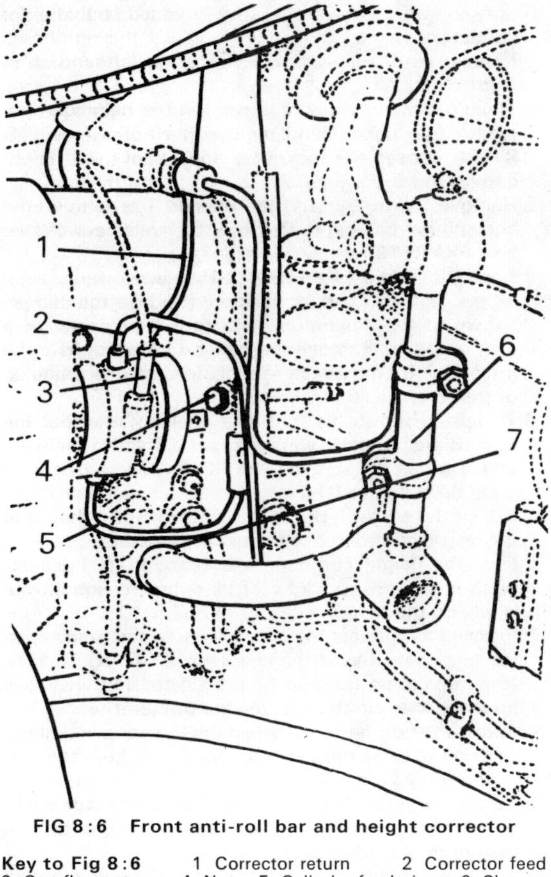

FIG 8:6 Front anti-roll bar and height corrector

Key to Fig 8:6 1 Corrector return 2 Corrector feed 3 Overflow return 4 Nut 5 Cylinder feed pipe 6 Sleeves 7 Bearing

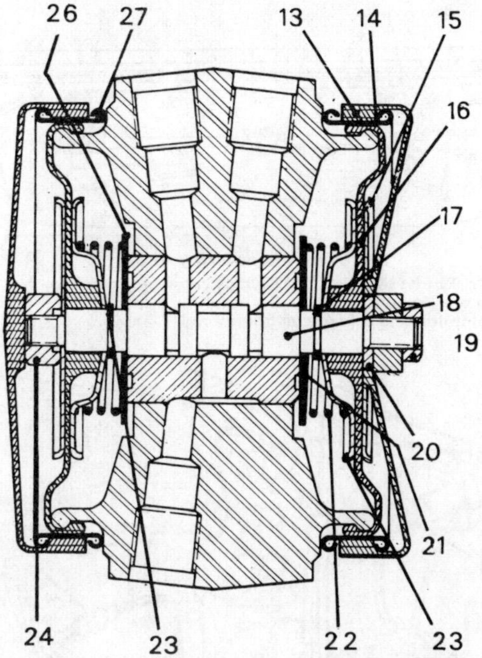

FIG 8:7 A sectional view of a height corrector

Key to Fig 8:7 13 Sealing cup 14 Metal retainers 15 Outer metal cups 16 Diaphragms 17 Circlip 18 Slide valve 19 Locknut 20 Washer 21 Disc valve 22 Springs 23 Inner metal cups 24 Nut 25 Circlip 26 Disc valve 27 Sealing cup

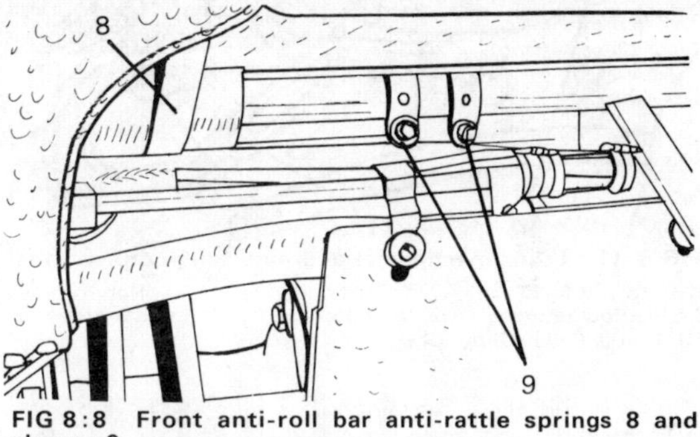

FIG 8:8 Front anti-roll bar anti-rattle springs 8 and clamps 9

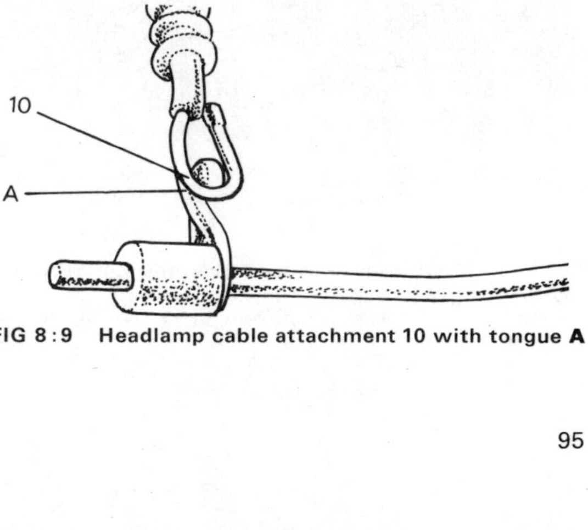

FIG 8:9 Headlamp cable attachment 10 with tongue A

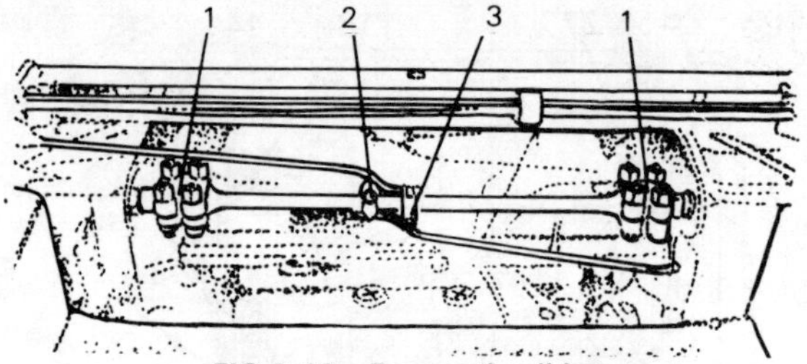

FIG 8:10 Rear anti-roll bar

Key to Fig 8:10 1 Clamps connecting anti-roll bar to wheel arm spindles 2 Clamp for headlamp control rod 3 Clamp for height corrector control rod

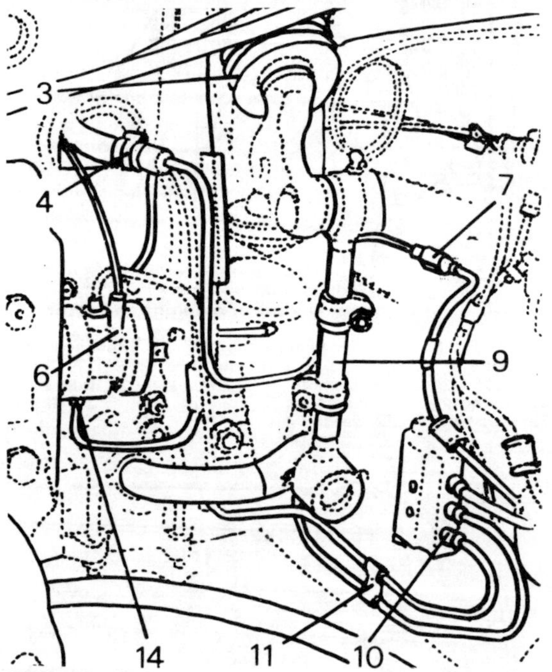

FIG 8:11 Front mechanical and hydraulic connections

Key to Fig 8:11 3 Dust cover 4 Return pipe 6 Overflow return 7 Union 9 Lefthand sleeve 10 Union 11 Clip 14 Union

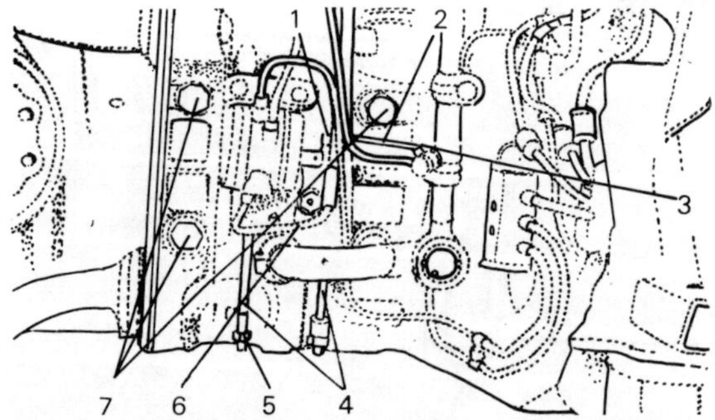

FIG 8:12 Front mechanical and hydraulic connections

Key to Fig 8:12 1 Retaining nut 2 Height control rod 3 Locknut 4 Clamps 5 Nuts 6 Anti-roll bar bearing 7 Retaining screws

2 of the headlamp control rod. Disconnect the clamps 1 connecting the anti-roll bar to the wheel-arm spindles and remove the anti-roll bar.

Refit by carrying out the removal operations in reverse order, distributing the clearance on the anti-roll bar equally on each side. Tighten the clamp nuts diagonally to a torque of 72 lb ft (10.5 kg m). Adjustment of the rear heights, if required, should be undertaken by a service agent with the necessary facilities.

8:4 Front half-axle removing and refitting

Initial preparations on the side of the half-axle to be removed are undertaken as for a front anti-roll bar described in **Section 8:3.** Proceed as follows:

1 Remove the drive shaft as described in **Chapter 7.**

2 On the anti-roll bar, loosen the two screws of the clips on the height control corrector and the headlamp beam control rod.

3 Referring to **FIG 8:11,** mark with paint the position of the sleeve 9, then loosen the clamp screws and remove the two sleeves. The lefthand sleeve has a lefthand thread at one end and a righthand thread at the other. The righthand sleeve has a righthand thread at both ends.

4 Disconnect the unions 14, 10 and 7, the overflow return 6 and the return pipe 4.

5 Loosen the screws 11 and remove the height corrector.

6 Remove the suspension cylinder as described in **Section 8:2.**

7 Place the manual height control in the high position, loosen the locknut and remove the nut 1 (see **FIG 8:12**). Loosen the locknut 3 and remove the height control rod 2.

8 Remove the nuts 5 and the clamps 4 to remove the anti-roll bar bearing 6. Remove the five screws 7 (see also **FIG 8:13**).

9 Bend the pipe 8 (see **FIG 8:14**) to allow withdrawal of the half-axle, then position the anti-roll bar as shown in the illustration, and turn it a quarter of a turn upwards. Remove the half-axle. Do not lose the thrust ball for the piston rod located in the housing 'a' of the lever.

10 To refit, offer up the half-axle, making sure that the dowels are correctly engaged in the holes in the front unit. Tighten the screws 7 in **FIG 8:12** to a torque of 50 to 65 lb ft (7 to 9 kg m).

11 Adjust the anti-roll bar (see **Section 8:3**), then refit the height control rod with nut and locknut.

12 Refit the height corrector and connect up the pipework in the reverse order of its removal. Tighten the screw on the securing clip 11 in **FIG 8:11.**

13 Proceed to connect the anti-roll bar to the suspension levers. Screw the lefthand sleeve 9 in **FIG 8:11** a few threads on the end of the suspension lever ball joint and then on the anti-roll bar ball joint.

14 Screw the righthand sleeve on the threaded end of the anti-roll bar ball joint until about 5 mm from the end of the thread.

15 Screw the lefthand sleeve up to the marks made when dismantling. If new parts have been fitted, obtain on the righthand side a dimension 'e' (see **FIG 8:15**) of 198 mm between the centre-lines of the ball joints on the anti-roll bar and on the lever.

16 Screw the righthand sleeve so that the number of threads engaged on the end of the lever ball joint is the same as that on the anti-roll bar ball joint.
17 Adjust the lefthand sleeve to obtain a dimension 'e' of 199 mm on this side, then tighten the screws in the clamps securing the right and lefthand sleeves. Obtain a check on the front heights (see **Section 8:3**).
18 Refit the suspension cylinder (see **Section 8:2**) and the drive shaft (see **Chapter 7**). Fit the front wheels, lower the car to the ground and refit the remaining items removed in the preparatory work in the reverse order of their dismantling. Adjust the cam for straight-line steering (see **Chapter 9**).

8:5 Rear half-axle removal and refitting

Raise the rear of the car on firm supports, remove the rear wing and the wheel and release the pressure in the system. Remove the upper and lower protection panels for the swivel union and, in the boot, the closing panel for the rear crossmember. Then proceed as follows:

1 Mark the angular position of the clamps on the anti-roll bar and disconnect the clamps for the height corrector and the headlamps (see **FIG 8:10**). Also disconnect the coupling clamps at each end of the anti-roll bar and free the bar.
2 Referring to **FIG 8:16**, clear the metal from the groove in the sidemember to release the ring nut 4 and remove the nut, for which a special spanner No. 1757.T is available.
3 Disconnect the feedpipe from the wheel cylinder, remove the bleed screw and raise the pipe clip. Disconnect the three-way union from the feedpipe and from the righthand brake pipe for the lefthand side. Loosen the locknut, remove the screw and free the swivel union.
4 In order to remove the righthand half-axle it is necessary to remove the rear wing, the wheel and the lefthand mud shield, also to remove the pipes from the retaining bushes in the sidemember in order to remove the pipe assembly.
5 Disconnect the piston rod as described in **Section 8:2.**
6 Remove the three nuts 7 fixing the bearing housing on the sidemember. Disengage the arm, if necessary by striking the end of the spindle with a mallet.
7 Drive out the housing fixing screws 8 only if they are damaged or worn and take care not to lose them inside the sidemember.
8 Clean the housing with petrol in order to remove the the thrust ball from the buffer support. Remove the half-axle.
9 When refitting, if removed hammer in position the screws 8 fixing the bearing housing in the sidemember.
10 Fit the arm in the sidemember and provisionally screw on the ring nut 4 (see **FIG 8:16**), the thin collar in contact with the sidemember.
11 Tighten the three shouldered nuts 7 fixing the bearing housing. Do not fit washers. Check that there is not less than .5 mm clearance between the arm and the metal bump stop on the chassis at J in **FIG 8:17.** Otherwise remove the front rubber buffer and file the stop.

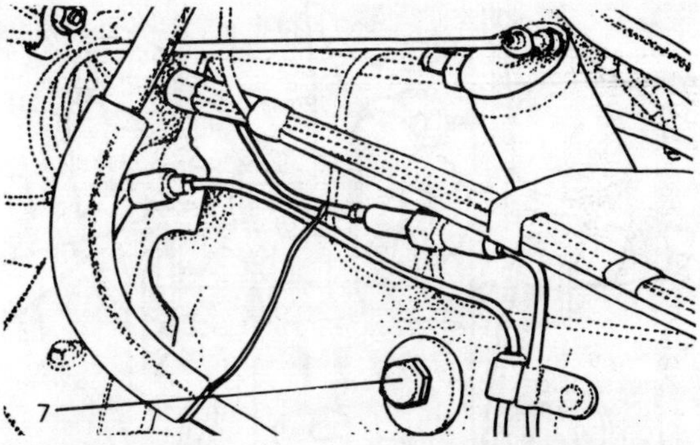

FIG 8:13 Removal of half-axle, showing the retaining screws 7

12 Finally tighten the ring nut 4 (see **FIG 8:16**). Knock over the metal of the nut at one point into the grooves in the sidemember.
13 Assemble the piston rod as described in **Section 8:2.** Before fitting the retaining clip, make sure that the piston rod is in good contact with the ball, so that when raising the arm, the piston rod will not slip out of the buffer support.
14 Fit the anti-roll bar, giving equal clearance on both sides and so as to line up the marks made when dismantling the corrector control rod. Tighten the flange screws to a torque of 36 lb ft (5 kg m).

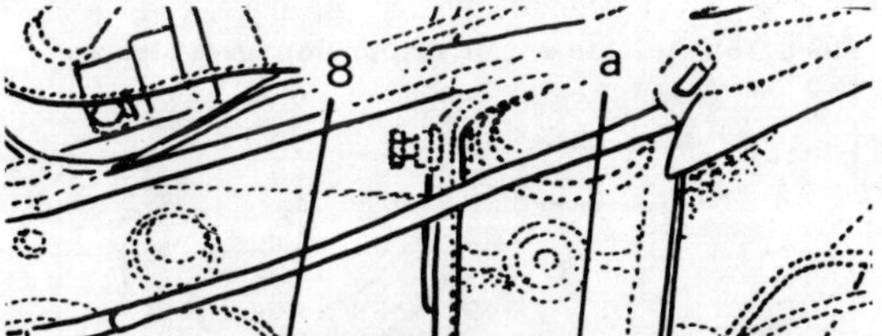

FIG 8:14 Removal of half-axle, showing the pipe 8 and the lever housing at 'a'

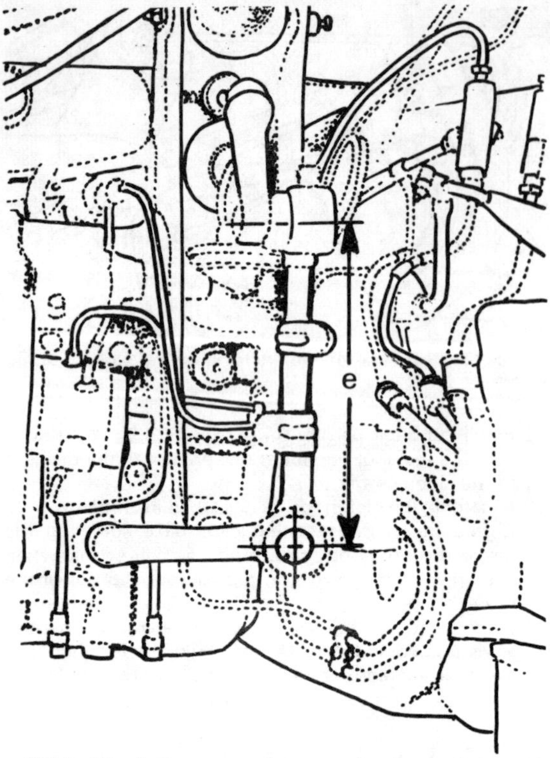

FIG 8:15 Adjustment of suspension lever sleeves

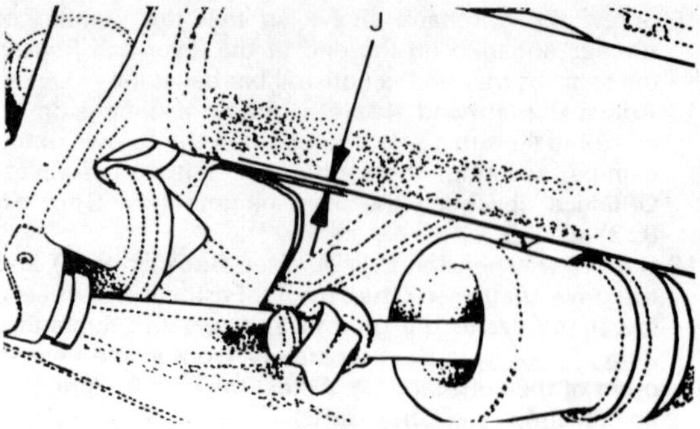

FIG 8:17 Wheel arm clearance J

15 Fit the corrector control rod clamp to the marks made when dismantling. If an anti-roll bar with a corrector control rod has been replaced, the heights should be pre-adjusted with the assistance of a service agent.
16 Fit the brake pipe in cars before February, 1969, by engaging the trunnion of the union in the bore of the arm spindle. Tighten moderately the locking screw and tighten the locknut. Make sure that the lever preventing rotation is in its housing. Connect the pipe to the wheel cylinder and fit the bleed screw. Align and connect the feedpipes for the brakes in the three-way union.
17 Put the systems under pressure by running the engine, refit the items removed during the preliminary operations and lower the car to the ground. Finally bleed the brake system as described in **Chapter 10**.

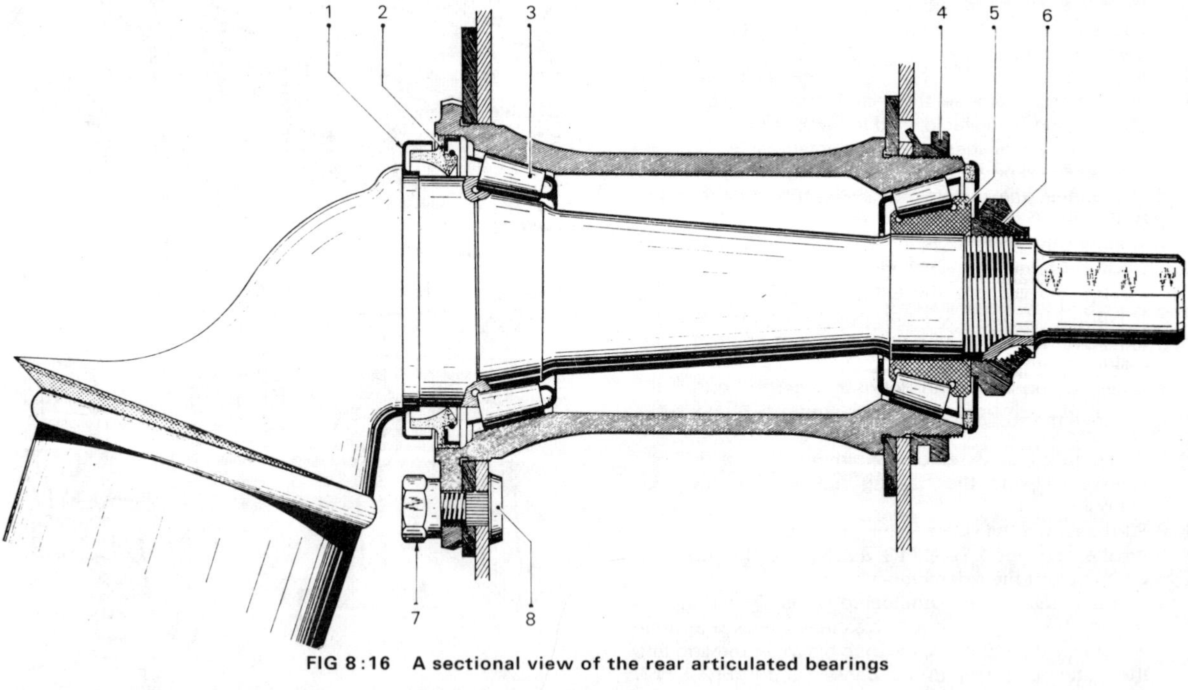

FIG 8:16 A sectional view of the rear articulated bearings

Key to Fig 8:16 1 Seal protector 2 Seal 3 Taper roller bearing 4 Ring nut 5 Taper roller bearing 6 Nut with dished cover 7 Bearing housing nut 8 Bearing housing screws

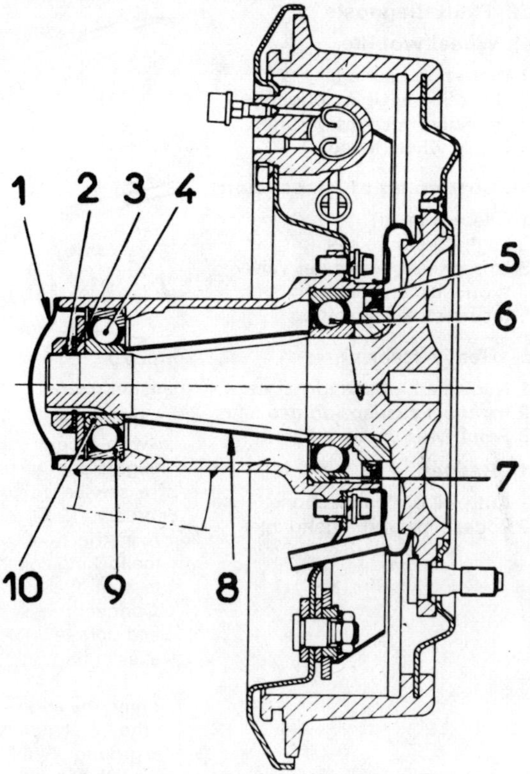

FIG 8:18 A sectional view of a rear stub axle

Key to Fig 8:18 1 Hub sealing cap 2 Nut 3 Thrust washer 4 Inner bearing 5 Seal 6 Outer bearing 7 Outer race of outer bearing 8 Spacer 9 Outer race of inner bearing 10 Outer cage of inner bearing

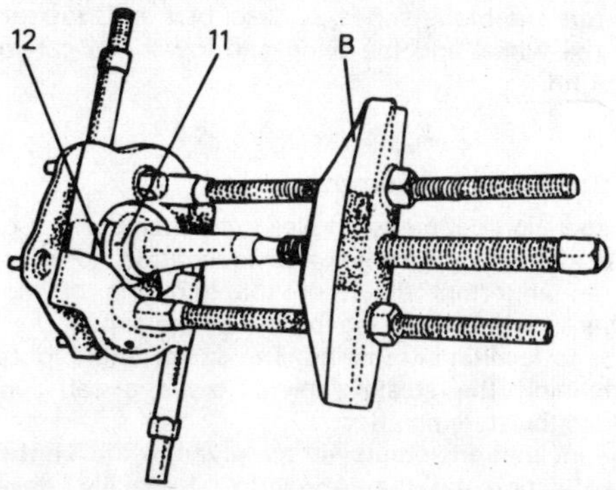

FIG 8:19 Removing the inner cap 11 of the outer bearing and the stop 12 with the Wilmonda universal extractor B

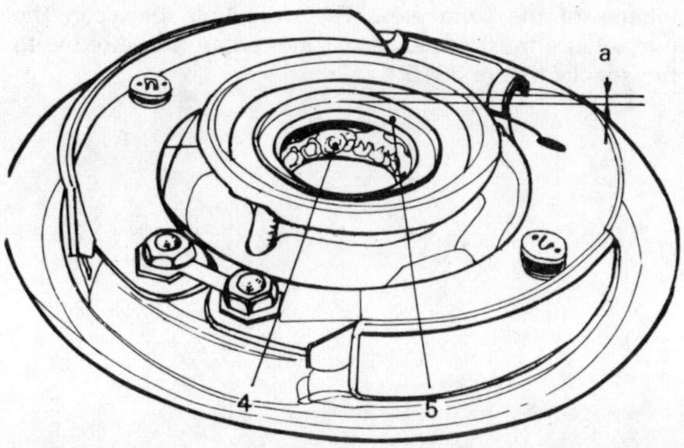

FIG 8:20 Fitting the outer bearing 4 and the sealing joint 5 at a distance 'a' of 4.5 mm from the outer face of the axle arm

8:6 Rear wheel stub axle removal, servicing and refitting

Raise the rear of the car on firm supports and remove the wing and the wheel. To remove and refit the stub axle, operations are as follows:

1 Referring to **FIG 8:18,** remove the hub sealing cap 1. Lock the brake drum by tightening the brake shoe adjusting cams. Remove the nut 2, the lockplate and the thrust washer 3.

2 Unscrew the brake adjusting cams. Unscrew the brake drum fixing screws and remove the drum after having marked its position.

3 Remove the stub axle, for which service agents use an extractor No. 2018.T.

4 Remove (a) the balls and cage 4 from the inner bearing, (b) the outer cage 10 of the inner bearing, (c) the spacer 8, (d) the seal 5 and (e) the balls and cage 6 of the outer bearing.

5 Remove the outer race 7 of the outer bearing with the aid of an extractor 2019.T, also the outer race 9 of the inner bearing using a tube of 53.5 mm outside diameter.

6 To remove the inner cup of the outer bearing, use a 'Wilmonda' universal extractor as shown in **FIG 8:19.**

7 When reassembling, fit the outer race of the inner bearing and the outer race of the outer bearing with the aid of the screw MR.4114. If the arm, the spacer or one or both bearings are to be renewed, the correct length of the adjusting spacer has to be determined. To do this a special fixture 2021.T in association with a dial gauge and a surface plate is employed, for which the assistance of a service agent should be obtained.

8 Referring to **FIG 8:20,** grease the balls and cage 4 of the outer bearing and fit it in position. Fit the sealing joint 5 at a distance 'a' of 4.5 mm from the outer face of the axle arm, using a mandrel MR.3676.170.

9 Fit the inner race of the outer bearing in a press, using a piece of tube of 40 mm inside diameter and length 250 mm.

10 Offer up the stub axle on the axle arm. Insert 50 g of special bearing grease in the housing and locate the spacer 8 (see **FIG 8:18**) and the outer bearing washer.

11 Fit the cage and balls 4 previously greased, the inner race, the thrust washer 3 with the recessed portion against the bearing, the lockwasher and the nut 2. Tighten the latter to a torque of 72 lb ft (10 kg m). Turn over the lockwasher tabs. Fit the sealing cap 1 for grease filling.

12 Centre the brake shoes as described in **Chapter 10**, fit the wheel and the wing and lower the car to the ground.

8:7 Suspension geometry

Suspension geometry applies to the camber and castor angles and also the swivel hub inclination, all of which have an important effect on the handling of the car. Camber is an outward inclination of the top of the front wheels to facilitate cornering. The castor angle, obtained by inclining the steering pivot, gives a self-centring action to the steering effort.

The inclinations employed are given in the **Technical Data** Section of the Appendix. Specially designed gauges are available to check the camber and castor angles if necessary, for which the assistance of a well-equipped service agent should be obtained. Camber is not adjustable but can be distributed between the two wheels of the front axle. The difference between the two wheels must not exceed 1 mm when measured with the special fixture 2315.T.

8:8 Fault diagnosis

(a) Wheel wobble

1 Worn hub bearings
2 Defective flexible couplings
3 Defective suspension units
4 Loose wheel fixings

(b) Bottoming of suspension

1 Check 3 in (a)
2 Faulty pressure system
3 Unserviceable damper valves
4 Worn suspension buffers
5 Incorrect buffer setting

(c) Heavy steering

1 Neglected lubrication of front suspension pivots
2 Incorrect suspension geometry
3 Front tyres under-inflated

(d) Rattles

1 Anti-roll bar connections loose
2 Loose pipework anchorages

CHAPTER 9

THE STEERING GAR

9:1 Operating principles

The steering gear consists of a rack and pinion unit with two separate track rods, one for each front wheel. Under manual operation (see **FIG 9:1**) a pinion at the bottom of the steering column moves the rack from side to side. Hydraulic operation (see **FIG 9:2**) is undertaken through two main units, a piston/cylinder assembly with a double-acting piston connected to the rack and control valves with a rotating union.

On each side of the piston slide valves controlled by hydraulic pressure in a valve block are connected to the steering by a coupling fork and move when the steering wheel is turned. The rotating union maintains the hydraulic connections. The effect is that one slide valve moves down in relation to its sleeve in the valve block and the other rises. The valve which moves down connects high pressure to one side of the piston and the valve which rises allows the fluid on the other side of the piston to return to the reservoir. A residual pressure is maintained on either side of the piston when the steering is at rest. Any movement of the steering wheel, therefore, causes an immediate response of the rack, with rising pressure on one side of the piston and falling pressure on the other side.

The steering wheel and the steering column are of integral construction, the single spoke of the wheel being formed by bending over an extension of the column into the wheel rim and thus improving safety and visibility.

9:2 Steering adjustments

Adjustments which may be made on the steering are concerned with (a) the lateral position, (b) the angular position, (c) the alignment, (d) the straight-ahead position, (e) the steering lock and (f) the cross-over pressure. For these operations, it is usually necessary to raise the front of the car, fit firm supports and remove the wing or wings, the battery, tray and support, as required for the work to be undertaken.

To adjust the lateral position, loosen the bearing cap screws and move the steering in its bearings to obtain a dimension of 122.5 ± 2.5 mm between the centre line of the lower relay lever and the centre line of the rack pressure pad as at 'g' in **FIG 9:3.** Fit the bearing cap screws without tightening and adjust the angular position by fitting the fixture No. 1955.T (see **FIG 9:4**). Rotate the steering assembly in its clamps to bring the control pinion 2 into contact with the central gauge pin A of the fixture. Tighten the bearing cap screws and remove the fixture.

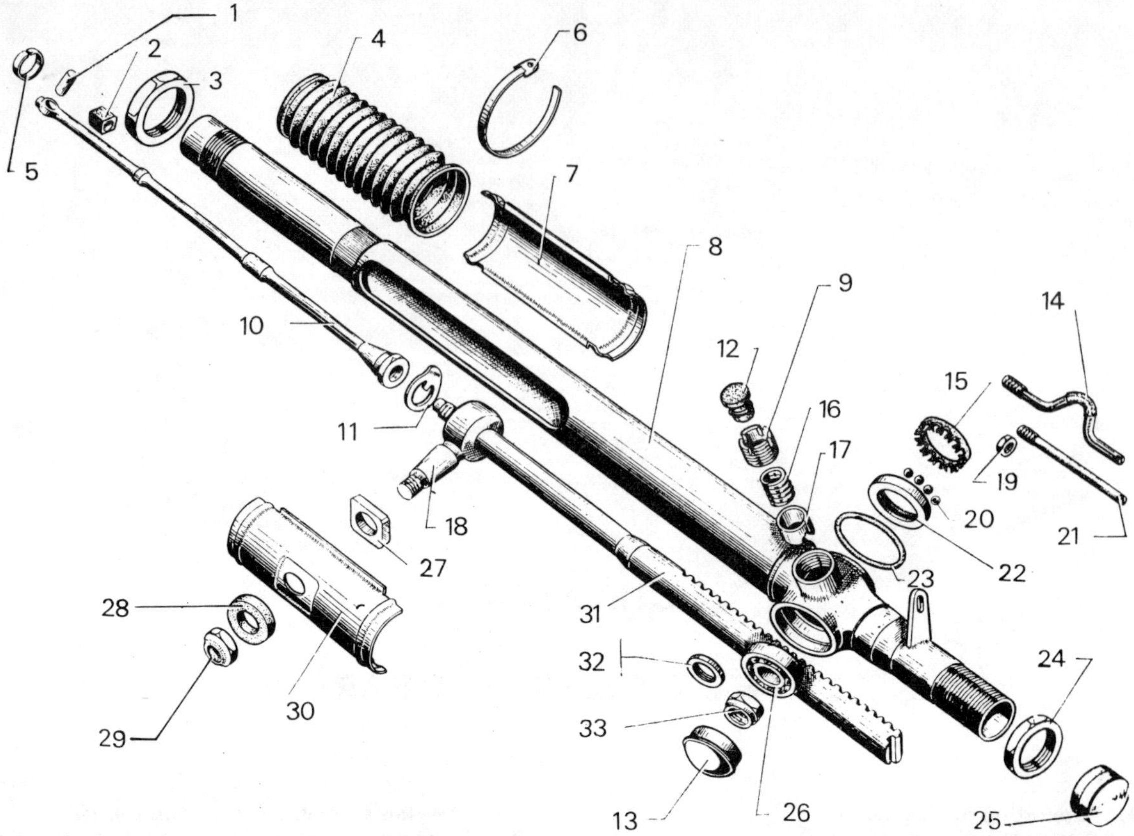

FIG 9:1 An exploded view of a manual steering assembly

Key to Fig 9:1 1 Connecting pin 2 Anti-rattle rubber bush 3 Locknut 4 Rack sealing sheath 5 Split ring locking connecting pin 6 Clip 7 Lower slide 8 Rack housing 9 Nut for plunger guide 10 Rack control rod 11 Lockwasher 12 Rubber dust seal 13 Cap 14 Stop rod 15 Ball cage 16 Spring 17 Plunger guide 18 Pivot ballpin 19 Nut 20 Balls 21 Rod securing rotating union 22 Ballbearing outer cage 23 Rubber sealing joint 24 Thrust cap locking nut 25 Adjustable thrust cap 26 Ballbearing 27 Guide block 28 Rubber sealing ring 29 Nut for ballpin 30 Upper slide 31 Steering rack 32 Adjusting washer 33 Rack pinion nut

For the adjustment of the alignment the wheels should toe-in at the front from 1 to 3 mm or 2 to 4 mm since September, 1966. This can be precisely determined by using special proprietary equipment or somewhat less accurately by ordinary measurement, when it is necessary to have the car at its normal height and on level ground with both front tyres inflated to the same pressure. With the wheels in the straightahead position, measure the distance between the rims at wheel centre height at the front. Mark these two points of measurement and then roll the car forward for exactly half a revolution of the wheels, so that the marks finish up at the rear. Measure again between the marked points. The difference between the measurements is the amount of toe-in. The alignment is set by altering the length of the righthand track rod. Referring to **FIG 9:5,** loosen the clamps 11 and turn the sleeve 12, on which a quarter of a turn corresponds to an alignment alteration of approximately 1 mm. Retighten the clamps to a torque of 7 lb ft (1 kg m) and recheck the adjustment in the manner described. Position the clamps so that the locking screws are opposite the slots in the sleeve (see **FIG 9:11**) and ensure that the ball joint of the track rod is not strained. Turn the steering fully each way to see that the clamp screws are clear of the front crossmember or radiator intake cowl.

Adjustment of the position of the steering in which the car runs in a straight line can only be carried out on the road. Travel on a straight flat road and hold the steering wheel to follow a straight line. Stop the car and mark the rim of the steering wheel with chalk in line with a similar mark on the dashboard. Adjust the position of the centring cam (see 2 in **FIG 9:9**) if required. Turn the steering wheel so that the marks made previously correspond. Loosen the securing clamp 3 and turn this until the roller is in the hollow of the cam. Tighten the clamp to a torque of 3 lb ft (.4 kg m). The roller should be parallel to the cam and in the centre of it to within approximately 2 mm. Again drive along the road and check that the car runs in a straight line.

The steering lock should be set at $42 \pm ^{0}_{1}$ deg. in order to avoid undue strain on the driveshafts. Place the steering

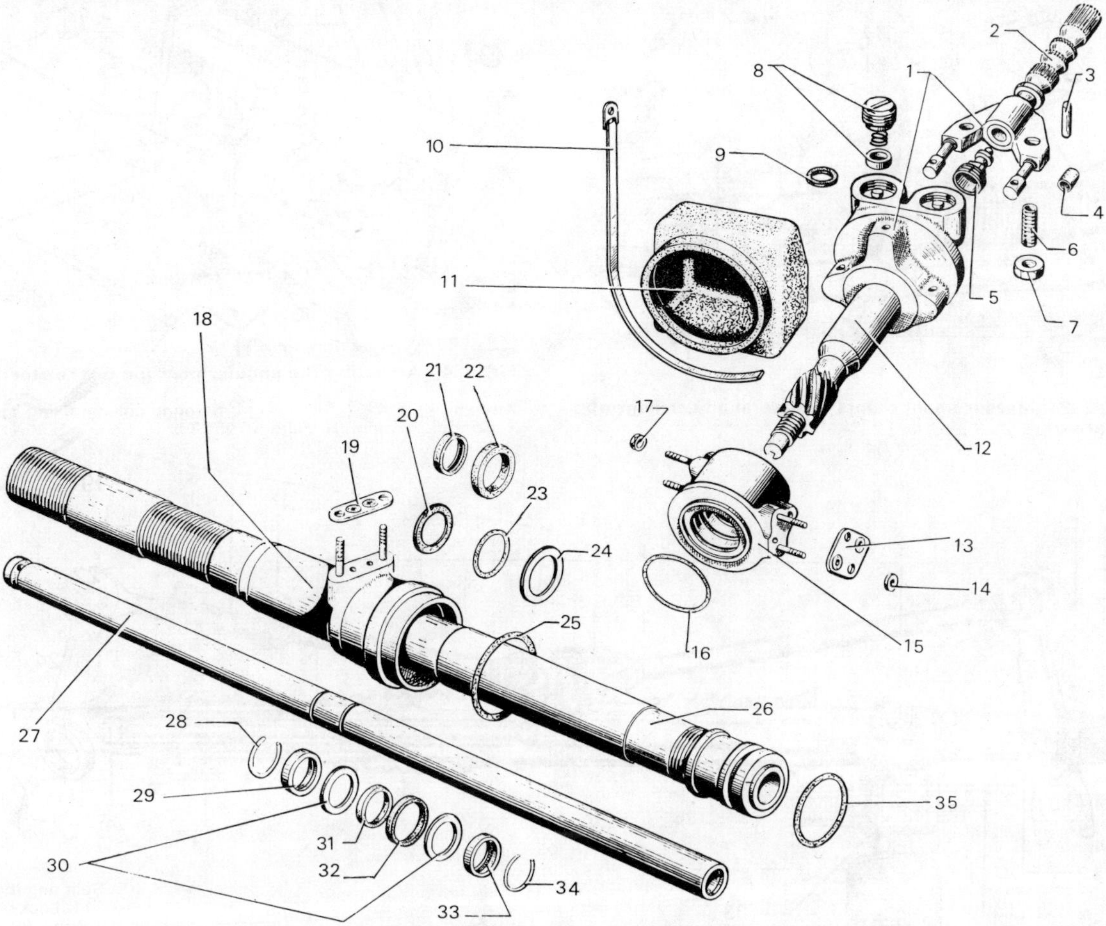

FIG 9:2 An exploded view of the steering hydraulic components

Key to Fig 9:2 1 Pinion assembly, complete with rotating union and coupling fork 2 Coupling fork for pinion 3 Needle operating slide valve 4 Rubber bush 5 Pinion spherical end piece 6 Adjusting screw for rotating union slide valve 7 Nut 8 Cap for dashpot, spring and thrust washer for valve 9 Sealing ring 10 Cover clip 11 Rubber cover 12 Pinion 13 Seal plate 14 Ring seal 15 Rotating union 16 Ring seal 17 Nut 18 Control for rack, with casing end piece, cylinder and piston 19 Seal plate 20 Washer 21 Joint for piston rod 22 Joint for piston rod 23 Ring seal 24 Sealing washer 25 Ring seal 26 Control cylinder for rack 27 Control rod for piston 28 Circlip 29 Shouldered washer 30 Washer 31 Ring seal 32 Joint 33 Shouldered washer 34 Circlip 35 Ring seal

wheel as for running in a straight line and turn the wheel exactly $1\frac{1}{2}$ turns towards the left. Adjust the cap 9 in **FIG 9:5** if necessary and tighten the locknut 10. Carry out the same operation to the right with exactly $1\frac{1}{2}$ turns of the wheel. Adjust the cap 18 and tighten the locknut. When the wheels are at maximum lock there must remain a clearance of 10 mm between the tyre and the relay shields. If necessary reduce the lock angle.

Adjustment of the cross-over pressure involves removing the pipe assembly and connecting it to two pressure gauges on a test bench (see **FIG 1:3, Chapter 1**) for which the assistance of a service agent should be obtained Briefly, the operation is to turn the steering wheel to the right or left to obtain a pressure difference of about 850 lb/sq inch (60 kg/sq cm), then reversing the wheel direction and observing the pressure when the two gauges show the same reading, which should be 710 ± 70 lb/sq inch (50 ± 5 kg/sq cm). Adjustment is made on one of the adjusting screws (see 8 in **FIG 9:2**) in the pressure distributor.

The need for adjustment of the cross-over pressure may arise in the case of a knocking in the steering, if the steering flickers in the central position or if the steering is abnormally harsh in operation or stiff on the locks. In the first instance, the knocking can equally be caused by excessive clearance on the joint between the piston washers, a clearance on the shackle pin 32 (see **FIG 9:6**), an excessive clearance on the rack support plunger 6, or a harsh spot on the slide valves or dashpots. In these cases it is necessary to overhaul the steering.

If the steering flickers in the central position the plug and cup assemblies 8 in **FIG 9:2** should also be checked

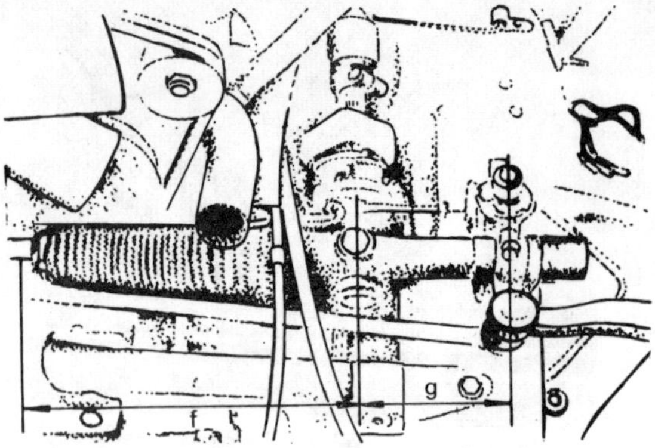

FIG 9:3 **Measurement points for lateral adjustment of steering**

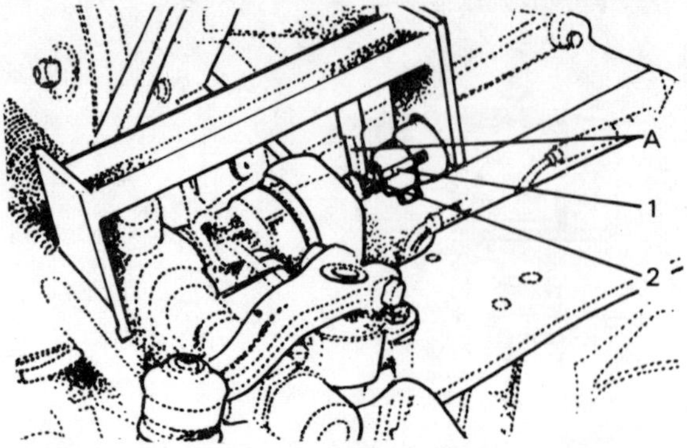

FIG 9:4 **Adjusting the angular position of the steering**

Key to Fig 9:4 1 Steering column fixing screw 2 Control pinion **A** Fixture 1955.T

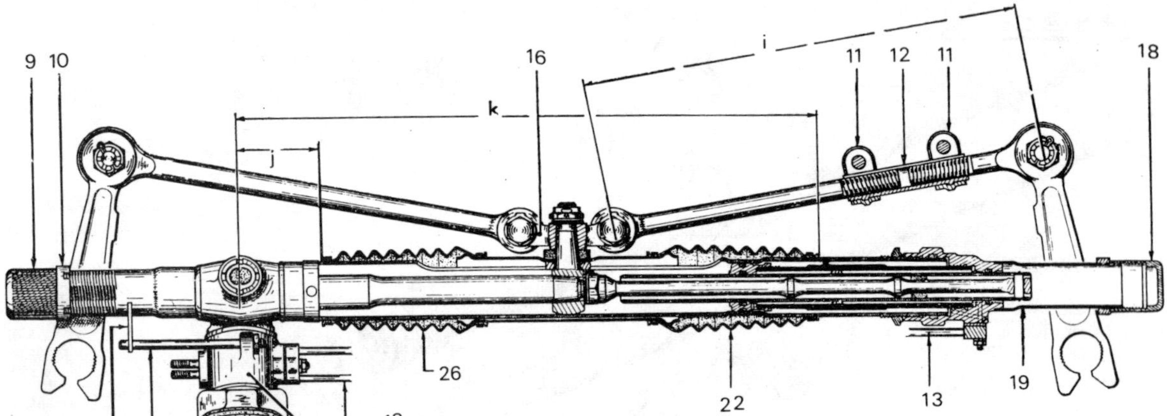

FIG 9:5 **Steering linkage and pressure distributor**

Key to Fig 9:5 3 Stop screw 9 Cap 10 Locknuts 11 Collars 12 Sleeve 13 Control pipe assembly 14 Nut 15 Retaining spring 16 Central shackle 17 Ballpin 18 Cap 22 Dust cover 23 Steel dust cover 26 Dust cover 27 Rack support plunger and pressure pad 28 Steel cap 29 Nut 30 Bearing balls 31 Rear upper bearing 32 Front lower bearing 33 Rotating union 34 Pins 35 Spring 36 Silent blocks 37 Rubber sealing joint 38 Stop rod on rotating union 39 Support 41 Rubber sealing washer 68 Nut **j** 56 ± 2.5 mm **k** 574 ± 2.5 mm **i** 402 mm

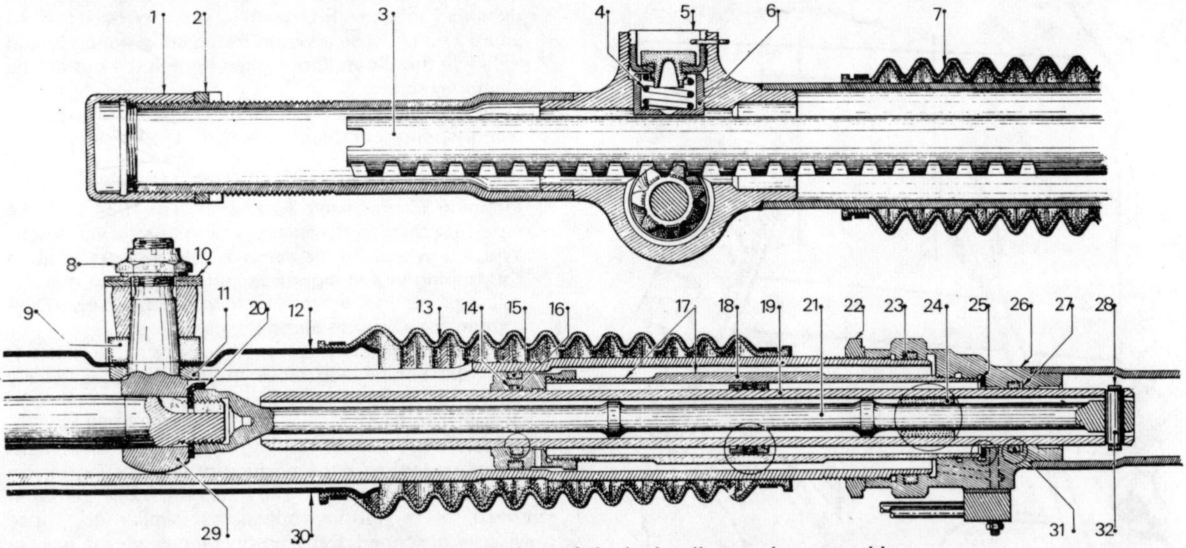

FIG 9:6 A sectional view of the hydraulic steering assembly

Key to Fig 9:6 1 Cap 2 Locknuts 3 Rack 4 Spring 5 Nut 6 Pressure pad 7 Dust cover 8 Nut 9 Rubber sealing washer 10 Spring 11 Ball guide 12 Steel tube 13 Dust cover 14 Rilsan washer 15 Seal 16 Seal 17 Engraving 18 Cylinder 19 Piston 20 Locking plate 21 Control rod 22 Locknut 23 Seal 24 Anti-rattle bush 25 Fibre joint 26 Steering housing end piece 27 Rilsan washer 28 Circlip 29 Ballpin 30 Steel cover tube 31 Seal 32 Connecting pin

after releasing the pressure and disengaging the dust cover from the rotating union (see 15 in **FIG 9:2**) to reach the plugs. Check for ease of operation and absence of any burrs. Note that each cup is paired with its plug and the parts must not be mixed. For harsh operation, the alignment and the lateral and angular positions of the steering must also be checked, as already described.

If the steering shows signs of leakage it may be either a leakage causing a noise resembling an escape of gas when turning the steering a few degrees without moving the wheels or a leak causing the inflation of the rubber dust covers, leading to exterior leakage of fluid, when it is necessary to overhaul the steering assembly. In the first instance disconnect the pipe assembly controlling the rack from the steering end housing and close the openings with seal plates. If the leak persists it comes from the rotating union, which must be renewed or repaired. If the leak disappears, it came from the rack piston and cylinder assembly, which must similarly be renewed or repaired.

Note that before doing any work on the hydraulic control of the steering assembly it should be ensured that the ball joints of the steering or track rods are in good condition. Using a suitable extractor, disconnect the ballpin on the pivot lever and ensure that the ballpins on the pivot lever and relay spindle (see **FIG 9:11**) move without binding and without tight spots even at the limits of their movement.

9:3 Steering wheel removal and refitting

Operations to remove a steering wheel assembly are commenced by releasing the pressure in the suspension units and removing the front suspension sphere. Fit a plug on the cylinder and disconnect the battery.

If the same steering wheel is to be refitted, mark (with a scriber), the position of the steering centralizing cam 2 in **FIG 9:7** in relation to the steering column. Mark also with a spot of paint the position of the slot on the steering pinion splines. Loosen the securing screw on the cam and remove the cam towards the front.

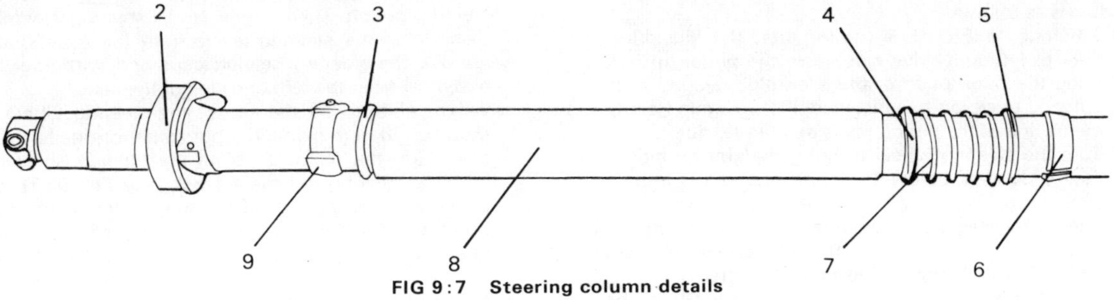

FIG 9:7 Steering column details

Key to Fig 9:7 2 Cam 3, 4, 5 Cups 6 Cone 7 Spring 8 Tube 9 Clamp

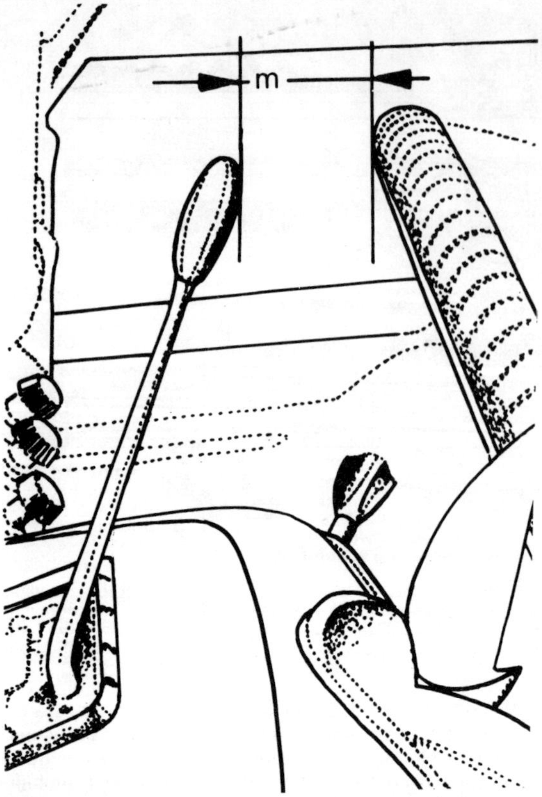

FIG 9:8 Correct position of gearlever after steering pinion adjustment, with a dimension 'm' of about 40 to 60 mm

Then loosen the screw in the clamp 9 (see **FIG 9:7**) using the spanner 1994.T shown in **FIG 9:9** and allow the spring 7 to extend. Remove the clamp screw securing the steering column to the steering pinion and disengage the column.

By pulling on the column from inside the vehicle free the cam 2, the clamp 9, the cup 3, the tube 8, the cup 4, the spring 7, the cup 5 and the cone 6. Remove the steering wheel via the inside of the vehicle.

Refitting is undertaken by following the removal operations in reverse order. Engage the steering wheel on the rack pinion according to the marks made when dismantling.

If a new steering wheel assembly is to be fitted, procedure is as follows:

1 Referring to **FIG 9:3** (noting that the illustrations refer to lefthand drive cars) turn the pinion in order bring the outer bush of the silentbloc bearing in the lefthand track rod to a distance 'f' of 275 mm from the centre line of the pinion pressure plunger nut.
2 Turn the steering wheel to bring the arm to approximately 30 deg. below the horizontal at the lefthand side.
3 Engage the steering pinion in the splines in the steering column and fit the screw 9. Only screws No. DM. 441.100 with smooth shanks must be fitted.
4 Move the gearlever to the second gear position, then push slightly on the steering wheel, when the distance 'm' (see **FIG 9:8**) should lie between 40 and 60 mm. Chose a slot in the steering pinion which will give these conditions, then tighten the nut on the clamping screw.
5 With the aid of an assistant, compress the spring using spring compressor A No. 1991.T shown in **FIG 9:9.**
6 When the spring coils are touching tighten the retaining clamp using spanner B No. 1994.T. Make sure that there is no axial play in the steering wheel.
7 With the wheels of the car in an approximate position for running in a straight line, turn the cam so that the roller is resting in the hollow of the cam. Then tighten the screw securing the cam.
8 Fit the suspension sphere, reconnect the battery, start the engine and close the bleed screw. Finally adjust the straight line steering position as described in **Section 9:2.**

In cars with manual steering, remove the instrument panel cover and mark the position of the steering pinion as previously described. The retaining collar is then removed, with further operations similar to those previously described. Refitting operations are the reverse of those used in removal, noting that the spring must be fully compressed (see Operation 5) when tightening the screw of the collar.

9:4 Steering assembly removal and refitting

To remove and refit a steering rack assembly as a unit, operations are as follows:

1 Remove the spare wheel, the spare wheel support and the front wing, also the battery and battery tray if necessary. The battery has been mounted on the righthand side of the car since 1967. Release the pressure and free the reservoir bracket assembly as much as possible.
2 Disconnect the steering column tube 1 (see **FIG 9:10**) from the steering pinion and the pipe assembly from the steering pinion housing 2. Free the sealing plate and fit a closing plate on the pipe assembly flange to prevent draining the reservoir. Disconnect the steering levers 3 from the steering relay spindles.
3 Remove the steering clamp caps 4 and the steering rack assembly from the steering column. Withdraw the steering rack from the side of the car.
4 In the case of manual steering arrangements, the battery, tray and instrument panel cover are removed. Further procedure is to slacken the screw of the collar, in this instance above the spring, and disconnect the steering pinion. Then to release the steering assembly disconnect the steering levers from the relay shafts, remove the steering bearing caps and withdraw the assembly from the lefthand side of the car.
5 When refitting, set the arm of the steering wheel so that it is 30 deg. below the horizontal on the lefthand side. Turn the pinion to bring the outer bush of the lefthand steering rod silent block (see **FIG 9:3**) to a distance 'f' of 275 mm from the centre of the rack pressure pad. A difference of more than 1 mm in this dimension will give excessive play on the steering wheel.
6 Offer up the assembly from the side of the car and engage the pinion into the splines of the steering

column. Fit the steering into its bearings. Adjust the lateral position, in order to obtain a distance 'g' of 122.5 ± 2.5 mm, between the centre line of the lower lefthand relay lever and the centre of the rack pressure pad as shown in **FIG 9:3.** Fit the bearing caps and the screws without tightening, inserting spring washers. Fit the screw 1 (DM.441.100) coupling the steering column to the pinion (see **FIG 9:4**) and tighten the nut and a spring washer. Make sure that the screw is correctly positioned in the groove of the pinion. The dimensions stated in this and the preceding Operation also apply when refitting a manual steering assembly in the reverse manner of its removal as described in Operation 4.

7 Adjust the angular position of the steering (see **Section 9:2**).

8 Fit the fixture No. 1955.T, then turn the steering assembly in its bearings in order to bring the control pinion 2 into contact with the gauge pin 'A' of the fixture. Tighten the fixing screws of the bearing caps and remove the fixture.

9 Connect the steering levers to the relay shafts with the nuts towards the outside. Tighten the nuts to a torque of 18 lb ft (2.5 kg m).

10 Connect the feed pipe assembly to the pinion housing. Fit the seal plates, so that the holes for the fluid correspond to those on the union plate. Tighten the nuts and spring washers.

11 Refit the items removed when commencing operations. Refill or top up the reservoir, start the engine, put the systems under pressure and check for leaks. Adjust the alignment, the straight-ahead position and the steering lock as described in **Section 9:2.**

A rack hydraulic control can be removed without removing the steering as follows:

1 Raise the front of the car on firm supports and remove the front righthand wing and wheel. Release the pressure.

2 Disconnect the steering pipe assembly flange from the steering housing. Place a cloth under the flange to avoid spilling fluid on the brake unit. Drain the steering system by turning the steering on full lock on both sides.

3 Remove the protection shield from the righthand steering relay housing. Unscrew the locknut of the righthand steering lock cap and remove the cap.

4 Turn the steering fully to the left. Referring to **FIG 9:6,** remove the circlip 28. Remove the connecting pin holding the piston to the rack control rod, for which service agents use an extractor No. 1969.T. Remove the righthand bearing cap.

5 Unscrew the locknut 22 of the steering casing piece and hold the steering in a straight line.

6 Unscrew the rack control assembly and remove by pulling towards the front of the car within the limit permitted by the steering column.

7 When refitting, make sure that the piston-cylinder assembly and the bore of the casing are well cleaned, also that the seals 15 and 23 are in position on the cylinder end piece and in the casing end piece. Dip the parts in hydraulic fluid before assembly.

8 Engage the rack control in the steering tube by pulling the steering towatds the front, within the limits permitted. Screw up the rack control assembly until

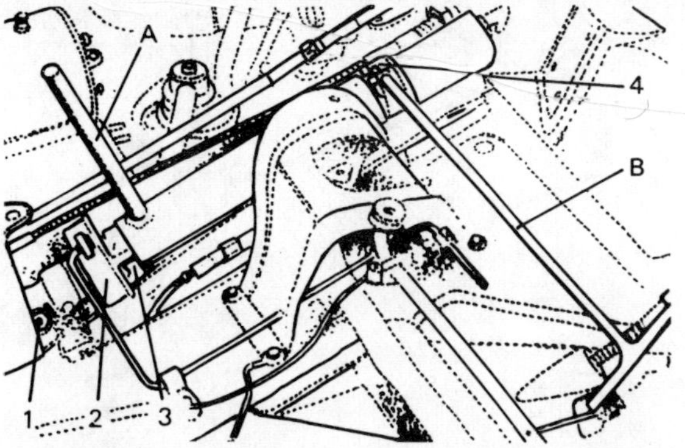

FIG 9:9 Centralizing cam and spring compressor

Key to Fig 9:9 1 Coupling screw 2 Cam 3 Securing screw 4 Clamp **A** Compressor tool No. 1991.T **B** Spanner No. 1994.T

the pipe assembly flange is in position, without using force. Fit the righthand bearing cap and tighten the fixing screws and spring washers.

9 Hold the steering housing end piece 26 and tighten the locknut 22. Connect the control pipe assembly flange, inserting a seal plate. Tighten the nuts and spring washers.

10 Turn the steering so that the hole in the control rod 21 is in line with the holes at the end of the piston 19. Align the two parts with a conical drift. Locate the connecting pin 32 in position and fit the circlip 28.

11 Refit the items removed when commencing operations, lower the car to the ground, start the engine, put the systems under pressure and check the unions for leakage.

Complete dismantling, overhaul and reassembly of the steering mechanism requires not only special tools, equipment and fixtures but also precise measurement methods and careful selection of seals and washers for correct adjustment on reassembly. Work of this nature comes within the province of an experienced service agent with the necessary facilities.

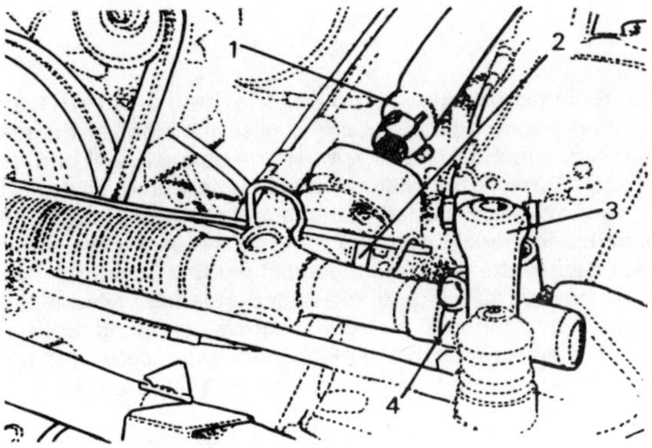

FIG 9:10 Steering rack assembly

Key to Fig 9:10 1 Steering column tube 2 Pinion housing 3 Steering lever 4 Steering clamp cap

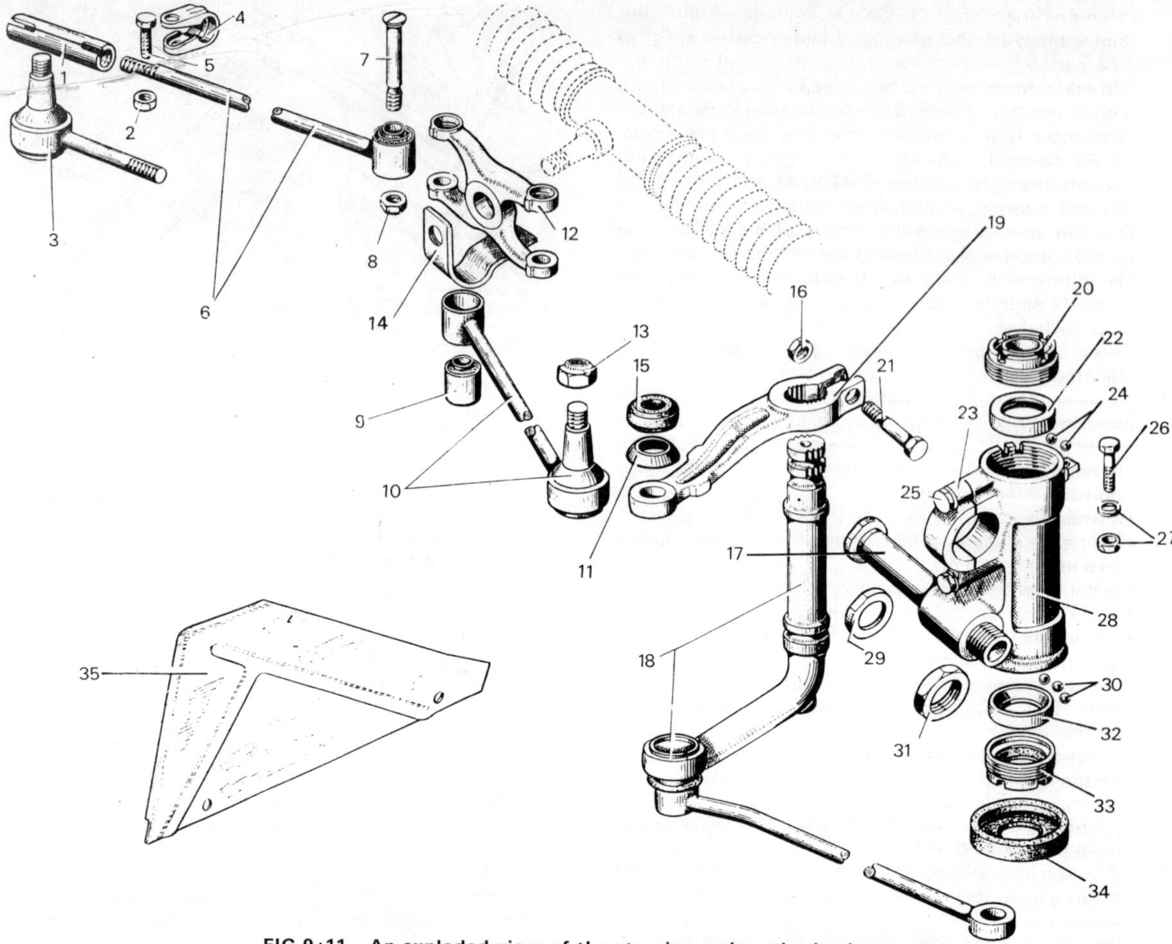

FIG 9:11 An exploded view of the steering rods and relay levers

Key to Fig 9:11 1 Adjusting sleeve on steering rod 2 Nut 3 Endpiece with ballpin 4 Clamp for adjusting sleeve 5 Screw 6 Steering rod 7 Bolt for steering rod shackle 8 Nut 9 Flexible bush 10 Steering rod and ballpin 11 Sealing cup 12 Shackle for steering rods 13 Ballpin nut 14 Spring, retaining rack ballpin 15 Rubber washer 16 Nut 17 Bolt securing housing 18 Relay lower lever with tie-rod 19 Relay upper lever 20 Nut, top of relay housing 21 Screw 22 Outer bearing cup 23 Cap 24 Balls 25 Cap screw 26 Screw 27 Adjusting washer and nut 28 Relay housing 29 Washer 30 Balls 31 Nut 32 Outer bearing cup 33 Nut, relay housing 34 Protective cap 35 Shield

9:5 Steering relay removal, overhaul and refitting

Preliminary operations are to raise the front of the car on firm supports and to remove the spare wheel and its support, the front wing and the battery and its tray if necessary. In cars fitted with manual steering remove the instrument panel cover and turn the steering wheel so as to unscrew the collar mentioned in the first Operation 4 in **Section 9:4**. For power-assisted steering, release the pressure, drain the reservoir, remove its fixing collars, the battery support, the bonnet lock control cable and the relay housing mud shield (see **FIG 9:11**). Then proceed as follows:

1 Disconnect the lower relay lever from the outer steering track rod, for which the extractor No. 3505.T shown in **FIG 9:12** is available, also the upper steering lever from the relay spindle.

2 Mark the position of the steering in the relay bearings with paint. Remove the bearing caps and lower the steering assembly and column assembly slowly, in order to avoid damage to the steering wheel assembly.

3 Referring to **FIG 9:11**, remove the screw 26 fixing the relay assembly on the sidemember. Remove the nut from the relay fixing spindle 17 and disengage the relay assembly and steering rod. Keep carefully the relay assembly adjusting washer 27.

4 Disengage the rubber bush 34. Remove the retaining metal to disengage the lower nut 33. Note that in later models items 33 and 34 have been replaced by an assembly of a metal cup, sealing joint, circlip and lower bearing cup. Continue by removing the lower lever 18, the steering rod assembly and the lower bearing race 32. Take care of the ballbearings.

5 Remove the retaining metal to disengage the upper nut 20 and remove the upper bearing race 22. Clean the parts.

6 To reassemble, refit the upper bearing race 22 and the upper nut 20 until the upper face is about 1 mm from the upper face of the relay housing. Insert about $\frac{3}{4}$ oz of EP grease into the housing.

7 Locate the 14 ballbearings in the upper bearing race 22 and secure with grease.

8 On the lower lever fit the rubber bush 34, the lower nut 33, and the lower bearing race 32.

9 Holding the lower lever 18 in a vice, fit the bearing race 32 slightly below the lower groove in the lever. Put 14 balls in the race and secure them with grease Also use grease to hold the lower nut 33 on the bearing race 32. Fit the race on the lever with the balls in position in their bearing groove. Turn the housing over and engage the lever 18 vertically.

10 Hold the bearing race 32 and screw up the nut 33. If necessary, use a tube to position the race in the housing. Refit the closing items removed when dismantling (see Operation 4).

11 Tighten the upper nut 20 to a torque of 43 lb ft, then unscrew the nut and retighten to a torque of 14 to 22 lb ft. Lock the nut by turning down the metal.

12 If the work carried out has been made necessary by seizure of a ball joint, even at the limit of its movement, the operation of the ball joints of the other relay lever and the pivot levers should be checked.

13 Refit by offering up the relay and steering rod assembly. Put the relay fixing spindle 17, fitted with its washer and previously oiled, in position. Fit the nut on the spindle without tightening. The spindle is fitted with a washer under the head. Note that the washer is fitted with the concave part towards the head of the spindle and the flat positioned downwards.

14 Connect the rod of the steering lever on the pivot. Insert a nylon cup and the rubber seal 15. Tighten the not to a torque of 29 lb ft and insert a new splitpin.

15 Fit the steering in its bearings, noting the paint marks made when dismantling. Put the roller in position on the steering locating cam. Fit the bearing cap fixing screws 25. Adjust the angular position of the steering, using the fixture No. 1955.T as described in the first Operation 8 in **Section 9:4.**

16 Connect the steering lever to the top of the relay spindle with the nut on the engine side. Connect also the outer steering track rod to the lower relay lever, tightening the nuts in each case to a torque of 50 lb ft (7 kg m).

17 Fit the relay housing mud shields and other items removed when commencing operations.

18 Refill the reservoir, lower the car to the ground, start the engine and put the systems under pressure. Check the unions for leakage and recheck the fluid level in the reservoir. Check the alignment, the straight-ahead position and the steering lock.

9:6 Fault diagnosis

(a) Wheel wobble

1 Unbalanced wheels and tyres
2 Slack steering connections
3 Incorrect steering geometry
4 Excessive play in steering gear
5 Worn hub bearings

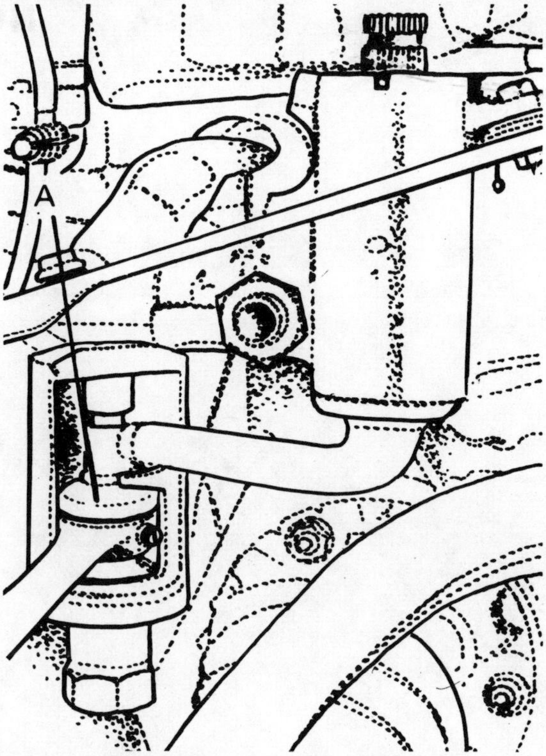

FIG 9:12 Disconnecting the lower relay lever from the track rod with the extractor A No. 3505.T

(b) Wander

1 Check 2, 3 and 4 in (a)
2 Uneven tyre pressures
3 Uneven tyre wear

(c) Heavy steering

1 Check 3 in (a)
2 Very low tyre pressures
3 Neglected lubrication
4 Wheels out of alignment
5 Steering shaft bent
6 Lateral or angular positions maladjusted
7 Incorrect cross-over pressure

(d) Lost motion

1 Worn pinion splines
2 Loose pinion coupling
3 Worn rack and pinion teeth (manual steering)
4 Worn ball joints

(e) Steering knocks

1 Check 7 in (c)
2 Worn shackle pin
3 Excessive clearance on rack support plunger
4 Worn pressure distributor components

(f) Flickering in central position

1 Check 7 in (c) and 4 in (e)

NOTES

CHAPTER 10

THE BRAKING SYSTEM

10:1 Description of layout

Two braking arrangements are employed, the DS system which applies to all DS models and the ID system used in the ID19B and ID20 or D Special and D Super models. The general layout of the former is to be seen in **FIG 2:1** in **Chapter 2** and of the latter in **FIG 10:1**.

Both front and rear brakes are operated hydraulically from the main servo system by foot pressure on a plunger with a small circular pad. This has very limited travel, sufficient only to open two distribution valves, one each for the front and rear hydraulic circuits. As described in **Chapter 2**, the proportion of effort applied to front and rear braking is automatically adjusted in the DS system according to the loading of the car.

Disc-type front brakes are mounted on the end of each front wheel drive shaft. Two pistons, one on each side of the disc, compress the pads against the disc when hydraulic pressure is applied. Air inlets from the front of the car provide for brake cooling. The rear brakes are of the expanding type, the drums incorporating leading and trailing shoes and mounted on the rear hubs. Separate cable-operated parking brakes acting on the front wheels are incorporated in calipers situated behind the main brake units, operated by a pendant pedal in the DS system or by a swivelling handbrake lever in cars equipped with the ID system. In each case locking and safety devices are provided.

Referring to **FIGS 2:1** and **10:1** similar features of the DS and ID braking systems are (a) the front and rear circuits are separate (b) the connection of the rear brake circuit to the rear suspension pressure and (c) the reserve of pressure for the front brake circuit.

The main features of the DS braking system are that separate front and rear hydraulic circuits are provided, with the brake accumulator in the front circuit. The front brakes are pressurized from the front suspension in earlier models and directly from the source of pressure in models since December, 1967, when a priority valve (see **FIG 10:2**) was fitted on the main accumulator supply line to isolate the suspension units if the main pressure falls below a specified limit. With the priority valve closed, only the front brake circuit, the steering circuit and the changespeed circuit (if fitted) are operative. The rear brakes are pressurized from the rear suspension circuit, which also supplies the pressure acting on the piston

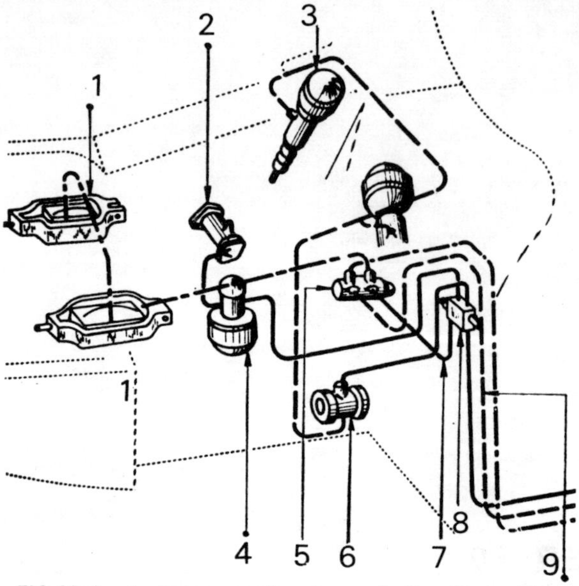

FIG 10:1 A diagrammatic view of the ID braking system

Key to Fig 10:1 1 Front brake housing 2 High pressure pump 3 Front suspension cylinder 4 Pressure regulator 5 Brake control 6 Front height corrector 7 High pressure supply to brake control system, front brake slide valve 8 Security valve 9 To brake control, rear brake slide valve, rear suspension pressure

in the brake distributor cylinder (see **FIG 10:3**). The brake pressure distribution unit includes the pedal knob assembly, the control valves, the distributor piston and cylinder, the stop lamp switch and the pressure warning light switch, the general operation of which is described in **Section 2:10** in **Chapter 2.**

The ID braking system incorporates a security valve and a hydraulic brake control as shown in the flow diagram in **FIG 10:1.** The front brake circuit is supplied from the main accumulator and the rear brake circuit from the rear suspension.

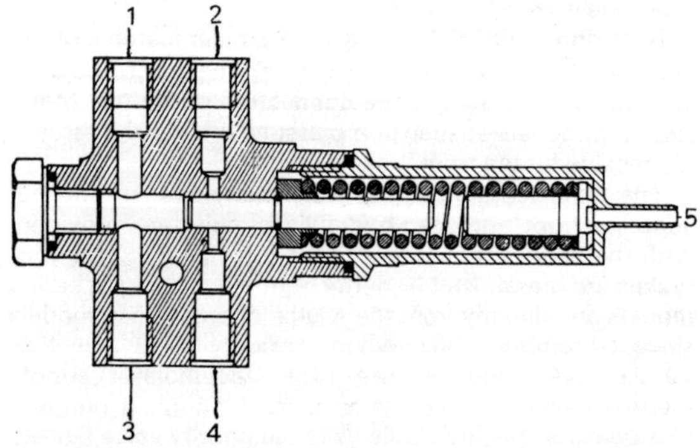

FIG 10:2 A sectional view of a priority valve

Key to Fig 10:2 1 High pressure supply 2 Front height correctors 3 Front brake accumulator 4 Rear height correctors 5 Overflow return

The security valve (see **FIG 10:4**), which takes the form of a four-way union, ensures that when the pressure rises in the circuits priority is given to the front brakes. The two outlets to the front and rear suspensions are closed by a slide valve when there is no pressure. The brake control valve (see **FIG 10:5**) includes two pressure control valves and pressure rises in the front brake circuit first. When this pressure is sufficient to compress the spring 3 the rear brakes are pressurized. The distribution of braking pressure is independent of the load in the car.

10:2 Routine maintenance, brake shoe adjustment

The gauge showing the level of the hydraulic fluid in the reservoir should be inspected at intervals of not more than 500 miles and the fluid topped up as necessary. It is essential that only an approved fluid should be used, as described in **Chapter 2, Section 2:1** together with the necessary attention to be given to the reservoir filter. When adding fluid according to the instructions on the outside of the reservoir the maximum mark should not be exceeded, otherwise excess fluid may be forced through the breather hole in the filler cap with a low suspension setting. Bleeding will be necessary after cleaning the filter. Open the bleed screw on the pressure regulator (see **FIG 2:1**) one full turn, take the cap off the reservoir and start the engine. When it is seen that the fluid entering the reservoir is free from air bubbles, tighten the bleed screw and refit the cap.

The disc brakes are self-adjusting. As the lining material of the brake pads becomes worn, fluid under pressure in the caliper cylinders and pipelines will compensate for wear. Adjustment of a front brake unit requires firstly the removal of the spare wheel and its crossmember, the headlamp control crossbar and the radiator air intake duct. Then loosen the screws holding the brake unit on the gearbox outlet housing and obtain an assistant to apply pressure to the hydraulic brake pedal. Tighten the screws to a torque of between 94 and 100 lb ft (13 to 14 kg m) and release the pedal. Refit the items removed for access. To adjust the rear brake shoes, raise the rear of the car on firm supports and remove the wing and the wheel on the side of the brake to be adjusted. Further operations are as follows:

1. Bring the shoes into contact with the drum by turning the adjusting cams in the direction shown by the arrows in **FIG 10:6.** It must still be possible to turn the drum by hand. Remove the two screws 1 and remove the drum 2.
2. Fit the gauge 3565.T shown in **FIG 10:7.** Turn the apparatus and find the highest point on the linings by means of the arm A. Fix it with a wing nut.
3. Loosen the locknuts 3 on the eccentric bushes 4 and position the eccentric so that the smaller throw is downwards.
4. Adjust the shoes by means of the cams and eccentrics 4 so as to obtain a clearance between the straight edge A and the shoes of .15 mm at the points M and M1 and of .25 mm at the points M2 and M3.
5. Tighten the nut 3 and knock over the lockwasher 5. Refit the brake drum and the items removed for access.

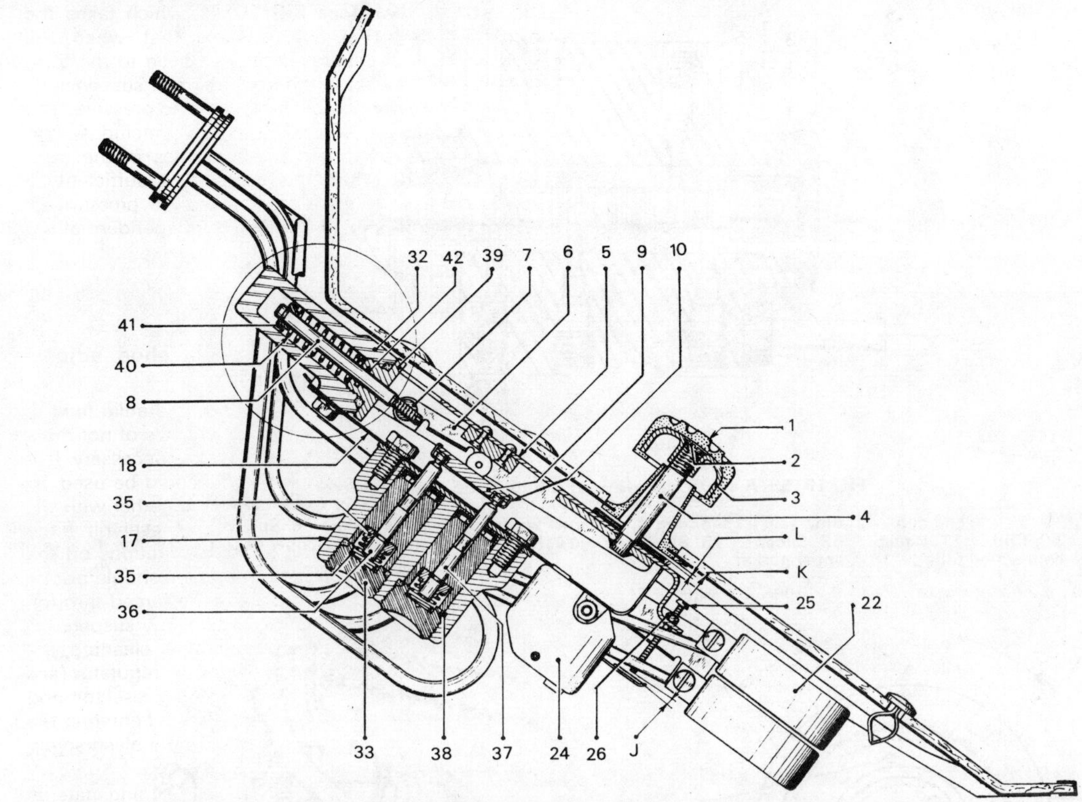

FIG 10:3 A typical sectional view of the hydraulic brake pressure distributor

Key to Fig 10:3 1 Pedal rubber 2 Screw 3 Pedal knob 4 Control rod 5 Pedal 6 Roller trolley 7 Spindle 8 Screwed control rod 9 Compensator plate 10 Spring retaining plate 17 Distribution unit 18 Bracket 22 Pressure switches 24 Stop lamp switch 25 Adjusting screw 26 Locknut 32 Braking distributor 33 Plug 34 Springs 35 Spring cups 36 Valve 37 Valve 38 Joint 39 Guide cap 40 Spring 41 Cup 42 Ring seal **j** Clearance .4 to .6 mm **k** Measuring base **l** Maximum clearance 2 mm

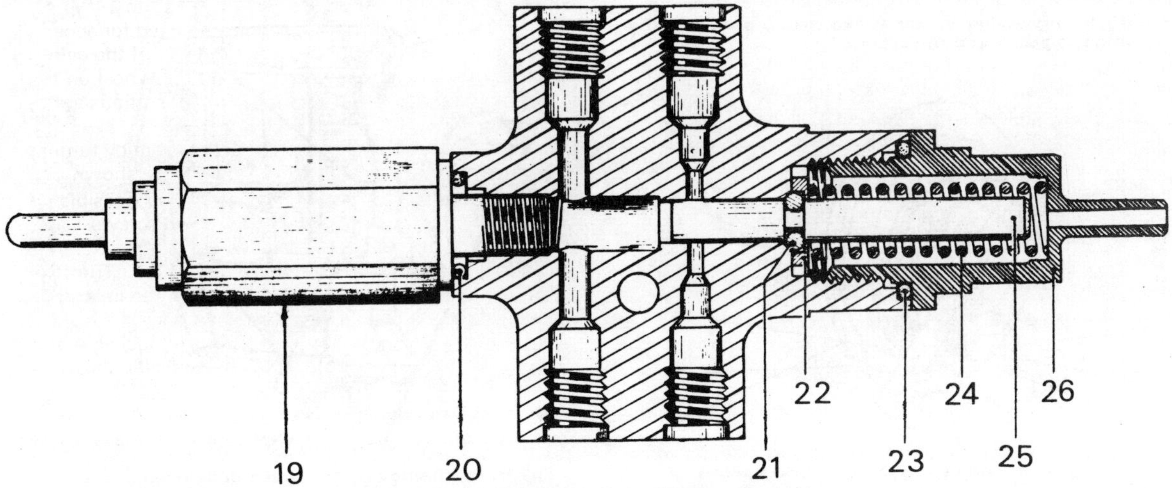

FIG 10:4 A sectional view of a security valve

Key to Fig 10:4 19 Pressure switch 20 Ring seal 22 Thrust washer 23 Ring seal 24 Spring 25 Slide valve 26 Plug

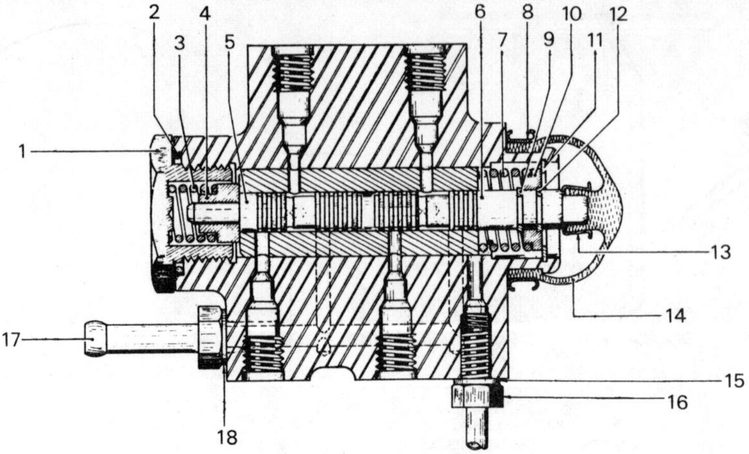

FIG 10:5 A sectional view of a hydraulic brake control

Key to Fig 10:5 1 End cap 2 Ring seal 3 Spring 4 Thrust washer 5 Slide valve 6 Spindle 7 Spring 8 Clip 9 Circlip 10 Cup 11 Circlip 12 Circlip 13 Steel cup 14 Rubber protector 15 Copper gasket 16 Overflow return 17 Exhaust connecting tube 18 Copper gasket

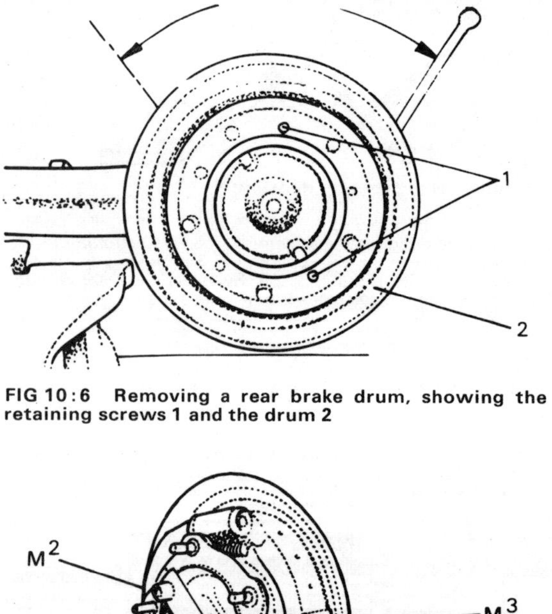

FIG 10:6 Removing a rear brake drum, showing the retaining screws 1 and the drum 2

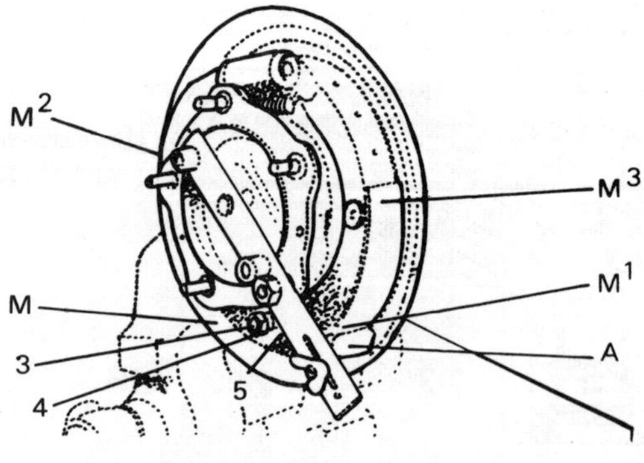

FIG 10:7 Adjusting the rear brake shoes

Key to Fig 10:7 3 Nut 4 Cams 5 Lockwasher **A** Arm of gauge 3565.T **M** Measurement points

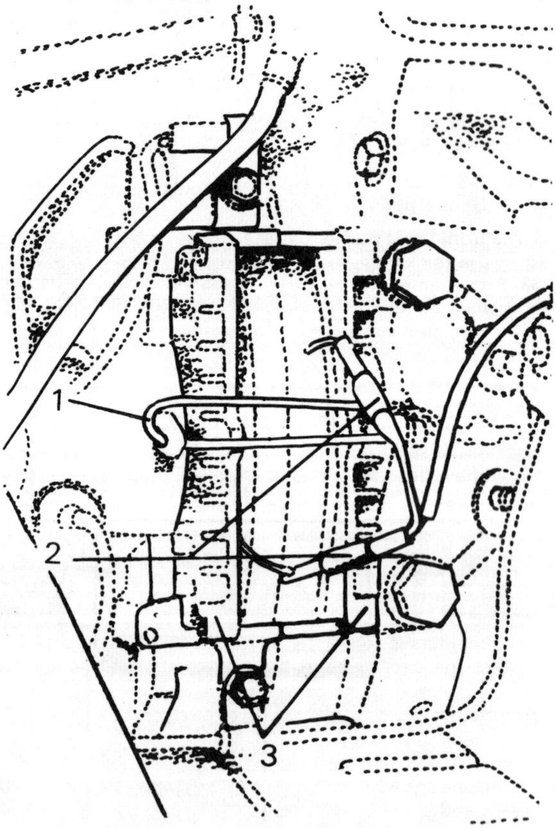

FIG 10:8 Removing the brake pads from a front brake

Key to Fig 10:8 1 Spring clips 2 Leads for brake pad wear warning light 3 Pads

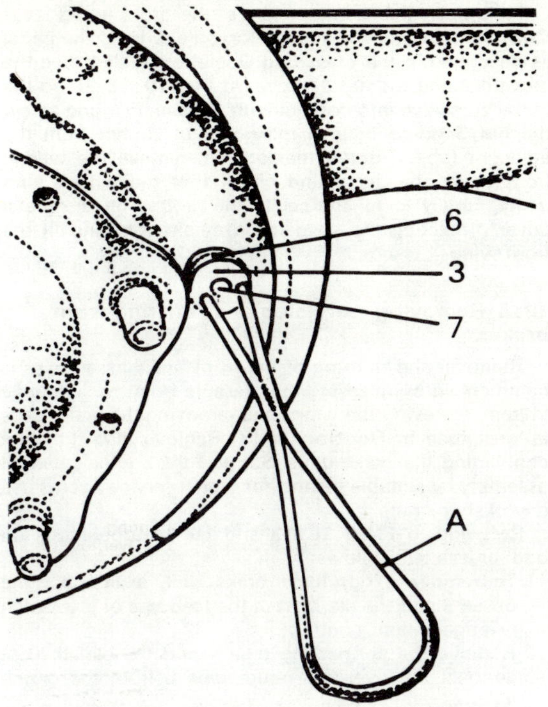

FIG 10:9 Removing the rear brake shoes

Key to Fig 10:9 3 Cups 6 Springs 7 Pins
A Tool No. 3556.T

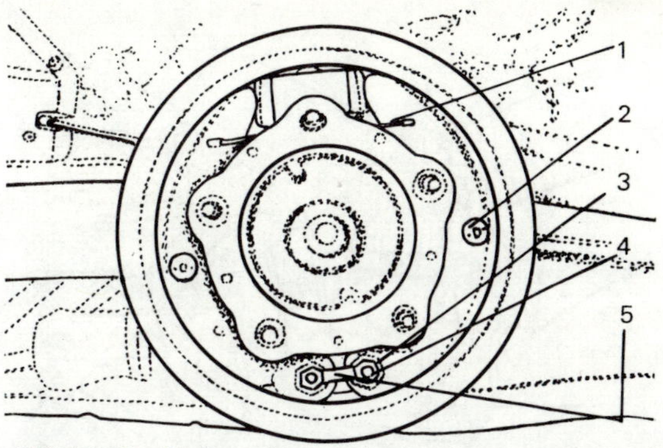

FIG 10:10 Fitting the rear brake shoes on the backplate

Key to Fig 10:10 1 Brake shoe spring 2 Cups
3 Adjusting bushes 4 Nuts 5 Lockplate

10:3 Brake pads and brake shoe linings

The front brake pads or shoe linings should be renewed when the thickness of the linings is less than .3 mm. On DS21 cars an earth wire is embedded in the brake pads so that when the pads are worn the wire touches the brake disc and closes the warning lamp circuit. A red lamp lights up on the dashboard to warn the driver that the pads need renewal. Scoring on the linings presents no danger but they must be dry and free from oil. In order to equalize the braking it is necessary to renew the four shoes at the same time.

To renew the pads, first obtain access to the brake units as described in the preceding Section. Remove the spring clips 1 (see **FIG 10:8**) and disconnect the leads 2 for the brake pad wear warning light. Then remove the pads 3, withdrawing them towards the front, and carefully clean the parts of the pistons exposed to dust.

Using the disc as a fulcrum, push the pistons back in their cylinders using a piece of wood. Fit the pads 3, connect the cables 2 and fit the clip 1. Adjust the unit on the gearbox housing and complete refitting as described in **Section 10:2**.

Renewal of the rear brake shoe linings is undertaken as follows. As for the front brakes, to ensure even braking it is necessary to renew the brake linings on both rear wheels at the same time.

1 Raise the rear of the car on firm supports and remove the wings and the wheels. Mark the position of the brake drum on the stub axle, remove the fixing screws and then the drum.

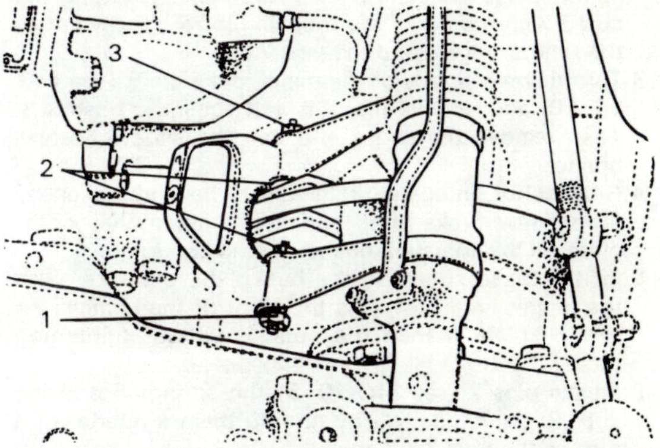

FIG 10:11 Adjusting clearance of brake pads, showing the nuts 1 and 3 and the screws 2

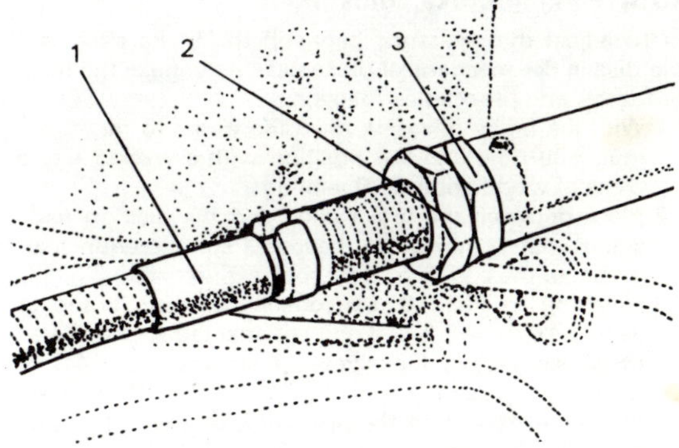

FIG 10:12 Adjusting the mechanical brake cable

Key to Fig 10:12 1 Cable sheath 2 Locknut 3 Nut

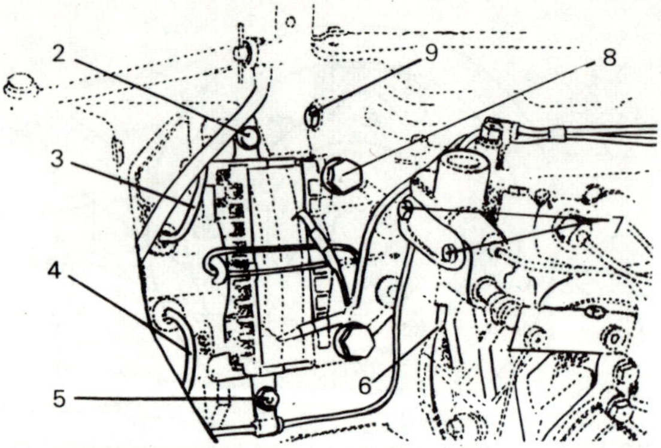

FIG 10:13 Removing the righthand front brake unit

Key to Fig 10:13 2 Clip 3 Union 4 Connecting pipe 5 Clip 6 Clutch lock overflow return pipe 7 Clutch lock screws 8 Retaining screws on gearbox 9 Retaining screws on crossmember

2 Unhook the springs 6 (see **FIG 10:9**), for which spring pliers No. 2110.T are available. Remove the cup 3 with the aid of the tool No. 3556.T shown at A, then the springs 6 and the pins 7.
3 Turn down the tabs of the metal lockplate 5 (see **FIG 10:10**) and remove the nuts and eccentric bushes 3. Then remove the shoes and free the shoe adjusting bushes.
4 Renewal of linings is preferably to be undertaken by fitting new brake shoe and lining assemblies complete. Fit the adjusting bushes on the brake shoes.
5 Fit the brake shoes on the backplate, the shoe with the longer lining towards the front of the vehicle. Fit the lockplate 5 then the nuts 4 without tightening them.
6 Fit the pins 7 (see **FIG 10:9**) the springs 6 and the cups 3. Lock the cups by turning them a quarter of a turn on the rods 7.
7 Hook on the brake shoe spring and adjust the brakes as described in **Section 10:2.**
8 Tighten and lock the nuts 4, then refit the drums and tighten the retaining screws. Refit the wheel and wing and lower the car to the ground.

10:4 Parking brake adjustment

To adjust the clearance between the brake pads and the disc in the mechanical brake assembly, raise the front of the car and proceed as follows:

1 With the brake released, raise the pedal to the maximum and hold it in this position with a wedge, e.g. a piece of wood about 210 mm high.
2 Place between the brake pads and the disc on each side a shim .1 mm thick, having a surface equivalent to that of the pad to prevent rocking.
3 Referring to **FIG 10:11,** loosen the nuts 1 and 3, using a 16 mm 12-sided ring spanner reduced to 3 mm thickness. Adjust the screws 2 with a thin 14 mm open-ended spanner, so that the pads just contact the highest spots on the disc. Tighten the nuts 1 and 3.
4 Carry out the same adjustment on the other brake unit and lower the vehicle to the ground.

To adjust the cable, remove the front wing (see **Chapter 12**) and the suspension shield. Hold the pedal as described in the preceding Operation 1, then free the locknut 2 and the nut 3 shown in **FIG 10:12.** Bring the threaded sleeve into contact with the sheath 1 and screw the nut 3 up to or at a maximum of .1 mm from the adjacent tube. Tighten the locknut, remove the wedge from under the pedal and check that the wheels turn freely. Finally lower the car to the ground, fit the metal cover protecting the suspension mechanism and fit the front wing.

10:5 Removing, servicing and refitting front brakes

Removal and refitting of the front brake assemblies is commenced by releasing the pressure from the hydraulic system, removing the wings and removing the brake pads as described in **Section 10:3.** Remove also the tube connecting the brake units. Support the engine-gearbox assembly by suitable means, for which service agents use a workshop crane.

Referring to **FIGS 10:13** and **10:14,** operations on both units are as follows:

1 To remove a righthand brake unit, disconnect the union 3 and the clip 2 from the feedpipe of the clutch re-engagement control.
2 Remove the connecting pipe 4 and the clip 5. Disconnect the overflow return pipe 6 from the clutch lock.
3 Remove the screws 7 securing the clutch lock, the two screws 8 securing the brake unit on the gearbox and the two screws 9 securing the brake unit on the crossmember. Use a ratchet spanner with a 6 inch (150 mm) extension with a universal joint, located between the steering and the track rod.
4 Remove the brake unit, withdrawing it downwards and forwards, at the same time raising the clutch lock and bringing it forward without forcing it.
5 To remove a lefthand brake unit, disconnect the feed union 14 and the clip 13 (see **FIG 10:14**).
6 Remove the connecting pipe 12, the clip 13, the two screws 11 securing the brake unit on the gearbox and the two screws 10 securing the brake unit on the front crossmember. Use a ratchet spanner with an extension and a universal joint, located parallel to the drive shaft through the wheel arch.
7 Remove the brake unit, withdrawing it downwards and forwards and passing under the five-pipe assembly of the gearbox control.

To overhaul a brake unit, dismantling and reassembly are undertaken as follows, referring to **FIG 10:15:**

1 Remove the piping 1 with its securing clip 2 and the four screws 8 securing the two halves of the unit together.
2 From each of these two halves withdraw the piston 3, the felt ring 4 and the ring seal 5.
3 Remove the distance piece 6 from the silentblocs 7 using a hammer and a small punch. Free the silentbloc after dipping them in water. Clean all parts very carecarefully in alcohol, then blow dry with compressed air.
4 The pistons and cylinders must show no signs of knocks or scores. If they do, they must be renewed. Fit new seals.

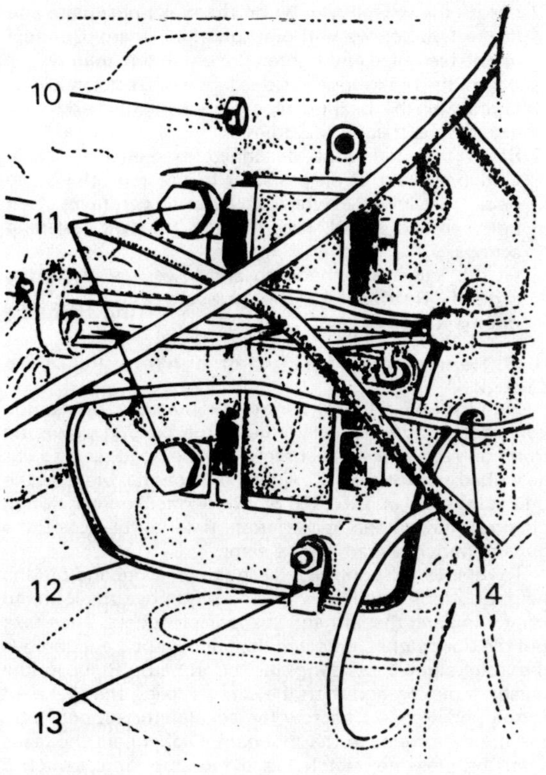

FIG 10:14 Removing the lefthand front brake unit

Key to Fig 10:14 10 Retaining screws on crossmember 11 Retaining screws on gearbox 12 Connecting pipe 13 Clip 14 Feed union

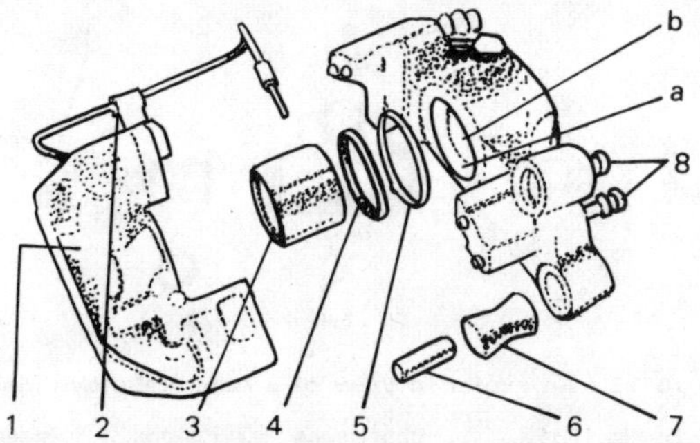

FIG 10:15 An exploded view of a front brake caliper

Key to Fig 10:15 1 Piping 2 Clip 3 Piston 4 Felt ring 5 Ring seal 6 Distance piece 7 Silentblocs 8 Screws **a** Felt ring groove **b** Ring seal groove

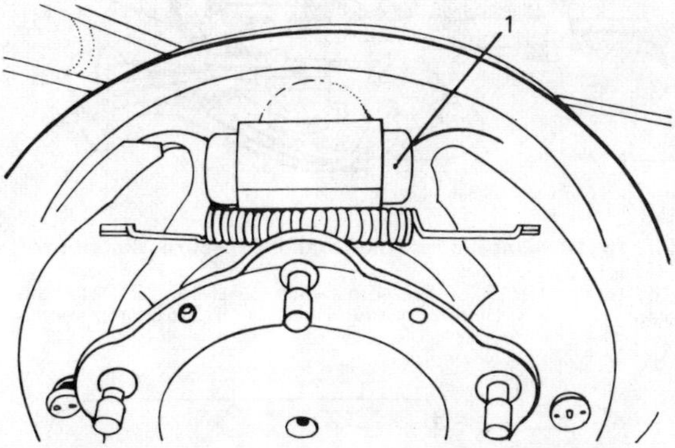

FIG 10:16 A rear brake cylinder, showing the cups 1

5 To reassemble, dip the silentblocs in water and refit them by hand. Fit the distance pieces 6 into the silentblocs with the aid of a mallet.

6 Smear with the approved hydraulic fluid the ring seals 5, the felts 4, the pistons 3 and the cylinders.

7 In each of the two halves of the unit fit a ring seal in the groove 'b' and a felt ring in the groove 'a'. Fit the pistons by hand.

8 Assemble the two halves of the brake unit with the four screws 8 with plain washers. Tighten to a torque of 36 lb ft (5 kg m).

9 Fit the piping and its securing clip and close all holes with plugs.

Refitting the brake units is undertaken by following the removal operations in reverse order, noting the following requirements:

1 Tighten the securing screws on the crossmember to a torque of between 28 and 31 lb ft (3.9 to 4.3 kg m).

2 Adjust the clutch lock if required (see **Chapter 6, Section 6:9**) and connect up the overflow return pipe.

3 Fit the brake pads (see **Section 10:3**) and adjust the units (see **Section 10:2**).

4 Reconstitute the pressure, check the unions for leaks and bleed the brakes as described in **Section 10:8.**

10:6 Removing and refitting rear brakes

Raise the rear of the car on firm supports and remove the rear wing, rear wheel and brake drum as previously described. Release the pressure, remove the brake shoes as instructed in **Section 10:3** and proceed as follows:

1 Using the cams, spread the brake shoes apart as shown in **FIG 10:16** to facilitate the removal of the cylinder without damaging the cups 1.

2 Disconnect the feed pipe from the wheel cylinder and plug the openings of the cylinder and feed pipe.

3 Remove the two retaining screws and disengage the wheel cylinder.

4 Referring to **FIG 10:17**, remove the rubber cups 1, the pistons 2, the circlips 4, the bleed screw 3 and the ring seals 5 from the pistons, using a brass wire hook flattened at one end.

5 Clean all the parts with alcohol and blow with compressed air. When reassembling, dip all the parts in new approved hydraulic fluid.

6 Locate the circlip 4 in position and fit the ring seals 5 on the pistons 2. Insert the pistons in the wheel cylinders after having made sure that there are no scratches or burrs or signs of seizure. Refit the rubber cups and the bleed screw.

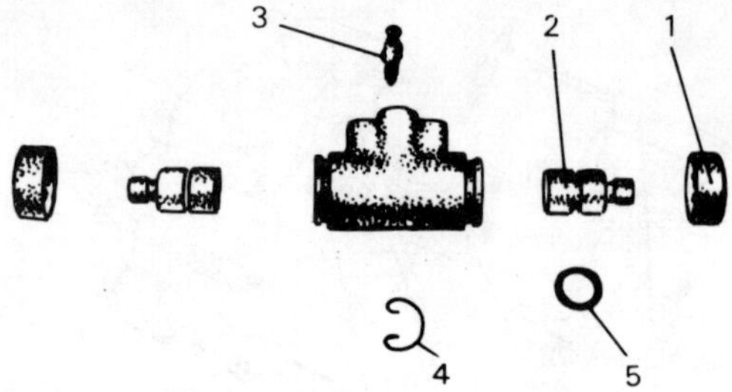

FIG 10:17 An exploded view of a rear brake cylinder

Key to Fig 10:17 1 Rubber cups 2 Pistons 3 Bleed screw 4 Circlips 5 Ring seals

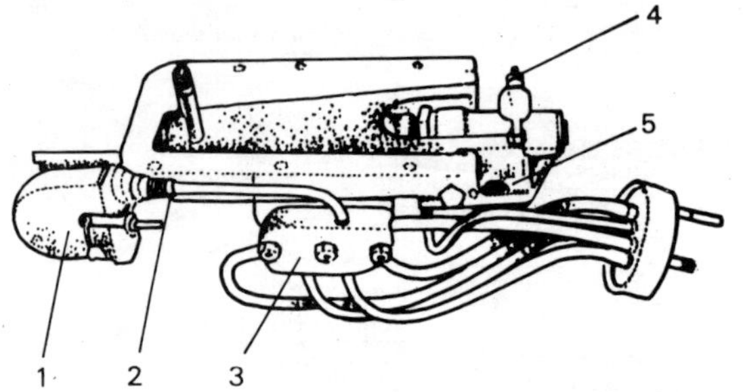

FIG 10:18 Details of the brake pressure distributor

Key to Fig 10:18 1 Pressure switch 2 Union 3 Retaining plate 4 Distributor union 5 Stop lamp switch

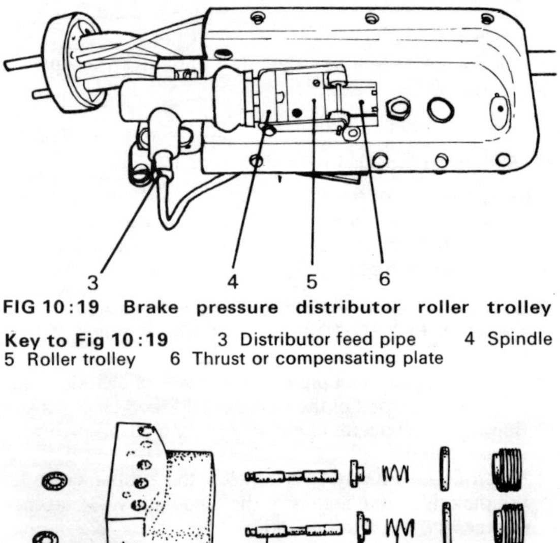

FIG 10:19 Brake pressure distributor roller trolley

Key to Fig 10:19 3 Distributor feed pipe 4 Spindle 5 Roller trolley 6 Thrust or compensating plate

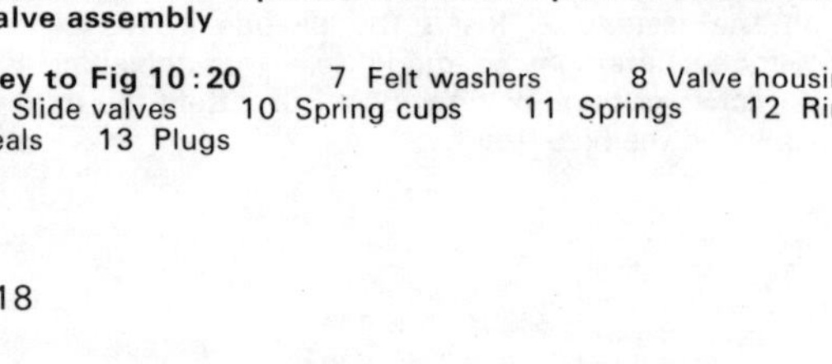

FIG 10:20 An exploded view of the pressure distributor valve assembly

Key to Fig 10:20 7 Felt washers 8 Valve housing 9 Slide valves 10 Spring cups 11 Springs 12 Ring seals 13 Plugs

7 Locate the wheel cylinder on the brake backplate and fit the two screws without tightening them. Connect up the feed pipe and tighten the union moderately.

8 Adjust the brake shoes as described in **Section 10:2.**

9 Lightly oil the bearing face between drum and stub axle flange, then fit the drum.

10 Bleed the brakes as described in **Section 10:8.** Obtain the aid of an assistant to press on the brake pedal to allow the wheel cylinder to centralize itself between the shoes, then tighten the two retaining screws.

11 Fit the wheel and the wing and lower the car to the ground. Reconstitute the pressure and check all unions for leaks.

10:7 Removing and refitting a hydraulic brake control

The hydraulic brake control or pressure distributor, when fitted, automatically adjusts the braking power on front or rear brakes according to the load carried, as described in **Chapter 2.** A typical sectional view of the unit is shown in **FIG 10:3.** Minor mechanical design changes have been made from time to time but the general principles remain the same.

To remove the control, release the pressure and put the height control in the 'low' position. Remove the lefthand front wing and the lefthand suspension sphere. Then take out the floor carpet, unfasten the felt covering and remove the four screws securing the floorboard. Remove the plastic trimming and then the screws fixing the toeboard to the pedal gear. Unscrew the accelerator support from the floor and remove the toeboard. Disconnect the leads from the pressure switch 1 and the stop lamp switch 5 (see **FIG 10:18**), disengage the studs from the union flanges and withdraw the pedal gear towards the interior of the car. Remove the rubber pedal pad and the pedal disc with its retaining screw.

Remove the two articulating screws to remove the pedal, then disengage the roller trolley 5 (see **FIG 10:19**), lifting it up by a quarter of a turn to free it from its spindle 4. Remove the thrust plate 6 and leaf spring from the slide valves. Remove the brake pressure distributor after disconnecting the feedpipe union 3 and the two retaining screws.

Disconnect the pipe assembly from the pressure switch and valve housing and remove the valve housing from the casing. Hold the housing in a vice with lead inserts, then remove the plugs 13 (see **FIG 10:20**), the felt washers 7, the springs 11, the spring cups 10, the slide-valves 9 and the ring seals 12. Keep all parts in strict order for refitting in the same positions as they are paired.

Examine the valves carefully. If they are scratched it is preferable to renew the control unit because of possible internal leakage. Clean the components carefully, especially in the fluid holes, and moisten them with hydraulic fluid for reassembly. Reassemble and refit the unit in the reverse order of the removal operations. When fitting the roller trolley line up the distributor to ensure that the rollers are correctly positioned on the compensating plate 6. Also, when fitting the valve housing, make quite sure that the contact faces on the housing and the bracket are perfectly clean. If required, the unit may be finally adjusted on a test bench with the aid of a service agent. Refit the items removed for access and reconstitute the pressure.

10:8 Bleeding the brake system

To bleed the brake system, raise the rear of the car on firm stands or position it over a pit and proceed as follows:

1 Release the pressure in all the circuits including the brake accumulator and place the manual height control lever in the high position.
2 Fit a flexible tube on the rear bleed screw of the centrifugal regulator to bleed the front righthand brake and on the accelerated idling control to bleed the front lefthand brake. Insert the ends of the tubes in the hydraulic reservoir after removing the cap.
3 Remove the rubber caps protecting the rear cylinder bleed screws. Fit a flexible tube on each rear cylinder bleed screw and dip the end of these tubes in a clean container already holding a small quantity of the approved hydraulic fluid.
4 Loosen the front and rear bleed screws, then tighten the bleed screw on the pressure regulator. Depress the brake pedal and hold it in this position with a weight of about 22 lb (10 kg). Start up the engine, allow the fluid to flow through the tubes until it is free from air bubbles then tighten the bleed screws.
5 Remove the bleed tubes. Leave the engine idling in order to put the circuits under pressure and check the bleed screws for leakage by depressing fully the brake pedal for about one minute.
6 Stop the engine. Replace the rubber protecting caps on the four bleed screws and lower the car to the ground.
7 Start up the engine and top up the level of fluid in the hydraulic fluid reservoir with the manual height control lever in the high position.

10:9 Renewing a rear brake articulated or flexible pipe

To renew a rear brake pivoting pipe, firmly support the rear of the car and remove the wheel. Release the pressure regulating screw about one-third of a turn and set the height control in the low position. Remove the rear wing, the corrector mudshield and the lower mudshield panel, then proceed as follows:

1 Referring to **FIG 10:21**, on the lefthand side disconnect the three-way union 2 from the feedpipe 1 and from the pipe 3 feeding the righthand brake.
2 Disconnect the feedpipe 9 from the wheel cylinder and raise the retaining clip 8.
3 Loosen the locknut 7 and remove the screw 6, then disengage the pivoting pipe from the rear wheel-arm.

To reassemble, insert the articulating spindle in the bore in the arm and follow the removal operations in reverse. Ensure that the conical hole in the articulating spindle lines up with the pointed screw 6 and that the locating lever 5 is central in its housing 4. Fit a new seal when connecting the tube 9 to the wheel cylinder. On completion bleed the brakes as described in **Section 10:8**.

As from February, 1969, the rear brake articulated pipe was replaced by a flexible pipe. With the pressure released, renewal of the flexible pipe is simply concerned with undoing and reconnecting the unions. When fitting the pipe, take care to hold it by the metal hexagon when tightening the nuts, to avoid damage by twisting.

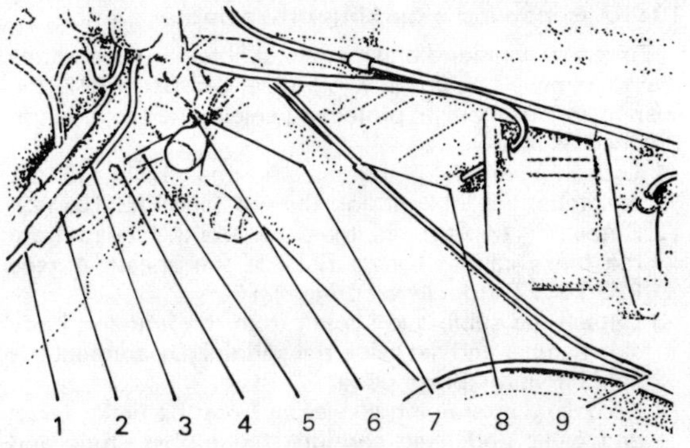

FIG 10:21 Rear-brake articulating pipe assembly

Key to Fig 10:21 1 Feed pipe 2 Three-way union 3 Pipe to righthand brake 4 Lever housing 5 Locating lever 6 Pointed screw 7 Locknut 8 Retaining clip 9 Pipe to brake cylinder

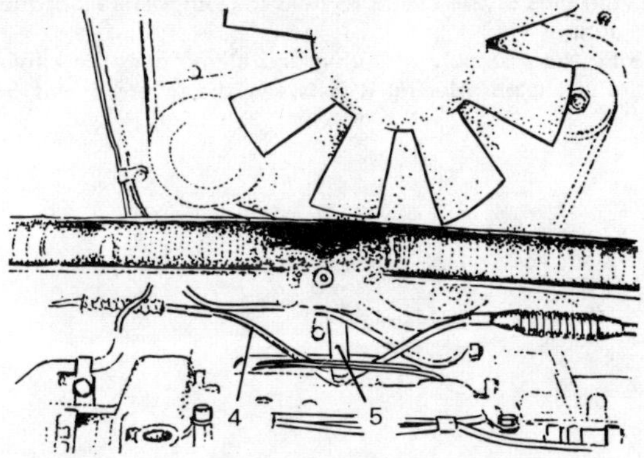

FIG 10:22 Showing parking brake cable 4 and securing clip 5

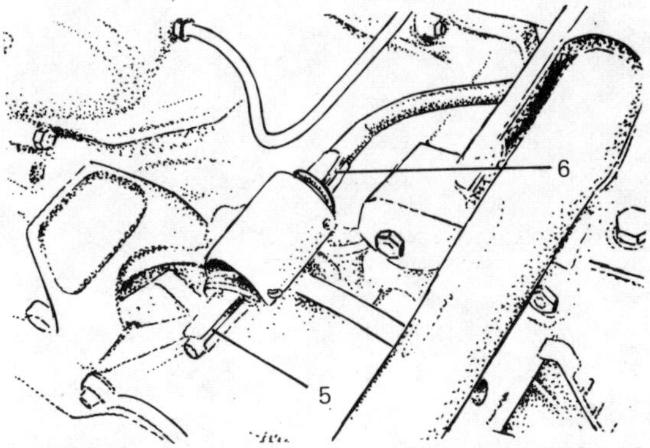

FIG 10:23 Parking brake cable spring clamp MR. 4158-50 with retaining pins located between the lefthand levers 5 and 6

10:10 Renewing a parking brake cable

To renew a parking brake cable, preliminary operations are to remove the front wing (see **Chapter 12**), the suspension mechanism protecting shield and the radiator. Proceed as follows:

1 Loosen completely the sheath, unscrewing to the maximum the locknut and the nut (see **FIG 10:12**).

2 Detach the two springs, the cable and the sheath from the brake caliper levers. Release the sheath 4 (see **FIG 10:22**) from its securing clip 5.

3 Detach the cable and sheath from the lefthand body sidemember and set aside the springs. Disconnect the cable from the brake pedal.

4 Remove the retaining clevis pin from the brake pedal and cable and keep carefully the rubber stops and plain washers. Remove the cable from the car.

5 Connect the new cable to the pedal. Fit a new clevis pin fitted with a lefthand rubber stop and then the other rubber stop and plain washer. Spread the metal at the end of the clevis pin.

6 Insert the cable through the lefthand body side-member. Fit the springs on the brake levers.

7 Place the spring in the clamp MR.4158-50 shown in **FIG 10:23,** compress the spring in a vice and place the pins of the clamp to hold the outer spirals of the spring.

8 Fit the assembly of spring and clamp over the cable and sheath, placing it between the levers 5 and 6. Engage the cable in the grooves of the levers, then remove the pins so that the spring positions itself on the lever bosses. Do the same for the second spring.

9 Insert the sheath in its securing clip and adjust the cable as described in **Section 10:4.** Refit the radiator, the suspension shield and the front wing.

10:11 Fault diagnosis

(a) Braking inefficiency

1 Leaks in the system
2 Leakage in hydraulic brake controls
3 Choked orifices or unserviceable slide valves in controls
4 Air in the system

(b) Brakes grab or pull to one side

1 Rear brake backplate loose
2 Scored, cracked or distorted drum
3 High spots on drum
4 Unbalanced rear shoe adjustment
5 Wet or oily linings
6 Worn steering connections
7 Uneven tyre pressures
8 Broken rear shoe return springs
9 Seized mechanical brake cable
10 Disc brake caliper piston sticking

CHAPTER 11

THE ELECTRICAL EQUIPMENT

11 :1 The system, exchange units, test equipment

A 12-volt electrical system is used with a negative earth return. Until July, 1967, a Ducellier or Paris-Rhone DC generator controlled by a regulator is used to charge the battery. In all later D models a Ducellier or Paris-Rhone alternator, in conjunction with a voltage regulator, generates an alternating current which is converted to direct current for charging the battery through silicon diodes. These are in the nature of one-way valves which prevent the current being returned to the alternator under low voltage conditions. The battery in turn supplies electrical energy to operate the starter motor, the ignition (see **Chapter 4**) the lights and other accessories, of which the general arrangement is shown in the wiring diagrams in the Appendix.

Major mechanical and electrical defects in the generator, starter motor and other integral features of the system are best remedied by fitting new units on an exchange basis, but instructions are given on overhaul and adjustments which can be undertaken with some basic understanding of electrical theory and practice and without elaborate equipment. The wiring diagrams will assist in tracing wiring faults. In the absence of a voltmeter a useful item of equipment is a test lamp, consisting of a small 6-volt or 12-volt bulb in a holder with two well-insulated leads ending in crocodile clips. If one lead is earthed, the bulb will light if the other lead is connected to any terminal or point in the system which is 'live'.

11 :2 Battery maintenance and testing

Regular attention is necessary to keep the battery in good working order and to extend its life. The top of the battery should be kept clean and dry. Any signs of corrosion may be removed by a weak solution of ammonia and hot water. The terminals should be coated with petroleum jelly and anti-sulphuric paint may be used for adjacent parts such as battery bolts and support. If the electrolyte level is less than $\frac{1}{4}$ inch above the plates, distilled water should be added. Should leakage or spilling require the addition of dilute sulphuric acid of the correct specific gravity it can usually be obtained already diluted. But if strong sulphuric acid is used, remember when diluting **always to add acid to water** and on no account add the water to the acid.

The specific gravity of the electrolyte in each cell may be checked by using a hydrometer. Readings as follows should be obtained for an electrolyte temperature of

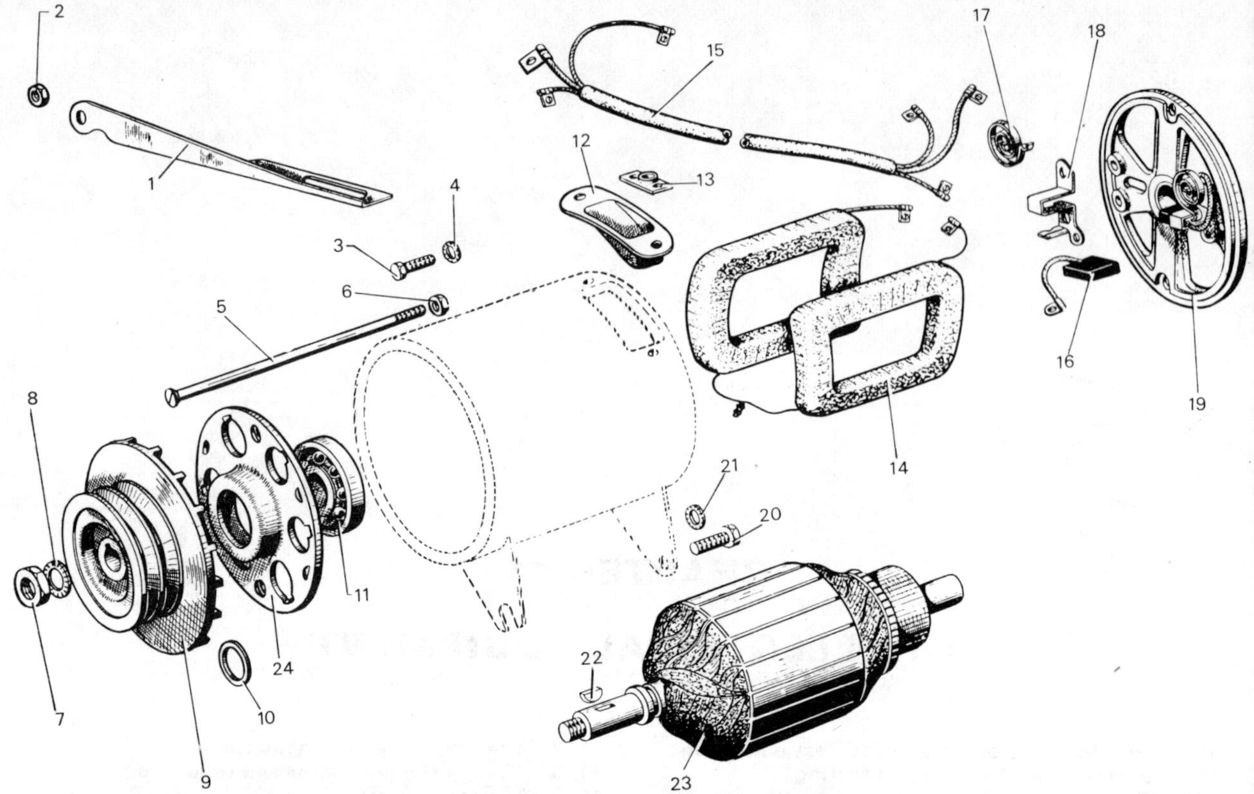

FIG 11 :1 A typical exploded view of the generator

Key to Fig 11 :1 1 Belt tensioning arm 2 Nut 3 Screw securing adjusting stay 4 Shakeproof washer 5 Assembly rod 6 Nut 7 Pulley nut 8 Shakeproof washer 9 Pulley 10 Adjusting washer 11 Bearing 12 Wiring support 13 Wiring plate 14 Field coils 15 Generator wiring 16 Brush 17 Brush spring 18 Brush holder, positive and negative 19 Commutator bracket or bearing end plate 20 Screw securing generator to flywheel housing 21 Shakeproof washer 22 Woodruff key 23 Armature 24 Drive bracket or bearing end plate

16°C (60°F). The readings should be corrected by adding or subtracting .002 for each 3°C (5°F) rise or fall from that temperature.

Cell fully charged	1.270 to 1.290
Cell half discharged	1.190 to 1.210
Cell fully discharged	1.110 to 1.130

11 :3 Generator maintenance, electrical tests in situ

Maintenance requirements are limited to checking and, if necessary, adjusting the belt tension at periodic intervals, as described in **Chapter 5.** Every 1250 miles (2000 km) a few drops of engine oil should be inserted into the oiler for the generator spindle. Apply sparingly to avoid any oil reaching the commutator or generator brushes.

To test the output of the generator, first make sure that there is no belt slip and that the output and field terminals on the generator are correctly connected to their respective terminals on the regulator. Operations are then as follows:

1 Disconnect the wires from the output and field terminals of the generator and join the terminals together with a short piece of wire.

2 Connect a 0–30 voltmeter between this junction and earth. Run the engine at a fast idling speed when the voltage reading should rise rapidly without fluctuation. Do not increase the engine speed above a fast idle or the generator may be damaged.

3 If there is no reading, first check the generator leads, brushes and brush connections. If the reading is very low, the field or armature windings may be at fault.

4 If the generator is in good order, leave the temporary link in position between the terminals and restore the original connections correctly. Remove the output lead from the regulator and connect the voltmeter between this lead and a good earth. Run the engine as before, when the reading should be the same as that measured directly on the generator. No reading indicates a break in the cable from generator to regulator. Repeat the test on the field cable and finally remove the temporary link from the generator.

Regulators of either Ducellier or Paris-Rhone manufacture are connected to the generator to control the output charge to the battery. The charging rate will be high when the battery is discharged and low when the battery is fully charged, independent of the speed of rotation of the generator. The regulators fitted include

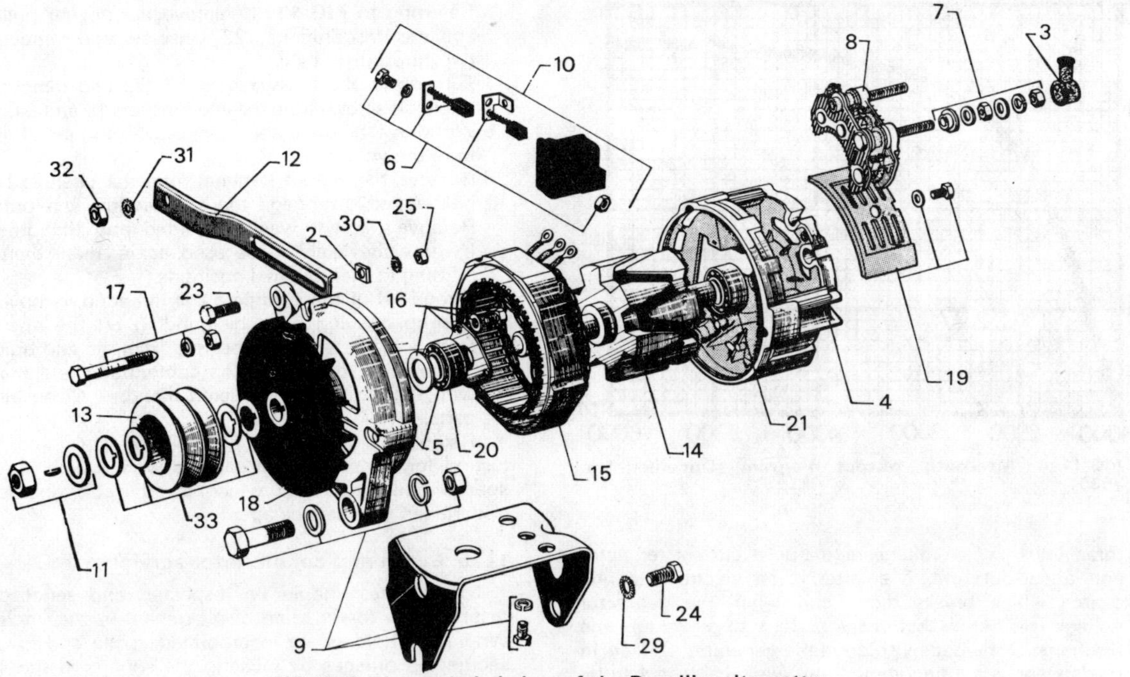

FIG 11 : 2 An exploded view of the Ducellier alternator

Key to Fig 11 : 2 2 Washer 3 Terminal 4 Slip ring end shield 5 Drive end bracket 6 Brush assembly 7 Terminal fasteners 8 Diode carrier 9 Assembly bolts 10 Brush assembly 11 Pulley nut and key 12 Belt tensioning arm 13 Pulley 14 Rotor 15 Stator 16 Retaining rings 17 Assembly bolts 18 Fan 19 Cover 20 Drive end bearing 21 Rear end bearing 23 Bolt 24 Bolt 25 Nut 29 Serrated washer 30 Serrated washer 31 Serrated washer 32 Nut 33 Assembling washers

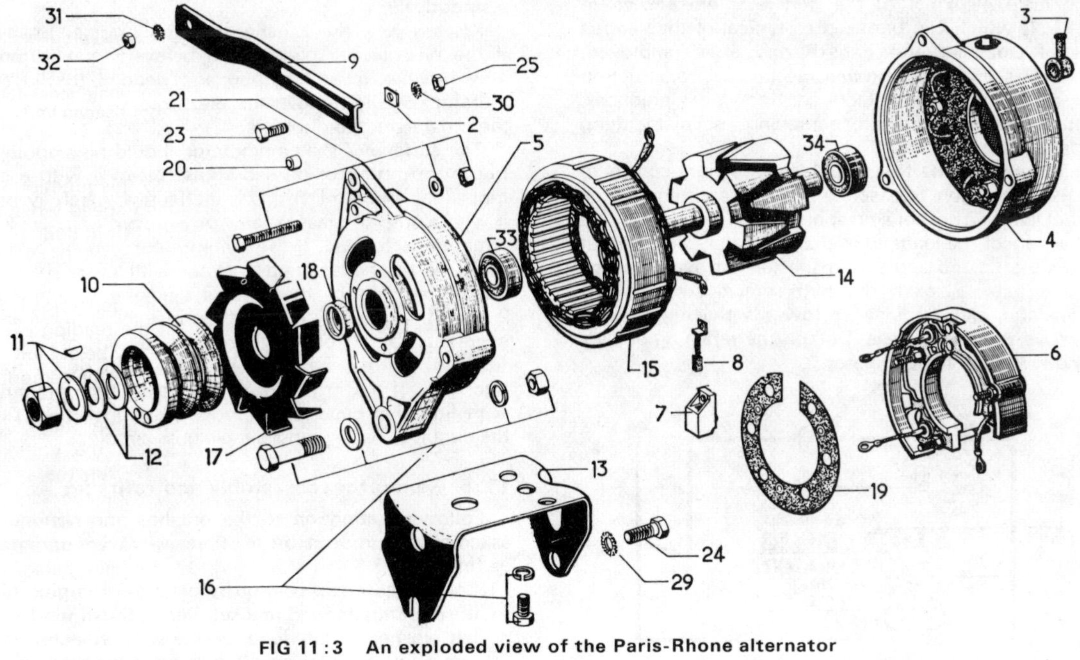

FIG 11 : 3 An exploded view of the Paris-Rhone alternator

Key to Fig 11 : 3 2 Washer 3 Terminal 4 Slip ring end shield 5 Drive end bracket 6 Diode carrier 7 Brush holder 8 Brush assembly 9 Belt tensioning arm 10 Pulley 11 Pulley nut and key 12 Washers 13 Bracket 14 Rotor 15 Stator 16 Assembly bolts 17 Fan 18 Retaining ring 19 Joint 20 Nut 21 Assembly bolts 23 Bolt 24 Bolt 25 Nut 29 Serrated washer 30 Serrated washer 31 Serrated washer 32 Nut 33 Drive end bearing 34 Rear end bearing

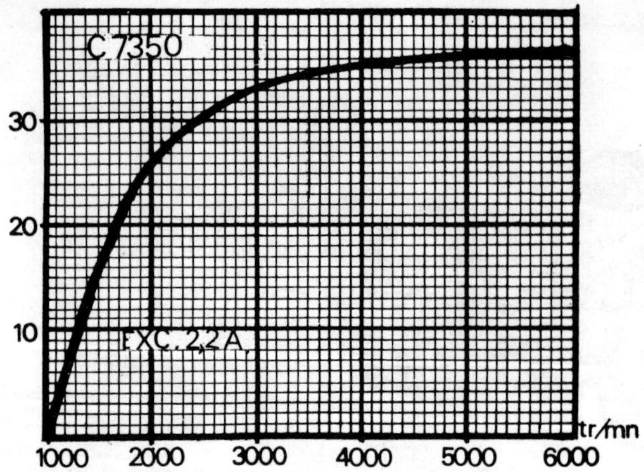

FIG 11 : 4 **Alternator output diagram (Ducellier No. 7530)**

three units, i.e., a voltage regulator, a current regulator and a cut-out unit. The latter is an electro-magnetic switch which breaks the circuit when the generator voltage falls below that of the battery, so preventing the discharge of the battery through the generator. Defects in this apparatus are uncommon, but electrical tests can be carried out if required by a service agent with the necessary facilities and experience.

11 : 4 Removing and dismantling generator

The main elements of the generator are shown in **FIG 11 : 1,** which can be taken as typical of the various types of Ducellier and Paris-Rhone units employed. Details of assembly design and mechanical construction differ according to manufacturers' individual practices, but the general principles of removing and dismantling a generator are as follows:

1 Disconnect the battery and place the height control in the low position, release the pressure and remove the front lefthand suspension sphere.
2 Disconnect the leads from the generator, also the nut from the tie-rod and swing the tie-rod over towards the engine. Slacken the two screws securing the generator, move the latter towards the engine and remove the pulley belts. Detach the retaining screws and withdraw the generator.

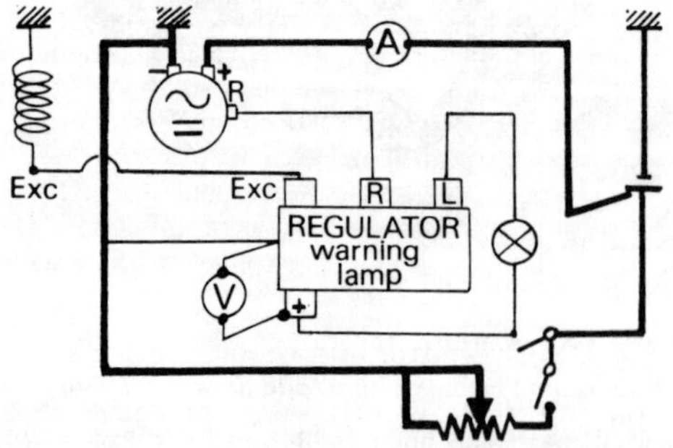

FIG 11 : 5 **Alternator regulator test connections**

3 Referring to **FIG 11 : 1,** remove the driving pulley 9 and the Woodruff key 22. Unscrew and remove the two through-bolts 5.
4 Turn down the lockwashers if fitted and remove the retaining screws from the end brackets 19 and 24.
5 Withdraw the drive end bracket with the armature 23 from the yoke.
6 Remove the output terminal from the positive brush holder and disengage the commutator end bracket. Remove the felt washer if fitted and the brushes. If these are likely to be used again, mark them for refitting in their original positions.
7 If renewal of the bearing 11 is intended, remove the bearing hosuing plate by grinding off the retaining rivets and press out the bearing from the end bracket.
8 Remove the bush from the commutator end bracket with the aid of a shouldered mandrel. Clean all the parts.

Removal and refitting of the field coils and their testing for continuity and earth is work which requires special equipment and which is advisable should be undertaken by a service agent.

11 : 5 Brush and commutator servicing

The brushes should be inspected and serviced by testing them for freedom of movement in their holders. Where the holders are incorporated in the end bracket, secure the brushes by locating the springs at the sides of the holders. Temporarily fit the commutator end bracket over the commutator, hold up each brush spring in turn and gently move the brush by pulling on the connector. If the movement is sluggish, remove the brush from its holder and ease the sides by slightly polishing them with a smooth file.

Always refit the brushes in their original positions. If the brushes are badly worn below 8 mm in length, new brushes must be fitted and bedded to the commutator. Finally remove the end bracket and reconnect the brushes to their holders.

The surface of the commutator should be smooth and free from pitting or burned spots. Clean it with a cloth moistened in petrol. If this is ineffective, carefully polish it with a strip of glasspaper, **not emerycloth,** while the armature is rotated. If the commutator is badly worn or scored it may be faced up in a lathe with a very sharp tool, but do not reduce the original diameter by more than 2 mm. If necessary, undercut the insulation between the segments after rectification to a depth of $\frac{1}{32}$ inch (.8 mm) with a hacksaw blade ground down to the thickness of the insulation. Then polish the commutator with fine glasspaper and remove all copper dust. Check the circuit to earth with a simple bulb circuit.

11 : 6 Generator reassembly and refitting

Following attention to the brushes and commutator assemblies as in **Section 11 : 5,** reassembly is undertaken as follows:

1 Locate the bush, previously oiled with engine oil, in the commutator end bracket. Refit a thrust washer or a felt washer, as provided, on the shaft adjacent to the armature. If a closing plate is fitted, knock back the metal of the bracket lightly to retain the plate. Insert a few drops of oil on the felt washer and in the oiler on the bracket.

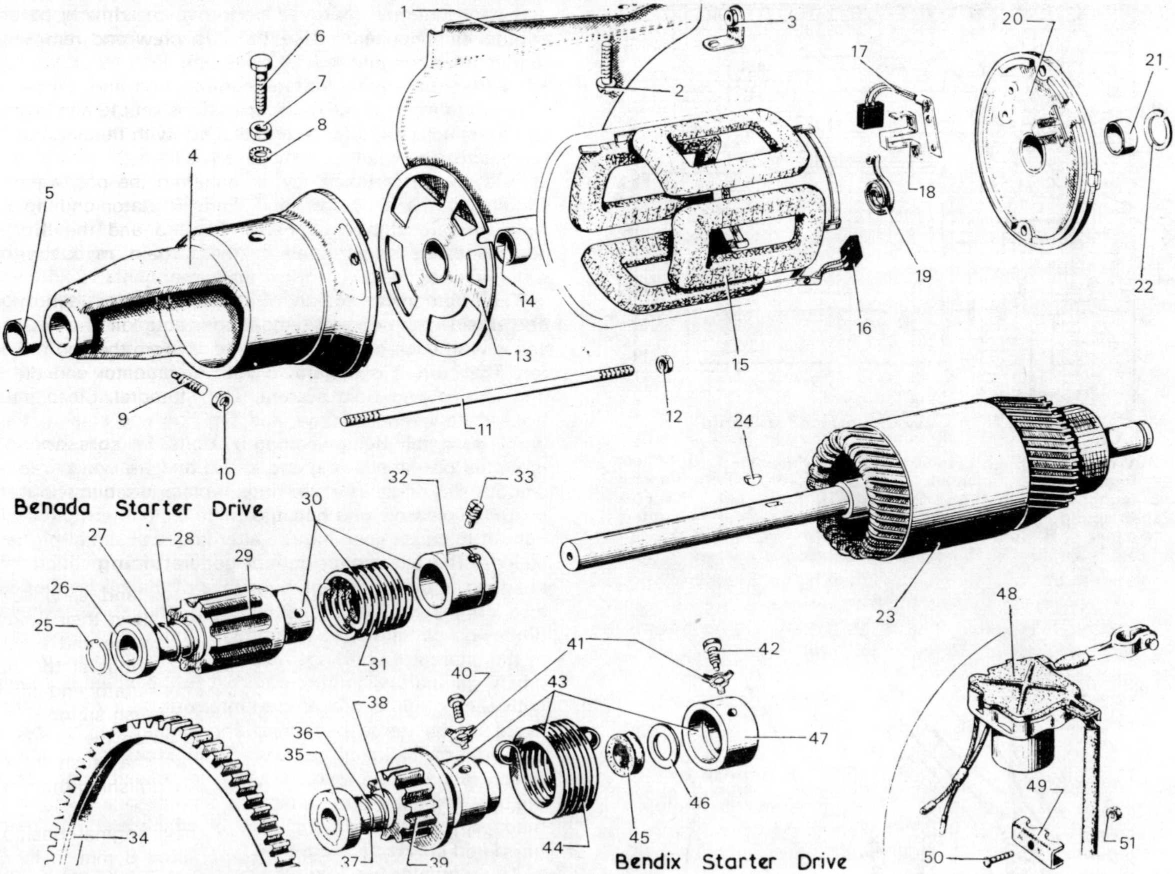

FIG 11:6 An exploded view of a starter motor

Key to Fig 11:6 1 Shield 2 Terminal 3 Screen support 4 Bearing housing 5 Bush 6 Screw securing motor 7 Nut 8 Shakeproof washer 9 Grubscrew for starter motor reaction 10 Nut 11 Assembly rod 12 Nut 13 Intermediate bearing plate 14 Bush 15 Field coils 16 Brush 17 Brush 18 Brush holder 19 Brush spring 20 Brush gear end plate 21 Bush 22 Circlip 23 Armature 24 Key for pinion drive 25 Circlip for thrust ring 26 Pinion thrust ring 27 Threaded sleeve 28 Spring 29 Pinion 30 Starter drive complete 31 Driving spring 32 Driving sleeve 33 Grubscrew 34 Gear ring 35 Pinion spring thrust nut 36 Threaded sleeve 37 Spring 38 Distance washer 39 Pinion 40 Screw for threaded sleeve 41 Lockplate 42 Screw for driving sleeve 43 Starter drive complete 44 Driving spring 45 Rubber bush for damper 46 Washer 47 Driving sleeve 48 Solenoid 49 Clamp 50 Screw 51 Nut

2 Assemble the drive end bracket. Grease the bearing with high melting point grease and if it has been removed insert it into the end bracket and refit the housing plate. Replace original rivets by round-headed screws, nuts and serrated washers.

3 Fit the brushes, connect the cables and bring the brushes into contact with the armature. Make sure that the brushes are correctly positioned with free movement. Retain the brushes in a raised position by means of the springs.

4 Insert the assembly of the armature and end bracket in the body of the generator, also the driving end bracket on the armature shaft. Release the brushes and ensure that they bear on the commutator. Attach the two end brackets by the screws and nuts fitted with insulating and serrated washers, or turn over lockwashers if fitted. Note that dowels may position the end brackets.

5 Connect the output terminal to the positive brush holder. Fit the key on the shaft and the driving pulley, with a shakeproof washer under the retaining nut.

6 Refit the generator by locating the slot in the front fixing plate between the plain washer of the fixing screw and the bellhousing. Locate the retaining screws with spring and plain washers.

7 Swing the generator towards the engine and fit the belts on the pulley. Couple up the tie-rod and tension the belts as described in **Chapter 5**.

8 Tighten the retaining screws, connect the generator leads to the regulator and finally refit and connect the battery.

11:7 The alternator and regulator

The advantages of an AC alternator in the electrical system instead of the normal DC generator are that the alternator can operate at higher speeds than the generator

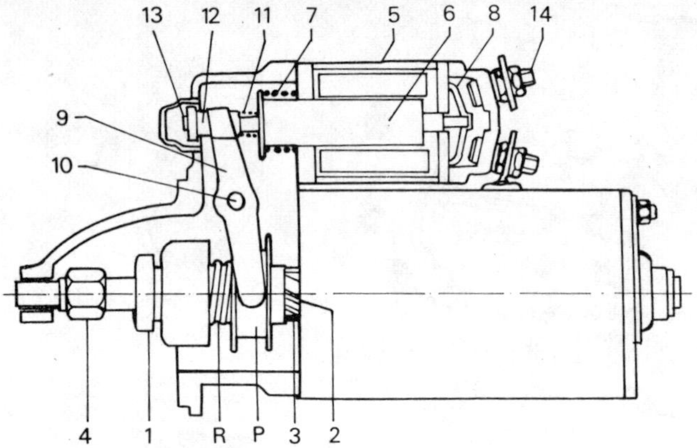

FIG 11:7 A view of a starter solenoid

Key to Fig 11:7 1 Pinion 2 Spiral splines 3 Spacer 4 Pinion nut 5 Solenoid 6 Plunger core 7 Return spring 8 Plunger contact plate 9 Fork 10 Fork shaft 11 Fork shaft spring 12 Fork rod 13 Plunger rod 14 Battery terminal **R** Spring **P** Fork collar

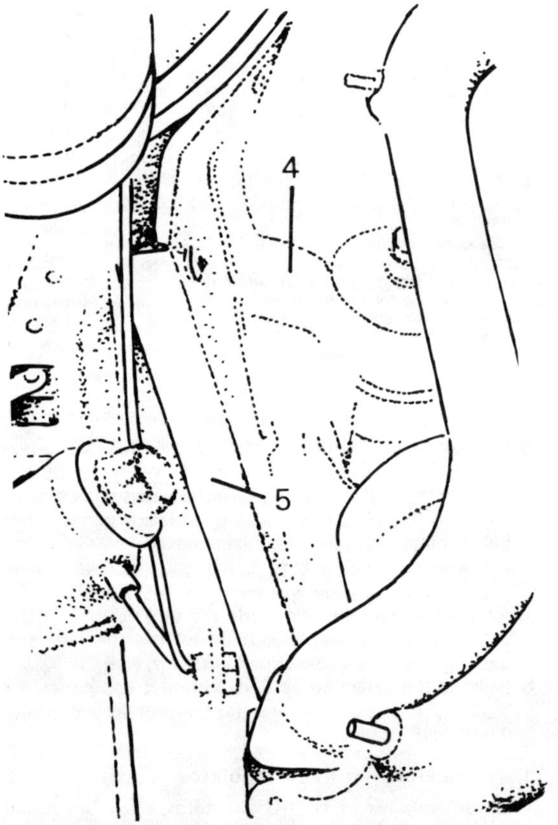

FIG 11:8 Starter damping weight 4 and anti-drumming plate 5

and consequently improved performance is obtained at engine idling speeds. Also there is no commutator to require attention and regulation is simplified by providing an instrument only for voltage control.

Dismantling and overhaul operations on the alternator call for special experience and test equipment, especially for electronic details, and it is advised that such work should be undertaken by a qualified service agent. Details of the Ducellier and Paris-Rhone alternators, however, are shown in **FIGS 11:2** and **11:3.** Both alternators are constructed on the same lines but with differences of design of individual components.

The unit consists mainly of a rotor, a stator, a slip ring end shield with two rectifying diodes and a safety fuse in series with each diode, a drive end shield, a pulley and a fan. The current is generated with a stationary armature and a revolving field system. The stator and rotor are housed between the drive and slip ring end shields, the whole assembly being secured by bolts. Two brushes are mounted on the slip ring end shield and bear on the two smooth slip rings. The slip rings replace the commutator on DC generators and because there is no interruption of current to cause sparking the alternator can run at higher speeds. The alternating current generated is rectified, or changed to direct current, by means of the silicon diodes also contained within the slip ring end shield. These diodes do not allow the return of current from the battery to the alternator windings and hence the normal cut-out on DC generators is not required. A fuse element in series with each diode is provided to interrupt the circuit in the event of the diode becoming shortcircuited. The rotor, mounted on ballbearings, carries the excitation winding which receives the feed through the collector rings and the brushes. The stator consists of a single-phase winding made up of two coils, the ends of which are separately fused and connected together.

The regulator has two terminals, one connected to the positive terminal of the ignition coil and the other connected to the EXC terminal of the alternator. The regulator base plate must be carefully earthed. The main purpose of the regulator is to keep the output voltage of the alternator within defined limits, which is achieved by varying the excitation current of the alternator.

11:8 Testing the alternator and regulator

Whenever work is undertaken on an alternator charging system care must be taken as follows to avoid serious damage to the diodes:

1 All alternator systems have negative earth and the leads of the battery must never be reversed, otherwise the diodes will be burned out and the wiring possibly damaged.

2 Battery leads, or any wires in the charging system, must not be disconnected whilst the engine is running.

3 Disconnect the battery leads if charging the battery from an outside source.

4 The alternator must never be run with the output disconnected.

5 Never check the operation of the unit by shortcircuiting either the positive terminal and earth or the excitation terminal and earth.

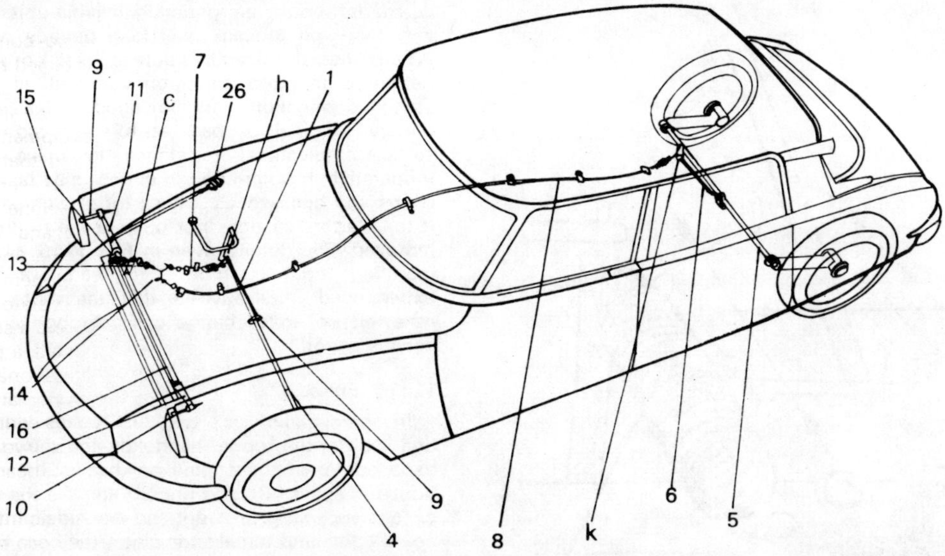

FIG 11 : 9 Main headlights mechanism

Key to Fig 11 : 9 1 Headlamp control torsion rod, front 4 Anti-roll bar, front 5 Anti-roll bar, rear 6 Headlamp control torsion rod, rear 7 Cable for front control 8 Cable for rear control 9 Control rod, righthand 10 Control rod, lefthand 11 Control lever, righthand 12 Control lever, lefthand 13 Adjuster 14 Integrator 15 Return spring 16 Headlamp control cross bar, front 26 Delay device **e** Lever for control rod **g** Clamp for control torsion rod, front **h** Cable hook lever

6 Disconnect the battery when removing the sparking plug nearest the alternator in case the plug spanner touches the alternator positive terminal.

7 The regulator should never operate without being earthed, otherwise the regulator windings will be destroyed.

Faults in the charging system are first to be sought in the condition of the battery, defective wiring connections or the loose adjustment of the driving belt. If the alternator is then suspect, proceed as follows:

1 Connect an ammeter in series on the output circuit, i.e., the thick cable.

2 Disconnect the excitation cable at the alternator to cut off the excitation circuit.

3 Using a separate cable, connect the alternator excitation circuit to the positive terminal of a battery for the full feed (14V) of the excitation circuit.

4 Check the driving belt tension and run the alternator at 3500 rev/min just for the time required to obtain the current reading. If the current reading gives a result not far away from the values indicated on the output diagram in **FIG 11 : 4**, the alternator is working correctly and the fault lies in the regulator circuit.

To check the regulator, connect as indicated in **FIG 11 : 5.** Maintain an output of 5 amps with battery and resistances connected in parallel until the meters have stabilized and then the voltage reading at 5 amp should be 13.4V to 14.2V and at 30 amp 13.0V to 13.8V.

Removal of the alternator is attained by disconnecting the leads from the terminals, slackening the driving belt and unbolting the unit from the engine. A visual check of the stator should be made to ensure that the windings are not burned or damaged. Examine the brushes, which should have a minimum length of 3 mm. Testing of the insulation may be made with the aid of a test lamp in series, after disconnecting the diodes. A similar test may be made between the slip ring and one of the pole clamps, using a 110V source. If the test lamp lights up, the rotor is faulty.

11 : 9 The starter motor

Starter motors may be of either the Ducellier or Paris-Rhone inertia type, the main components of which are generally similar and are shown in **FIG 11 : 6.** Also shown are details of the Benada and Bendix types of starter drive and a view of the separate solenoid used to energize the starter (No. 13 in the wiring diagram in the Appendix). Since September, 1968, however, the solenoid is incorporated on the starter (see **FIG 11 : 7**). In operation, when the starter switch is closed the solenoid is energized and the pinion drive moves forwards, causing the pinion to engage with the ring gear on the flywheel.

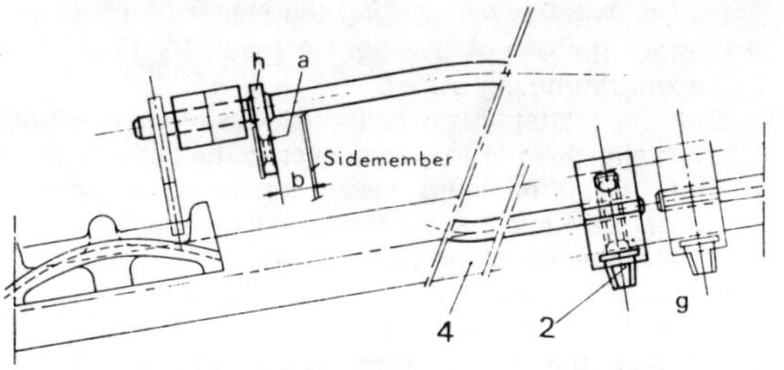

FIG 11 : 10 Adjustment of main headlights

Key to Fig 11 : 10 2 Clamp screw 4 Anti-roll bar **a** Lever **b** 8.5 to 10.5 mm **g** Clamp **h** Cable hook

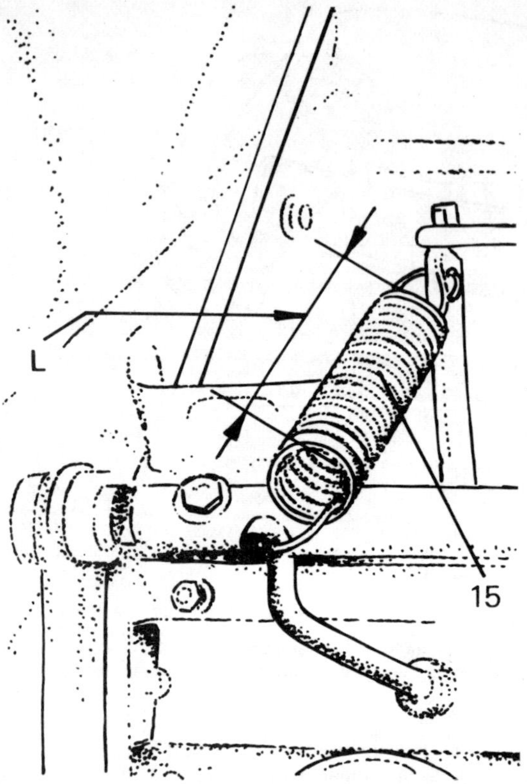

FIG 11 :11 Adjusting the length L of the return spring 15

The armature starts turning slowly until at the end of the solenoid stroke the starter receives full current and turns the engine. Release of the starter switch enables the solenoid to withdraw the gear and disconnect the supply to the motor.

Operations to remove and refit the starter motor are as follows:

1. Release the pressure, place the manual height control in the low position and remove the righthand front suspension sphere. Fit a sealing plug on the cylinder.
2. Disconnect the negative cable from the battery, and the starter cable from the starter motor.
3. Bend upwards the protective shield of the engine mounting and remove (a) the air filter and its bracket, (b) the protection shield for the exhaust manifold and (c) the two screws securing the starter motor shield.
4. Remove the damping weight 4 (see **FIG 11 :8**) and the anti-drumming plate 5.
5. Slide the starter shield as far as possible to the front of the engine so as to gain access to the collar.
6. Remove the retaining screw from above, using a 12 mm box spanner to remove the collar, sliding it towards the rear of the starter motor.
7. Remove the motor shield and the three securing screws from the starter motor.
8. Withdraw the starter motor towards the rear and upwards. To facilitate its removal a cable may be fixed on the rear stud of the starter motor.
9. Refit in the reverse order of the removal operations.

Starter motors are generally reliable units which give very little for concern over long periods of operation. When checking starter troubles, first ensure that the battery is in good condition and that all battery and starter connections are in good order. A corroded battery terminal or bad earth connection may have sufficient electrical resistance to make the starter inoperative, though enough current may be available for lamps and accessories. Check for a jammed pinion and if the starter still does not operate the motor should be removed. The details given in **FIG 11 :6** will guide dismantling and reassembly if required, but if trouble is experienced it is advised that the motor should be renewed on an exchange basis through an accredited service agent.

11 :10 Fuses

In some earlier cars two fuse boxes were installed, one each at the top lefthand side and the bottom righthand corner of the engine bulkhead. The lefthand box houses a spare fuse and one 30-amp fuse protecting the circuits supplying the front and rear sidelights, the dashboard lights and the electric clock, the boot light and the number plate light. On the righthand side are two 30-amp fuses, one with a yellow lead serving the circuits of the wiper motor, cigar lighter and the spare terminal for supplementary accessories, the other with a white lead protecting all other circuits excepting the ignition coil, horn and headlights high beam.

In all cars after September, 1969, a single fuse box is situated at the top lefthand side of the bulkhead and houses two 10-amp and two 16-amp fuses from left to right facing the car. The circuits protected are as follows:

1. Green lead (16-amp): Interior lights, direction indicators and warning lights, charging circuit warning light, cigarette lighter, righthand heating system and rear window heating (where fitted).
2. Red lead (16-amp): Revolution counter, fuel gauge, warning light dial, windscreen washer pump, wiper motor, accessory terminal, stoplights, clock, heater motor and glove compartment lighting (Pallas only).
3. Blue lead 10-amp: Parking lights.
4. Yellow lead (10-amp): Rear number plate light, boot light/sidelight warning lamp, dashboard lighting, town lights/clock light and heating control light (Pallas only).

11 :11 Headlight operation and adjustment

A four-headlight system is installed with the headlights in pairs behind moulded glass covers, but only the outer ones dip up and down. These have twin-filament lamps and are connected to the front and rear suspensions to give a constant beam height irrespective of the pitch of the car when accelerating or braking. Cables run from each anti-roll bar to be hooked on a lever on a transverse bar connecting the two headlights and a dashpot is incorporated to prevent immediate response to minor road irregularities. Sidelight bulbs are fitted in the reflectors of the main headlights.

The inner or auxiliary headlights are long-distance ones which extinguish when the outer pair is dipped and which are brought into use by a switch on the dashboard.

In Pallas models in 1967 and optionally on other models a year later, a swivelling system connected to the

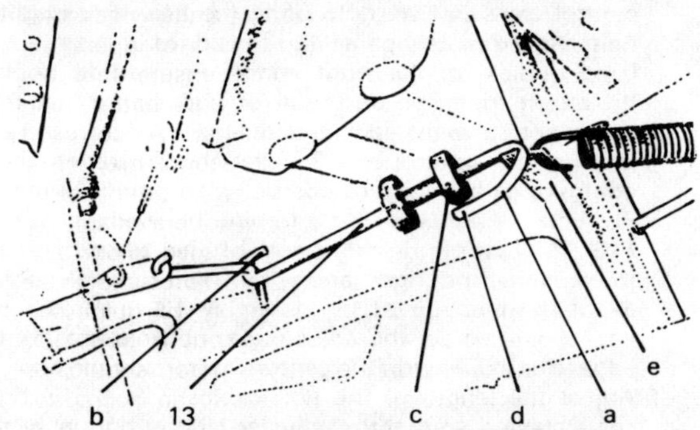

FIG 11:12 Adjusting the main headlights

Key to Fig 11:12 **a, b** Hooks at each end of the front rod **c** Adjusting knob **d** Central mark on front hook 13 Front rod assembly

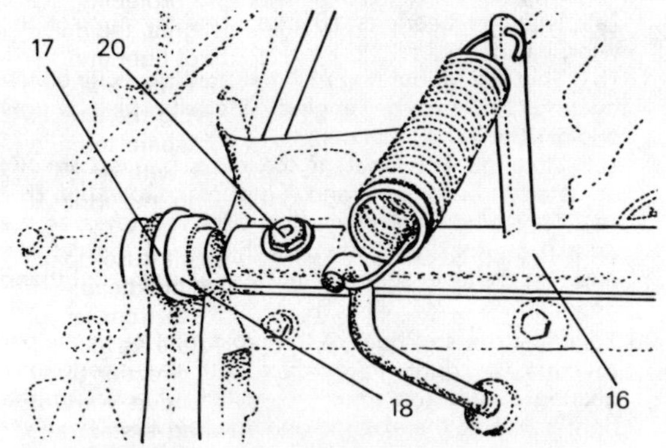

FIG 11:13 Adjusting cross bar end float

Key to Fig 11:13 16 Cross bar 17 Rubber rings 18 Bearing 20 Retaining screws

steering mechanism was incorporated in the auxiliary headlights, enabling them to rotate so that the beams automatically follow the movement of the front wheels. The system is designed so that the lights do not rotate by the same amount; the light on the inside of a turn follows the nearer side of the road more than the light on the outside. On full lock the beams swing through an arc of nearly 90 deg. Another feature is that the beams tilt slightly to compensate for body roll on short bends. At the same time, as standard on Pallas cars and optional on other models, tungsten/iodine quartz bulbs were provided for the auxiliary headlights, giving a longer life and proportionately higher brilliance than the usual tungsten bulbs.

Adjustments of the control mechanism for the main headlamps is carried out with the height control in the normal position, the tyres correctly inflated and the engine idling. Referring to **FIGS 11:9** and **11:10**, adjustments may be made as follows:

1 For the lateral position of the headlamp control torsion rod on the front anti-roll bar 4, measure the distance between the face 'a' of the cable hook lever and the outer side of the righthand sidemember,

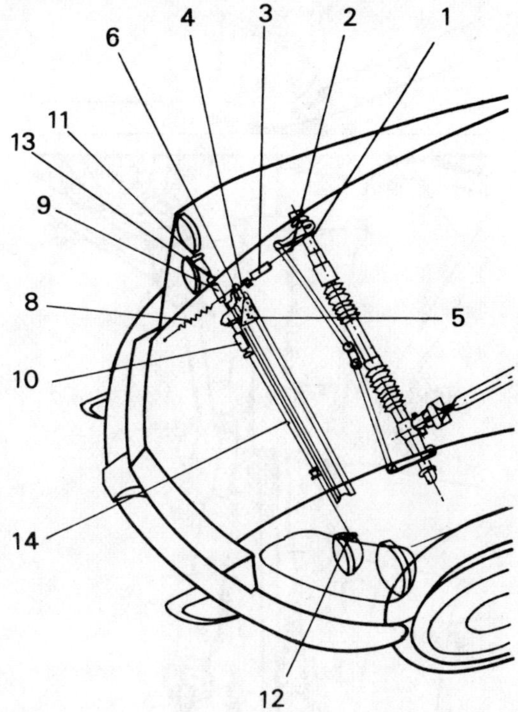

FIG 11:14 Auxiliary headlights control mechanism

Key to Fig 11:14 1 Control lever 2 Rear control rod 3 Adjusting sleeve 4 Front control rod 5 Bell lever support 6 Bell lever 8 Return spring 9 Righthand adjusting sleeve 10 Lefthand adjusting sleeve 11 Lever for righthand lamp 12 Lever for lefthand lamp 13 Righthand cable 14 Lefthand cable

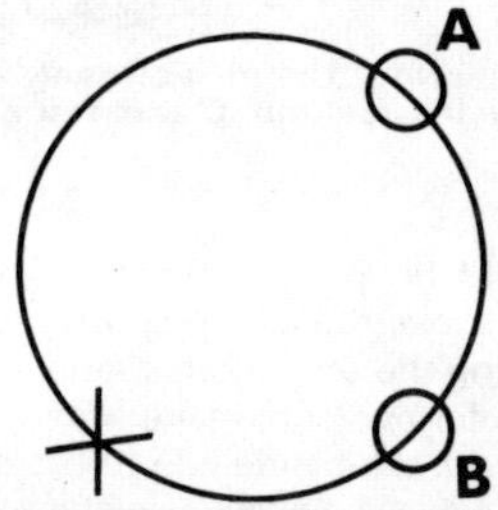

FIG 11:15 Location of adjusting screws, movable main headlights

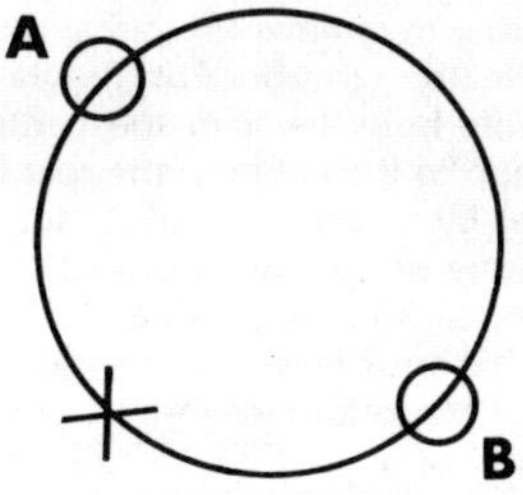

FIG 11:16 Location of adjusting screws, fixed main headlights

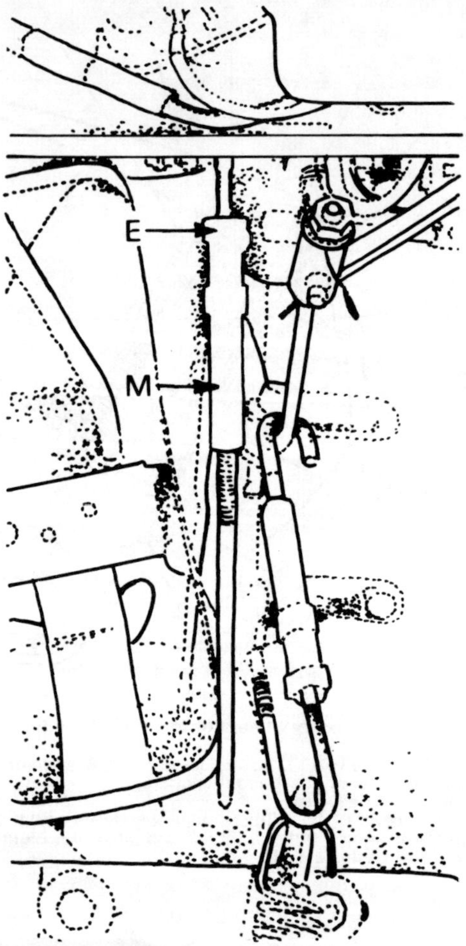

FIG 11:17 Adjusting the directional auxiliary headlights, showing the locknut E and the adjusting sleeve M

which should be 8.5 to 10.5 mm as shown at 'b'. If necessary move the clamp 'g' on the anti-roll bar 4, after loosening the screw 2 in clamp 'g'.

2 For the angular position, make an angle of 90 deg. ± 5 deg. between the centre line of the cable hook lever 'h' and the cable 7 by moving the clamp 'g' on the anti-roll bar. Tighten the screw 2 holding the clamp on the anti-roll bar.

3 To position the headlamp control torsion rod 6 on the rear anti-roll bar 5, remove the metal panel protecting the rear corrector control. For the lateral position, place the cable hook lever in the centre of the hole for the passage of the cable in the rear unit. The lever may be offset by a maximum of 2 mm to the right or left of the centre of the hole. For the angular position, make an angle of 90 deg. ± 5 deg. between the centre line of the cable hook lever and the cable.

4 The length of the return spring 15 should be 75 ± 5 mm as shown at L in **FIG 11:11.** To adjust, disconnect the adjuster 13 from the lever on the cross-bar 16. Then position the lever 'e' of the headlamp control cross-bar so as to bring the headlamps light units approximately parallel to the edges of the headlamp bodies on the front wings. Proceed to hook the return spring 15 on the lever, choosing a hole in the lever to give the specified dimension. If necessary, readjust the control rod 9. After this operation the control rods should protrude between 8 and 28 mm.

5 Position the adjuster 13 by turning the hook 'a' (see **FIG 11:12**) of the front rod of the assembly 13 towards the front righthand wing. Then turn the hook 'b' of the rear rod of the assembly 13 towards the engine and screw the adjusting knob until the front edge 'c' is in line with the central mark 'd' on the hook.

6 Adjust the length of the two cables 7 and 8 using cable clamps, so that the adjuster 13 is at right angles to a line passing through the holes in the cable clamps on the ingegrator 14 and so that the headlamp light units are approximately parallel to the edges of the headlamp bodies on the front wings.

7 For the cross-bar 16 to operate without any strain, referring to **FIG 11:13** it is necessary to ensure:

(a) That the bearings 18 butt correctly against the wing valance.

(b) That the rubber rings 17 are fitted correctly on the bearings 18 on the engine side and also snugly against the wing valance.

(c) That the end float of the cross-bar is correctly adjusted to between 2 and 4 mm (see Operation 8).

(d) That when the cross-bar is moved towards the right it returns freely towards the left of the vehicle, and that the lever seats correctly against the righthand bearing.

8 To adjust the end float of the cross-bar, push the bar towards the right, in contact with the spring, the bearing 18 and the adjacent washer. Measure on the righthand side the existing end float between the lever and the bearing, which should be 2 to 4 mm. To adjust, loosen the screws 20 holding the bar. Move the rod laterally in the slots provided, tighten the screws 20 and again check the end float.

The control system for the auxiliary headlights is shown in **FIG 11:14.** A bracket on the righthand side steering lever is connected to a rear control rod 2, which acts on a bell lever 6 through an adjusting sleeve 3 and a front control rod 4. The bell lever is supported on a bracket 5 attached by three bolts to the internal face of the spare wheel crossmember. Movement of the steering lever is thus transmitted to the headlights operating cables 13 and 14 through two threaded rods and two adjusters. A main return spring keeps the steering/bell lever control under

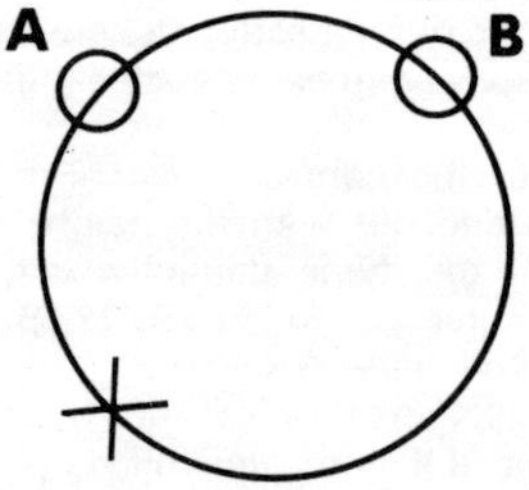

FIG 11:18 Location of adjusting screws for fixed auxiliary headlights

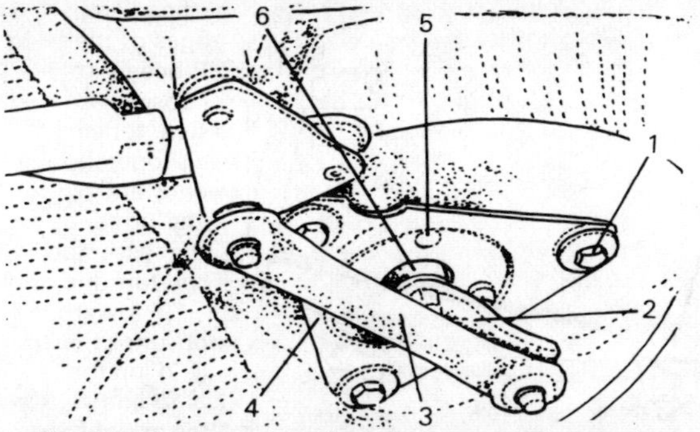

FIG 11:19 Removing the windscreen wiper motor

Key to Fig 11:19 1 Retaining screws 2 Motor connecting rod 3 Control arm 4 Backplate 5 Screws 6 Distance piece

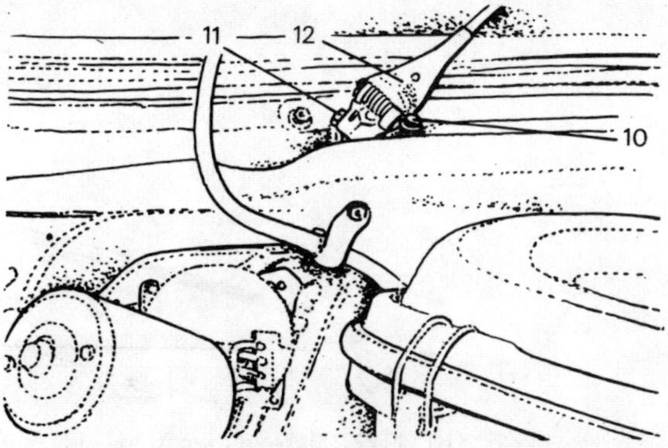

FIG 11:20 Wiper arm linkage, showing the arm 12 and securing screws 10 and 11

tension and two return springs, one for each headlight, ensure the correct tension of the operating cables.

For the adjustment of the control it must be ensured that the steering is in the straight-ahead position (see **Chapter 9**). Adjust the sleeve 3 until the bell lever 6 is exactly at a right-angle to the crossmember, then tighten the locknut. Turn the steering wheel to the full righthand lock and check that the end of the bell lever does not touch the ventilation duct of the radiator. If necessary, move the duct to the left by altering the position of the screws in the slots to obtain a minimum clearance of 2 mm.

The positions of the screws for adjusting the main large diameter headlights are shown in **FIGS 11:15** (movable type) and **11:16** (fixed type) showing a lefthand light viewed from the rear, the righthand one being symmetrical. To adjust the height turn the screw A and to adjust in the horizontal plane turn the screw B.

In the case of the small diameter auxiliary headlights, the lights should be directed along the axis of the car when driving straight-ahead. Simultaneous adjustment is obtained by means of the white sleeve M (see **FIG 11:17**) in the tie-rod. Slacken the locknut E at the rear end of the sleeve. Unscrew the sleeve to position to the right and screw up the sleeve to position to the left. Stop the car facing a wall at least 50 feet (15 m) away and assess the angle which the headlights should traverse while driving. Turn the sleeve to obtain the required correction then tighten the locknut E. Repeat the process as necessary to obtain a satisfactory setting. For fixed lights, refer to **FIG 11:18,** showing a lefthand light viewed from the rear with the righthand one symmetrical. Turn the screw A for vertical adjustment and the screw B for horizontal adjustment. For comprehensive alignment of the headlights the assistance of a service agent with the necessary equipment should be obtained.

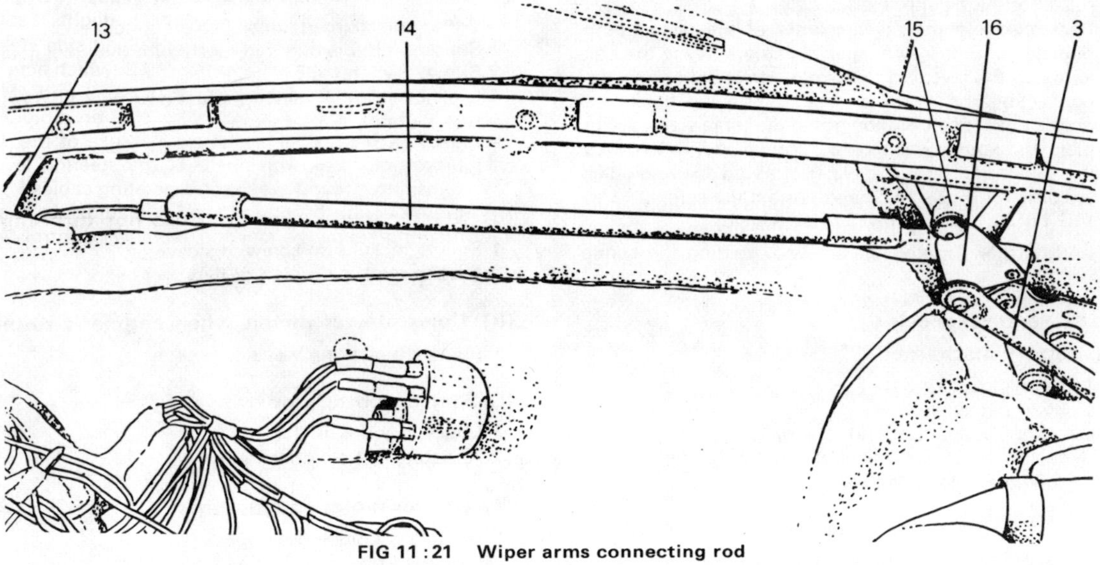

FIG 11:21 Wiper arms connecting rod

Key to Fig 11:21 3 Control arm 13, 15 Supports for arm spindles 14 Connecting rod

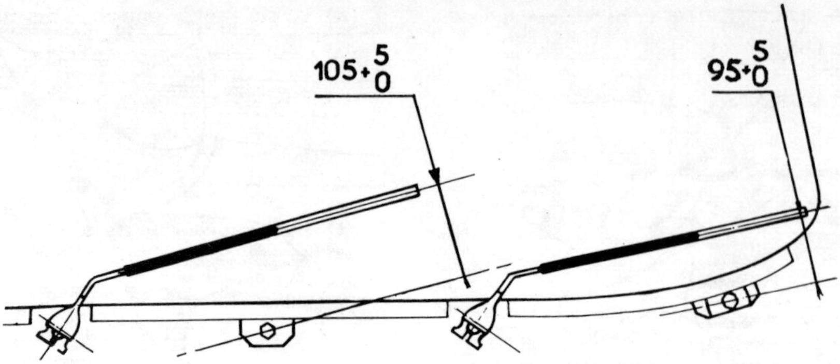

FIG 11 : 22 Correct locations of windscreen wiper arms. Dimensions are in mm

11 : 12 Wiper motor removal and refitting

To remove the windscreen wiper motor, first remove the facia panel as described in **Chapter 12** and then proceed as follows:

1 Remove with a screwdriver the nylon bush securing the control arm 3 (see **FIG 11 : 19**) to the ballpin on the motor connecting rod 2 and disconnect the arm.
2 Remove the three retaining screws 1 and the backplate 4. Disconnect the supply leads from the motor noting the colour order and remove the motor with its plate and locators.
3 Loosen the screw 11 (see **FIG 11 : 20**) and free the wiper arms 12. Remove the angled packing piece and the rubber sealing gasket, then with a screwdriver remove the sealing compound from the windscreen round the heads of the screws 10.
4 On both righthand and lefthand sides remove the three screws 10 securing the bracket for the wiper arm spindle.
5 Remove the supports 13 and 15 (see **FIG 11 : 21**) for both wiper arm spindles together with the connecting rod 14 and the control arm 3.
6 Reassemble in the reverse order of the dismantling operations. Smear with special cardan grease the ball joints on the levers of the wiper arm spindles and the connecting rod nylon bushes. Centre the backplate on the three locators and tighten the three screws with plain and spring washers to a torque of 6 lb ft (.8 kg m). Finally position the wiper arms on their spindles as shown in **FIG 11 : 22** and tighten the screws 11 in **FIG 11 : 20** to a torque of 3 lb ft (.4 kg m).

11 : 13 Fault diagnosis

(a) Battery discharged

1 Terminals loose or dirty
2 Lighting circuit shorted
3 Generator or alternator not charging
4 Regulator or cut-out units not working properly
5 Battery internally defective

(b) Insufficient charging current

1 Loose or corroded battery terminals
2 Generator or alternator driving belt slipping

(c) Battery will not hold a charge

1 Low electrolyte level
2 Battery plates sulphated
3 Electrolyte leakage from cracked casing or top sealing compound.
4 Plate separators ineffective

(d) Battery overcharged

1 Voltage regulator needs adjusting

(e) Generator output low or nil

1 Belt broken or slipping
2 Regulator unit out of adjustment
3 Worn bearings, loose polepieces
4 Commutator worn, burned or shorted
5 Armature shaft bent or worn
6 Insulation proud between commutator segments
7 Brushes sticking, springs weak or broken
8 Field coil wires shorted, broken or burned

(f) Starter motor lacks power or will not operate

1 Battery discharged, loose cable connections
2 Starter pinion jammed in mesh with flywheel gear
3 Starter switch faulty
4 Brushes worn or sticking, leads detached or shorting
5 Commutator dirty or worn
6 Starter shaft bent
7 Engine abnormally stiff

(g) Starter motor runs but does not turn engine

1 Pinion sticking on screwed sleeve
2 Broken teeth on pinion or flywheel gears

(h) Noisy starter pinion when engine is running

1 Restraining spring weak or broken

(j) Starter motor inoperative

1 Check 1 and 4 in (f)
2 Armature or field coils faulty

(k) Starter motor rough or noisy

1 Mounting bolts loose
2 Damaged pinion or flywheel gear teeth
3 Main pinion spring broken

(l) Lamps inoperative or erratic

1 Battery low, bulbs burned out
2 Faulty earthing of lamps or battery
3 Lighting switch faulty, loose or broken wiring connections

(m) Wiper motor sluggish, taking high current

1 Faulty armature
2 Bearings out of alignment
3 Commutator dirty or shortcircuited

(n) Wiper motor operates but does not drive arms

1 Gearbox components worn

(o) Fuel gauge does not register

1 No battery supply to gauge
2 Gauge casing not earthed
3 Cable between gauge and tank unit earthed

(p) Fuel gauge registers 'FULL'

1 Cable between gauge and tank unit broken or disconnected

NOTES

CHAPTER 12

THE BODYWORK

12:1 Removing door trim

Removal of a door interior trimming panel is undertaken by first removing the window winder handle 30 in **FIG 12:1**. The handle escutcheon is pressed down strongly with a suitable forked tool, as shown in the illustration, to give access for driving out the retaining pin. Then withdraw the handle, the escutcheon, the cup and the spring.

Insert a screwdriver between the trimming panel and the steel panel and lever out the panel clips all round the panel, which is withdrawn by lifting it upwards to disengage it from the armrest support plate. Do not remove the three felt pads attached to the steel panel, but detach the vinyl sealing panels from the interior openings if access to the door mechanism is required. The same operations in reverse order are undertaken when refitting. Attach the vinyl sealing panels on the edges of the interior openings with a good adhesive and fit the trimming panel by sliding it towards the bottom of the door and anchoring it on the armrest support plate.

12:2 Servicing door locks, remote control gear

A door is opened from the interior by gripping the handle (see **FIG 12:2**) and pressing the catch A with the thumb. The catch moves backwards. Then push the door open. When the door is closed, lock it by moving the catch forwards. To unlock it, press the button B. The two front doors must be locked with a key and cannot be locked from the inside.

The removal and refitting of a door lock and its controls are undertaken as follows:

1 Remove the door by lifting it upwards after unscrewing the door lower pivot bracket screw. Do not unscrew the upper pivot bracket screw in order to avoid altering the adjustment of the door.

2 Remove the glass guide on the lock side, the glass and the trimming panel (see **Section 12:1**).

3 Referring to **FIG 12:3**, remove the three lock fixing screws and then the lock by disconnecting the interior handle control rod 15.

4 Remove the interior handle 21. Referring to **FIG 12:1**, unscrew the handle fixing screw 17 by turning the hexagon 19 in a clockwise direction. Turn the handle a quarter of a turn to remove it from the door together with the control rod.

5 Remove the exterior door handle 14 (see **FIG 12:3**) by unscrewing the retaining screw 1 from the inside. Disengage the handle from the door by turning it a quarter of a turn.

6 To reassemble, fit the interior door handle 21 together with the shouldered rubber washer 24, the control rod 15 and the anti-rattle plate 26, introducing the

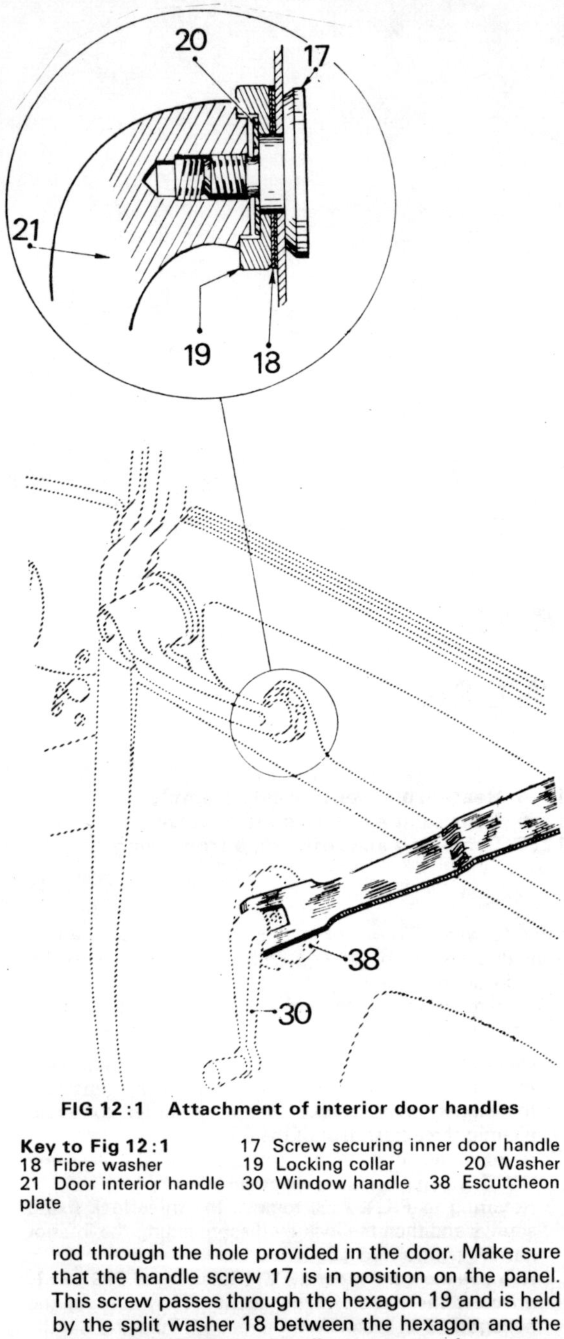

FIG 12:1 Attachment of interior door handles

Key to Fig 12:1 17 Screw securing inner door handle 18 Fibre washer 19 Locking collar 20 Washer 21 Door interior handle 30 Window handle 38 Escutcheon plate

rod through the hole provided in the door. Make sure that the handle screw 17 is in position on the panel. This screw passes through the hexagon 19 and is held by the split washer 18 between the hexagon and the door panel. Turn the handle a quarter of a turn to bring its end opposite the second fixing hole and secure it by turning the hexagon in an anticlockwise direction.

7 Fit the lock on the door and connect the control rod 15 on the lock catch 16. Secure the lock by the three screws 3 and check its operation.

8 Fit the exterior handle 14, also the rubber washer 7, then turn the handle a quarter of a turn.

9 Locate the fixing plate 4 on the hub of the handle from the inside of the door. Turn the plate a quarter of a turn. Fit the washer 2 between the handle and the door handle and secure by the screw 1 through the interior of the door.

10 Refit the door on the car. Fit the glass guide, the glass and the door panel (see **Section 12:1**).

To renew a door lock barrel, close the window and remove the window winder and door panel as previously described. Partially detach the vinyl sheet and from the inside of the door take out the retaining screw 1 (see **FIG 12:3**) and remove the door handle 14 by turning it through a quarter of a turn. Withdraw the retaining plate. Now remove the locknut 6 and the adjusting screw 5, slide out the pushbutton 11 and its return spring 13, then remove the circlip 9 and the lock barrel 10. Note the direction in which the barrel is fitted for later reassembly.

When reassembling, fit the ignition key in the lock barrel 10 and the barrel in the pushbutton 11. Press the barrel right to the bottom of the pushbutton so that it can be secured by its circlips. Fit the return spring 13 and the pushbutton in the door handle. Press down the pushbutton and screw together the adjusting screw 5 and the locknut 6 in the button. Fit the handle as described in the foregoing Operations 8 and 9. Refit the vinyl door lining with a good adhesive and then the trimming panel and the window winder.

12:3 Removing and refitting the facia panel

Operations to remove and refit the facia panel are as follows:

1 Disconnect the negative lead from the battery.

2 Remove the screws holding the finisher 9 (see **FIG 12:4**) over the steering aperture and move the finisher back.

3 Remove the cover 4 from the electrical control bracket. Then remove the screws securing the speedometer surround 5, the reset knob 3 from the speedometer and the buttons 1 from the ventilation shutter controls. Remove the speedometer surround.

4 Disconnect the wiring harness from behind the switches next to the speedometer and behind the speedometer itself. Disconnect the flexible cable and remove the speedometer.

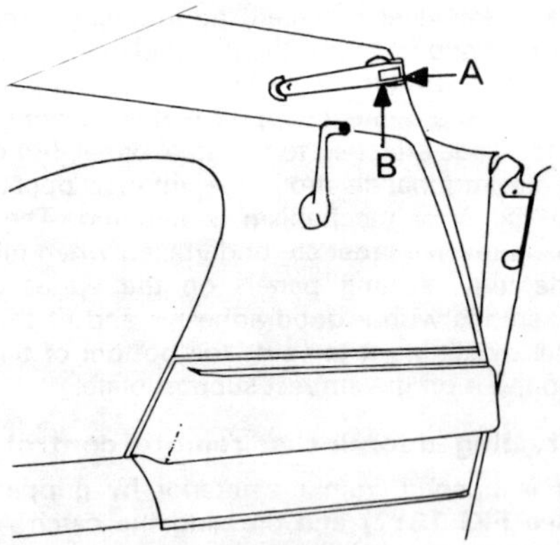

FIG 12:2 Door opening and locking mechanism, showing the catch A and the button B

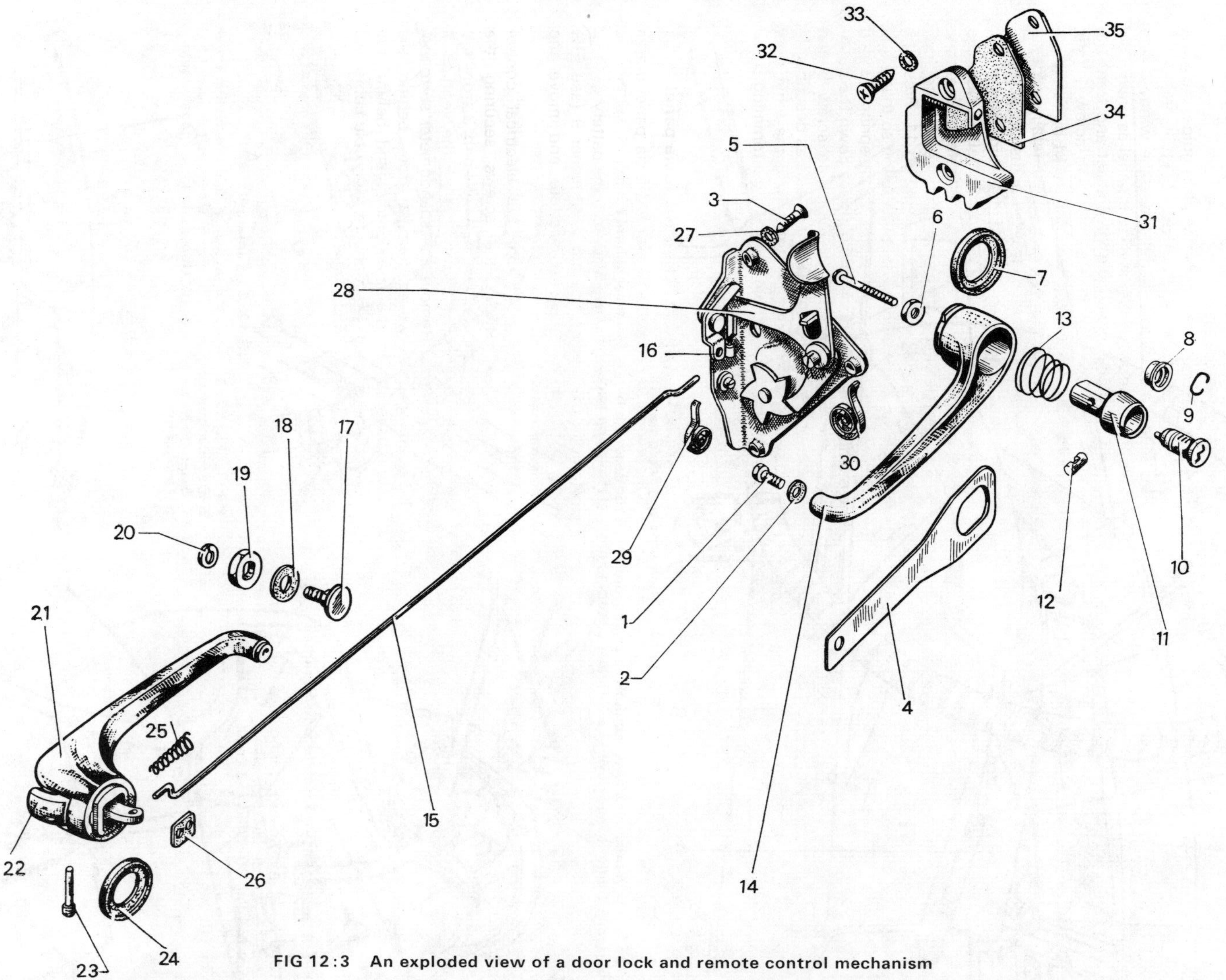

FIG 12:3 An exploded view of a door lock and remote control mechanism

Key to Fig 12:3 1 Screw, exterior door handle 2 Fibre washer 3 Screws securing lock 4 Locking plate 5 Screw for adjusting push button 6 Nut 7 Shouldered rubber washer 8 Cup retaining push button 9 Circlip 10 Lock barrel 11 Push button 12 Locking pin 13 Return spring 14 External handle 15 Remote control rod 16 Lock catch for control rod 17 Screw securing inner handle 18 Fibre washer 19 Locking collar 20 Washer 21 Interior handle 22 Tongue for safety catch 23 Pin for safety catch 24 Shouldered rubber washer 25 Return spring 26 Anti-rattle plate for control rod 27 Washer 28 Door lock 29 Spring for locking catch 30 Return spring, door lock lever 31 Striking plate 32 Screw 33 Washer 34 Plate on pillars 35 Adjusting plate

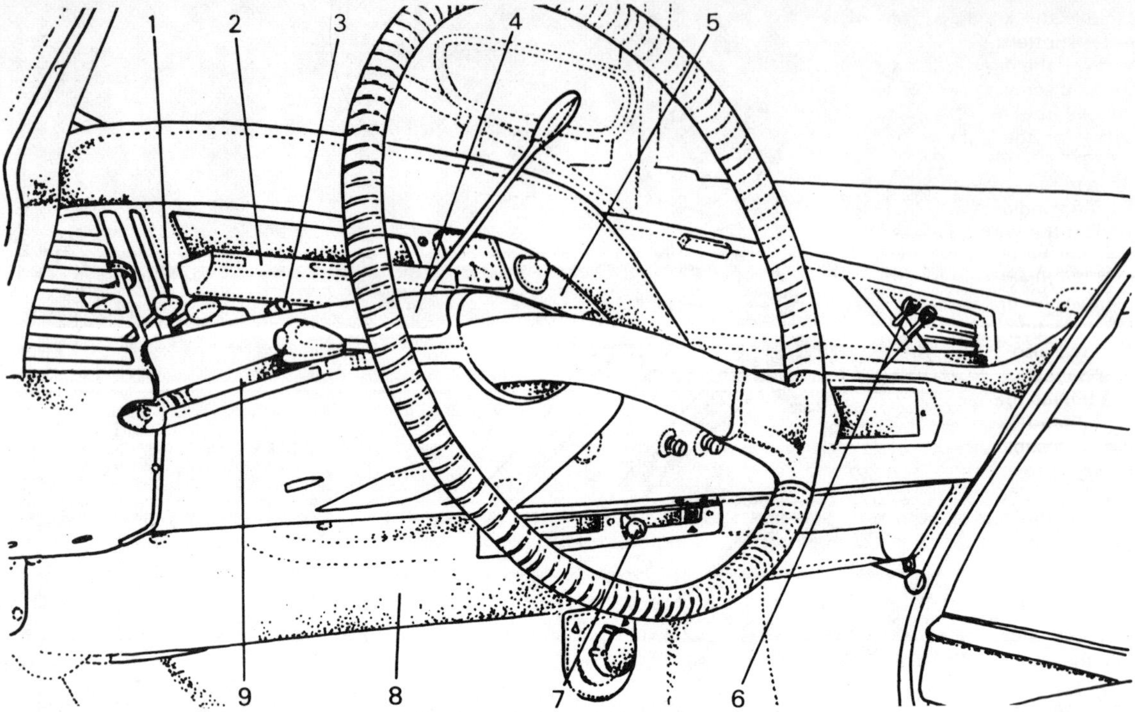

FIG 12:4 A view of the facia panel

Key to Fig 12:4 1 Ventilation shutter controls 2 Speedometer 3 Reset knob 4 Electrical control cover 5 Speedometer surround 6 Heater shutter control levers 7 Heater control knobs 8 Finishing panel 9 Finisher

FIG 12:5 Facia switch locations

Key to Fig 12:5 6 Support for electrical control unit 7 Switch for lighting and horns 8 Switch for direction indicators with headlamp flashers

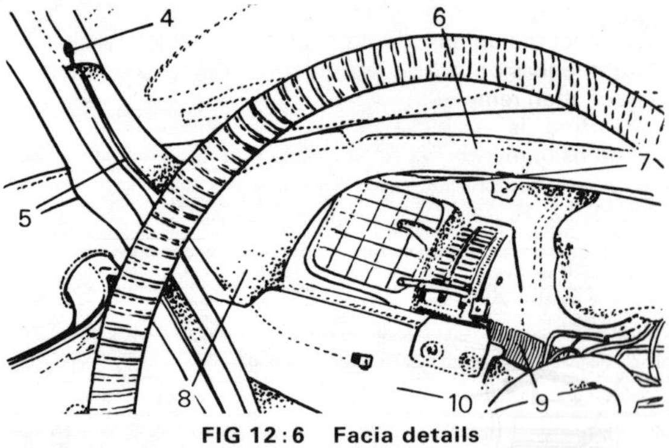

FIG 12:6 Facia details

Key to Fig 12:6 4 Screw securing demisting nozzle 5 Demisting nozzle 6 Upper part of facia panel 7 Securing nuts 8, 10 Upper and lower panel assembly 9 Flexible tube

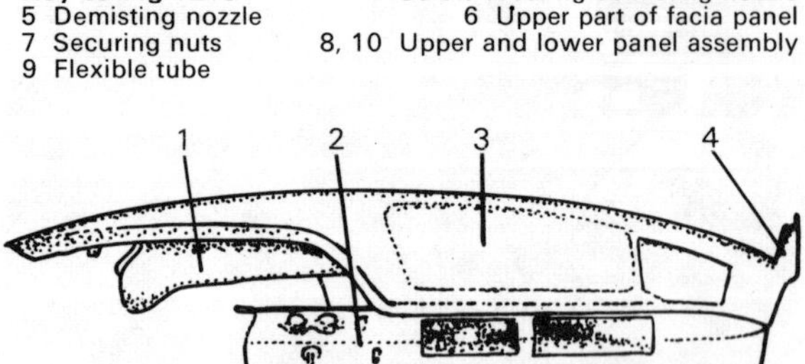

FIG 12:7 Righthand facia panel assembly

Key to Fig 12:7 1 Demisting duct 2 Lower facia panel 3 Upper facia panel 4 Demisting nozzle

5 Remove the knobs 6 from the control levers of the heater shutters.
6 Remove the finishing panel 8 after taking out the retaining screws under the facia.
7 Remove the nuts securing the switch 7 (see **FIG 12:5**) for the lighting and horns together with its wiring.
8 Remove the screw holding the 'AXO' switch 8 for the direction indicators with headlight flashers and disconnect the wiring harness.
9 Remove the electrical control unit 6 with the switch 8 for the direction indicators.
10 Remove the upper screw 4 (see **FIG 12:6**) securing the demisting nozzle 5 for the lefthand front door window, also the screw securing the lower lefthand facia panel.
11 Disconnect the assembly of the upper 8 and lower 10 lefthand facia panel and disconnect the nozzle from its flexible tube 9.
12 Remove the ashtray and the screw securing the map pocket, placing the map pocket towards the rear.
13 Remove the rubber stop from the rear view mirror support and remove the mirror. Remove the righthand ventilation grille.
14 Remove the nuts on both righthand and lefthand sides securing the upper part of the facia panel 6 on the righthand side. Remove the upper securing screw from the demisting nozzle for the front righthand door window.
15 Disconnect the choke cable from the carburetter, the harnesses and the rubber tubes from the windscreen washer pump.
16 Referring to **FIG 12:7,** free the assembly of upper 3 and lower 2 righthand facia panel and the nozzle 4 for demisting the righthand front window glass. Disconnect the union pipe 6 (see **FIG 12:8**) between the righthand side nozzle and the windscreen demisting duct, then remove the righthand facia panel assembly.

Refitting is undertaken by following the removal operations in reverse order. Note that the upper part of the facia panel must be engaged fully under the finishing strip 5 in **FIG 12:8.** Allow a small clearance when connecting the choke cable to the carburetter. When connecting the leads to the switches, refer as necessary to the wiring diagram in the Appendix.

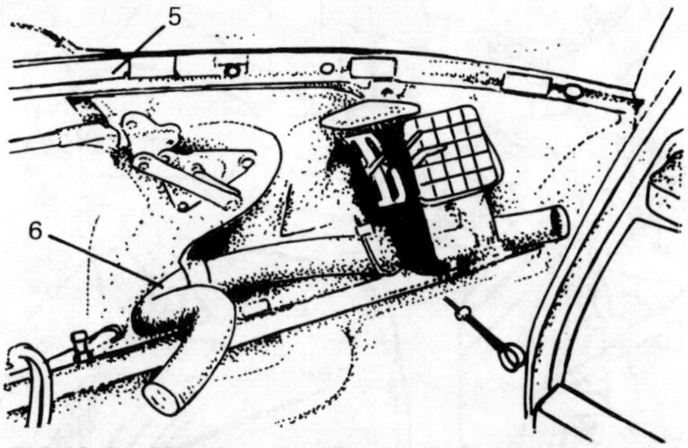

FIG 12:8 Showing finishing strip 5 between windscreen and facia panel and union pipe 6 between windscreen demisting duct and righthand side nozzle

12:4 Heating and ventilating assembly

Air ventilation and heating for the interior of the car, also for demisting and defrosting the windscreen and front door windows, is obtained from an inlet between the front bumpers. Insect screens are provided which should be periodically cleaned, otherwise the efficiency of the system will be reduced. A centrifugal blower ensures that the heating and ventilation remain effective with the car at rest with the engine running or when travelling at low speed. Three central levers 40, 41 and 42 (see **FIG 12:9**) control the distribution, temperature and volume of the air supply, in conjunction with the switch 33 for the booster fan. There are three controls for each of the facia vents and additional outlets above the ventilator grilles direct heated air on the side windows for demisting.

Operations to remove and refit the heating and ventilating assembly are as follows:

1 Disconnect the negative lead from the battery and remove the lefthand front wing (see **Section 12:6**).
2 Disconnect the flexible water return pipes 4 (see **FIG 12:10**) and feedpipes 1. Plug them with conical wooden plugs.
3 Remove the three screws securing the heater unit on its bracket, retaining the rubber bushes and plain washers.

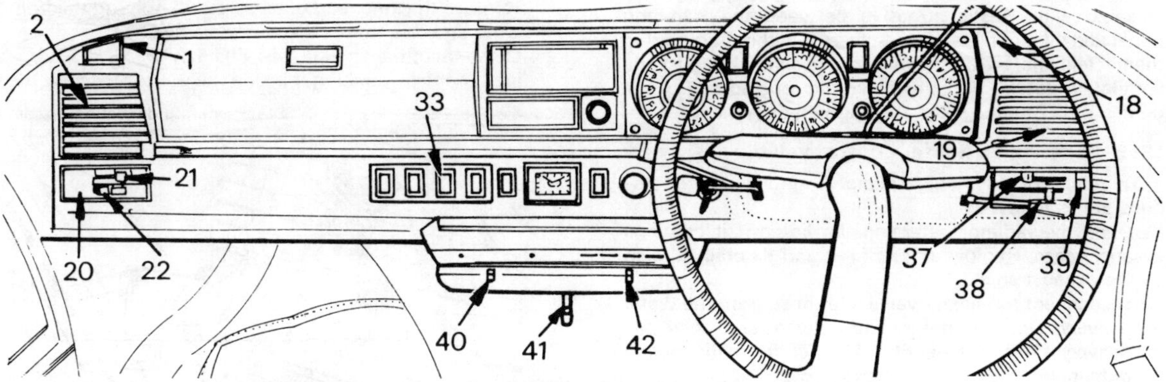

FIG 12:9 A view of the heating and ventilating outlets and controls

Key to Fig 12:9 1, 18 Side window vent 2, 19 Facia vents 20, 22, 38, 39 Directional controls 21, 37 Volume controls 33 Blower motor switch 40 Distribution control 41 Temperature control 42 Warm air volume control

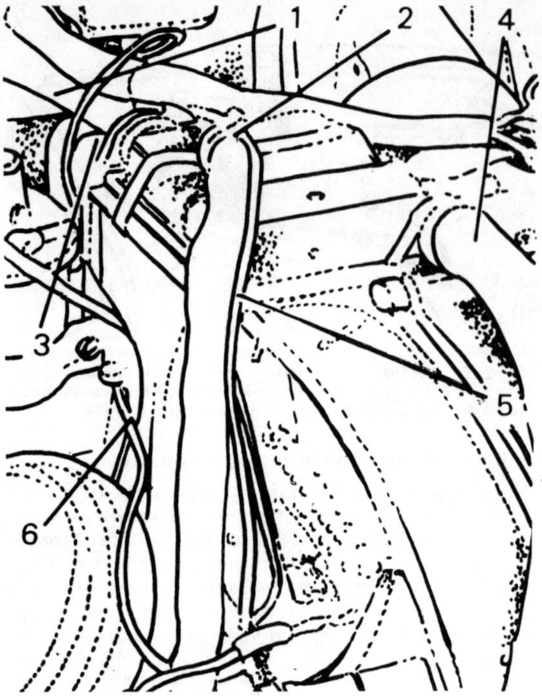

FIG 12:10 A view of the heater connections

Key to Fig 12:10 1 Water feed pipes 2 Rubber clip 3 Flexible hose from radiator and heater assembly 4 Flexible water return pipes 5 Feed wire 6 Earth wire

4 Disconnect the earth wire 6 and the feed wire 5, remove the rubber clip 2 and withdraw the heater unit.
5 Refit by following the removal operations in reverse order.

Removal of the ventilation ducts necessitates first the removal of the facia as described in **Section 12:3.** Then remove the two securing screws 8 shown in **FIG 12:11,** the flexible ducts between the heater assembly and the ventilation ducts and finally the ventilation ducts on each side.

When refitting, insert the polyester sponge gasket smeared with Bostik adhesive between the trimming panel and the duct. Insert the screws 8 without tightening them. Refit the facia as previously described, adjust the ventilation ducts to obtain the correct positioning of the control rods 7 in the grilles, then tighten the screws.

12:5 Renewing a heater control valve

To renew or overhaul a heater control valve, operations are as follows:

1 Drain the radiator, retaining the liquid if it contains anti-freeze. Remove the air filter and its bracket, also the exhaust shield.
2 Disconnect the heater valve inlet hose from the water delivery pipe on the cylinder head and then the delivery hose 2 (see **FIG 12:12**) from the heater radiator.
3 Remove the supporting clip 1 from the hose on the scuttle panel, loosen the clip supporting the hose at A in the engine recess and remove the hose.
4 Take off the rubber cover from the valve knob and remove the nut holding the operating knob.
5 From the valve remove the operating knob, the indicating disc and the valve stop.
6 From the body remove the heater valve indicating plate and the three screws securing the valve in the engine recess.
7 Withdraw the valve and hose assembly by passing it under the exhaust manifold and remove the hoses.
8 To overhaul the valve, remove the stop and securing screw 1 (see **FIG 12:13**). Then remove the rubber insulation washer 6 (see **FIG 12:14**) and the plate 5 securing the valve.
9 Withdraw the valve stem 3 from the valve body 2 and the ring seal 4 from the stem.
10 Fit a new ring seal in the groove 'a' of the valve stem and insert the stem in the body of the valve.
11 Engage the securing plate 5 and the rubber insulation washer on the valve stem, tightening the screws 1 after inserting the washers 7.
12 Fit the heater valve in the engine housing recess, passing the assembly under the exhaust manifold. Insert the rubber washer between the engine recess and the anti-rattle plate and tighten the three screws securing the valve to the body.
13 Refit the valve assembly in the reverse order of the removal procedure described in the previous Operations 1 to 7. Finally turn the heater control to the 'on' position, fill up the radiator and check all unions for leaks.

12:6 Removing and refitting a front wing

Mark the position of the wing lengthwise and across at the front fixing point with the aid of a scriber, also mark the lateral position on the two wings of the crossmember for the spare wheel support. This allows for removing and refitting the wings without having to adjust the bonnet, and it should also be unnecessary to readjust the headlamp height. Proceed to remove the wing as follows:

1 Remove the adjuster 11 (see **FIG 12:15**) and the return spring 12, marking the hole in which it hooks.
2 Remove the securing screw 1 (see **FIG 12:16**) from the headlamp control cross-bar 2, also the securing screws 3 for the spare wheel crossmember support.
3 Disconnect the cable 4 for releasing the bonnet catch. Remove the inner and outer screws 5 holding the front wing and disconnect the wiring harness.
4 Disconnect the lever 6 (see **FIG 12:17**) of the headlamp control, pushing it inside the wing. Unscrew the

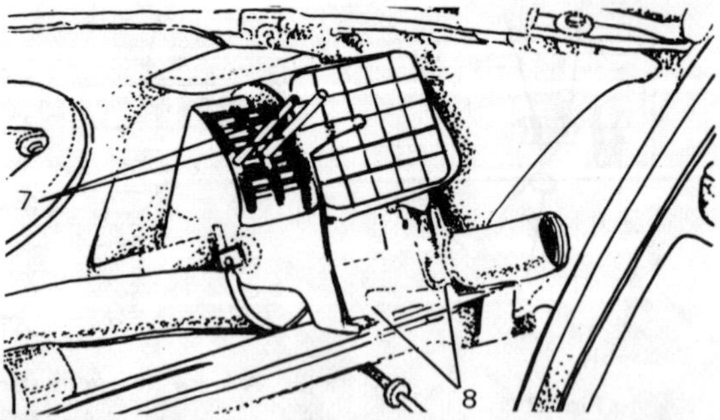

FIG 12:11 Showing the air grille controls 7 and securing screws 8

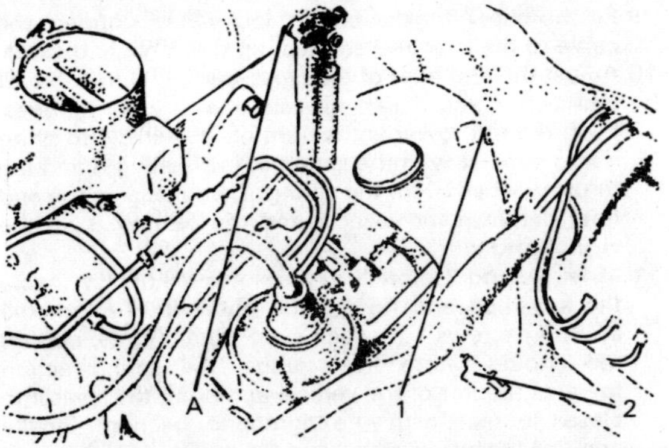

FIG 12:12 Heater hoses securing clips 1, 2 and at A

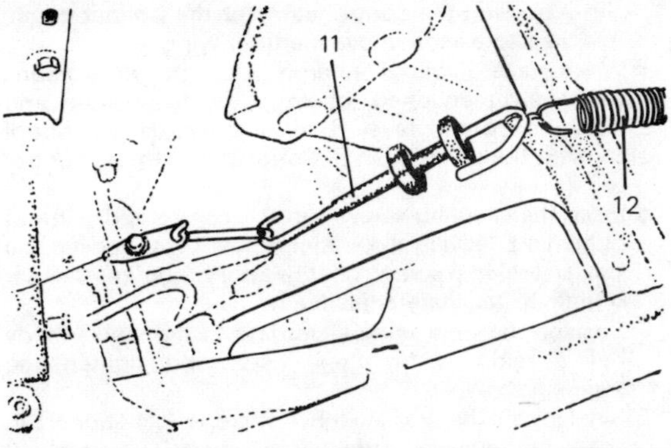

FIG 12:15 Headlamp adjuster 11 and return spring 12

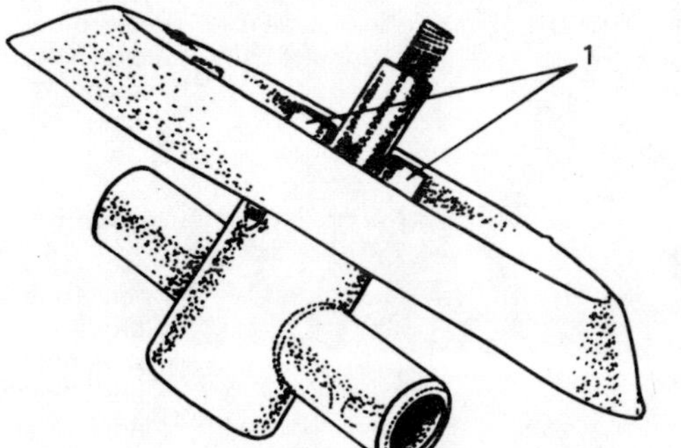

FIG 12:13 Heater valve assembly showing the securing screws 1

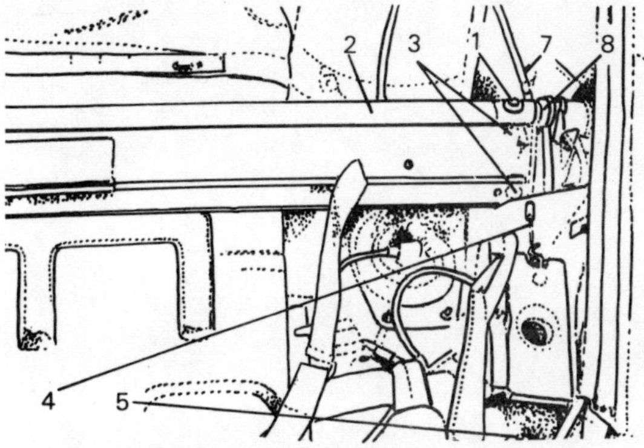

FIG 12:16 Front wing connections

Key to Fig 12:16 1 Screw 2 Headlamp cross bar 3 Screws 4 Bonnet catch cable 5 Wing screws 7 Clip screw 8 Bearing

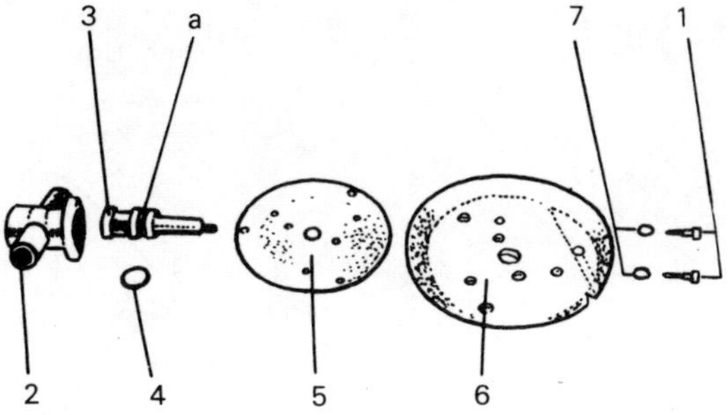

FIG 12:14 An exploded view of the heater valve assembly

Key to Fig 12:14 1 Screws 2 Valve body 3 Valve stem 4 Ring seal 5 Securing plate 6 Insulating washer 7 Washers

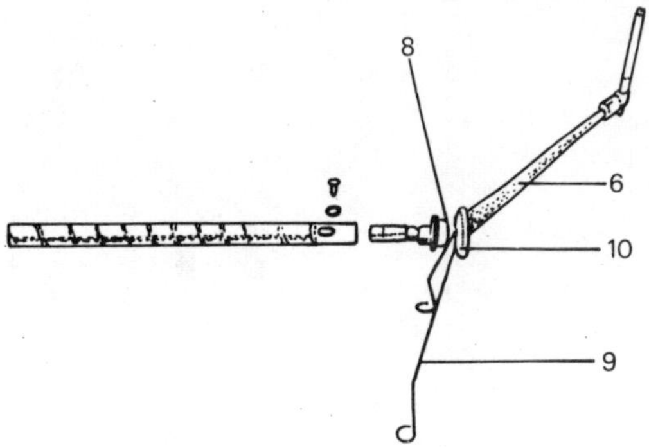

FIG 12:17 Headlamp control

Key to Fig 12:17 6 Headlamp control lever 8 Nylon bush 9 Spring 10 Thrust washer clip 7 holding the control cable of the bonnet catch, free the cable and remove the front wing.

5 When reassembling, referring to the illustrations previously mentioned, offer up the front wing and pass the control lever 6 for the headlamp control through the nylon bush 8. Connect it with the control rod 2.

6 Insert the securing screw 1 in the control rod without tightening, leaving it for later adjustment. Loosen the similar locking screw on the other side of the car slightly to facilitate adjustment.

7 Position the front wing according to the marks made before removing it, then insert and tighten the securing screws 5.

8 Similarly fit the crossmember spare wheel support in line with the marks made before removal.

9 Fit the clip 7 for the bonnet lock cable, connect the cable to the lock and connect up the cable harnesses.

10 Adjust the end float of the cross-bar 2 to a freedom of between 2 and 4 mm measured with feeler gauges. Push the rod towards the right of the vehicle to bring it into contact with the spring 9, the bearing 8 and the thrust washer 10 for the spring. Then measure the end float between the lever 6 and the bearing 8 on the **righthand** side.

11 Move the rod 2 laterally in the slots provided to enable the specified end float to be obtained. Tighten the securing screws 1 on each side. Note that the control rod should return freely under the spring action towards the left of the vehicle and bring the lever into close contact with the righthand bearing. Finally connect the return spring and the adjuster 11.

APPENDIX

NOTES

TECHNICAL DATA

ENGINE DETAILS

Types and works codes	DS21(DX), DS21M(DJ), DS19A(DY), DS19MA(DL), DS20(DY), DS20M(DL), ID19B(DV), D Special (DV), ID20(DT), D Super (DY), D Super 5 (DX)	
Description	4-cylinder in-line, ohv	
Dimensions:	*DS21, D Super 5*	*All except DS21*
Bore and stroke	90 x 85.5 mm	86 x 85.5 mm
Capacity	2175 cc	1985 cc
Firing order	1-3-4-2, No. 1 at flywheel end	
Brake horsepower (SAE):		
DS21, 8.75:1 cr	109 at 5500 rev/min	
DS21, 8.75:1 cr, October, 1968	115 at 5750 rev/min	
DS19A, 8.75:1 cr	90 at 5250 rev/min	
DS20, 8.75:1 cr	103 at 6000 rev/min	
ID19B, 8.0:1 cr	84 at 5230 rev/min	
D Special, 8.0:1 cr	91 to 5500 rev/min (1970)	
8.75:1 cr	98 at 5750 rev/min (1972)	
D Super 5, 8.75:1 cr	106 at 5500 rev/min	
Camshaft:		
End float	.05 to .07 mm	
Thrust plates	Five thicknesses of 2 mm available 5.44—5.46 to 5.56—5.58 mm	
Bearing clearance	.075 to .12 mm (.003 to .0047 inch)	
Connecting rods:		
Big-end bearings:		
Type	Steel-backed, thin bi-metal shells	
Nominal diameter	54.00 mm	
Oversize diameter	53.50 mm	
Crankpin clearance in bearing	.013 to .05 mm (.0005 to .002 inch)	
Small-end bushes:		
Type	Steel-backed with bores of anti-friction metal. Removal requires special tools	
Gudgeon pins	Free in the bush	
Crankshaft:		
Main bearings:		
No.	5	
Type	Steel-backed, thin bi-metal shells. Top and bottom shells identical and interchangeable on all bearings	
Nominal diameter	64.00 mm	
Oversize diameter	63.50 mm	
Bore	68.700 ± .005 mm	
Radial play	.06 mm max.	
End float	.045 to .160 mm	
Centre bearing thrust washers thicknesses	(I) 3.10 to 3.14 mm, (II) 3.14 to 3.18 mm	
Engine lubrication:		
Lubricant	SAE.10.W30 or SAE.20	
Capacity:		
After dismantling or changing the filter/element	5 litre (8$\frac{3}{4}$ pints)	
After draining	4.5 litre (8 pints)	
Difference between 'min' and 'max' on dipstick	1 litre (1$\frac{3}{4}$ pints)	
Oil pressure, hot at 2000 rev/min	54 lb/sq inch	

Pistons:

Type	Aluminium alloy, supplied complete with cylinder liners
Rings	1 compression, 1 scraper and 1 oil control
Groove clearance	.04 to .07 mm (.0016 to .0028 inch)
Gap, compression and scraper	.35 to .55 mm (.014 to .022 inch)
oil control	.25 to .40 mm (.010 to .016 inch)

Pushrods:

Length	189 mm (inlet valves) 213 mm (exhaust valves)

Valves:

Dimensions:	*Inlet*	*Exhaust*
Head angle	120 deg.	90 deg.
Head diameter	47 mm (49 mm after 1968)	39.0 ± .1 mm
Stem diameter	7.950 + .015 — 0 mm	8.950 + 0 — .015 mm
Clearance in guide	.025 to .065 mm (.001 to .0025 inch)	.04 to .08 mm (.0015 to .003 inch)
Length	115.47 + .60 — .25 mm	104.05 + .45 — .25 mm
Seat width	.8 to 1.5 mm	.8 to 1.5 mm
Seat angle	120 deg. inclusive	90 deg. inclusive
Valve guides:	*Inlet*	*Exhaust*
Length	60.00 mm	46.75 mm
Bore	8.000 + .015 — .010 mm	8.990 + .015 — .010 mm
Normal diameter	13 mm	13 mm
Oversize	13.25 mm	13.25 mm
Valve springs:	*Outer*	*Inner*
Free length	46.8 mm	40.0 mm
Length under load of:		
28.9 ± 1.6 kg	39.0 mm	
60.0 ± 3.2 kg	30.5 mm	
7.4 ± .5 kg		30.7 mm
12 ± 1 kg		22.0 mm
Valve clearances:	*Engine hot*	*Engine cold*
Inlet	.20 mm	.15 mm
Exhaust	.25 mm	.20 mm

FUEL SYSTEM

Carburetters:

Make and types:

DS21 (hydraulic gearchange)	Weber 28-36 DDE or DLE
DS21 (mechanical gearchange)	Weber 28-36 DDE A1 or DLE A1
DS19A (hydraulic gearchange)	Weber 28-36 DDE 2
DS19A (mechanical gearchange)	Weber 28-36 DDE A2
DS20 (hydraulic gearchange)	Weber 28-36 DLE 2
DS20 (mechanical gearchange)	Weber 28-36 DLE A2
D Super	Weber 28-36 DLE A2 or Solex SFIF
ID19B and D Special	Solex 34 PBIC or Weber DMA.3
D Special	Solex 28-36 SFIF
D Super 5	Weber 28-36 DMA.2

Component details:

	28/36 DDE Primary bore	28/36 DDE Secondary bore	28/36 DDE 2 and DDE A2 Primary bore	28/36 DDE 2 and DDE A2 Secondary bore	28/36 DLE Primary bore	28/36 DLE Secondary bore	28/36 DLE A1 Primary bore	28/36 DLE A1 Secondary bore
Venturi diameter (mm) ...	23	27	23	27	23	27	23	27
Main jet	130	175	120	170	130	175	130	175
Compensating jet	155	155	140	140	AB	AB	AB	AB
Emulsion tube ...	F16	F16	F16	F16	F16	F16	F16	F16
Diffuser	3.5	3.5	3.5	3.5	3.5	3.5	3.5	3.5
Idling jet* ...	50	70	45	55	45	65	45	65
Idling air jet ...	185	85	185	85	AD	AA	AD	AA
Float	11g	—	11g	—	—	—	—	—
Float level ...	—	—	—	—	4.75±.25	—	4.75±.25	—
Needle valve ...	175	—	175	—	175	—	175	—
Pump jet	60	—	60	—	60	—	60	—
Pump bypass valve	55	—	55	—	55	—	55	—
Primary butterfly opening, choke closed (mm) ...	.90	—	.90	—	.85±.05	—	.95±.05	—

**Since December, 1968, the idling jets in DJ, DL and DT engines (mechanical gearchange) are modified to 50 and 70 for primary and secondary bores respectively. In engines DX, DY (hydraulic gearchange) the idling jets are similarly modified to 50 and 75*

	28/36 DLE 3 Primary	28/36 DLE 3 Secondary	28/36 DLE A2 Primary	28/36 DLE A2 Secondary	SOLEX 34 PB1C
Venturi diameter (mm) ...	20	26	20	26	—
Main jet	110	155	110	155	135
Compensating jet ...	AD	AA	AD	AA	210
Emulsion tube	F16	F16	F16	F16	19
Diffuser	3.5	3.5	3.5	3.5	26
Idling jet	45	65	45	65	50
Idling air jet	AD	AA	AD	AA	130
Float	—	—	—	—	57g
Float level	4.75±.25	—	4.75±.25	—	—
Needle valve	175	—	175	—	1.7
Pump jet	60	—	60	—	50
Pump bypass valve ...	55	—	55	—	—
Primary butterfly opening, choke closed (mm) ...	.85±.05	—	.96±.05	—	—
Starting jet	—	—	—	—	145
Starting air jet	—	—	—	—	6

Solex 28/36 SFIF	Primary barrel	Secondary barrel
Diffuser	20	26
Main jet	120	145
Compensating jet...	1AD	2AA
Idle air jet	55	65
Idle air jet	90	90
Progression holes 1	90	100
2	90	100
3	110	—
Primary butterfly opening with choke closed...	1.40+.10 mm	

Slow-running adjustments:	Before September, 1968	Since September, 1968
	rev/min	rev/min
Normal idling	550	625
Accelerated idling	875 to 925	850 to 900
Clutch drag	700 to 750	725 to 775

Weber 28/36 DMA-2:	Primary	Secondary
Choke diameter (mm)	23	27
Main jet	115	175
Compensating jet	AC	AC
Emulsion tube	F20	F6
Diffuser	3.5	3.5
Idle jet	50	70
Idle air jet	AC	AA
Extra idle jet	50	—
Air calibration	4	—
Float weight (g)	11	
Needle	1.75	
Pump jet	50	
Float chamber level (mm)	5±.25	
Weber 28/36 DMA-3:		
Choke diameter	20	26
Main jet	105	150
Compensating jet	1AD	2AA
Emulsion tube	F20	F6
Diffuser	3.5	3.5
Idle jet	45	70
Idle air jet	AC	AA
Air calibration	4	—

Fuel pump:
Make and type ... ... SEV or AC, mechanical
Fuel tank capacity ... ... 65 litre (14.3 gallons)

HYDRAULIC SYSTEM

Hydraulic fluid ... ... Green mineral-based LHM hydraulic fluid since September, 1966. The former LHS2 fluid continued to be used in vehicles for the USA and Canada up to December, 1968

System contents:	DS	ID
	6 litre (10.5 pints)	5 litre (8.8 pints)
Difference 'min' to 'max'	1 litre (1.75 pints)	

High pressure pumps:
Single cylinder pump ... ... Fitted to standard ID19 and ID20 models, driven by eccentric on camshaft
Seven-cylinder pump ... ... Fitted to all other D models, also to ID19 and ID20 with optional power steering. Driven at half engine speed by two belts and pulleys

Pressure regulator, 7-cyl. pump:
Cutting out:
Before May, 1969 ... ... 150 to 175 kg/sq cm (2130 to 2490 lb/sq inch)
After May, 1969 ... ... 163 to 175 kg/sq cm (2305 to 2490 lb/sq inch)
Cutting in:
Before May, 1969 ... ... 125 to 140 kg/sq cm (1775 to 1990 lb/sq inch)
After May, 1969 ... ... 140 to 147 kg/sq cm (1990 to 2090 lb/sq inch)

IGNITION SYSTEM

Distributor:	
Type	Ducellier, SEV Marchal
Contact breaker points gap	.45 ± .05 mm
Dwell angle, Ducellier	57 deg.
SEV-Marchal	59 deg.
Sparking plugs:	
Up to 1970	AC 42 FF, Champion L85, SEV 35G
1970 onwards	AC 42 FS, Bosch W225T35, Champion L87Y, Lodge HNY, SEV 351-B
Gap	.6 mm (.024 inch)

COOLING SYSTEM

Capacity, including heater system	10.8 litre (19 pints)
Thermostat starts to open	75°C to 78°C (167°F to 172°F)
Fan	Nylon, 8 blades

CLUTCH

Type	Single dry plate
Height of clutch pedal from underside of pedal to the metal floor:	
Before February, 1967, DJ models	137 to 142 mm
Since February, 1967, all models except Pallas, without rubber pad	141 to 143 mm
Since February, 1967, Pallas models with rubber pad	136 to 138 mm

GEARBOX

Overall gear ratios (including final drive 8/35):

	Before September, 1967	*Since September, 1967*
First	.0703 (14.21:1)	.0703 (14.21:1)
Second	.1177 (8.49:1)	.1246 (8.03:1)
Third	.1795 (5.58:1)	.1922 (5.20:1)
Fourth	.2683 (3.73:1)	.2683 (3.73:1)
Reverse	.0724 (13.80:1)	.0724 (13.80:1)

Overall gear ratios (including final drive 7/34) 'D Special' (1969):

First	.0633 (15.8:1)
Second	.1123 (8.9:1)
Third	.1705 (5.9:1)
Fourth	.2416 (4.1:1)
Reverse	.0652 (15.4:1)

Overall gear ratios (5-speed box including final drive 7/34):

First	.0633 (15.8:1)
Second	.1123 (8.9:1)
Third	.1558 (6.5:1)
Fourth	.2123 (4.7:1)
Fifth	.2720 (3.7:1)
Reverse	.0652 (15.4:1)

Overall gear ratios. D Super 5 (including final ratio 8/35):

First	.0703 (14.2:1)
Second	.1177 (8.5:1)
Third	.1729 (5.78:1)
Fourth	.2356 (4.25:1)
Fifth	.2916 (3.42:1)
Reverse	.0724 (13.8:1)

Lubrication:

Grade of lubricant	SAE.90.EP
Gearbox oil capacity (4-speed)	2 litre (3.5 pints)
Gearbox oil capacity (5-speed)	2.25 litres (4 pints)

FRONT SUSPENSION

Type	Hydro-pneumatic springs, half wishbones each side, anti-roll bar and height correctors
Wheel alignment:	
Camber	Equal on both sides to within 1 mm
Castor angle	1 deg. 30′
Toe-in at the front	2 to 4 mm

REAR SUSPENSION

Type	Hydro-pneumatic springs on trailing arms, anti-roll bar and height correctors

STEERING

Type	Rack and pinion
Turning radius	5.5 m (18 ft $\frac{1}{2}$ inch)
Angle of steering lock	41 to 42 deg.
Lateral positioning	122.5 ± 2.5 mm between centre line of lower relay lever and centre line of rack plunger
Cross-over pressure	70 ± 10 kg/sq cm (995 ± 150 lb/sq inch)

BRAKES

Type	Hydraulically-operated, inboard disc-type front outboard drum-type rear
Front brake disc diameter	300 mm
Disc runout	.15 mm max.
Difference in disc thickness overall	.02 mm max.
Pedal free play	2 mm max.
Rear brake drum diameter	255 mm
Drum runout	.04 mm max.
Front brake pads	Ferodo 623, Textar V1431
Thickness	12 mm
Number of pads	4

ELECTRICAL EQUIPMENT

Battery	12-volt, 40 amp/hr (55 amp/hr for iodine lamps except where alternator is fitted)	
Generator:		
Types	Ducellier No. 7336A or Paris-Rhone No. G10.C44	
	Ducellier	*Paris-Rhone*
Commutator diameter after machining	36 mm min.	34.5 mm min.

Regulator:	
Types	Ducellier No. 8346A or Paris-Rhone No. YT.2116
Cut-in voltage	12 to 13.6 volt (cold and hot)
Cut-out voltage	At least 1-volt lower than the cut-in voltage
Alternator (since July, 1967):	
Type	Ducellier No. 7530A or 7558A or Paris-Rhone No. A13.R52 or A13.R119
Rectifying system	Incorporated in alternator
Direction of rotation	Clockwise, indicated by arrow stamped on fan
Nominal battery voltage	12-volt
Nominal capacity...	35 amp
Cut-in speed at 13.2 volt...	900 rev/min (hot)
Nominal speed or rotation	1200 rev/min
Regulator:	
Type	Paris-Rhone AY.212 or Ducellier 8360A, vibrating contact type
Starter motor:	
Types	Ducellier No. 6164A, 6201A, 6215A, 6225A or Paris-Rhone D.11B.116
	Ducellier / *Paris-Rhone*
Commutator diameter after machining ...	39.5 mm min. / 43 mm min.

TIGHTENING TORQUES

	kg m	*lb ft*
Brakes:		
Front brake unit to gearbox	13 to 14	94 to 101
Caliper halves	5	36
Mechanical brake unit to clutch housing...	10 to 11	72 to 80
Clutch:		
Clutch to flywheel	3.5	25
Engine:		
Cylinder head nuts:		
Pre-tightening	3	22
Final tightening	6 to 6.5	43 to 47
Chain tensioner	1.7	12.5
Connecting rod bolts	6.75 to 7.50	49 to 54
Fan	1 to 1.4	7 to 10
Flywheel	6.5 to 7	47 to 50
Main bearing bolts	10	72
Oil pump	.5 to .7	3.6 to 5
Rocker bracket bolts	2.2 to 2.8	16 to 20
Sump	1.4 to 1.9	7 to 14
Timing cover	1.4 to 1.8	7 to 13
Front axle:		
Pivot bearing nut...	80	580
Track rod ball joint	7	50
Track rod lever on pivot	5	36
Upper and lower arm nuts (finally slacken by $\frac{1}{24}$ to $\frac{1}{12}$ turn)	9	65
Wheel nuts	8 to 10	58 to 72
Hydraulic system:		
Pressure regulator cylinder nut	3	22
Pressure regulator cap	17 to 20	122 to 144
Sphere damper	1.9	14
Rear axle:		
Stub axle bearing	10	72
Articulating housing bearing	8 to 9	58 to 65
Brake plate	2.5	18
Steering:		
Ballpins	4	28
Casing end piece...	6	43
Casing end piece locknut	10	72
Centre yoke	4	29
Centring cam collar	.5	3.5
Pinion nut	5	36
Rack control rod	7	50
Relay shafts to steering levers	2.5	18
Suspension:		
Front anti-roll bar U-bolts	1.25	9
Rear anti-roll bar bearings	10.5	72
Rear anti-roll bar flanges	5	36
Transmission:		
Differential shaft nuts	15	108
Differential shaft bearing support ...	10	72
Starting dog	15 to 17	108 to 123

WIRING DIAGRAMS

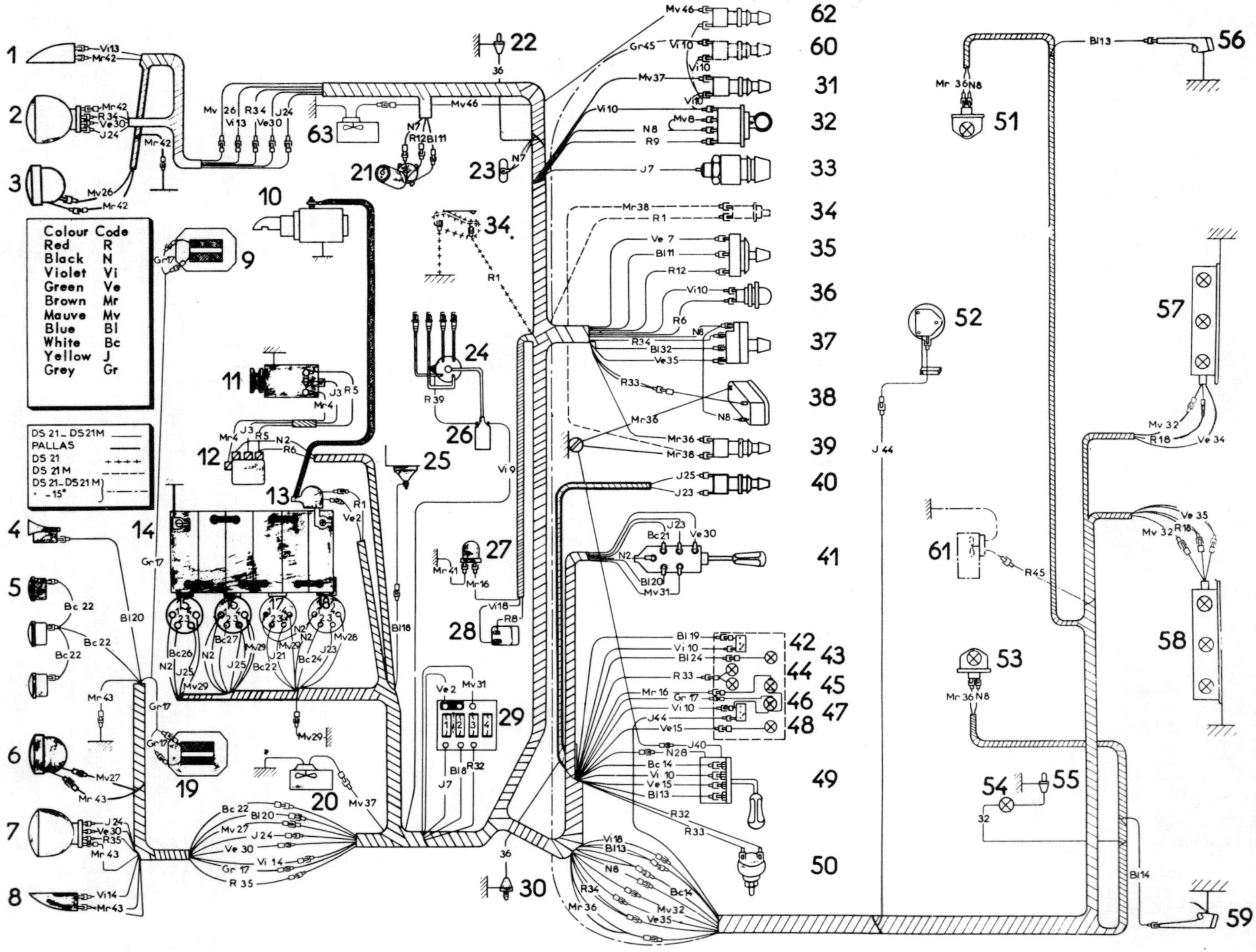

FIG 13:1 Wiring diagram, 1966

Key to Fig 13:1 1 Direction indicator lamp, front right 2 Headlamp, front right 3 Headlamp, quartz-iodine, front right 4 Horn, town use (low note) 5 Horns, country (high note) 6 Headlamp, quartz-iodine, front lefthand 7 Headlamp, front lefthand 8 Direction indicator lamp, front left 9 Brake unit, front, right 10 Starter motor 11 Generator 12 Regulator 13 Starter motor solenoid 14 Battery 15 Solenoid, SANOR, for quartz-iodine headlamp, front right 16 Solenoid, SANOR, for quartz-iodine headlamp, front left 17 Solenoid, SANOR, for horns, country (high note) 18 Solenoid, SANOR, for headlamp flasher 19 Brake unit, front left 20 Blower motor, heating, front 21 Motor for windscreen wiper 22 Switch for interior lamps operated by front righthand door 23 Terminal accessories 24 Distributor 25 Thermometer transmitter 26 Ignition coil 27 Pressure switch for brake 28 Stop light switch 29 Fuse box 30 Switch for interior lamps operated by door, front left 31 Switch for heating, front 32 Ignition switch 33 Cigar lighter 34 Switch for starter solenoid 35 Switch for windscreen wiper 36 Ignition and charge-lights 37 Switch for parking lights 38 Electric clock 39 Switch for interior lights 40 Switch for quartz-iodine headlamps 41 Switch for lighting and horns 42 Thermometer 43 Warning lamp for headlamp main beam 44 Instrument lighting bulbs 45 Warning lamp for brake pressure switch 46 Warning lamp for brake pad wear, front 47 Fuel gauge 48 Warning lamp for direction indicators 49 Switch for direction indicators with switch for headlamp flasher 50 Rheostat for instrument and clock lighting 51 Interior light, front right 52 Rheostat for fuel gauge unit 53 Interior light, front, lefthand 54 Boot light 55 Switch for boot light 56 Righthand rear direction indicator light 57 Lights for number plate—rear light and stoplights, righthand 58 Lights for number plate—rear light and stoplights, lefthand 59 Direction indicator light—rear, left 60 Switch for rear heater (—15 heating) 61 Blower motor for rear heating (—15 heating) 62 Switch for fresh air blower motor (optional) 63 Fresh air blower (optional)

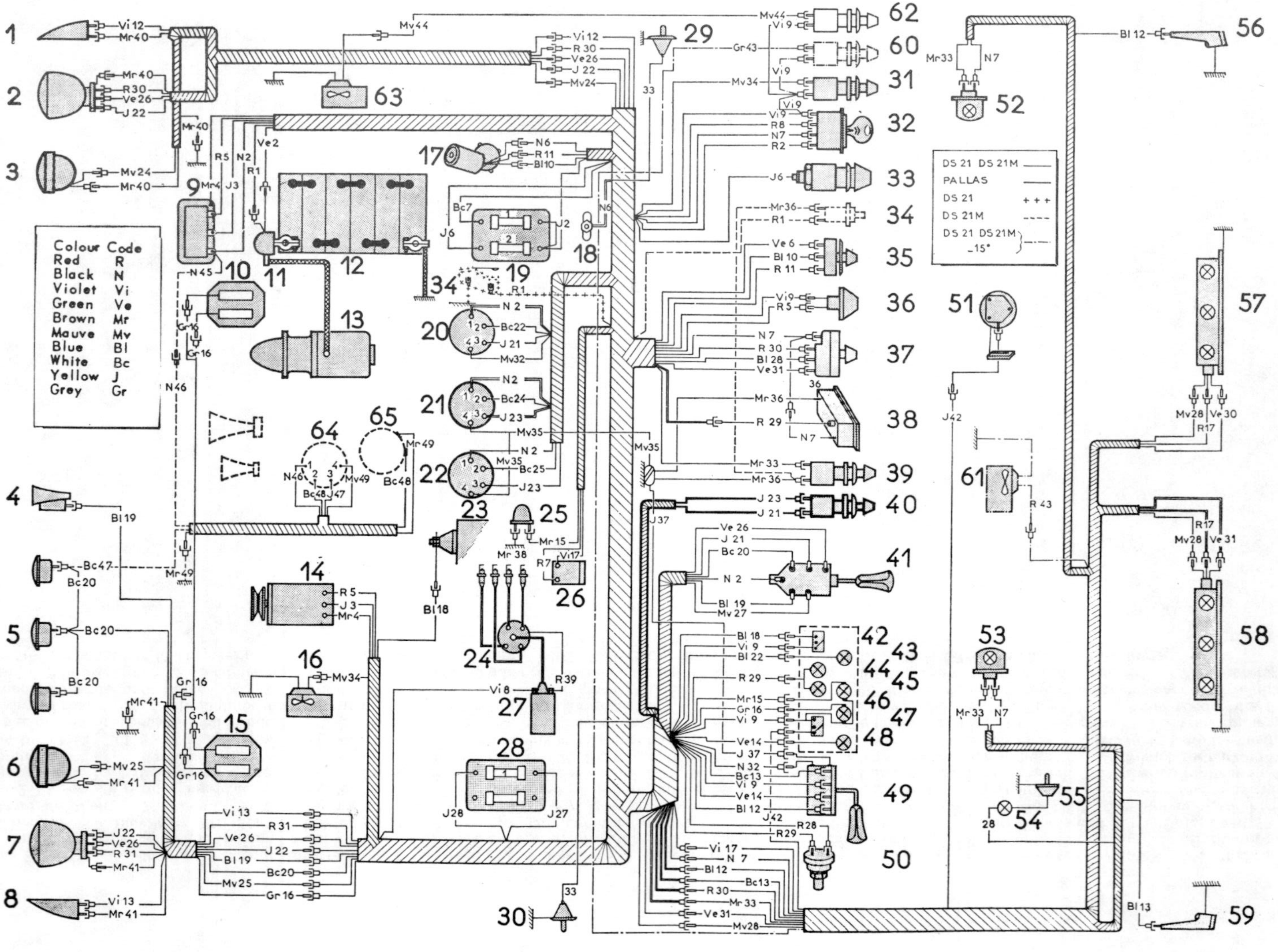

FIG 13:2 Wiring diagram, 1967-1969

Key to Fig 13:2 1 Righthand front flasher 2 Righthand headlamp 3 Righthand iodine lamp 4 Town horn 5 Road horn 6 Lefthand iodine lamp 7 Lefthand headlamp 8 Lefthand front flasher 9 Regulator 10 Righthand front brake unit 11 Starter relay 12 Battery 13 Starter 14 Generator 15 Lefthand front brake unit 16 Front heater blower 17 Wiper motor 18 Accessories terminal 19 Righthand fuse box 20 'Sanor' relay for headlamp flasher 21 'Sanor' relay of the righthand front iodine lamp 22 'Sanor' relay for lefthand front iodine lamp 23 Temperature sender 24 Distributor 25 Brake pressure switch 26 Stop switch 27 Ignition coil 28 Lefthand fuse box 29 Righthand front door switch 30 Lefthand front door switch 31 Front heater switch 32 Ignition switch 33 Cigar lighter 34 Starter relay switch 35 Windscreen wiper switch 36 Battery charge pilot light 37 Parking light switch 38 Electric clock 39 Interior light switch 40 Iodine lamp switch 41 Lighting and horn switch 42 Temperature gauge 43 Headlamp pilot light 44 Dashboard lamps 45 Brake pressure switch pilot light 46 Front brake pad wear warning light 47 Petrol gauge 48 Flasher indicating lamp 49 Flasher switch and headlamp flasher switch 50 Dashboard and clock light rheostat 51 Petrol gauge sender unit 52 Righthand front interior light 53 Lefthand front interior light 54 Boot light 55 Boot light switch 56 Righthand rear flasher 57 Righthand stoplight and number plate light 58 Lefthand stoplight and number plate light 59 Lefthand rear flasher 60 Rear heater (—15°C) switch (optional) 61 Rear heater booster (optional) 62 Switch for 63 (optional) 63 Fresh air fan (optional) 64 'Sonor' relay for horn compressor (optional) 65 Horn compressor (optional)

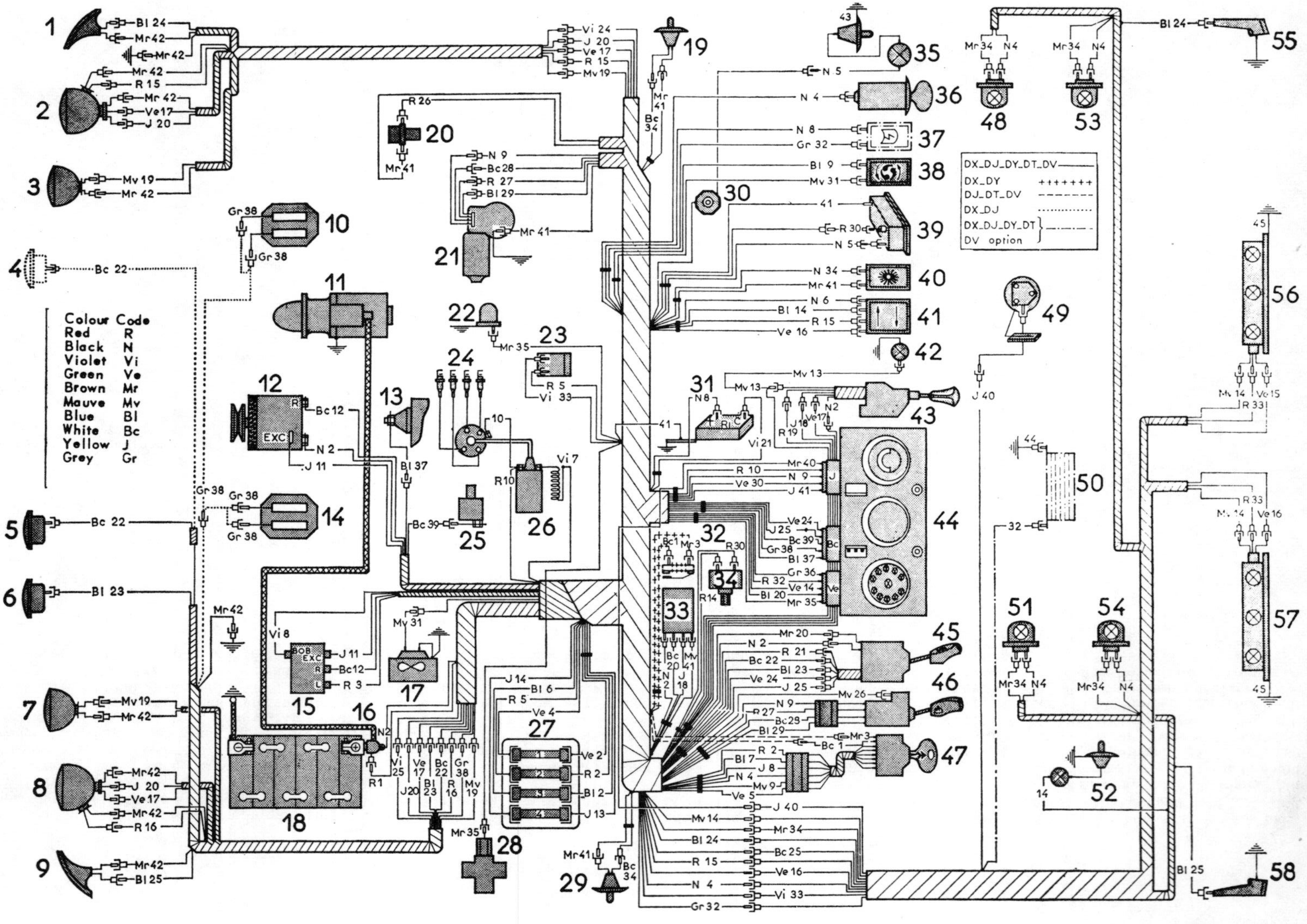

FIG 13:3 Wiring diagram. September 1969 to 1971

Key to Fig 13:3, 13:4 and 13:5 1 Righthand front flasher 2 Righthand headlight 3 Righthand auxiliary headlamp 4 Road horn, righthand 5 Road horn, lefthand 6 Main road horn 7 Lefthand auxiliary headlight 8 Lefthand headlamp 9 Lefthand front flasher 10 Righthand front brake unit 11 Starter with solenoid 12 Alternator 13 Temperature sender unit 14 Lefthand front brake unit 15 Regulator unit 16 Starter relay 17 Heater blower 18 Battery 19 Righthand front door switch 20 Screen washer pump 21 Wiper motor 22 Brake pressure switch (DX-DJ-DV) 23 Stop switch 24 Distributor 25 Engine oil pressure switch 26 Ignition coil 27 Fuse box 28 Safety valve pressure switch (DT-DV) 29 Lefthand front door switch 30 Accessories terminal 31 Flasher unit 32 Starter relay switch (DX-DY) 33 Headlamps relay 34 Lighting rheostat 35 Glove-box light (Pallas) 36 Cigar lighter 37 Rear window heater switch (optional) 38 Heater switch 39 Clock (except DV) 40 Interior light switch 41 Parking light selector switch 42 Heater control lighting (Pallas) 43 Lighting switch 44 Control unit 45 Flasher switch 46 Windscreen wiper and washer switch 47 Ignition switch 48 Righthand side interior light 49 Petrol gauge sender unit 50 Heated rear window (optional) 51 Lefthand side interior light 52 Boot light 53 Righthand rear interior light (DX-DJ-DY except Pallas) 54 Lefthand rear interior light (DX-DJ-DY except Pallas) 55 Righthand rear flasher 56 Righthand rear stop and number plate lights 57 Lefthand rear stop and number plate lights 58 Lefthand rear flasher 59 Horn compressor relay 60 Horn compressor 61 Cigar lighter lamp 62 Reverse light switch 63 Ash tray light 64 Righthand reverse light 65 Lefthand reverse light

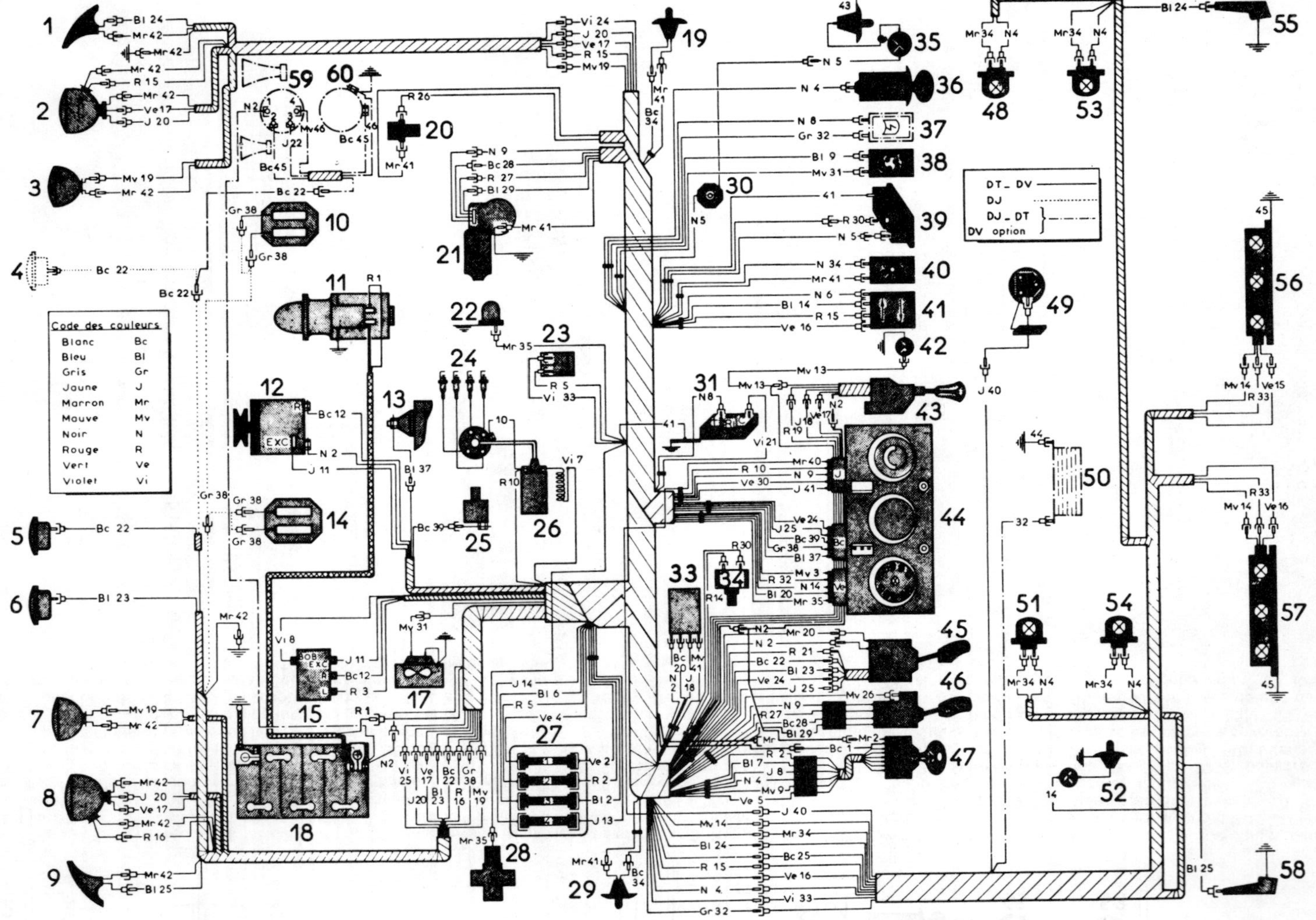

FIG 13:4 Wiring diagram 1971

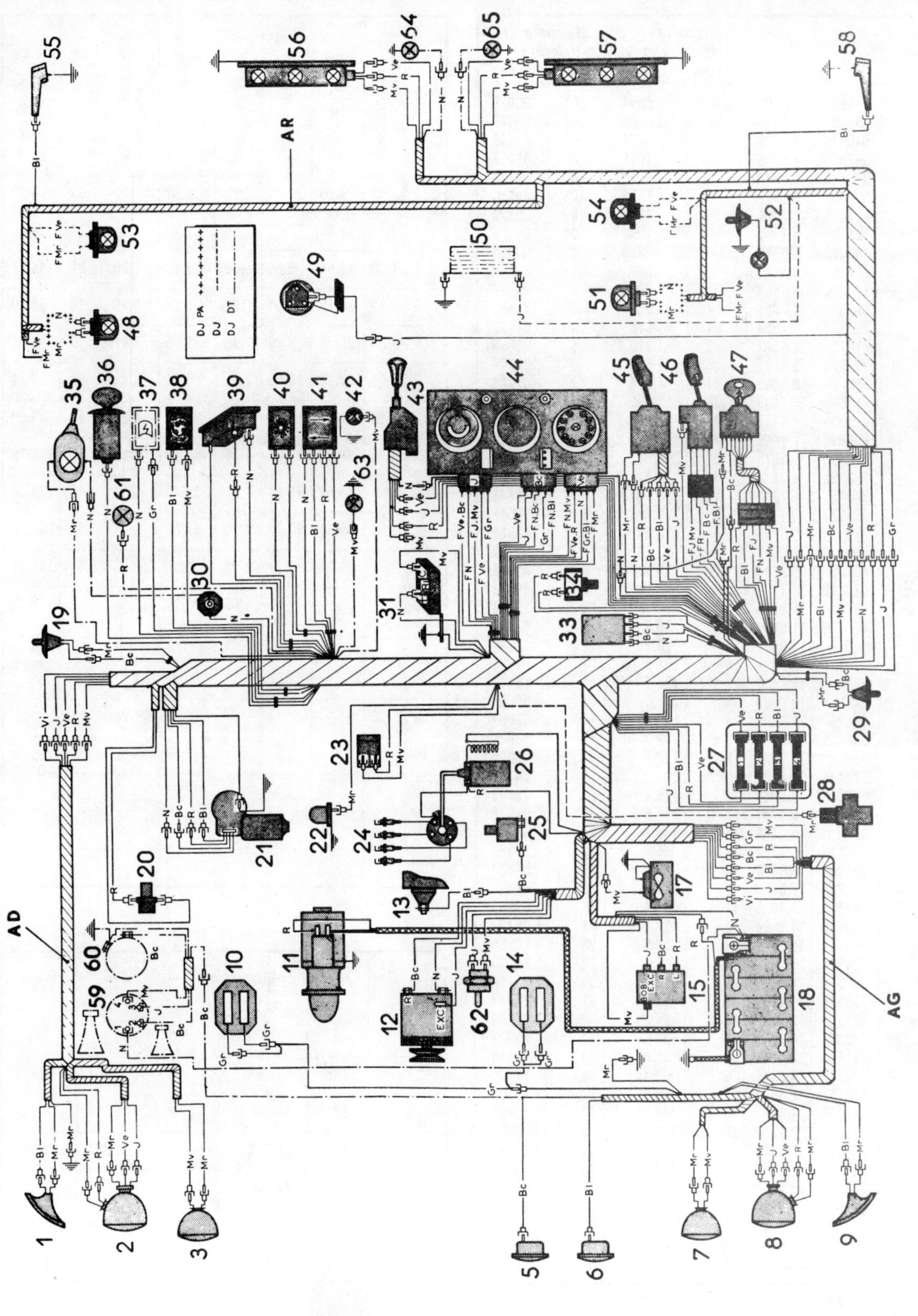

FIG 13:5 Wiring diagram 1972

Inches	*Decimals*	*Milli-metres*	*Inches to Millimetres*		*Millimetres to Inches*	
			Inches	*mm*	*mm*	*Inches*
1/64	.015625	.3969	.001	.0254	.01	.00039
1/32	.03125	.7937	.002	.0508	.02	.00079
3/64	.046875	1.1906	.003	.0762	.03	.00118
1/16	.0625	1.5875	.004	.1016	.04	.00157
5/64	.078125	1.9844	.005	.1270	.05	.00197
3/32	.09375	2.3812	.006	.1524	.06	.00236
7/64	.109375	2.7781	.007	.1778	.07	.00276
1/8	.125	3.1750	.008	.2032	.08	.00315
9/64	.140625	3.5719	.009	.2286	.09	.00354
5/32	.15625	3.9687	.01	.254	.1	.00394
11/64	.171875	4.3656	.02	.508	.2	.00787
3/16	.1875	4.7625	.03	.762	.3	.01181
13/64	.203125	5·1594	.04	1.016	.4	.01575
7/32	.21875	5.5562	.05	1.270	.5	.01969
15/64	.234375	5.9531	.06	1.524	.6	.02362
1/4	.25	6.3500	.07	1.778	.7	.02756
17/64	.265625	6.7469	.08	2.032	.8	.03150
9/32	.28125	7.1437	.09	2.286	.9	.03543
19/64	.296875	7.5406	.1	2.54	1	.03937
5/16	.3125	7.9375	.2	5.08	2	.07874
21/64	.328125	8.3344	.3	7.62	3	.11811
11/32	.34375	8.7312	.4	10.16	4	.15748
23/64	.359375	9.1281	.5	12.70	5	.19685
3/8	.375	9.5250	.6	15.24	6	.23622
25/64	.390625	9.9219	.7	17.78	7	.27559
13/32	.40625	10.3187	.8	20.32	8	.31496
27/64	.421875	10.7156	.9	22.86	9	.35433
7/16	.4375	11.1125	1	25.4	10	.39370
29/64	.453125	11.5094	2	50.8	11	.43307
15/32	.46875	11.9062	3	76.2	12	.47244
31/64	.484375	12.3031	4	101.6	13	.51181
1/2	.5	12.7000	5	127.0	14	.55118
33/64	.515625	13.0969	6	152.4	15	.59055
17/32	.53125	13.4937	7	177.8	16	.62992
35/64	.546875	13.8906	8	203.2	17	.66929
9/16	.5625	14.2875	9	228.6	18	.70866
37/64	.578125	14.6844	10	254.0	19	.74803
19/32	.59375	15.0812	11	279.4	20	.78740
39/64	.609375	15.4781	12	304.8	21	.82677
5/8	.625	15.8750	13	330.2	22	.86614
41/64	.640625	16.2719	14	355.6	23	.90551
21/32	.65625	16.6687	15	381.0	24	.94488
43/64	.671875	17.0656	16	406.4	25	.98425
11/16	.6875	17.4625	17	431.8	26	1.02362
45/64	.703125	17.8594	18	457.2	27	1.06299
23/32	.71875	18.2562	19	482.6	28	1.10236
47/64	.734375	18.6531	20	508.0	29	1.14173
3/4	.75	19.0500	21	533.4	30	1.18110
49/64	.765625	19.4469	22	558.8	31	1.22047
25/32	.78125	19.8437	23	584.2	32	1.25984
51/64	.796875	20.2406	24	609.6	33	1.29921
13/16	.8125	20.6375	25	635.0	34	1.33858
53/64	.828125	21.0344	26	660.4	35	1.37795
27/32	.84375	21.4312	27	685.8	36	1.41732
55/64	.859375	21.8281	28	711.2	37	1.4567
7/8	.875	22.2250	29	736.6	38	1.4961
57/64	.890625	22.6219	30	762.0	39	1.5354
29/32	.90625	23.0187	31	787.4	40	1.5748
59/64	.921875	23.4156	32	812.8	41	1.6142
15/16	.9375	23.8125	33	838.2	42	1.6535
61/64	.953125	24.2094	34	863.6	43	1.6929
31/32	.96875	24.6062	35	889.0	44	1.7323
63/64	.984375	25.0031	36	914.4	45	1.7717

UNITS	*Pints to Litres*	*Gallons to Litres*	*Litres to Pints*	*Litres to Gallons*	*Miles to Kilometres*	*Kilometres to Miles*	*Lbs. per sq. In. to Kg. per sq. Cm.*	*Kg. per sq. Cm. to Lbs. per sq. In.*
1	.57	4.55	1.76	.22	1.61	.62	.07	14.22
2	1.14	9.09	3.52	.44	3.22	1.24	.14	28.50
3	1.70	13.64	5.28	.66	4.83	1.86	.21	42.67
4	2.27	18.18	7.04	.88	6.44	2.49	.28	56.89
5	2.84	22.73	8.80	1.10	8.05	3.11	.35	71.12
6	3.41	27.28	10.56	1.32	9.66	3.73	.42	85.34
7	3.98	31.82	12.32	1.54	11.27	4.35	.49	99.56
8	4.55	36.37	14.08	1.76	12.88	4.97	.56	113.79
9		40.91	15.84	1.98	14.48	5.59	.63	128.00
10		45.46	17.60	2.20	16.09	6.21	.70	142.23
20				4.40	32.19	12.43	1.41	284.47
30				6.60	48.28	18.64	2.11	426.70
40				8.80	64.37	24.85		
50					80.47	31.07		
60					96.56	37.28		
70					112.65	43.50		
80					128.75	49.71		
90					144.84	55.92		
100					160.93	62.14		

UNITS	*Lb ft to kgm*	*Kgm to lb ft*	*UNITS*	*Lb ft to kgm*	*Kgm to lb ft*
1	.138	7.233	7	.967	50.631
2	.276	14.466	8	1.106	57.864
3	.414	21.699	9	1.244	65.097
4	.553	28.932	10	1.382	72.330
5	.691	36.165	20	2.765	144.660
6	.829	43.398	30	4.147	216.990

HINTS ON MAINTENANCE AND OVERHAUL

There are few things more rewarding than the restoration of a vehicle's original peak of efficiency and smooth performance.

The following notes are intended to help the owner to reach that state of perfection. Providing that he possesses the basic manual skills he should have no difficulty in performing most of the operations detailed in this manual. It must be stressed, however, that where recommended in the manual, highly-skilled operations ought to be entrusted to experts, who have the necessary equipment, to carry out the work satisfactorily.

Quality of workmanship:

The hazardous driving conditions on the roads to-day demand that vehicles should be as nearly perfect, mechanically, as possible. It is therefore most important that amateur work be carried out with care, bearing in mind the often inadequate working conditions, and also the inferior tools which may have to be used. It is easy to counsel perfection in all things, and we recognize that it may be setting an impossibly high standard. We do, however, suggest that every care should be taken to ensure that a vehicle is as safe to take on the road as it is humanly possible to make it.

Safe working conditions:

Even though a vehicle may be stationary, it is still potentially dangerous if certain sensible precautions are not taken when working on it while it is supported on jacks or blocks. It is indeed preferable not to use jacks alone, but to supplement them with carefully placed blocks, so that there will be plenty of support if the car rolls off the jacks during a strenuous manoeuvre. Axle stands are an excellent way of providing a rigid base which is not readily disturbed. Piles of bricks are a dangerous substitute. Be careful not to get under heavy loads on lifting tackle, the load could fall. It is preferable not to work alone when lifting an engine, or when working underneath a vehicle which is supported well off the ground. To be trapped, particularly under the vehicle, may have unpleasant results if help is not quickly forthcoming. Make some provision, however humble, to deal with fires. Always disconnect a battery if there is a likelihood of electrical shorts. These may start a fire if there is leaking fuel about. This applies particularly to leads which can carry a heavy current, like those in the starter circuit. While on the subject of electricity, we must also stress the danger of using equipment which is run off the mains and which has no earth or has faulty wiring or connections. So many workshops have damp floors, and electrical shocks are of such a nature that it is sometimes impossible to let go of a live lead or piece of equipment due to the muscular spasms which take place.

Work demanding special care:

This involves the servicing of braking, steering and suspension systems. On the road, failure of the braking system may be disastrous. Make quite sure that there can be no possibility of failure through the bursting of rusty brake pipes or rotten hoses, nor to a sudden loss of pressure due to defective seals or valves.

Problems:

The chief problems which may face an operator are:

1 External dirt.
2 Difficulty in undoing tight fixings
3 Dismantling unfamiliar mechanisms.
4 Deciding in what respect parts are defective.
5 Confusion about the correct order for reassembly.
6 Adjusting running clearances.
7 Road testing.
8 Final tuning.

Practical suggestion to solve the problems:

1 Preliminary cleaning of large parts—engines, transmissions, steering, suspensions, etc.,—should be carried out before removal from the car. Where road dirt and mud alone are present, wash clean with a high-pressure water jet, brushing to remove stubborn adhesions, and allow to drain and dry. Where oil or grease is also present, wash down with a proprietary compound (Gunk, Teepol etc.,) applying with a stiff brush—an old paint brush is suitable—into all crevices. Cover the distributor and ignition coils with a polythene bag and then apply a strong water jet to clear the loosened deposits. Allow to drain and dry. The assemblies will then be sufficiently clean to remove and transfer to the bench for the next stage.

On the bench, further cleaning can be carried out, first wiping the parts as free as possible from grease with old newspaper. Avoid using rag or cotton waste which can leave clogging fibres behind. Any remaining grease can be removed with a brush dipped in paraffin. If necessary, traces of paraffin can be removed by carbon tetrachloride. Avoid using paraffin or petrol in large quantities for cleaning in enclosed areas, such as garages, on account of the high fire risk.

When all exteriors have been cleaned, and not before, dismantling can be commenced. This ensures that dirt will not enter into interiors and orifices revealed by dismantling. In the next phases, where components have to be cleaned, use carbon tetrachloride in preference to petrol and keep the containers covered except when in use. After the components have been cleaned, plug small holes with tapered hard wood plugs cut to size and blank off larger orifices with greaseproof paper and masking tape. Do not use soft wood plugs or matchsticks as they may break.

2 It is not advisable to hammer on the end of a screw thread, but if it must be done, first screw on a nut to protect the thread, and use a lead hammer. This applies particularly to the removal of tapered cotters. Nuts and bolts seem to 'grow' together, especially in exhaust systems. If penetrating oil does not work, try the judicious application of heat, but be careful ot starting a fire. Asbestos sheet or cloth is useful to isolate heat.

Tight bushes or pieces of tail-pipe rusted into a silencer can be removed by splitting them with an open-ended hacksaw. Tight screws can sometimes be started by a tap from a hammer on the end of a suitable screwdriver. Many tight fittings will yield to the judicious use of a hammer, but it must be a soft-faced hammer if damage is to be avoided, use a heavy block on the opposite side to absorb shock. Any parts of the steering system which have been damaged should be renewed, as attempts to repair them may lead to cracking and subsequent failure, and steering ball joints should be disconnected using a recommended tool to prevent damage.

3 If often happens that an owner is baffled when trying to dismantle an unfamiliar piece of equipment. So many modern devices are pressed together or assembled by spinning-over flanges, that they must be sawn apart. The intention is that the whole assembly must be renewed. However, parts which appear to be in one piece to the naked eye, may reveal close-fitting joint lines when inspected with a magnifying glass, and, this may provide the necessary clue to dismantling. Left-handed screw threads are used where rotational forces would tend to unscrew a right-handed screw thread.

Be very careful when dismantling mechanisms which may come apart suddenly. Work in an enclosed space where the parts will be contained, and drape a piece of cloth over the device if springs are likely to fly in all directions. Mark everything which might be reassembled in the wrong position, scratched symbols may be used on unstressed parts, or a sequence of tiny dots from a centre punch can be useful. Stressed parts should never be scratched or centre-popped as this may lead to cracking under working conditions. Store parts which look alike in the correct order for reassembly. Never rely upon memory to assist in the assembly of complicated mechanisms, especially when they will be dismantled for a long time, but make notes, and drawings to supplement the diagrams in the manual, and put labels on detached wires. Rust stains may indicate unlubricated wear. This can sometimes be seen round the outside edge of a bearing cup in a universal joint. Look for bright rubbing marks on parts which normally should not make heavy contact. These might prove that something is bent or running out of true. For example, there might be bright marks on one side of a piston, at the top near the ring grooves, and others at the bottom of the skirt on the other side. This could well be the clue to a bent connecting rod. Suspected cracks can be proved by heating the component in a light oil to approximately 100°C, removing, drying off, and dusting with french chalk, if a crack is present the oil retained in the crack will stain the french chalk.

4 In determining wear, and the degree, against the permissible limits set in the manual, accurate measurement can only be achieved by the use of a micrometer. In many cases, the wear is given to the fourth place of decimals; that is in ten-thousandths of an inch. This can be read by the vernier scale on the barrel of a good micrometer. Bore diameters are more difficult to determine. If, however, the matching shaft is accurately measured, the degree of play in the bore can be felt as a guide to its suitability. In other cases, the shank of a twist drill of known diameter is a handy check.

Many methods have been devised for determining the clearance between bearing surfaces. To-day the best and simplest is by the use of Plastigage, obtainable from most garages. A thin plastic thread is laid between the two surfaces and the bearing is tightened, flattening the thread. On removal, the width of the thread is compared with a scale supplied with the thread and the clearance is read off directly. Sometimes joint faces leak persistently, even after gasket renewal. The fault will then be traceable to distortion, dirt or burrs. Studs which are screwed into soft metal frequently raise burrs at the point of entry. A quick cure for this is to chamfer the edge of the hole in the part which fits over the stud.

5 **Always check a replacement part with the original one before it is fitted.**

If parts are not marked, and the order for reassembly is not known, a little detective work will help. Look for marks which are due to wear to see if they can be mated. Joint faces may not be identical due to manufacturing errors, and parts which overlap may be stained, giving a clue to the correct position. Most fixings leave identifying marks especially if they were painted over on assembly. It is then easier to decide whether a nut, for instance, has a plain, a spring, or a shakeproof washer under it. All running surfaces become 'bedded' together after long spells of work and tiny imperfections on one part will be found to have left corresponding marks on the other. This is particularly true of shafts and bearings and even a score on a cylinder wall will show on the piston.

6 Checking end float or rocker clearances by feeler gauge may not always give accurate results because of wear. For instance, the rocker tip which bears on a valve stem may be deeply pitted, in which case the feeler will simply be bridging a depression. Thrust washers may also wear depressions in opposing faces to make accurate measurement difficult. End float is then easier to check by using a dial gauge. It is common practice to adjust end play in bearing assemblies, like front hubs with taper rollers, by doing up the axle nut until the hub becomes stiff to turn and then backing it off a little. Do not use this method with ballbearing hubs as the assembly is often preloaded by tightening the axle nut to its fullest extent. If the splitpin hole will not line up, file the base of the nut a little.

Steering assemblies often wear in the straight-ahead position. If any part is adjusted, make sure that it remains free when moved from lock to lock. Do not be surprised if an assembly like a steering gearbox, which is known to be carefully adjusted outside the car, becomes stiff when it is bolted in place. This will be due to distortion of the case by the pull of the mounting bolts, particularly if the mounting points are not all touching together. This problem may be met in other equipment and is cured by careful attention to the alignment of mounting points.

When a spanner is stamped with a size and A/F it means that the dimension is the width between the jaws and has no connection with ANF, which is the designation for the American National Fine thread. Coarse threads like Whitworth are rarely used on cars to-day except for studs which screw into soft aluminium or cast iron. For this reason it might be found that the top end of a cylinder head stud has a fine thread and the lower end a coarse thread to screw into the cylinder block. If the car has mainly UNF threads then it is likely that any coarse threads will be UNC, which are not the same as Whitworth. Small sizes have the same number of threads in Whitworth and UNC, but in the $\frac{1}{2}$ inch size for example, there are twelve threads to the inch in the former and thirteen in the latter.

7 After a major overhaul, particularly if a great deal of work has been done on the braking, steering and suspension systems, it is advisable to approach the problem of testing with care. If the braking system has been overhauled, apply heavy pressure to the brake pedal and get a second operator to check every possible source of leakage. The brakes may work extremely well, but a leak could cause complete failure after a few miles.

Do not fit the hub caps until every wheel nut has been checked for tightness, and make sure the tyre pressures are correct. Check the levels of coolant, lubricants and hydraulic fluids. Being satisfied that all is well, take the car on the road and test the brakes at once. Check the steering and the action of the handbrake. Do all this at moderate speeds on quiet roads, and make sure there is no other vehicle behind you when you try a rapid stop.

Finally, remember that many parts settle down after a time, so check for tightness of all fixings after the car has been on the road for a hundred miles or so.

8 It is useless to tune an engine which has not reached its normal running temperature. In the same way, the tune of an engine which is stiff after a rebore will be different when the engine is again running free. Remember too, that rocker clearances on pushrod operated valve gear will change when the cylinder head nuts are tightened after an initial period of running with a new head gasket.

Trouble may not always be due to what seems the obvious cause. Ignition, carburation and mechanical condition are interdependent and spitting back through the carburetter, which might be attributed to a weak mixture, can be caused by a sticking inlet valve.

For one final hint on tuning, never adjust more than one thing at a time or it will be impossible to tell which adjustment produced the desired result.

NOTES

GLOSSARY OF TERMS

Allen key — Cranked wrench of hexagonal section for use with socket head screws.

Alternator — Electrical generator producing alternating current. Rectified to direct current for battery charging.

Ambient temperature — Surrounding atmospheric temperature.

Annulus — Used in engineering to indicate the outer ring gear of an epicyclic gear train.

Armature — The shaft carrying the windings, which rotates in the magnetic field of a generator or starter motor. That part of a solenoid or relay which is activated by the magnetic field.

Axial — In line with, or pertaining to, an axis.

Backlash — Play in meshing gears.

Balance lever — A bar where force applied at the centre is equally divided between connections at the ends.

Banjo axle — Axle casing with large diameter housing for the crownwheel and differential.

Bendix pinion — A self-engaging and self-disengaging drive on a starter motor shaft.

Bevel pinion — A conical shaped gearwheel, designed to mesh with a similar gear with an axis usually at 90 deg. to its own.

bhp — Brake horse power, measured on a dynamometer.

bmep — Brake mean effective pressure. Average pressure on a piston during the working stroke.

Brake cylinder — Cylinder with hydraulically operated piston(s) acting on brake shoes or pad(s).

Brake regulator — Control valve fitted in hydraulic braking system which limits brake pressure to rear brakes during heavy braking to prevent rear wheel locking.

Camber — Angle at which a wheel is tilted from the vertical.

Capacitor — Modern term for an electrical condenser. Part of distributor assembly, connected across contact breaker points, acts as an interference suppressor.

Castellated — Top face of a nut, slotted across the flats, to take a locking splitpin.

Castor — Angle at which the kingpin or swivel pin is tilted when viewed from the side.

cc — Cubic centimetres. Engine capacity is arrived at by multiplying the area of the bore in sq cm by the stroke in cm by the number of cylinders.

Clevis — U-shaped forked connector used with a clevis pin, usually at handbrake connections.

Collet — A type of collar, usually split and located in a groove in a shaft, and held in place by a retainer. The arrangement used to retain the spring(s) on a valve stem in most cases.

Commutator — Rotating segmented current distributor between armature windings and brushes in generator or motor.

Compression ratio — The ratio, or quantitative relation, of the total volume (piston at bottom of stroke) to the unswept volume (piston at top of stroke) in an engine cylinder.

Condenser — See capacitor.

Core plug — Plug for blanking off a manufacturing hole in a casting.

Crownwheel — Large bevel gear in rear axle, driven by a bevel pinion attached to the propeller shaft. Sometimes called a 'ring gear'.

'C'-spanner — Like a 'C' with a handle. For use on screwed collars without flats, but with slots or holes.

Damper — Modern term for shock-absorber, used in vehicle suspension systems to damp out spring oscillations.

Depression — The lowering of atmospheric pressure as in the inlet manifold and carburetter.

Dowel — Close tolerance pin, peg, tube, or bolt, which accurately locates mating parts.

Drag link — Rod connecting steering box drop arm (pitman arm) to nearest front wheel steering arm in certain types of steering systems.

Dry liner — Thinwall tube pressed into cylinder bore

Dry sump — Lubrication system where all oil is scavenged from the sump, and returned to a separate tank.

Dynamo — See Generator.

Electrode — Terminal, part of an electrical component, such as the points or 'Electrodes' of a sparking plug.

Electrolyte — In lead-acid car batteries a solution of sulphuric acid and distilled water.

End float — The axial movement between associated parts, end play.

EP — Extreme pressure. In lubricants, special grades for heavily loaded bearing surfaces, such as gear teeth in a gearbox, or crownwheel and pinion in a rear axle.

EP Extreme pressure. In lubricants, special grades for heavily loaded bearing surfaces, such as gear teeth in a gearbox, or crownwheel and pinion in a rear axle.

Fade Of brakes. Reduced efficiency due to overheating.

Field coils Windings on the polepieces of motors and generators.

Fillets Narrow finishing strips usually applied to interior bodywork.

First motion shaft Input shaft from clutch to gearbox.

Fullflow filter Filters in which all the oil is pumped to the engine. If the element becomes clogged, a bypass valve operates to pass unfiltered oil to the engine.

FWD Front wheel drive.

g Gramme.

Gear pump Two meshing gears in a close fitting casing. Oil is carried from the inlet round the outside of both gears in the spaces between the gear teeth and casing to the outlet, the meshing gear teeth prevent oil passing back to the inlet, and the oil is forced through the outlet port.

Generator Modern term for 'Dynamo'. When rotated produces electrical current.

Grommet A ring of protective or sealing material. Can be used to protect pipes or leads passing through bulkheads.

Grubscrew Fully threaded headless screw with screwdriver slot. Used for locking, or alignment purposes.

Gudgeon pin Shaft which connects a piston to its connecting rod. Sometimes called 'wrist pin', or 'piston pin'.

Halfshaft One of a pair transmitting drive from the differential.

Helical In spiral form. The teeth of helical gears are cut at a spiral angle to the side faces of the gearwheel.

Hot spot Hot area that assists vapourisation of fuel on its way to cylinders. Often provided by close contact between inlet and exhaust manifolds.

HT High Tension. Applied to electrical current produced by the ignition coil for the sparking plugs.

Hydrometer A device for checking specific gravity of liquids. Used to check specific gravity of electrolyte.

Hypoid bevel gears A form of bevel gear used in the rear axle drive gears. The bevel pinion meshes below the centre line of the crownwheel, giving a lower propeller shaft line.

Idler A device for passing on movement. A free running gear between driving and driven gears. A lever transmitting track rod movement to a side rod in steering gear.

Impeller A centrifugal pumping element. Used in water pumps to stimulate flow.

Journals Those parts of a shaft that are in contact with the bearings.

kg Kilogramme.

kg m Metric measure of twist or torque. A pull of 10 kg at a radius of 1 m is a torque of 10 kg m.

kg/sq cm Kilogrammes per square centimetre.

Kingpin The main vertical pin which carries the front wheel spindle, and permits steering movement. May be called 'steering pin' or 'swivel pin'.

l Litre.

Layshaft The shaft which carries the laygear in the gearbox. The laygear is driven by the first motion shaft and drives the third motion shaft according to the gear selected. Sometimes called the 'countershaft' or 'second motion shaft.'

lb ft A measure of twist or torque. A pull of 10 lb at a radius of 1 ft is a torque of 10 lb ft.

lb/sq in Pounds per square inch.

Little-end The small, or piston end of a connecting rod. Sometimes called the 'small-end'.

LT Low Tension. The current output from the battery.

m Metre.

Mandrel Accurately manufactured bar or rod used for test or centring purposes.

Manifold A pipe, duct, or chamber, with several branches.

Needle rollers Bearing rollers with a length many times their diameter.

Oil bath Reservoir which lubricates parts by immersion. In air filters, a separate oil supply for wetting a wire mesh element to hold the dust.

Oil wetted In air filters, a wire mesh element lightly oiled to trap and hold airborne dust.

Overlap Period during which inlet and exhaust valves are open together.

Panhard rod Bar connected between fixed point on chassis and another on axle to control sideways movement.

Pawl	Pivoted catch which engages in the teeth of a ratchet to permit movement in one direction only.
Peg spanner	Tool with pegs, or pins, to engage in holes or slots in the part to be turned.
Pendant pedals	Pedals with levers that are pivoted at the top end.
Phillips screwdriver	A cross-point screwdriver for use with the cross-slotted heads of Phillips screws.
Pinion	A small gear, usually in relation to another gear.
Piston-type damper	Shock absorber in which damping is controlled by a piston working in a closed oil-filled cylinder.
Preloading	Preset static pressure on ball or roller bearings not due to working loads.
Radial	Radiating from a centre, like the spokes of a wheel.
Radius rod	Pivoted arm confining movement of a part to an arc of fixed radius.
Ratchet	Toothed wheel or rack which can move in one direction only, movement in the other being prevented by a pawl.
Ring gear	A gear tooth ring attached to outer periphery of flywheel. Starter pinion engages with it during starting.
Runout	Amount by which rotating part is out of true.
Semi-floating axle	Outer end of rear axle halfshaft is carried on bearing inside axle casing. Wheel hub is secured to end of shaft.
Servo	A hydraulic or pneumatic system for assisting, or, augmenting a physical effort. See 'Vacuum Servo'.
Setscrew	One which is threaded for the full length of the shank.
Shackle	A coupling link, used in the form of two parallel pins connected by side plates to secure the end of the master suspension spring and absorb the effects of deflection.
Shell bearing	Thinwalled steel shell lined with antifriction metal. Usually semi-circular and used in pairs for main and big-end bearings.
Shock absorber	See 'Damper'.
Silentbloc	Rubber bush bonded to inner and outer metal sleeves.
Socket-head screw	Screw with hexagonal socket for an Allen key.
Solenoid	A coil of wire creating a magnetic field when electric current passes through it. Used with a soft iron core to operate contacts or a mechanical device.
Spur gear	A gear with teeth cut axially across the periphery.
Stub axle	Short axle fixed at one end only.
Tachometer	An instrument for accurate measurement of rotating speed. Usually indicates in revolutions per minute.
TDC	Top Dead Centre. The highest point reached by a piston in a cylinder, with the crank and connecting rod in line.
Thermostat	Automatic device for regulating temperature. Used in vehicle coolant systems to open a valve which restricts circulation at low temperature.
Third motion shaft	Output shaft of gearbox.
Threequarter floating axle	Outer end of rear axle halfshaft flanged and bolted to wheel hub, which runs on bearing mounted on outside of axle casing. Vehicle weight is not carried by the axle shaft.
Thrust bearing or washer	Used to reduce friction in rotating parts subject to axial loads.
Torque	Turning or twisting effort. See 'lb ft'.
Track rod	The bar(s) across the vehicle which connect the steering arms and maintain the front wheels in their correct alignment.
UJ	Universal joint. A coupling between shafts which permits angular movement.
UNF	Unified National Fine screw thread.
Vacuum servo	Device used in brake system, using difference between atmospheric pressure and inlet manifold depression to operate a piston which acts to augment brake pressure as required. See 'Servo'.
Venturi	A restriction or 'choke' in a tube, as in a carburetter, used to increase velocity to obtain a reduction in pressure.
Vernier	A sliding scale for obtaining fractional readings of the graduations of an adjacent scale.
Welch plug	A domed thin metal disc which is partially flattened to lock in a recess. Used to plug core holes in castings.
Wet liner	Removable cylinder barrel, sealed against coolant leakage, where the coolant is in direct contact with the outer surface.
Wet sump	A reservoir attached to the crankcase to hold the lubricating oil.

NOTES

INDEX

NOTES

Alfa Romeo Giulia 1600, 1750, 2000 1962 on
Aston Martin 1921-58
Auto Union Audi 70, 80, Super 90, 1966-72
Audi 100 1969 on
Austin, Morris etc. 1100 Mk. 1 1962-67
Austin, Morris etc. 1100 Mk. 2, 3, 1300 Mk. 1, 2, 3 America 1968 on
Austin A30, A35, A40 Farina 1951-67
Austin A55 Mk. 2, A60 1958-69
Austin A99, A110 1959-68
Austin J4 1960 on
Austin Allegro 1973 on
Austin Maxi 1969 on
Austin, Morris 1800 1964 on
Austin, Morris 2200 1972 on
Austin Kimberley, Tasman 1970 on
Austin, Morris 1300, 1500 Nomad 1969 on
BMC 3 (Austin A50, A55 Mk. 1, Morris Oxford 2, 3 1954-59)
Austin Healey 100/6, 3000 1956-68
Austin Healey, MG Sprite, Midget 1958 on
Bedford CA Mk. 2 1964-69
Bedford CF Vans 1969 on
Bedford Beagle HA Vans 1964 on
BMW 1600 1966 on
BMW 1800 1964-71
BMW 2000, 2002 1966 on
Chevrolet Corvair 1960-69
Chevrolet Corvette V8 1957-65
Chevrolet Corvette V8 1965 on
Chevrolet Vega 2300 1970 on
Chrysler Valiant V8 1965 on
Chrysler Valiant Straight Six 1963 on
Citroen DS 19, ID 19 1955-66
Citroen ID 19, DS 19, 20, 21 1966 on
Citroen Dyane Ami 1964 on
Daf 31, 32, 33, 44, 55 1961 on
Datsun Bluebird 610 series 1972 on
Datsun Cherry 100A, 120A 1971 on
Datsun 1000, 1200 1968 on
Datsun 1300, 1400, 1600 1968 on
Datsun 240C 1971 on
Datsun 240Z Sport 1970 on
Fiat 124 1966 on
Fiat 124 Sport 1966 on
Fiat 125 1967-72
Fiat 127 1971 on
Fiat 128 1969 on
Fiat 500 1957 on
Fiat 600, 600D 1955-69
Fiat 850 1964 on
Fiat 1100 1957-69
Fiat 1300, 1500 1961-67
Ford Anglia Prefect 100E 1953-62
Ford Anglia 105E, Prefect 107E 1959-67
Ford Capri 1300, 1600 OHV 1968 on
Ford Capri 1300, 1600, 2000 OHC 1972 on
Ford Capri 2000 V4, 3000 V6 1969 on
Ford Classic, Capri 1961-64
Ford Consul, Zephyr, Zodiac, 1, 2 1950-62
Ford Corsair Straight Four 1963-65
Ford Corsair V4 1965-68
Ford Corsair V4 2000 1969-70
Ford Cortina 1962-66
Ford Cortina 1967-68
Ford Cortina 1969-70
Ford Cortina Mk. 3 1970 on
Ford Escort 1967 on
Ford Falcon 6 1964-70
Ford Falcon XK, XL 1960-63
Ford Falcon 6 XR/XA 1966 on
Ford Falcon V8 (U.S.A.) 1965-71
Ford Falcon V8 (Aust.) 1966 on
Ford Pinto 1970 on
Ford Maverick 6 1969 on
Ford Maverick V8 1970 on
Ford Mustang 6 1965 on
Ford Mustang V8 1965 on
Ford Thames 10, 12, 15 cwt 1957-65
Ford Transit V4 1965 on
Ford Zephyr Zodiac Mk. 3 1962-66
Ford Zephyr Zodiac V4, V6, Mk. 4 1966-72
Ford Consul, Granada 1972 on
Hillman Avenger 1970 on
Hillman Hunter 1966 on
Hillman Imp 1963-68
Hillman Imp 1969 on
Hillman Minx 1 to 5 1956-65
Hillman Minx 1965-67
Hillman Minx 1966-70
Hillman Super Minx 1961-65
Jaguar XK120, 140, 150, Mk. 7, 8, 9 1948-61
Jaguar 2.4, 3.4, 3.8 Mk. 1, 2 1955-69
Jaguar 'E' Type 1961-72
Jaguar 'S' Type 420 1963-68
Jaguar XJ6 1968 on
Jowett Javelin Jupiter 1947-53
Landrover 1, 2 1948-61
Landrover 2, 2a, 3 1959 on
Mazda 616 1970 on
Mazda 808, 818 1972 on
Mazda 1200, 1300 1969 on
Mazda 1500, 1800 1967 on
Mazda RX-2 1971 on
Mazda R100, RX-3 1970 on
Mercedes-Benz 190b, 190c, 200 1959-68
Mercedes-Benz 220 1959-65
Mercedes-Benz 220/8 1968 on
Mercedes-Benz 230 1963-68
Mercedes-Benz 250 1965-67
Mercedes-Benz 250 1968 on
Mercedes-Benz 280 1968 on
MG TA to TF 1936-55
MGA MGB 1955-68
MGB 1969 on
Mini 1959 on
Mini Cooper 1961-72
Morgan Four 1936-72
Morris Marina 1971 on
Morris (Aust) Marina 1972 on
Morris Minor 2, 1000 1952-71
Morris Oxford 5, 6 1959-71
NSU 1000 1963-72
NSU Prinz 1 to 4 1957-72
Opel Ascona, Manta 1970 on
Opel GT 1900 1968 on
Opel Kadett, Olympia 993 cc 1078 cc 1962 on
Opel Kadett, Olympia 1492, 1698, 1897 cc 1967 on
Opel Rekord C 1966-72
Peugeot 204 1965 on
Peugeot 304 1970 on
Peugeot 404 1960 on
Peugeot 504 1968 on
Porsche 356A, B, C 1957-65
Porsche 911 1964 on
Porsche 912 1965-69
Porsche 914 S 1969 on
Reliant Regal 1952-73
Renault R4, R4L, 4 1961 on
Renault 5 1972 on
Renault 6 1968 on
Renault 8, 10, 1100 1962-71
Renault 12, 1969 on
Renault 15, 17 1971 on
Renault R16 1965 on
Renault Dauphine Floride 1957-67
Renault Caravelle 1962-68
Rover 60 to 110 1953-64
Rover 2000 1963-73
Rover 3 Litre 1958-67
Rover 3500, 3500S 1968 on
Saab 95, 96, Sport 1960-68
Saab 99 1969 on
Saab V4 1966 on
Simca 1000 1961 on
Simca 1100 1967 on
Simca 1300, 1301, 1500, 1501 1963 on
Skoda One (440, 445, 450) 1955-70
Sunbeam Rapier Alpine 1955-65
Toyota Carina, Celica 1971 on
Toyota Corolla 1100, 1200 1967 on
Toyota Corona 1500 Mk. 1 1965-70
Toyota Corona Mk. 2 1969 on
Triumph TR2, TR3, TR3A 1952-62
Triumph TR4, TR4A 1961-67
Triumph TR5, TR250, TR6 1967 on
Triumph 1300, 1500 1965-73
Triumph 2000 Mk. 1, 2.5 PI Mk. 1 1963-69
Triumph 2000 Mk. 2, 2.5 PI Mk. 2 1969 on
Triumph Dolomite 1972 on
Triumph Herald 1959-68
Triumph Herald 1969-71
Triumph Spitfire, Vitesse 1962-68
Triumph Spitfire Mk. 3, 4 1969 on
Triumph GT6, Vitesse 2 Litre 1969 on
Triumph Stag 1970 on
Triumph Toledo 1970 on
Vauxhall Velox, Cresta 1957-72
Vauxhall Victor 1, 2, FB 1957-64
Vauxhall Victor 101 1964-67
Vauxhall Victor FD 1600, 2000 1967-72

Continued on following page

THE AUTOBOOK SERIES OF WORKSHOP MANUALS

Vauxhall Victor 3300, Ventora 1968-72
Vauxhall Victor FE Ventora 1972 on
Vauxhall Viva HA 1963-66
Vauxhall Viva HB 1966-70
Vauxhall Viva, HC Firenza 1971 on
Volkswagen Beetle 1954-67
Volkswagen Beetle 1968 on
Volkswagen 1500 1961-66
Volkswagen 1600 Fastback 1965-73
Volkswagen Transporter 1954-67
Volkswagen Transporter 1968 on
Volkswagen 411 1968-72
Volvo 120 series 1961-70
Volvo 140 series 1966 on
Volvo 160 series 1968 on
Volvo 1800 1960-73